Vadsø

Kirkenes

FINNMARK

Tromsø

NORTHERN NORWAY

TROMS

Bodø

NORDLAND

Northern Norway and Svalbard
See pp206–225

Trøndelag
See pp192–205

NORD-
ØNDELAG

Eastern Norway
See pp130–147

AKERSHUS

VESTFOLD

ØSTFOLD

Around Oslofjorden
See pp116–129

0 kilometres   200

0 miles   100

EYEWITNESS TRAVEL

NORWAY

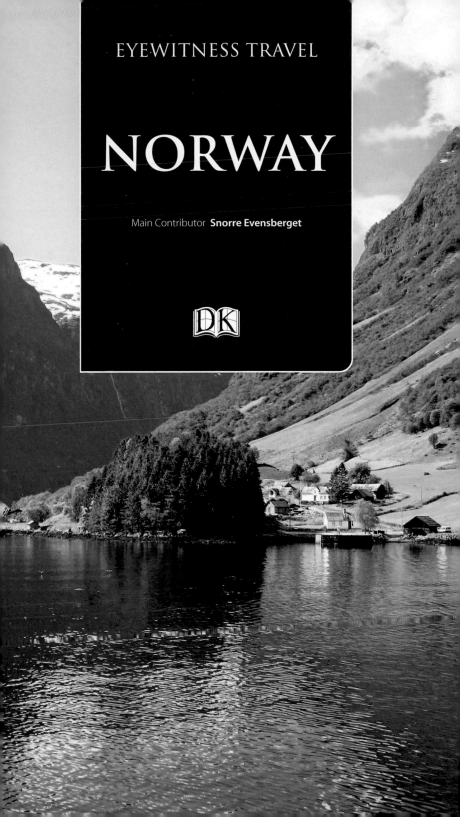

EYEWITNESS TRAVEL

NORWAY

Main Contributor **Snorre Evensberget**

DK

LONDON, NEW YORK, MELBOURNE, MUNICH AND DELHI
www.dk.com

Produced for Dorling Kindersley by
Streiffert Förlag AB, Stockholm

Senior Editor & Design Bo Streiffert

Project Editor Guy Engström

Main Contributer Snorre Evensberget

Other Contributors
Alf G. Andersen, Hans-Erik Hansen,
Tine Flinder-Nyquist, Annette Mürer

Photographers
Jørn Bøhmer-Olsen, Frits Solvang, Rolf Sørensen

Cartographer Stig Söderlind

Illustrators
Richard Bonson, Gary Cross,
Claire Littlejohn, John Woodcock

English Translation Fiona Harris
Dorling Kindersley Limited

Editor Jane Hutchings

Senior DTP Designer Jason Little

Production Sarah Dodd

Printed and bound in China by L.Rex Printing Co. Ltd

First American edition 2003

14 15 16 17 10 9 8 7 6 5 4 3 2 1

Published in the United States by DK Publishing,
345 Hudson Street, New York, NY 10014

Reprinted with revisions 2008, 2010, 2012, 2014

Copyright © 2003, 2014 Dorling Kindersley Limited, London

A Penguin Random House Company

ISSN 1542-1554

ISBN 978-1-4654-1181-5

Floors are referrd to throughout in accordance with European usage; ie the "first floor" is the floor above ground level.

MIX
Paper from
responsible sources
FSC™ C018179
www.fsc.org

**The information in this
DK Eyewitness Travel Guide is checked regularly.**
Every effort has been made to ensure that this book is as up-to-date as possible at the time of going to press. Some details, however, such as telephone numbers, opening hours, prices, gallery hanging arrangements and travel information are liable to change. The publishers cannot accept responsibility for any consequences arising from the use of this book, nor for any material on third party websites, and cannot guarantee that any website address in this book will be a suitable source of travel information. We value the views and suggestions of our readers very highly. Please write to: Publisher, DK Eyewitness Travel Guides, Dorling Kindersley, 80 Strand, London, WC2R 0RL, UK, or email: travelguides@dk.com.

Front cover main image: The spectacular Geirangerfjorden in Møre and Romsdale, Norway

◄ Songefjorden, the longest fjord in Norway

View of Geirangerfjorden

Contents

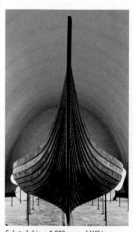

Gokstad ship, a 1,000-year-old Viking vessel *(see pp88–9)*

Skiers taking a break at a cabin
in Trysil, Eastern Norway

Oslo Area by Area

Bridal crown from Hallingdal
(see pp28–9)

Norway Area
by Area

Travellers'
Needs

Geitost and Jarlsberg cheeses

Survival Guide

Borgund Stavkirke
(see p187)

HOW TO USE THIS GUIDE

This guide helps you to get the most from your visit to Norway by providing detailed practical information and expert recommendations. *Introducing Norway* maps the country and sets it in its historical and cultural context. The Oslo section and the six regional chapters describe important sights using maps, photographs and illustrations. Restaurant and hotel recommendations can be found in *Travellers' Needs*, while the *Survival Guide* has tips on everything from making a telephone call to using local transportation, as well as information on money, etiquette and safety.

Oslo

The centre of the capital is divided into three areas, each with its own chapter which opens with a list of the sights to be covered. A fourth chapter, *Further Afield*, covers the peripheral areas of Bogstad, Frogner and Toyen. All sights are numbered and plotted on each chapter's area map. Information on each sight is easy to locate as the entries follow the numbering used on the map.

Sights at a Glance lists the chapter's sights by category: Churches, Museums and Galleries, Historic Buildings, Parks and Gardens.

All pages relating to Oslo have the same colour thumb tabs.

A locator map shows you where you are in relation to other areas in the city centre.

1 Area Map
For easy reference, sights are numbered and located on a map. The central sights are also marked on the Oslo Street Finder maps on pages 108–113.

2 Street-by-Street Map
This gives a bird's eye view of the key areas covered in each chapter.

Stars indicate the sights that no visitor should miss.

Walking routes are shown in red.

3 Detailed Information
City sights are described individually. Addresses, phone numbers and opening times are given, as well as admission charges, wheelchair access, guided tours and transport.

Story boxes talk about subjects of interest linked to the sights.

1 Introduction
The landscape, history and character of each area is described here, along with an account of how the area has developed and what it has to offer the visitor.

Norway Area by Area

Apart from Oslo, Norway has been divided into six areas, each of which has a separate chapter. The most interesting towns and sights in each region are located on a *Regional Map* at the beginning of each chapter.

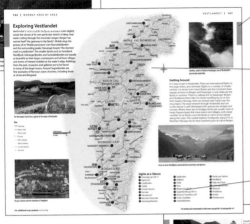

Each area of Norway can be quickly identified by its colour-coded thumb tags (*see inside front cover*).

2 Regional Map
This map shows the most important roads and gives an illustrated overview of each area. Interesting places to visit are numbered, and there are useful tips on getting around the region by car and train.

Sights at a Glance shows all sights covered in the chapter.

3 Detailed Information
All the main towns and places to visit are described individually. Listed in order, they follow the numbering on the Regional Map. Within each town or city, there is detailed information on important buildings and other sights.

A Visitors' Checklist provides the practical information you will need to plan your visit.

4 Norway's Top Sights
National parks have maps showing places of interest. Illustrations reveal the interiors of historic buildings. Museums and galleries have floorplans. Large towns have maps showing selected sights.

INTRODUCING NORWAY

DISCOVERING NORWAY

The following itineraries have been designed to include as many of the country's highlights as possible, while keeping long-distance travel to manageable proportions. First come three 2-day tours of Norway's most important cities: Oslo, Bergen and Trondheim. Visitors can fly between these cities to create a week-long city tour, or make it a 10-day tour by travelling on the train from Oslo to

Bergen, then getting the bus, train or ferry (which will add an additional day to the tour) from Bergen to Trondheim. Next come two week-long tours, covering the Western Fjords and the Far North of the country, including Svalbard. Pick and follow your favourite tours based on the time you have available for your trip, or simply dip in and out of the various options and be inspired.

Ålesund
This enchanting town, spanning several islands, is well-known for its interesting architecture and stunning coastal location.

A Week in the Western Fjords

- Stand near the edge of the **Preikestolen** rock at the mouth of Lysefjorden and dare to look down.

- Enjoy a remarkable train journey on the steeply winding **Flåmsbanen** line.

- Brave the icy crevices of the **Jostedalsbreen** glacier on a guided hike.

- Wonder at the magnificent natural beauty of the **Sognefjorden**.

- Admire the exquisite Art Nouveau architecture of **Ålesund**.

◄ *The Bridal Procession in Hardanger by A Tidemand and H Gude, 1848*

A Week in the Far North and Svalbard

- Explore Norway's strong seafaring tradition at the old trading station of **Kjerringøy**, near Bodø.
- Sample extreme sports in the busy port town of **Narvik**.
- Saunter the streets of **Tromsø** and admire its fascinating assortment of old wooden houses.
- Boat, hike and skidoo amongst the wild, icy tracts of **Svalbard**.
- Study the superb prehistoric rock carvings at **Alta's** Hjemmeluft.

Two Days in Oslo, Bergen and Trondheim

- Delight in the superb paintings at **Oslo**'s **Nasjonalgalleriet**, with Edvard Munch taking prime slot.
- Imagine the sea-faring skills of the Vikings as you gaze at their longships in Oslo's **Vikingskipshuset**.
- Enjoy the convivial atmosphere and handsome timber houses of the **Bryggen**, **Bergen**'s oldest quarter.
- Head up the flanks of **Mount Fløyen** in Bergen's funicular for the views and a hike in the woods.
- Admire the sterling medieval architecture of **Trondheim cathedral**, the Nidarosdomen.

Key

— Far North and Svalbard Tour

— Western Fjords Tour

Tourists on a guided kayak tour watch a Beluga whale

Two Days in Oslo

Oslo is a city in an unsurpassed location, with a fascinating history, excellent museums and galleries, and a lively harbour and waterfront area.

- **Arriving** Oslo airport is approximately 35 km (22 miles) from the city centre. There are good bus and train services connecting the airport and city.

- **Moving on** The train from Oslo to Bergen takes 6–7 hours; the flight takes 1 hour.

Day 1
Morning Begin the day by strolling up **Karl Johans Gate** *(p54)*, Oslo's pleasant and busy main drag, alive with buskers during the summer. Pause to admire the imposing edifice of the **Universitet** *(p54)* and make the brief detour over to the **Nasjonalgalleriet** *(pp56–7)*, which holds a huge collection of Norwegian paintings, including prime works by Edvard Munch. Push on up to the **Royal Palace** (Det Konelige Slottet) *(p55)* – an expansive 19th-century structure, which you can visit on a guided tour. Wander the leafy park around the palace before dropping by the **Ibsensmuseet** *(pp62–3)*, the restored former home of the playwright and polemicist Henrik Ibsen.

Afternoon Relax down on the harbourfront, watching the ferries shuttling in and out and walking along the main boardwalk adjoining the **Aker Brygge** *(p61)*, a sprawling retail and leisure complex that was formerly the city's main shipyard. Be sure to pop into the **Nobel Peace Center** *(p61)*, which commemorates both the Nobel Peace prize itself and all those who have received it. Also allow time for a visit to **Rådhuset** (City Hall) *(pp60–61)*, a landmark brick building behind the harbour. Take the free guided tour of the Rådhuset and admire its magnificent murals.

The 9th-century Gokstad Ship in Oslo's Vikingskipshuset

Day 2
Morning Explore the hilly headland overlooking Oslo harbour, where the prime attraction is the **Akershus Slott** *(pp70–71)*, the old medieval castle with its **Royal Mausoleum** *(p71)*. Afterwards, be sure to visit the **Norges Hjemmefrontmuseum** *(p72)*, which honours those Norwegians who joined the Resistance against the German occupation of World War II. Continue onto the **Museet for Samtidskunst** *(pp74–5)*, where you can enjoy Oslo's widest collection of contemporary art, and then proceed onto the **Opera House** *(p76)*, a striking example of modern design.

Afternoon Catch the passenger ferry over to the leafy **Bygdøy peninsula** *(p81)*, which is home to no fewer than five of Oslo's biggest and best museums. Enthusiasts will want to see them all, but the pick is the **Norsk Folkemuseum** *(pp86–7)*, a sprawling complex with an outdoor section comprising more than 150 old wooden buildings brought here from all over southern Norway. Don't miss the indoor section, which is devoted to the costumes and customs of rural Norway. Finish the day with a visit to the world-famous **Vikingskipshuset** *(pp88–9)*, where three magnificent Viking longboats are displayed.

Two Days in Bergen

A sprawling but charming town, Bergen has long been a major fishing and trade centre, and is still an important hub for the shipping industry.

- **Arriving** Bergen airport is 20 km (12 miles) from the city centre, and well served by public bus, airport shuttle bus and taxi.

- **Moving on** The ferry to Trondheim sails daily and takes about a day and a half. Alternatively, get an overnight train or bus (14–15 hours), or fly (1 hour).

Day 1
Morning Begin the day by investigating the oldest and prettiest part of Bergen, the **Bryggen** *(p175)*, where a string of old timber buildings overlook the harbourfront. Drop into one of the best preserved, the **Hanseatiske Museum** *(p175)*, where German merchants once held sway. Spend time in the **Bryggens Museum** *(p174)*, which is packed with archeological finds dug out of the Bergen mud, and call in at the **Mariakirken** *(p174)*, the city's oldest and most engaging church. Round off the morning by wandering the fortifications

Colourful buildings in Bryggen Historic District, Bergen

Nidarosdomen, Trondheim's vast cathedral dating from around 1320

of the **Bergenhus** *(p174)* castle and park before clambering up the **Rosenkrantztårnet** *(p174)* – for the views over the harbour.

Afternoon Detour out to one of the region's most popular attractions, **Troldhaugen** *(p181)*, celebrated across Norway as the one-time home of the composer Edvard Grieg. Visit the house, which has changed little since Grieg's death in 1907 and wander around the museum that traces Grieg's life and times. If possible, try to arrange your visit to coincide with a performance at the concert hall.

Day 2
Morning Delve into the wooded, rocky valleys surrounding Bergen en route to the tiny quay at Buena Kai, where you catch the passenger ferry over to **Lysøen** *(p181)*, once the island hidey-hole of the violinist Ole Bull. Take the guided tour of Bull's ornate villa and enjoy the tales associated with this famous musician.

Afternoon Spend the afternoon wandering the lively streets of downtown Bergen, popping into the city's most interesting art museum, the Rasmus Meyer Collection, which forms one distinct part of the **Bergen Kunstmuseum** *(p177)*. Round off the day by taking the little funicular to the top of **Mount Fløyen** *(p180)*, from where there are wonderful views over the city and a network of easy footpaths into the surrounding forest.

Two Days in Trondheim

With a rich variety of sights including a cathedral dating from the 14th century, Trondheim is a rewarding town to explore.

- **Arriving** Trondheim airport is 35 km (22 miles) north of the city centre, with good connections by train, bus or taxi.

- **Transport** A car is the best way to get to Stiklestad, or take the train to Verdal and then a taxi or local bus.

- **Moving on** The train to Oslo takes about 7 hours, or take a flight (1 hour).

Day 1
Morning Visit Trondheim's pride and joy, its magnificent cathedral, the **Nidarosdomen** *(p203)*, whose mighty stone tower soars high above the city. Inside, admire the cavernous nave and look at Norway's Crown Jewels. Then explore the neighbouring **Erkebispegården** *(p200)*, the former Archbishop's Palace and now home to two museums – one dedicated to medieval sculpture, the other devoted to the resistance against the German occupation of World War II.

Afternoon Stop for lunch at one of the cafés near the cathedral and then proceed to the excellent **Trondheim Kunstmuseum** *(p200)*, which

features challenging temporary exhibitions of contemporary art. Head next to the **Nordenfjeldske Kunstindustrimuseum** *(p200)*, which holds an exemplary collection of Norwegian furniture, glassware, ceramics, silverware and evocative tapestries. Finish the day by catching the boat to the offshore islet of **Munkholm** *(p197)*, where you can explore a ruined fort and take a dip in the fjord – no matter what the locals say, the water is cold.

Day 2
Morning Venturing out from Trondheim, travel to the hamlet of **Stiklestad** *(p204)*, where a famous Viking battle was fought in 1030: King Olav Haraldsson came to a grisly end here, but in a twist of fate he was later to become a saint and national icon. Visit the **Nasjonale Kultursenter** *(p204)*, which explores the history of this battle, and wander the battlefield with its medieval kirke (church) and amphitheatre, where costumed dramas reenact these events.

Afternoon Head back to downtown Trondheim and stroll around the attractive streets, pausing at the main square, the Torvet. Pop into the **Stiftsgården** *(p202)*, a former Royal residence with a Rococo interior. Then go to the **Bryggen** *(p201)*, with its long line of restored wooden warehouses, and push on up to **Bakklandet** *(p202)*, the coolest part of town with its cobbled lanes, wonky timber houses, and boho cafés and bars.

A Week in the Western Fjords

- **Arriving** Stavanger is well connected to the rest of Norway by plane with daily flights here from every other major town. There are also daily trains from Oslo and frequent buses from Bergen.

- **Transport** Buses, ferries and trains combine to make this fjord itinerary possible by public transport, though it is much more convenient by car. Even in winter, despite the harsh conditions, all the main roads are passable almost all of the time.

- **Moving on** There are flights from Ålesund to Oslo, Bergen and Stavanger as well as boats to Bergen and bus connections for the Oslo train.

Day 1: Stavanger

Start your tour of the Western Fjords in **Stavanger** (pp168–9), a bright and cheerful city that spreads out over a hilly peninsula. Don't miss a visit to the city's proudest building, its cathedral – the **Domkirken** (p169) – dating back to around 1100. Drop by the **Norsk Hermetikkmuseum** (p168), which gives a fascinating insight into the fish canning industry that was once Stavanger's mainstay. Nowadays it's oil that keeps Stavanger prosperous, so be sure to explore the **Norsk Oljemuseum** (p168), which tracks through the oil industry's short but remarkable history.

To extend your trip…

Catch the car ferry from Stavanger as it nudges slowly up the **Lysefjorden** (p170), where sheer cliffs shadow dark waters. Detour out to the **Preikestolen** (p170), a dramatic hunk of mountain with three sheer sides towering over the Lysefjord: dangle your legs over the edge if you dare.

Day 2: Bergen

Select a day from the Bergen itineraries (pp12–13).

Day 3: Voss to Undredal

Heading out from Bergen, pause at **Voss** (p173), an agreeable little town and extreme sports centre, whose speciality is whitewater rafting and kayaking. Proceed to Flåm for your first taste of the magnificent scenery of the **Sognefjorden** (pp184–6), arguably Norway's most beautiful fjord, running east–west for 206 km (128 miles). Consider taking the dramatic **Flåmsbanen** (p186) railway up from Flåm to Myrdal (50 minutes each way) or spend time visiting the ancient stave church perched high above the fjord at the tiny hamlet of **Undredal** (p186), where goats outnumber villagers by about ten to one.

Day 4: Sognefjorden and surrounds

Travelling east from Flåm, negotiate the longest road tunnel in the world (at 24.5 km/15 miles) before journeying inland and up the valley to **Borgund Stavkirke** (p187), arguably the country's finest stave church. Afterwards, regain the Sognefjorden at Fodnes and proceed to **Sogndal** (p186), a medium-sized town that strings along the fjord within comfortable striking distance of a second exquisite stave church, **Urnes Stavkirke** (p188). Doubling back to Sogndal, head west to **Balestrand** (p186), one of the region's most alluring villages,

its higgledy-piggledy houses rolling down the hill to the fjord with imposing mountains standing behind.

Day 5: Nordfjorden and glacier

Sample the rugged scenery of the **Nordfjord** (pp188–9), which is seen to fine advantage at the hamlet of **Loen** (p189), with the mountains on one side and the glassy fjord on the other. Go inland to the shaggy flanks of the **Jostedalsbreen** glacier (p188) – or even better, sign up for a glacier walking tour.

Day 6: Geraingerfjorden

Marvel at the serenely magnificent scenery of the **Geraingerfjorden** (p189), a narrow S-shaped stretch of water hemmed in on all sides by mighty mountains. See the whole length of the fjord by car ferry or hike up to one of the abandoned mountain farms that dot the fjord's eastern recesses. Allow time for **Gerainger** (p189), the fjord's most appealing village.

Day 7: Ålesund

Spend the day exploring the delightful town of **Ålesund** (p190), a pocket-sized port framed by its dainty harbours and in a prime coastal location. Investigate the town's most distinctive feature, its bevy of Art Nouveau buildings, which line up along the main streets of the centre, hastily rebuilt following a devastating fire in 1904.

A passenger train on the Flåmsbanen scenic mountain railway

For practical information on travelling around Norway, see pp286–91

A Week in the Far North and Svalbard

- **Arriving** There are daily flights from several Norwegian cities to Bodø; the port can also be reached by bus and train.

- **Transport** The best way to complete this tour is by car: the itinerary has been divided up into manageable day-long drives – and the main roads are well maintained. Svalbard can only be reached by plane with several flights daily from Tromsø and Oslo.

- **Book ahead** If planning a tour of the Svalbard wilderness consider arranging this in advance. Choose from dog-sledding, skidoos, kayaking, glacier walking, wildlife excursions, hiking or a boat trip. Longer tours allow you to get close to the polar bears for which Svalbard is famous.

- **Moving on** There are daily flights between Honningsvåg, about 30 km (19 miles) from Nordkapp, and Oslo, but note that the Honningsvåg to Nordkapp road is closed in winter.

Day 1: Bodø
Begin your tour of northern Norway in **Bodø** (p211), a bustling sea-port with excellent ferry and plane connections to points north. Wander the harbour and explore the old part of town before driving to the neighbouring village of **Kjerringøy** (p211), a 19th-century trading station where time seems to have stood still

---

To extend your trip…
Experience the beautiful scenery of the **Lofoten islands** (pp212–13) on a three-day excursion. Take the car ferry from Bodø to Moskenes. Pause at the islands' most beguiling villages, Å and Nusfjord, and enjoy the charms of fishing village **Stamsund** (p214).

Waterfront buildings overlooking Tromsø's old port

Day 2: Narvik
Drive up the coast, past snow-tipped mountains and deep fjords. Stop at **Narvik** (p218), a small town that occupies a dramatic setting and is a centre for extreme sports. Find out about the fierce battles fought here in World War II at the **Krigsminnesmuseet** (p218).

Day 3: Tromsø
Enjoy the charms of **Tromsø** (pp220–21), the prettiest city in northern Norway. Stroll the old part of town, which drapes itself along the waterfront, and drop by one of the several museums that celebrate Tromsø's key role in the exploration of the Arctic: the pick is the **Polarmuseet** (p220), which has a display on the redoubtable Norwegian explorer Roald Amundsen.

Day 4: Svalbard
Take the first flight of the day north from Tromsø to **Svalbard** (pp224–5), a 2-hour journey that takes you to this wild and icy, mountainous and unforgiving archipelago lying about halfway between mainland Norway and

Lyngen, located inside the Arctic Circle between Tromsø and Alta

the North Pole. Spend the afternoon wandering around the main settlement of **Longyearbyen** (p224).

Day 5: Svalbard
Sample the wild, frozen wastes of Svalbard on your chosen guided tour: you are not permitted to wander off into the wilderness on your own because it is much too dangerous. Catch the last flight of the day back to Tromsø.

Day 6: Alta, Hjemmeluft and Hammerfest
Savour a decent slice of wild and wonderful scenery on the coastal drive from Tromsø to **Alta** (pp218–19), a sprawling township that was once a centre of Sami settlement. In Alta, make a beeline for the most amazing manmade sight in northern Norway, the ochre-tinted, rock carvings of **Hjemmeluft** (see p219), now designated a UNESCO World Heritage site. Pushing on, it is another beautiful drive onto former hunting and trapping centre **Hammerfest** (p222), a solitary seaport with a fine coastal setting.

Day 7: Nordkapp
Continuing north, the determined tourist eventually reaches **Nordkapp** (p222), whose gloomy, slate-black cliffs stand at the end of a bare and treeless, wind-battered promontory. Do not despair, the Norwegians have matters in hand with the **Nordkapphallen** (North Cape Hall) (p222), a tourist complex with viewpoints, tunnels, a cinema, shops, bars and cafés. Get your postcards specially franked at the post office to prove you really have reached this far north.

Putting Norway on the Map

The kingdom of Norway is one of the largest countries in Europe, covering 324,219 sq km (125,148 sq miles). The most southerly point, Lindersnes, lies at about the same latitude as Aberdeen in Scotland, and the northernmost tip, near the North Cape, is at latitude 71°11'8" N. The coastline bordering the Skagerrak, the North Sea, the Norwegian Sea and the Arctic Ocean measures 20,000 km (12,400 miles). Much of the country is habitable thanks to the warming effects of the Gulf Stream. The country has more than 5 million inhabitants, 600,000 of whom live in the capital, Oslo.

Key

▬▬	Motorway
▬▬	Major road
═══	Minor Road
──	Train line
▬▬	International border
– –	Ferry Route

For additional map symbols *see back flap*

Hammerfest
Vardø
Vadsø E75
Barents Sea
Lakselv
Alta
Kirkenes
Liinakhamari
Karasjok
Nikel
Murmansk
Tromsø
Andenes
NORWAY
Kautokeino
4
RUSSIA
Vesterålen
Inarijärvi
FINLAND
Monchegorsk
Revda
ofoten
Narvik
Abisko E6
Torneträsk
Karesuando
Lokan Tekojärvi
Svolvær
E10
Kiruna
Torneälven
Vest-
orden
E6
Gällivare
Bodø
Arctic Circle
Jokkmokk
Kalixälven
Mo i Rana
95
Arjeplog
97
E12
Hemavan
Boden
Arvidsjaur
Luleå
Storuman
Skellefteälven
95
Piteå
Gäddede
Skellefteå
E45
E12
Umeå

Northern Europe

Greenland
Svalbard
Greenland Sea
Barents Sea
ICELAND
Arctic Circle
Norwegian Sea
NORWAY
FINLAND
Oslo
SWEDEN
ESTONIA
RUSSIA
DENMARK
LATVIA
U.K.
LITHUANIA
GERMANY
POLAND
BELARUS
CZECH
FRANCE
REPUBLIC
UKRAINE
AUSTRIA
HUNGARY
ROMANIA

Östersund
Örnsköldsvik
Vaasa
SWEDEN
Härnösand
E14
Sundsvall
Jyväskylä
Sveg
84
Hudiksvall
8
Gulf of Bothnia
FINLAND
Mora
Pori
11
Tampere
Ladozhskoye Ozero
rlänge
Falun
Gävle
12
Priozersk
70
Grisslehamn
Åland
8
2
6
Vyborg
50
Fagersta
Mariehamn
3
4
7
St Petersburg
Turku
1
Helsinki
Kapellskär
Örebro
Stockholm
Tallinn
Nynäshamn
Baltic Sea
Norrköping
ESTONIA
Linköping
önköping
Västervik
Visby
Riga
Ventspils
Oskarshamn
Gotland
LATVIA
Växjö
Kalmar

Greater Oslo

Oslo Airport
4
2
Tyrifjorden
E6
E16
Lille-
strøm
Sandvika
Oslo
E18
E18
E6
22
Drammen
Oslofjorden
283
23
Drøbak
E18
0 kilometres   30
E18
319
0 miles   20

A PORTRAIT OF NORWAY

Norway's magnificent scenery and untamed nature have long captivated visitors. Spectacular fjords indent the rugged coastline, mountains rise above tranquil valleys. This is a country where music, art and literature are part of its soul, where sports such as skiing and football and outdoor activities such as hiking and fishing are actively pursued, and current affairs are hotly debated. It is also the home of the Nobel Peace Prize.

Wrapped around northwestern Scandinavia like a protective bastion against the North Sea, Norway is one of the most scenically beautiful places in Europe. The country stretches an incredible 1,752 km (1,089 miles), from southernmost Lindesnes across the Arctic Circle to the North Cape. It is barely 430 km (267 miles) at its widest point, and only 6 km (4 miles) at its narrowest.

Geological processes such as the land rising, the Ice Age and erosion have created a remarkably varied landscape. Deep fjords penetrate the coastal mountain ranges, their glassy green waters extending far inland to waterside towns and settlements. More than 75,000 islands lie offshore, providing sheltered harbours and passageways for the numerous ferries, cruise ships and fishing boats that ply the coast.

The capital, Oslo, is a vibrant city centred round a harbour and guarded by a castle. It is an eclectic place of traditional timber houses, stately Neo-Classical buildings and the latest in ultra-modern architecture, with a thriving café-life that spills outdoors in summer. Around Oslofjorden – a summer playground teeming with boats – evidence of Norway's Viking heritage abounds. The Vikings were a warrior-like maritime race whose voyages took them as far as America in one direction and the Caspian Sea in the other, and whose raiding parties inspired terror in the coastal communities of Northern Europe. Fascinating archaeological finds

Fishermen at the former trading post of Sund in the Lofoten Islands

◀ An antique violin and case at Hardanger Folk Museum, Utne

Pumping riches from the bottom of the sea on the Ekofisk oil field

from this time, including 9th-century sailing vessels, are on show in museums such as Oslo's Viking Ship Museum.

Northeast of the capital, fertile farmland and forests give way to lofty mountains with peaks reaching 2,500 m (8,200 ft) and long, slender valleys with lakes and rivers. The south coast is lined with silver-sand beaches set against a backdrop of the 1,400-m (4,593-ft) high mountain plateau of Hardangervidda. Vestlandet, on the west coast, with the fishing port and World Heritage City of Bergen and Norway's "oil capital", Stavanger, is picturesque fjord country.

Northern Lights

Pilgrims in days of old would make the treacherous journey north across the mountains to the sacred Nidaros Cathedral in Trondheim. Here lie the remains of the country's patron saint, Olav Haraldsson. The northernmost point in Norway, the North Cape, is a place of pilgrimage for modern-day travellers, its precipitous cliffs standing proud against the Barents Sea.

Northern Norway is the land of the midnight sun and shimmering Northern Lights. In the height of summer it basks in daylight around the clock; in winter the sun disappears altogether and its rearrival in the New Year is marked by joyous festivities.

Climate

It is possible to live so far north in Norway because of the warming effects of the Gulf Stream. On the west coast this results in warm winters and cool summers. The south and west of the country have the highest average temperatures: 22° C (72° F) in Oslo in July. The coldest temperatures can be found in the mountains, particularly Finnmarksvidda, where –51.4° C (–60.5° F) was recorded in December 1886.

Riches of the Land and Sea

Fishing, particularly herring, and the timber industry have formed the backbone of the Norwegian economy. This has always been a seafaring country, renowned for shipbuilding, and foreign trade has played an important role in its development. Industrialization gathered momentum in the 19th century; small sawmills and factories gave way to larger enterprises powered by hydro-electricity. In the 20th century, Norway made its fortune in offshore oil production, creating one of the world's richest countries. How the oil revenue should be spent has been the subject of much political controversy. The state of the environment is also a matter of fierce debate. Top of the list of concerns are pollution of the waterways,

National coat of arms

high energy consumption and which type of power stations should be built.

King and Government

Norway is a constitutional, hereditary monarchy. The current monarch is King Harald V, who succeeded to the throne in 1991. He is married to Queen Sonja, a commoner, and their two children, Crown Prince Haakon Magnus and Princess Märtha Louise, are also both married to commoners. Most Norwegians are traditionally fiercely proud of their royal family, who in turn are close to their people and are seen as modern, down-to-earth monarchs.

According to the constitution, the executive power rests with the king, but in practice it is the Council of State which governs. The Norwegian Parliament (Stortinget) has the decisive power when it comes to the management of the country. Elections to the 165-representative parliament are held every four years. Of the six principal parties jostling for power, the Labour Party held the majority from 1945–61; since then there have been both socialist and non-socialist governments.

The main political aims have been welfare, social stability and equality. The Equal Opportunities Act of 1978 established a series of principles aiming to improve the balance of men and women in the workplace and ensuring

A Sami wedding party, Kautokeino, Finnmark

equal pay for equal work. As a result, women entered political life in large numbers, and when Gro Harlem Brundtland formed her government in 1986, 44.4 per cent of the ministers were women, which caused an international sensation.

The People

Norwegians are hospitable people who will, more often than not, go out of their way to welcome a guest in their home and offer cake and a drink. This is a tradition that has its roots in the remote rural settlements of old when visitors needed sustenance after an arduous journey. Major investment in road-building, tunnels and bridges has meant that few Norwegian communities are so isolated today, but old traditions live on.

The Norwegians are a deeply patriotic race, as can be seen on National Day (17 May), when young and old dress in folk costume (the *bunad, see pp20–9*) and parade through the streets. Yet this nationalistic outlook does not prevent them from accepting refugees and immigrants.

On the one hand Norwegians are regarded as a liberal, tolerant people, but on the other they still adhere to laws that hark back to a bygone era. The sale of alcohol, for instance, is restricted to government-owned shops known as Vinmonopolet.

The marriage of Crown Prince Haakon Magnus and Mette-Marit in Oslo Cathedral, 2001

Norway was a Catholic country until the Reformation in 1537, when the state church became Evangelical-Lutheran by royal decree.

Language

Norway has had vigorous and at times heated discussions over the status of its two languages, *bokmål* ("book language"), which is a derivation of Danish, and *nynorsk*, an amalgamation of the many Norwegian dialects nationwide.

Both *bokmål* and *nynorsk* have had equal official status since 1885. *Nynorsk* is most widely spoken in the west of the country (Vestlandet) and in the central valleys to the south and east. Norway's oldest minority language, Sami, is spoken by some 20,000 people *(see p219)*.

Jubliant crowds on Holmenkoll Sunday for the ski-jumping highlight of the annual skiing festival

A Nation of Avid Readers

Norwegians read more newspapers than anyone else in the world. On average, each household buys a remarkable 1.4 newspapers a day.

Sales of books are also high. Thor Heyerdahl's *The Kon-Tiki Expedition* continues to be a top seller. It has been translated into nearly 70 languages and has sold millions of copies worldwide since it was published in 1948. Jostein Gaarder's *Sophie's World* was the world's bestselling book in 1996; Herbjørg Wassmo's *Tora-trilogy* has been translated into 22 languages, and several Norwegian crime novels have been published in as many as 30 countries.

Thor Heyerdahl's best-selling book, *The Kon-Tiki Expedition.*

Art, Music and Drama

The 19th-century passion for National Romanticism in Norway laid the foundations for what has become a rich heritage of visual arts, music and literature. Artists working at this time, such as Adolph Tidemand and Hans Gude, captured the countryside and its

people in their paintings. Edvard Munch followed with his deeply emotional Expressionist works. In music, the violinist Ole Bull and the pianist and composer Edvard Grieg looked to Norwegian folk songs for inspiration. The playwrights Bjørnstjerne Bjørnson and Henrik Ibsen put Norwegian issues firmly centre stage in their dramas.

The importance of traditions is obvious in the country's many open-air museums. It seems that no town is complete without its own collection of rustic timber buildings representing local building style and crafts such as wood-carving and decorative painting (known as *rosemaling).*

Folk music is rooted in the country's ancient songs and sagas, and musicians can often be heard playing the Hardanger fiddle, particularly at festivals. A multitude of school brass bands form a happy and harmonious part of the children's National Day parade on 17 May and other festive occasions.

Sports and the Outdoors

Renowned as the cradle of skiing, during the 2010 Winter Olympics in Vancouver, Canada, Norway won nine gold medals and came fourth in the overall competition. The country has hosted two Winter Olympics: in Oslo in 1952 and Lillehammer in 1994.

Skiing is a popular winter pastime and with the first snowfalls, trails are prepared and people of all ages venture out on skis. Events such as the Holmenkollen Ski Festival attract thousands of spectators.

Football has a strong following with 1,800 clubs throughout the country. In other fields, the women's handball and football teams have had great successes, followed closely by the whole nation on TV.

The nature-loving Norwegians still spend much of their spare time outdoors, by the sea, sailing, fishing or walking in the forests and mountains, where a network of mountain huts *(hytte)* provides overnight accommodation *(see p229).*

Skier taking a break at a hut in Rondane National Park during Easter holidays

Norway and the World

A member of NATO since 1949, Norway has remained a nation with a strong sense of "self". The referenda for joining the European Union (in 1972 and 1994) both resulted in a "no" vote; the latter with 52.2 per cent against and 47.8 per cent in favour. Opinion polls today indicate the same standpoint. However, the issue of Norways's EU membership is still regularly debated, so it remains to be seen whether the country will have a further referendum.

When it comes to international welfare and peace issues, however, Norway plays a central role. In relation to its gross national product, Norway is the world's third largest donor. It has also sent nearly 60,000 soldiers to take part in United Nations peacekeeping missions, and awards the Nobel Peace prize every year.

Norway is becoming more dependent on the outside world, and there are concerns about the future and what will happen when its oil supplies run out.

The annual award ceremony for the Nobel Peace Prize in the main hall of Oslo Town Hall

The Fjords

Among the world's most spectacular geological formations, the Norwegian fjords are long, narrow inlets stretching deep into the surrounding mountains. At their innermost reaches, their depth often matches the height of the cliffs above, while shallower waters connect them to the sea. They were created by a gradual process of glacier erosion during the last Ice Age (around 110,000 to 13,000 BC) when enormous glaciers crept through the valleys, gouging steep-sided crevices into the landscape, often far below the surface of the sea. When the glaciers melted, sea water burst in and filled the hollows left by the ice.

Waterfalls can be seen where glaciers and torrents of water once cut vertical precipices into the mountain sides.

The tree line in Vestlandet is usually at 500–1,000 m (1,640–3,280 ft).

Where the fjords meet the sea on the west coast of Norway, the tree-covered mountains rise steeply. Spruce and birch are the most common species. In the north, the cliff faces are often bare all the way down to the shore.

The threshold between the fjord and the sea often has a depth of just one-tenth of the fjord at its deepest point.

Sediment

Sandstone

Granite and gneissic rock

The Structure of a Fjord

This cut-away artwork shows a typical fjord, with a threshold of shallow water at the mouth falling steeply to great depths further inland, and inlets radiating from the main fjord. The sea bed, like the surrounding mountains, consists of granite and gneiss with sediment on top.

Fruit and vegetable cultivation is a thriving industry at the inner reaches of the southern fjords. Here the climate is more favourable than by the coast.

Glaciers such as Jostedalsbreen *(see p182)* gouged out the fjords. Toward the end of the last Ice Age, the glaciers covered all of what was to become Sognefjorden. As the ice melted, the seawater forced its way into the basin.

The mountain peaks can reach as high as 1,500 m (4,900 ft) just a short distance from the shore. In inner Sognefjorden, the mountains rise to 2,000 m (6,560 ft).

The inner arms of the fjord can extend 200 km (124 miles) from its mouth.

Small villages have developed in sheltered bays where the soil is good for fruit-growing and farming.

The inlets can be very long and often branch into several tributaries. The glaciers carved through the rock wherever the surface was weak.

A fjord's depth can be more than 1,200 m (3,930 ft).

Car ferries criss-cross the fjords at many points. Although not as quick an alternative as road tunnels and bridges, they remain a popular choice for the scenic views they offer.

Road Tunnels Under the Fjords

Communications along the Atlantic coast of Norway have always been a challenge, with fjords cutting long clefts into the land and the risk of avalanches and the mountains themselves creating other obstacles. Great improvements to the infrastructure have nevertheless been made possible thanks to the riches from the North Sea oil fields. Using modern engineering techniques, huge tunnels have been driven through mountain ranges and under fjords, making transport easier between the small communities.

The 24.5-km (15-mile) long Lærdal Tunnel *(see p180)*

Landscape and Wildlife

Norway has an immensely varied landscape. The plains and rolling hills of the southwest give way to rounded mountains cut by rivers and lakes where Arctic char, salmon and trout can be fished. Reindeer inhabit the high plateaus; elk, wolf and roe deer the forests. Further north the terrain becomes more rugged. This is the habitat of bear, lynx and Arctic fox. Polar bears can be seen on the islands of Svalbard *(see pp224–5)*. The coast is punctuated by fjords where seals and even whales may be spotted. Skerries and islands provide ideal nesting sites for some of the country's 250 species of birds. Out to sea the waters are rich in cod, coley, mackerel and herring.

The brown bear was once found throughout the country, but today lives in limited numbers in the far north.

The Atlantic Coast

The nesting cliffs of Runde, near Ålesund, Lofoten, Troms, Finnmark and Svalbard are home to several hundred thousand birds. Species include white-breasted guillemot, kittiwake, auk and puffin. Northern fulmar and northern gannet can also be seen in fewer numbers.

The Forests

Half of Norway's land area is forest, creating a natural habitat for elk and roe deer, hare, fox and squirrel. It is possible to witness a capercaillie mating game or the migration of woodcock, or even hear the call of the black grouse and the cry of the common crane from the marshes.

Puffins, "the parrots of the nesting cliffs", can be found in large numbers in northern Norway. The population varies according to feeding conditions.

The elk is Norway's largest member of the deer family, which includes wild reindeer, red deer and roe deer. It is found throughout the country.

White-tailed eagles nest high on coastal mountain shelves. Other predatory birds include the golden eagle, osprey, goshawk, buzzard and gyrfalcon.

The lynx prowls the area north from Trøndelag. Of the large predators, Norway also has bear and wolverine. The wolf, now an endangered species, inhabits the southeast.

Sea Mammals

The killer whale is a relatively frequent visitor to the coast, especially to Tysfjord in northern Norway. Those people who take part in a whale and seal safari off Andøya (see p211) may be lucky to spot a sperm whale, which can be up to 18-m (60-ft) long. The Greenland whale occasionally appears off Svalbard. Porpoises swim close to the Norwegian shore and six species of seals live along the coast. Herds of walruses can be seen around Svalbard.

The grey seal (fjordkobbe) and the common seal (steinkobbe) are found off mainland Norway. Four other species can be seen on the islands of Svalbard.

The killer whale is one of the ocean's feared predators. It eats vast quantities of seals and fish, especially herring, and will attack other whales.

Fjords and Mountains

Red deer is the biggest game animal to be seen in the coastal areas and around the fjords. Reindeer rule the mountain plateaus, where the willow grouse lives in copses and willow thickets. The common ptarmigan is found on higher ground. The wolverine thrives in the mountains.

The Far North

Animals associated with the high mountains and forests, as well as Arctic species, are found in the far north of Norway. Wildlife on Svalbard is relatively limited, but Svalbard reindeer, Arctic fox and the polar bear in particular have adjusted well to the harsh environment. Bird life along the northern coast is particularly rich.

Wild reindeer roam Hardangervidda, in the mountains of Dovrefjell and Rondane, and in the Bykle and Setesdal hills. The population fluctuates at around 70,000 animals.

The Arctic fox, or polar fox, was close to extinction in 1920 when it became an officially protected species. The population is growing, but is still very vulnerable.

Musk oxen can be found mainly in the Arctic, but a population has existed on the Dovrefjell plateau since 1932.

The common ptarmigan has pure white winter plumage, apart from near its eyes and beak. It may nest as high as 1,650 m (5,400 ft) above sea level.

The Norwegian Bunad

National Day on 17 May draws crowds of Norwegians on to the streets dressed either in traditional folk costumes or in the national dress, known as *bunad*. The two outfits differ: folk costumes have long-standing traditions in the regions, whereas the *bunad* is a modern interpretation of the traditional outfits. The large migration of rural people to the towns has made the *bunad* a symbol of their identity and for many an important link with their roots. Its use for festive occasions is becoming increasingly popular.

① Bunad from Vestfold

The Vestfold *bunad* was recreated piece-by-piece. It was first presented in its final form in 1956. Vestfold's lively foreign trade probably led to the garments being made in lighter, imported materials, rather than thick homespun fabric, but these disintegrated more easily and no complete costumes have survived. There are two versions of the Vestfold *bunad (see left)*.

Bonnet worn with the *bunad*

Silver-buckled woollen belt

② Hallingdal Bunad

The traditional *bunad* in Hallingdal consists of a black, sometimes layered skirt, a floral apron and a black cloth bodice embroidered with wool. It has a white shirt with white-work embroidery on the neckband and wristbands, just like the exquisite bridal *bunad (see left)*, which is on display in Hallingdal District Museum in Nesbyen.

The bridal bodice in luxurious cream brocade

Bridal crown in red woollen broadcloth

③ Amli Bunad from Aust-Agder

The Åmli *bunad* is considered the last link in the development of a national folk costume. The ensemble has, since the 1920s, been based on original single garments used in Åmli and neighbouring rural settlements between 1700 and the mid-1800s. A striking part of this *bunad* is the shoulder piece, in red (or green) damask. It has three pairs of silver eyes which are cross-laced over the chest with a silver chain.

Embroidered linen headscarf with a fringe

Double collar stud fastenings for a blouse

④ Bridal Bunad from Voss

The most eye-catching part of the bridal *bunad* from Voss is the splendid crown, or *Vosseladet* as it is known. It is covered in red fabric embroidered with beads. Silver coins and filigree silver ornaments inset with semi-precious stones hang from the brim. Apart from the crown and a special black jacket, the bridal costume is largely the same as the normal Voss *bunad* worn for festive occasions.

Agnus Dei pendant worn with bridal gown

Voss's bridal crown dating from the early 19th century

⑤ Bunads from Oppdal

There is one *bunad* that can be used in the whole of Trøndelag, although many counties have their own version. The Oppdal *bunad* was reconstructed in 1963 from the fragments of old costumes. The multi-coloured woollen skirt is worn with a red, green or blue bodice. The man's *bunad* is based on an 18th-century garment. The breeches can be made of leather or black homespun.

Agnus Dei pendant worn by the women

Man's waistcoat made from linen and wool

⑥ Bunads from Nordland and Troms

The Nordland *bunad*, created in 1928, was originally blue, but now also comes in green. It is based on a 200-year-old fabric from Vefsn. The bag or reticule is in the same colour and floral pattern as the skirt. The woman's *bunad* from Troms is inspired by costumes from Bjarkøy and Senja. The man's *bunad* is the same for Nordland and Troms.

A silver-clasped reticule for the woman

Traditional Sami Costumes

The colourful costume, an important part of Sami cultural identity *(see p219)*

Sami costumes made from cloth can be traced back to the Middle Ages. They developed from earlier versions which were made from animal hide. Today, the three most distinctive outfits come from Kautokeino, Varanger and Karasjok.

The Kautokeino costume comprises a tunic top for the men, a pleated skirt for the women and a belt with silver buttons. Each item is richly decorated with bands of embroidery. The Varanger costume is also colourfully embellished, while that from Karasjok is remarkably simple and retains much of the cut of the ancient hide costume, the *pesk*. The women of Karasjok wear a beautiful fringed shawl and may add an ornate oversized silver brooch.

The Home of Skiing

Norway is known as the "home of skiing" and, indeed, Morgedal in Telemark is considered by some aficionados to be the birthplace of the sport. The torch for the Winter Olympic Games in Oslo in 1952 and Lillehammer in 1994 was lit from ski veteran Sondre Norheim's fireplace in Morgedal. Norwegians excel in international skiing competitions, but it is as a leisure activity that skiing comes into its own. Long stretches of illuminated trails and floodlit pistes tempt both the young and the old on to the snowy tracks. Special family events and exercise competitions attract keen participants.

Poster for the 1952 Oslo Winter Olympics

The History of Skiing

Skiing is shown in ancient rock carvings and is mentioned in the Edda poems and Norse sagas. There is evidence of skiing for leisure and competition from the 1750s, with a rapid increase after 1850. Its popularity grew with Nansen's ski trek across Greenland in 1888 and Amundsen's journey to the South Pole in 1911. Since the first Winter Olympics in 1924, skiing in its various forms has been a key part of the programme.

A 4000-year-old rock carving, possibly the oldest recorded depiction of a skier

The Birkebeiner rescue of young Prince Håkon, 1206 (painting by K Bergslien, 1869)

Roald Amundsen's expedition to the South Pole, 1910–12

Liv Arnesen, first lone woman to reach the South Pole, 1994

The Arena holds up to 30,000 spectators.

Holmenkollen Ski Festival

The first skiing competition at Holmenkollen in 1892 combined an 18-km (11-miles) cross-country course with jumping. The longest jump was 21.5 m (70 ft). Today's record is more than 132 m (433 ft). A 50-km (31-miles) cross-country course was introduced in 1902. The trail event, Holmenkollmarsjen, and the Children's Day (see above), are held in March.

Skiing traditions are very important to the Norwegians. This is a popular modern ski, built according to an old cross-country model.

The annual Birkebeiner race every March from Rena to Lillehammer celebrates the rescue of baby Prince Håkon in 1206 by two Birkebeinere on skis. The race is 58-km (36-miles) long.

From Cross-country to High Jump

It all began with cross-country, because skis were the most efficient means of getting around on the snow. Ski-jumping and Alpine skiing were introduced as sports for fun, games and competition.

Classic cross-country was universal until 1987, when the faster "ski-skating" developed into a separate discipline.

The Hill size is 134-m (440-ft) long.

The Inrun is 97-m (318-ft) long.

Telemark style, such as the Telemark turn and landing, has been the model for cross-country and ski-jumping since 1860.

Alpine skiing developed in the Alps, but the word *slalom* is Norwegian (*sla*: hill; *låm*: track). Downhill skiing became a form of popular entertainment.

Cross-country trail in "Marka", the area around Oslo which comprises 2,000 km (1,243 miles) of prepared wide tracks for skiers. There are narrow tracks, too, for those who prefer to ski alone. Ski huts dotted at intervals along the routes are popular meeting places for a rest and a sandwich.

Ski-jumping has seen a rapid development with increasingly higher and longer ski jumps. The aerodynamic "Boklöv style" has been universally adopted.

NORWAY THROUGH THE YEAR

There are four clearly defined seasons in Norway, but as the saying goes: "Every season has its charm." Norwegians enjoy being one of the world's top skiing nations, and even town-dwellers will don their skis as soon as the first snow falls in November or December. The winter sports centres have something to offer everyone, both beginners and experienced skiers, and are extremely popular, particularly at Easter. The arrival of spring brings long light filled days. The arts and cultural scenes begin to stir after their winter slumber. Norway celebrates National Day on 17 May with children's parades and other festivities.

In summer Norwegians head for the islands and skerries. There are boat festivals, fairs and games all the way along the coast. Autumn is the season for theatre-going, concerts, opera, dance, film premieres and art exhibitions.

Norwegian Royals at Holmenkollen Ski Festival

Spring

When the severe "King Winter" loosens his grip, the country bursts into life. The spring sun at the end of April heralds the last of the season's skiing trips in the mountains and encourages an urge to get out and about and experience life anew. The tourist season starts in earnest in May when the countryside is crisp and fresh, and the arts and cultural festivals are beginning to blossom. At this time of year activities such as dancing and musical events move outdoors. There are markets and shows to visit.

March

Sun Party at Svalbard (1st week of Mar). The world's northernmost celebration of the return of the sun.
Holmenkollen Ski Festival (2nd week Mar, see pp30–31).
Alternative Fair, Bergen (mid-Mar). An exploration of the "Age of Aquarius".

Oslo Festival of Church Music (1st week of Mar) features a variety of concerts.
The Birkebeiner Race (3rd week of Mar). Ski marathon from Rena to Lillehammer (see pp31, 135 and 141).
Winter Festival, Røros (all month). Musical events in this old copper-mining town.
Vossajazz Hordaland (late Mar). International jazz festival, one of the first of the season.

April

Sami Easter celebrations and weddings (end of Mar or early Apr).
Scandinavian Ski Pride (2nd week of Apr). Gay and lesbian ski festival at Norway's largest ski resort, with a vibrant entertainment and après ski line-up.
Day of Dance (29 Apr). Celebrated all over the country with performances and dance stunts in the streets and squares by amateurs and professionals.

May

May Jazz, Stavanger (1st half of May). A fast-growing festival offering big stars and exciting new talent.
17 May, ("Syttende Mai"), Norway's National Day, is celebrated nationwide with children's parades and a host of festivities.
Bergen International Arts Festival (end of May/early Jun) offers ten days of music, dance, drama and artistic events of international standing attracting large numbers of visitors to venues across the city.
Night Jazz Bergen (end of May/early Jun). Staged around the same time as the Bergen Festival, Night Jazz Bergen organizes more than 70 different concerts featuring both Norwegian and international artists.

Norway's National Day, 17 May, on Karl Johans Gate, Oslo

Summer

The long, light summer nights are not for sleeping. Summer is the peak season for festivals and outdoor productions ranging from musicals to historical plays and classical dramas using nature as a backdrop.

In many parts of the country traditions centre around types of food, such as the Oslo Seafood Festival in August. Often they are combined with varying degrees of physical challenges. Tourist offices can recommend events off the beaten track, or check www.visitoslo.no.

Salmon fishing in Ågårdselva, Østfold

June

Salmon Fishing Season *(1 Jun–mid/end Aug)*. Dates may vary slightly.
Music Fest Olso, Oslo *(1st week of Jun)*. Classical, jazz, pop and rock.
Norwegian Mountain Marathon *(1st week Jun)*. A remarkable marathon in the spectacular mountains of Jotunheimen.
Bergen Fest *(mid-Jun)*. Voted the best Norwegian festival by its participants.
Summer Concerts at Troldhaugen, Bergen *(Wed, Sat and Sun, mid-Jun to mid-Aug; also Sun in Sep)*. The music of Edvard Grieg performed in his own home.
Norwegian Wood, Oslo *(mid-Jun)*. Rock music festival near Vigelandsparken *(see pp94–5)*.
Short Film Festival, Grimstad *(mid-Jun)*. Popular competition for short films.
St Hans Aften *(20–26 Jun)*. Midsummer is celebrated with bonfires and festivities.
Cultural Festival in Northern Norway Harstad *(around midsummer)*.
Midnight Sun Marathon, Tromsø *(21 Jun)*. At the world's northernmost marathon runners compete at night in broad daylight due to the midnight sun.
Risør Festival of Chamber Music, Risør *(last week of Jun)*. Top-class concerts in idyllic Sørlandet on the southern coast.

Skiing in summer

Extreme Sports Week, Voss *(last week of Jun)*. Mountain biking, mountain climbing, extreme skiing, plus music.
Vestfold Festival *(end of Jun/early Jul)*. Ten-day festival of music, dance and theatre.

July

Norsk Aften, Norsk Folkemuseum, Oslo *(Tue, Wed, Fri and Sat from 1 Jul)*. The "Norwegian Evening" offers guided tours in the stave church and museum area; folk dancing and food.
Kongsberg Jazz Festival *(early Jul)*, with top musicians such as Joshua Redman.
Fjæreheia Grimstad *(from mid-Jul)*. Agder Theatre's outdoor performances of Ibsen dramas and musicals.
Molde International Jazz Festival *(last week of Jul)*, starring the world's best performers and first-class Norwegian artists.
Gladmat Festival, Stavanger *(late Jul)*. Scandinavia's largest food festival draws the crowds with celebrity guest chefs and tasting events highlighting the latest culinary trends.

Thousands of fans at the Molde International Jazz Festival in July

Telemark Festival, Bø *(late Jul/early Aug)*. International folk music festival with something for all the family: song, dance, music, concerts, dance and instrument courses, and seminars.

August

Wooden Boat Festival, Risør *(early Aug)*. Exhibition of coastal culture, old and new wooden boats; outdoor concerts.
Notodden International Blues Festival *(1st week of Aug)*. Concerts in clubs and outdoors. There is a "blues cruise" for those without a boat of their own.
Peer Gynt Festival *(1–10 Aug)*. The Ibsen drama *Peer Gynt* is performed outdoors in beautiful surroundings by Gålå Lake.
Nordic Hunting and Fishing Days Elverum *(1st half of Aug)*.
Stavanger Chamber Music Festival and **Oslo Chamber Music Festival** *(mid-Aug)* attract large numbers of visitors to the summer evening concerts.
Sildajazz, Haugesund *(mid-Aug)*. Colourful festival featuring 20 concert venues, children's and street parades, harbour market and pleasure craft.
Bjørnson Festival, Molde *(last week of Aug)*. International festival of literature. Bjørnson was one of Norway's greatest writers.
Norwegian Film Festival Haugesund *(end of Aug)*. More than 100 new films are shown during the eight-day festival. Buy a season ticket. Presentation of the Amanda Awards.

Bearberries colouring the mountains red in the autumn

Autumn

Walking in the forests and mountains, picking berries and gathering mushrooms are ideal pastimes in autumn. As the evenings begin to close in, Norwegians retreat indoors and enjoy the many cultural events that are staged in theatres large and small. Autumn brings plenty to refresh the mind: new books are published and major art exhibitions often open at this time of year.

September

The National Theatre (Nationaltheatret), Oslo (1st half of Sep), alternates the start of the season each year with either the Ibsen Festival or the Contemporary Festival (Samtidsfestival) of new drama.

Ibsen Culture Festival, Skien (1st half of Sep). A celebration of the work of the 19th-century Norwegian

Chanterelle harvest

playwright in the town where he grew up.

Ultima Festival, Oslo (1st half of Sep). Scandinavia's largest contemporary music festival takes place over 10 days every year. Concerts, workshops and live music are enjoyed in various venues around the capital.

October

Oslo Beer Festival (10–12 Oct). Celebrating Oslo's growing craft beer culture with more than 60 events at bars and restaurants across the city. A beer "train" allows participants to hear talks and taste selected beers.

Fartein Valen Days, Haugesund (end of Oct). The composer Fartein Valen (1887–1952) is showcased with a series of lectures and concerts in churches, galleries and in his childhood home.

Kingsland Oslo Horse Show (mid-Oct). A popular family event held at Telenor Arena.

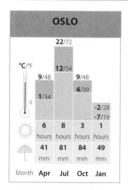

OSLO

	22/72		
9/48	12/54	9/48	
1/34		4/39	-2/28
			-7/19

°C/°F

6	8	3	1
hours	hours	hours	hours
41	81	84	49
mm	mm	mm	mm

Month | Apr | Jul | Oct | Jan

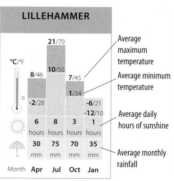

LILLEHAMMER

	21/70		
8/46	10/50	7/45	
-2/28		1/34	-6/21
			-12/10

°C/°F

6	8	3	1
hours	hours	hours	hours
30	75	70	35
mm	mm	mm	mm

Month | Apr | Jul | Oct | Jan

Average maximum temperature
Average minimum temperature
Average daily hours of sunshine
Average monthly rainfall

Climate

Western Norway has an Atlantic climate with warm winters and cool summers. The highest average temperatures are in Sørlandet and Vestlandet. Østlandet has an inland climate, with cold winters and warm summers. Vestlandet has the most rain; the north end of Gudbrandsdal and the depths of Finnmarksvidda have the least rain.

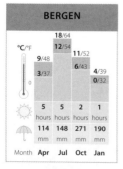

BERGEN

	18/64		
9/48	12/54	11/52	
3/37		6/43	4/39
			0/32

°C/°F

5	5	2	1
hours	hours	hours	hours
114	148	271	190
mm	mm	mm	mm

Month | Apr | Jul | Oct | Jan

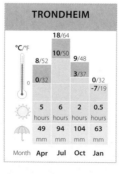

TRONDHEIM

	18/64		
8/52	10/50	9/48	
0/32		3/37	0/32
			-7/19

°C/°F

5	6	2	0.5
hours	hours	hours	hours
49	94	104	63
mm	mm	mm	mm

Month | Apr | Jul | Oct | Jan

TROMSØ

	15/59		
	9/48	5/41	
3/37		1/34	-2/28
-2/28			-7/19

°C/°F

5	7	1,5	0
hours	hours	hours	hours
64	77	131	95
mm	mm	mm	mm

Month | Apr | Jul | Oct | Jan

Winter

The Christmas season gets underway when the Christmas trees are lit, the first Christmas snow starts to fall and colourfully decorated gingerbread cookie houses start appearing. Restaurants are fully booked for their Christmas buffets, with the Norwegian speciality, *lutefisk* (dried fish treated with lye), on the menu.

New Year sees the start of the skiing season, and the prospect of fresh tracks lures many on to the slopes.

November

Rakfisk Festival, Fagernes, Valdres *(1st weekend in Nov)*. Fermented mountain trout is a delicacy, and visitors can choose from the best producers have to offer.

Museum of Children's Art, (Det Internasjonale Barnekunstmuseet), Oslo, has extended opening hours during the winter, on Tue, Wed, Thu and Sun morning. Paintings and drawings by children worldwide.

Lighting the Christmas Tree *(1st Sun of Advent)*. Trees are lit in towns and villages and there is music, speeches and group singing, as well as the traditional walk around the tree.

December

Christmas Concerts *(all Dec)*. Well-known singers and entertainers give church concerts, often with local choirs and orchestras.

Christmas Markets *(Sun)*. Folk museums such as the Norsk Folkemuseum, Oslo, and Maihaugen, Lillehammer, arrange special folk dancing displays and concerts, the sales of crafts and Father Christmas workshops.

Gingerbread Houses, Galleriet, Bergen *(all Dec)*. The world's biggest gingerbread town according to the *Guinness Book of Records*. A remarkable show of 150 gingerbread houses, ships, aeroplanes and ski jumps skilfully made by children, young people and professionals.

Full moon over a wintery scene at Lillehammer

January

Ski-Kite, Møsvann, Telemark *(early Jan)*. Skiing with the aid of a kite. Lessons at the Rauland Ski Centre.

Festival of Northern Lights, Tromsø *(end of Jan)*. Visitors from around the world come to see the magnificent northern lights *(aurora borealis)* and enjoy a musical extravaganza that features top Norwegian and international stars from a wide variety of musical genres.

Giant snowman at the Snow Sculpture Festival, Vinje

Polar Jazz Svalbard *(end of Jan)*. The world's most northerly jazz and blues festival. Four to five days of concerts and events staged throughout the Svalbard town of Longyearbyen.

February

Snow Sculpture Festival, Vinje *(mid-Feb)*. A sculpture park with a difference. Create your own masterwork in ice and snow and admire other people's eye-catching handiwork.

Opera Week, Kristiansund *(early Feb)*. Opera, ballet, art exhibitions and a number of other events are staged at Festiviteten.

Winter Arts Festival, Lillehammer *(mid-Feb)*. Concerts and ice and snow sculpture celebrating the season.

Røros Market *(3rd Tue of Feb)*. A fair celebrating traditional handicrafts with demonstrations, workshops and local food.

Public Holidays

New Year's Day (1 Jan)
Palm Sunday (Sunday before Easter)
Maundy Thursday
Good Friday
Easter Sunday
Easter Monday
Whit Sunday
Whit Monday
Labour Day (1 May)
National Day (17 May)
St Hans (24 Jun)
Christmas Day (25 Dec)
Boxing Day (26 Dec)

Traditional Christmas displays in a shopping centre

THE HISTORY OF NORWAY

When the Norwegian chieftain, Ottar, visited the court of King Alfred the Great in England 1,100 years ago, he was the first person to give an account of "Nor-weg", the homeland of the Northmen. The Viking Age was to follow, and centuries of strife and colonization, union, war and occupation. The country survived to achieve prosperity and international standing.

The first traces of human habitation in Norway are those of the Komsa and Fosna cultures, both more than 9,000 years old. Archaeological finds from the Stone Age to the Iron Age include crude implements and weapons, and realistic rock carvings of reindeer and fish. Later, symbols of sun wheels and boats appear. Iron Age burial mounds containing weapons and ornamental items, rune stones and ships have been uncovered.

The Viking Age (see pp38–9) marks a transition in the history of Norway. Viking warriors set forth on their voyages and brought home ideas that were to influence the country's political and cultural development.

Norway was united as one kingdom at the Battle of Hafrsfjord at Stavanger in AD 890. Here Harald Hårfagre (Harald Fine-hair) defeated his enemies and secured sufficient power to establish a permanent army and maintain unity. Those who failed to fall into line left the country, became outlaws or were killed.

Some of those who left Norway settled in Iceland. They included Erik the Red (Eirik Raude), who in 985 laid the foundations for a settlement on Greenland. His son, Leiv Eiriksson, discovered America in AD 1000. This led to temporary Norse settlements on the northern point of Newfoundland.

After Håkon Haraldsson (Håkon the Good), the popular younger son of Harald Fine-hair, conflict ensued over the kingship, until Olav Tryggvason (d. AD 1000), and Olaf II Haraldsson (Olav the Holy; see p208) united the kingdom and introduced Christianity. They tore down the pagan statues and built stave churches.

Over the centuries, Norway became a sovereign kingdom and built up an empire comprising the Faeroe Islands, Orkney Islands, Hebrides, Isle of Man and, after 1260, Iceland and Greenland.

From 1130, the conflict for leadership caused civil war until finally the line of Sverre Sigurdsson triumphed. Norway stood at the height of its power when his grandson, Håkon Håkonsson, was crowned king in 1247. After the death of Håkon V Magnusson in 1319, the order of royal succession did not work in Norway's favour. His grandson, Håkon VI was the last king of an independent nation.

10 000 BC	1500	AD 500	750	1000	1250
9300 BC The first inhabitants, the Komsa hunters, fishermen and gatherers, live around Alta, Finnmark	**c.500 BC** Early Iron Age. Iron extraction begins on Hardangervidda and in Aurland. The climate becomes colder			**c. 1000** Leiv Eiriksson discovers Vinland in North America	
				1030 Olav the Holy is killed at the Battle of Stiklestad	
c.4000 BC Growth of farming in Østfold	**1800–500 BC** Bronze Age people build large burial mounds on ridges, roadsides and on the coast, such as in Jæren	**793** The Viking Age begins with a raid on the monastery on Lindisfarne in northeast England		**890** Battle of Hafrsfjord: Norway is united under Harald Hårfagre	
				1247 Håkon Håkonsson is crowned king	

Viking Age sculpture of Odin

◄ *Håkon Håkonsson's coronation in Bergen, 1247, by Cardinal Vilhelm of Sabina (Gerhard Munthe, 1910)*

The Vikings

For more than 300 years, from the 8th to the 11th century, the Vikings took the world by storm. As traders, settlers and plunderers, they set sail from their homes in Norway, Sweden and Denmark in search of land, slaves, gold and silver. They carried out raids throughout Europe, sailed as far as Baghdad and even reached America. Terrified Christian monks wrote of dreadful attacks on monasteries and towns. But the Vikings were more than barbarians. They were clever traders, outstanding seafarers, craftsmen and shipbuilders, and they lived in an open society that was democratic for its time.

Conical helmet
Spear
Round shield
Sword
Axe

A Viking warrior with his equipment in a carving on a 10th-century stone cross from Middleton, England.

Shields along the ship's sides served as both protection and decoration.

Lindisfarne is a small island off the north-east coast of England. Its monastery was raided by Vikings in 793. This gravestone shows an attacking band of Vikings.

A tent provided the only shelter from the elements.

Leiv Eiriksson Discovers America

The Norse discoverers sailed in broad, robust ships that were heavier than the narrow longships used in battle. They had more room for a crew with goods and provisions. In his painting of 1893, Christian Krohg portrays the moment when Leiv points in wonder to the new continent, America. Leiv was the son of Erik the Red. He was known as the "lucky one".

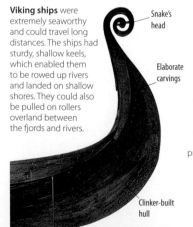

Viking ships were extremely seaworthy and could travel long distances. The ships had sturdy, shallow keels, which enabled them to be rowed up rivers and landed on shallow shores. They could also be pulled on rollers overland between the fjords and rivers.

Snake's head

Elaborate carvings

Clinker-built hull

An iron helmet and sword were essential items of Viking equipment. The helmets, like this one from Ringerike, were without horns, but had an ocularium to protect the eyes. Sword shafts were often beautifully decorated.

Viking women ran the household and the farm while the men were away. They were independent and self-sufficient.

The tiller was on the ship's starboard side.

The World of the Vikings

The Vikings raided, traded and invaded far and wide. They reached Iceland in about 870 and sailed west to Greenland in 982. Leiv Eiriksson discovered America in about 1000. In the east, the Vikings travelled to Russia and sailed on rivers as far as the Black Sea and Constantinople. Others travelled along the west coast of Europe and into the Mediterranean.

The ruins of a 9th-century Viking farm on the Shetland Islands. It had two rooms, a long hall and a kitchen. The inhabitants slept on benches along the sloping walls.

The important Viking gods were Odin, god of wisdom; Thor, god of thunder and Freya, goddess of fertility. This statue depicts Freya. Norway converted to Christianity in the 11th century.

Brooches such as this were used by men to fasten their cloaks. They were secured to the right shoulder so the sword arm was free.

793 Vikings raid the English monastery of Lindisfarne	**834** The ship *Oseberg* is used for a Viking burial	**890** Battle of Hafrsfjord: the kingdom is united	**911** Normandy is founded by the Viking chieftain, Rollo	**948** Håkon the Good attempts to convert his countrymen	**c.1000** Leiv Eiriksson discovers Vinland in North America	**1030** Battle of Stiklestad
	845 The sack of Hamburg and Paris					
800	**830**	**860**	**890**	**920**	**950**	**980**	**1010**
841 A large Viking fleet overwinters in Dublin	**870** Vikings colonize Iceland	**876** Vikings settle permanently in England		**985** Erik the Red settles in Greenland	**1066** Battle of Stamford Bridge: Vikings are defeated by Harold II of England
799 Viking raids begin in France		**912** Vikings reach the Caspian Sea	*Viking ship c.980*	**c.1000** Olav Tryggvason is killed at Svolder	

Sarcophagus in Roskilde Cathedral of Queen Margrete, ruler of Denmark, Sweden and Norway

The Kalmar Union

Håkon VI Magnusson married the Danish princess, Margrete. Their only child, Olav, became king of Denmark in 1375, and inherited the Norwegian throne on Håkon's death in 1380. This was the start of the 400-year-long Danish-Norwegian union.

When Olav died in 1388 at the age of 17, Margrete became ruler of both countries, and of Sweden, too. By adopting her nephew, Erik of Pomerania, as king of all three nations in 1397, she laid the foundation for the Kalmar Union, which was to last until 1523, when Gustav Vasa seceded from the Union and established a new dynasty in Sweden.

Union with Denmark

Margrete conducted a fair policy towards Norway. The country's position weakened in 1536 when Christian III declared that Norway would forever be a vassal state of Denmark.

Norway was unable to assert its authority in the union, because from the middle of 14th century the Black Death reduced the population by more than half. The Reformation forced Archbishop Olav Engelbrektsson, one of the few to campaign for Norwegian independence, to flee the country. Norway was ruled by feudal overlords as a dependency of Denmark. Its middle class was weakened by the Hanseatic merchants from northern Germany who ruled trading life on the west coast.

Christian IV

The union with Denmark was not without its high points. Norwegian industry gradually began to pick up. Fishing expanded; forestry and the export of timber became a new resource. As the Hanseatic League declined, Norwegian traders were able to step in. Mining became an important industry, especially under Christian IV (1577–1648), who took a great interest in Norwegian affairs. He visited the country on 30 occasions, founded the city of Christiania and streamlined the administration. The country was granted a new church ordination and its own military system.

Christian established Norwegian control of the north of the country. But his on-going conflict with Sweden resulted in Norway having to cede land in the east to Sweden. His son, Frederik III, introduced absolute rule in the "double monarchy" in 1660. This meant rule by officials appointed by the king

Bærums Verk, one of the first ironworks in Norway, dating from 1610

1380 Håkon VI Magnusson, the last king of an independent Norway, dies

1400 Hanseatic League, based in Bergen, reaches the height of its power, controlling imports and exports

1536 Christian III of Denmark declares that Norway will forever be a vassal state of Denmark

1350

1400

1450

1500

1550

1349 Black Death reduces Norway's population by 50 per cent

1397 Kalmar Union unites Norway, Denmark and Sweden under one king

Queen Margrete (r.1388–1412)

1537 The Reformation: Archbishop Olav Engelbrektsson is driven out of Norway

1558 Hanseatic grip weakens

Painting of the poets' nationalist society, *Det Norske Selskab*, in Copenhagen, by Eilif Peterssen (1892)

instead of rule by aristocrats. Increasingly, officials came from the Norwegian middle class, which worked in Norway's favour.

In the early 18th century, under Frederik IV, the wars with Sweden continued. They produced a national hero for Norway, the naval commander Peter Wessel Tordenskiold, who, in a surprise attack, obliterated the Swedish fleet.

The Swedish warrior king, Karl XII, twice tried to conquer Norway, but was killed during a siege on Halden in 1718.

Demands grew for Norwegian independence. This was due in part to a revival in interest in the country's history, brought about by a patriotic society of poets and historians, *Det Norske Selskab*, in Copenhagen. Calls for a national university in Norway were finally conceded to in 1811. Nevertheless, it was mostly affairs outside the country that led to the parting of the "double monarchy" in 1814.

Naval hero Peter Wessel Tordenskiold

In Napoleon's Shadow

The Danish-Norwegian king, Frederik VI, allied himself with Napoleon in 1807. As a result, Britain blockaded Norwegian harbours and halted all imports and exports. Isolation became total when, for a time, there was also a war with Sweden. Then followed the years of great need in 1808 and 1812. Crops failed, fishing yields were poor and there was much hunger.

In Sweden, the former French marshal, Jean Baptiste Bernadotte, became crown prince in 1810 under the name Karl Johan. He joined the coalition against Napoleon and was able to persuade his allies – Russia, Britain, Austria and Prussia – that he would be able to force Denmark to relinquish Norway to Sweden when Napoleon was defeated. When Napoleon was finally routed at Leipzig in 1813, Karl Johan marched toward Denmark, and at the Treaty of Kiel in January 1014, Norway was surrendered to Sweden.

1624 Oslo burns down. Christiania is established north of Akershus Castle

1709 The Great Nordic War takes place between Denmark-Norway and Sweden

1718 The Swedish king, Karl XII, is killed at Frederiksten Fortress during his second attempt to conquer Norway

1813 Karl Johan marches on Denmark

1814 Norway is ceded to Sweden at the Peace of Kiel

1600

1650

1700

1750

1800

Christian IV (1577–1648)

1660 Frederik III introduces absolute rule

1645 Under the Treaty of Bromsebro, Norwegian territories of Jemtland and Herjedalen are ceded to Sweden

1769 Norway's population totals 723,000 of whom 65,000 live in towns

1772 Patriotic society, *Det Norske Selskab*, is founded

1811 The University of Norway is founded in Oslo

A painting of *The National Assembly at Eidsvoll*, by O. Wergeland, 1885, hanging in the Storting in Oslo

The National Assembly at Eidsvoll

The Danish prince, Christian Frederik, was governor-general of Norway at the time of the Treaty of Kiel, which ceded Norway to Sweden. Both he and the Norwegian people opposed the agreement. An assembly of 21 of the most prominent men in Norway declared Christian Frederik to be the most suitable candidate for the throne of their country, but would not agree to his wish for an absolute monarchy. Instead, it was decided that the people should elect delegates to a national assembly. On Easter Sunday 1814, 112 representatives convened at Eidsvoll and on 17 May they adopted the Norwegian constitution. Christian Frederik was elected king of an independent, free Norway.

Meanwhile, Crown Prince Karl Johan of Sweden demanded that the Treaty of Kiel be implemented. There was a brief war. Karl Johan then accepted the Eidsvoll constitution and on 4 November 1814 the Storting (Norwegian Parliament) elected Sweden's elderly Karl XIII as king of Norway. He was followed in 1818 by Karl Johan himself.

Union with Sweden

The *riksakt*, the convention that was ratified by the Norwegian and Swedish parliaments, ruled that the two countries should have a common king and would stand united in war. Apart from this, they were equal and independent of one another. But there were no provisions in the *riksakt* for a Norwegian foreign service or a national flag. The demand for a flag was not resolved until 1898. The tug-of-war over the foreign service was one of the reasons that led to the dissolution of the union. Another area of dispute was whether the king should be entitled to appoint the governor-general in Norway.

By the time of his death in 1844, Karl Johan had become popular in Norway, despite attempting to suppress displays of national identity. *Torvslaget* (Battle in the Marketplace) on 17 May 1829 in Christiania (Oslo) was one such occasion. Norwegians were celebrating National Day when troops attacked. The poet Henrik Wergeland, who was in the crowd, received a blow from a sword. He was subsequently inspired to write with fervour in praise of a free Norway. *Torvslaget* had added new meaning to the 17 May festivities.

The Battle in the Marketplace, Christiania, 17 May 1829

1814 Norway's constitution is adopted on 17 May by the National Assembly

Henrik Wergeland

1829 Battle in the Marketplace: troops attack crowds on National Day, 17 May. The nationalist poet, Henrik Wergeland, is wounded

1837 First performance at Christiania Theatre

1844 Karl Johan dies; is succeeded by his son, Oscar I

| 1810 | 1820 | 1830 | 1840 | 1850 |

1816 Norges Bank is established

1818 Karl Johan is crowned king of Norway in Nidaros Cathedral

1819 The first edition of *Morgenbladet*, Norway's first daily newspaper, is published

1848 Marcus Thrane founds Norway's first workers' union

1854 The first railway line is opened for passenger trains from Christiania to Eidsvoll

The Christiania–Eidsvoll railway line, completed in 1854

Economic Growth

An economic crisis in the first few years after 1814 was short-lived. Norges Bank was established in 1816, the country stabilised

its currency and was free of debt by 1850. This period marked a watershed in the Norwegian economy. Industry was in the throes of change and growing rapidly. Shipping was experiencing a golden age, particularly between 1850 and 1880, with the transition from sail to steam. Norway

Textile worker at the Hjula weaving mill, 1887

built its first railway in 1854; the telegraph arrived in 1850 and the telephone in 1880.

An economic downturn in 1848–50 caused mass unemployment and prompted Marcus Thrane to establish the first workers' union. By 1865, Norway's population had doubled from 900,000 in 1800 to 1.7 million, and it continued to rise. Emigration to America began in 1825 and gradually increased in intensity – between 1879 and 1893 a quarter of a million people crossed the Atlantic.

A Vote for Freedom

Political life toward the end of the period of union with Sweden was characterized by turbulence and the transition to democracy. Parliamentary rule was introduced in 1884, universal suffrage for men in 1898, and for women in 1913.

The long-standing conflict over demands for a separate foreign minister finally brought the union to its knees. In 1905, Norway's Michelsen government resigned because the king would not sanction the Storting's bill on the consular service. The king refused to accept the government's resignation on the grounds that: "A new government cannot now be formed." Michelsen used these words as a pretext to declare the union dissolved. As the king was outside the government and was unable to form a new one – which he was obliged to do under the constitution – he could no longer fulfil his role and was thus no longer the Norwegian king. Without a common king, the union ceased to exist. On 7 June, it was dissolved by the Storting, but Sweden demanded a referendum: 368,208 people voted in favour of secession; 184 against. The Swedish-Norwegian union ended peacefully.

Postcard marking the dissolution of the union with Sweden after a "yes" vote in the 1905 referendum

1860

1865 Norway's population exceeds 1.7 million people

1871 Opening of the telegraph line to Kirkenes in Northern Norway

1870

1875 Norway's merchant navy becomes the third largest in the world

1879 Ibsen's play *A Doll's House* is published

1880

1882 The height of emigration to North America

1884 Parliamentary rule is introduced after a bitter struggle

Christian Michelsen

1889 Compulsory schooling introduced

1890

1898 Universal suffrage for men

1905 Under Prime Minister Christian Michelsen, the union with Sweden comes to a peaceful end

1900

1899 The Norwegian Federation of Trade Unions (LO) is established

Prime Minister Christian Michelsen greeting Prince Carl and the infant Olav, 25 November 1905

A New Royal Family

After 400 years of Danish and Swedish rule, in 1905 the Norwegian royal family had died out and the nation turned to Prince Carl, second son of the heir to the Danish throne, to be its head of state. His wife was the British princess, Maud, and they had a two-year-old son, Olav. Prince Carl adopted the name Haakon VII and was crowned in Nidaros Cathedral.

For the first period following the dissolution of the union, domestic policy concen- trated on social reforms. Roald Amundsen's successful expedition to the South Pole in 1911 created an enormous wave of national pride. With the writer Bjørnstjerne Bjørnson

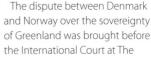

Fridtjof Nansen, polar researcher

leading the way, Norway made its presence strongly felt in peacekeeping efforts. In 1901, the Storting had been given the honourable task of awarding the annual Alfred Nobel Peace Prize.

Norway remained neutral during World War I, but half of her merchant fleet was lost. However, shipping and the export of iron ore provided good revenues and led to wild speculation in shares and a boom period. Toward the end of the war, a shortage of provisions caused difficulties.

Between the Wars

After the war, restrictions in many areas led to bankruptcies and industrial disputes. Farmers and fishermen who had invested heavily in new machinery and equipment in the boom-time were forced to sell up.

In 1930, as the Great Depression took hold in Norway, hardship increased. The banks failed, and people lost their savings. Some 200,000 people were unemployed, and many industrial disputes resembled armed conflicts. Shipping fared better: the modern Norwegian merchant fleet had become the third largest in the world.

Between 1918 and 1935, Norway had nine different governments. Then Johan Nygaardsvold's Labour Party came to power and remained in office until 1945. Norway joined the League of Nations and participated in its activities under the guidance of the scientist and diplomat, Fridtjof Nansen.

The dispute between Denmark and Norway over the sovereignty of Greenland was brought before the International Court at The Hague in 1931, and Norway lost its claim.

Under Occupation

Norway declared itself neutral when World War II broke out in September 1939. Regardless, Germany invaded on 9 April 1940. Norwegian troops succeeded in sinking the German cruiser, *Blücher*, in Oslofjorden, and held back the German advance for 62 days

1905 Haakon VII, Queen Maud and Crown Prince Olav take up residence in the palace in Oslo

Haakon VII

1931 Norway loses the Greenland case after a ruling by the court in The Hague

1940 Germany occupies Norway

1945 Norway is free. King Haakon returns on 7 June

1957 Haakon VII dies, and Olav V succeeds as king

1947 Thor Heyerdahl crosses the Pacific in *Kon-Tiki*

1910	1920	1930	1940	1950	1960

1911 Roald Amundsen reaches the South Pole

1905–07 Christian Michelsen is the first prime minister of an independent Norway

1920 Norway joins the League of Nations

1946 Trygve Lie becomes the first United Nations General Secretary

1949 Norway joins NATO

1960 Norway becomes a member of EFTA

before capitulating. On 7 June the king, the crown prince and the cabinet fled from Tromsø to continue the fight in exile in London.

Vidkun Quisling, with German backing, became prime minister of an occupied Norway, but he lacked popular support. There was mounting civil resistance. An underground military organization (Milorg) was formed, eventually comprising 47,000 men, which was controlled by the government in exile. They passed intelligence to the Allies and conducted numerous covert operations against the occupying forces, the most renowned of which was at Rjukan, where resistance fighters destroyed a heavy water plant (see pp160–61).

The Norwegian merchant navy played a major role in the war effort outside the country, but more than half the fleet was lost and 3,000 sailors perished. About 35,000 people were imprisoned during the occupation and 1,400 people, including 738 Jews, died in German concentration camps.

While retreating from Finnmark, the Germans forced the population to evacuate and scorched everything behind them. Germany capitulated on 7 May 1945; 8 May marked liberation day. A month later, King Haakon returned to Norway.

The Troll Platform is one of the largest and most co0mplex engineering projects in history

Modern Norway

Rebuilding the country after World War II took place faster than expected. During the first year of peace, output reached the pre-war level. Politically, Norway was more stable than during the interwar years. At the elections to the Storting in 1945, the Labour Party achieved a clear majority and, except for a short break, remained in power until 1963. Norway joined NATO in 1949 and EFTA in 1960. Many social reforms were introduced and Norway was on the road to becoming a welfare state.

Following the Gerhardsen period, parliamentary power shifted between Labour and the non-socialist coalition parties. The longest-serving prime minister since Einar Gerhardsen was Gro Harlem Brundtland. Since the 1970s the economy and welfare policies have been buoyed up by North Sea oil extraction and strong growth in the fishing industry. Two referenda on membership of the EU have ended in a "No", and Norway seems keen to keep its independent spirit.

German troops marching along Karl Johans Gate in Oslo, 9 April 1940

OSLO
AREA BY AREA

Oslo at a Glance

Oslo has changed its name several times in its history – from Oslo to Christiania and then to Kristiania. In 1925 the capital reverted to its original title, Oslo. The city enjoys an unsurpassed location. Within its boundaries, it is possible to swim in Oslofjorden in summer and ski on well-maintained ski trails in winter. The centre of Oslo is home to museums and galleries, a royal palace, parks and public institutions, all of which can be reached on foot. Its harbour is guarded by a 14th-century castle. There is a wide choice of shops, and in summer cafés spill out onto the pavements and waterfronts. Most sights are within walking distance from the centre, apart from those on Bygdøy.

Slottet
The Royal Palace is a Neo-Classical building on three floors. It was built as a royal residence in the reigns of King Karl XIV Johan and Oscar I, between 1825 and 1848 *(see p55)*.

Aker Brygge
Situated on the waterfront, this is a popular place to meet up for a drink, a meal or to shop. This former shipyard abounds with life. It is packed with shops and eating places *(see p61)*.

HENRIK IBSENS GAT

CENTRAL
OSLO WE
(see pp50–6

LØKKEVEIEN

MUNKEDAMSVEIEN

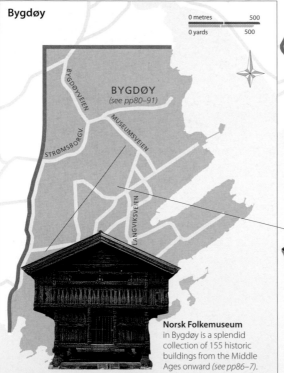

Bygdøy

BYGDØY
(see pp80–91)

BYGDØYVEIEN
MUSEUMSVEIEN
STRØMSBORGV.
LANGVIKSVEIEN

0 metres 500
0 yards 500

Norsk Folkemuseum
in Bygdøy is a splendid collection of 155 historic buildings from the Middle Ages onward *(see pp86–7)*.

Vikingskipshuse
This museum houses three of the best-preserved Viking ships in the world, and is one of Norway's cultural jewels *(see pp88–9)*

VISITORS' CHECKLIST

Practical Information
👥 600,000. ℹ Tourist
Information Office: Fridtjof
Nansens Plass 5, 24 14 77 00.
📅 17 May on Karl Johan, Ultima
Music Festival (first half Sep); Oslo
Church Music Festival (end Mar);
Oslo Horse Show (mid-Oct).

Transport
✈ Gardermoen 45 km (28 miles)
from the centre.

Locator Map

Karl Johans Gate
has been the city's main thoroughfare
for more than 100 years. The lower
part is pedestrianized; the
upper section is used for
parades *(see p54)*.

Stortinget
Constructed in yellow brick
on a granite base, this is where
Norway's National Assembly
meets. It was completed and first
used in 1866 *(see p78)*.

Akershus Festning
Norway's best-preserved
castle complex from the
Middle Ages was begun in
1300 and occupies a
spectacular harbour setting
on Oslofjorden *(see pp72–3)*.

0 metres 500
0 yards 500

CENTRAL OSLO WEST

Many of the capital's largest and most important institutions and sights are situated in the western part of central Oslo, and most of them are within walking distance of each other. In a historical context, this area of the city is relatively new. It became the capital's centre when the Royal Palace was completed and Karl Johans Gate had been laid out in the second half of the 19th century.

The area includes Oslo's most popular swathes of green: Studenterlunden, alongside

Karl Johans Gate, and Slottsparken, which surrounds the Royal Palace, are both used as recreational spaces. The bustling former wharfside at Aker Brygge, with its shops and bars, galleries and theatres, attracts the most visitors. This area of central Oslo is well served by all forms of public transport. During the summer, the streets teem with people, and cafés and restaurants open out onto the pavements in a way more normally associated with the capitals of southern Europe.

Sights at a Glance

Castles and Museums
- ❸ Nasjonalgalleriet pp56–7
- ❹ Historisk Museum pp58–9
- ❺ Slottet (Royal Palace)
- ❿ Nobel Peace Center
- ⓭ Stenersenmuseet
- ⓮ Ibsenmuseet
- ⓯ Kunstindustrimuseet
- ⓰ Oslo Reptilpark

Interesting Buildings
- ❷ Universitetet
- ❻ Nationaltheatret
- ❼ Theatercaféen
- ❽ Det Norske Teatret
- ❾ Rådhuset pp60–61
- ⓬ Oslo Konserthus

Streets and Squares
- ❶ Karl Johans Gate
- ⓫ Aker Brygge

See also Street Finder maps 2 and 3

For keys to symbols see back flap

Street-by-Street: Karl Johans Gate

Karl Johans Gate in the heart of Oslo is the best known and busiest thoroughfare in Norway. Every day 100,000 pedestrians use the street, better known as Karl Johan. Many of Norway's foremost institutions are situated here, including the Royal Palace (Slottet), Stortinget (the Norwegian Parliament), the university and the National Theatre. The street is lined with department stores, specialist shops and places to eat. The Historisk Museum and Nasjonalgalleriet are only a couple of minutes' walk away. The upper part of Karl Johan, beside the park known as Studenterlunden, is the venue for parades. In winter it is transformed into a skating rink, which attracts young and old.

❺ Slottet
The Royal Palace is situated on a hill at the end of Karl Johans Gate. It forms a natural and imposing focal point.

Dronningparken is an enclosed part of the large and open Slottsparken.

Queen Maud's statue was designed by Ada Madssen in 1959.

King Karl Johan
depicted on his horse in Slottsplassen. He built the Royal Palace and gave Oslo's main street its name. The statue is by Brynjulf Bergslien, 1875.

❶ Karl Johans Gate
Oslo's main thoroughfare is the focal point for both city life and national events such as the 17 May parades. It was planned by the palace architect, H D F Linstow, in 1840 and named after King Karl Johan.

Key

— Suggested route

4 ★ Historisk Museum
Housed in an Art Nouveau building dating from 1902 are the Ethnographic Museum, the National Antiquities Collection – comprising 36,000 archaeological finds – and the Collection of Coins and Medals.

Locator Map
See Street Finder maps 2 and 3

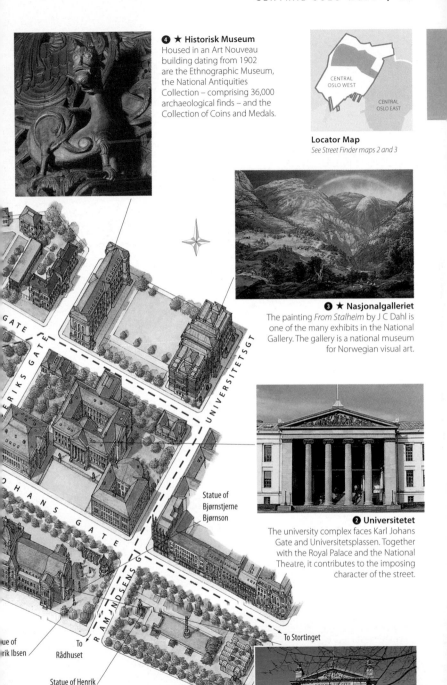

5 ★ Nasjonalgalleriet
The painting *From Stalheim* by J C Dahl is one of the many exhibits in the National Gallery. The gallery is a national museum for Norwegian visual art.

Statue of Bjørnstjerne Bjørnson

2 Universitetet
The university complex faces Karl Johans Gate and Universitetsplassen. Together with the Royal Palace and the National Theatre, it contributes to the imposing character of the street.

To Stortinget

ue of rik Ibsen

To Rådhuset

Statue of Henrik Wergeland

meters   100
yards   100

6 Nationaltheatret
The National Theatre is the principal stage for Norwegian drama. Designed by Henrik Bull, it was completed in 1899.

The upper part of Norway's foremost thoroughfare, Karl Johans Gate

❶ Karl Johans Gate

Map 3 D3. Ⓣ Stortinget, Nationaltheatret. 🚃 11, 13, 17, 18, 19. 🚌 32, 34.

Norway's best-known and busiest thoroughfare is Karl Johans Gate. It is named after the king of Norway and Sweden, Karl Johan (1818–44), and is known simply as Karl Johan by the people of Oslo. The street is flanked by stately, Neo-Classical buildings.

The upper section is the most imposing. Stortinget (the Norwegian parliament) is situated here and Slottet (the Royal Palace) takes pride of place at the western end of the street. Between these two buildings lie the university and Nationaltheatret, a park known as Studenterlunden, and a skating rink which is open to the public in winter (skates are available for hire). The lower part of Karl Johans Gate terminates at Central Station. Basarhallene (the market halls) at Kirkeristen can be found in this section.

Karl Johans Gate grew in importance after the Royal Palace, designed by the architect H D F Linstow, was completed in 1848. Linstow also planned Karl Johan.

In addition to the many public buildings, the street is lined with department stores, specialist shops and places to eat. Karl Johans Gate has been a popular meeting place since the 19th century. The citizens of Oslo used to stroll along Studenterlunden to see and be seen. Today, young people

continue to meet on the "Strip". It is also the focal point for royal occasions and state visits. Undoubtedly the biggest day of the year on Karl Johan is Norway's National Day, 17 May, when thousands of children, accompanied by singers and musicians, parade toward the palace to be greeted by the royal family who come out on to the balcony.

Each evening as darkness falls, lights switch on automatically, illuminating the façades along Karl Johans Gate. The street teems with life until the early hours. Visitors are often surprised by the vibrancy of the nightlife in and around Karl Johans Gate, which is more on a par with some of the larger capitals of Europe.

❷ Universitetet

Karl Johans Gate 47. **Map** 3 D3. **Tel** 22 85 50 50. Ⓣ National- theatret. 🚃 11, 13, 17, 18, 19. 🚌 32, 34.

The university dominates the northeast side of Karl Johans Gate. The Neo-Classical building was completed in 1852, 40 years after Frederik VI decreed that Norway could finally have its very own university. He gave it his name, the "Royal Frederik University in Oslo", by which it was known until 1939.

Over the years, most of the teaching, other than the Faculty of Law and some of the administration, has moved to Blindern on the outskirts of Oslo. The university complex is situated directly opposite the Nationaltheatret. It

comprises three buildings which encircle University Square. To mark its centenary in 1911, the university built a new auditorium, the Aula, in an extension to the main building. The Aula is renowned for its murals by the Norwegian artist Edvard Munch, installed in 1916. The powerful background motif, *The Sun*, symbolizes light in the form of an explosive sunrise over the coastline. The main canvas on the right, *Alma Mater*, depicts a nursing mother representing the university, while that on the left, *History*, represents knowledge and wisdom. Edvard Munch regarded the paintings in the Aula as his major work. Note that the Aula is not open to the public unless an event is taking place.

Politicians and humanitarians from all over the world have, over the years, visited the Aula. It was used as the venue for the presentation of the Nobel Peace Prize until 1990 when the award ceremony was moved to Rådhuset (Oslo City Hall).

On one day in mid-August every year, some 3,000 students descend upon University Square to register for a university place.

Oslo University's Aula with Edvard Munch's murals, 1916

❸ Nasjonalgalleriet

See pp56–7.

❹ Historisk Museum

See pp58–9.

Slottet (the Royal Palace) standing supreme on the hill at the top of Karl Johans Gate

⑤ Slottet

Drammensveien 1. **Map** 2 C2.
Tel 22 04 87 00. Ⓣ Nationaltheatret.
🚋 11, 13, 17, 18, 19. 🚌 32, 34.
Open guided tours only; end Jun–
mid-Aug: daily; tickets in advance
from post offices, 7 Eleven or Narvesen
stores and at 🔲 **royalcourt.no**
🎫 🎥 ♿ 📷 📷

The Royal Palace (Det Kongelige
Slottet) occupies an elevated
position overlooking the city
centre and forms a natural focal
point on Karl Johans Gate.

King Karl Johan decided to
build a royal residence in Oslo
on ascending to the Swedish-
Norwegian throne in 1818. He
commissioned the architect
Lieutenant H D F Linstow to
design the project.

Work on the interior, by the
architects H E Schirmer and
J H Nebelong, began in 1836.
Peter Frederik Wergmann was
responsible for the Pompeii-
style wall friezes in the
Banqueting Hall. The Palace
Chapel and the Ballroom were
designed by Linstow; the
painter Johannes Flintoe
decorated the Bird Room.

The palace was not
completed until 1848, by which
time Karl Johan had died. It was
inaugurated by Oscar I amid
great festivities.

The grand buildings did not
become a permanent residence
until 1905 when Norway finally
became an independent nation.
King Haakon and Queen Maud,
the newly crowned monarchs,
moved into what was then a
poorly maintained palace. It has
been gradually restored and
upgraded over time and at the
end of the 20th century
underwent a further
comprehensive restoration.

The palace is built of brick and
plaster. It has two wings of three
storeys each. Slottsparken, the
gardens surrounding the
buildings to the south and east,
are not fenced off and are open
to the public. Dronningsparken,
to the west, is private property
and is not open to visitors.

The palace has a splendid
collection of fine art. It wasn't
until the summer of 2000,
however, that the public were
able to view the collection
and some of the interior, on
guided tours. The tours are
now a regular feature every
year from the end of June
until mid-August.

A statue of Karl Johan stands
in front of the palace.

⑥ Nationaltheatret

Johannes Dybwads plass 1. **Map** 3 D3.
Tel 22 00 14 00. Ⓣ Nationaltheatret.
🚋 11, 13, 17, 18, 19. 🚌 32, 34. Ticket
Office: **Open** 9.30am–6.30pm Mon–
Fri, 11am–5pm Sat. **Closed** public
hols. 🎫 by arrangement. 📷
📷 open 1 hr before performances.

It was no coincidence that
a play by the Norwegian
dramatist Henrik Ibsen was
on the programme when the
National Theatre opened its
doors in 1899. The theatre's first
production was the socially
critical drama, *An Enemy of the
People*. Since then, Ibsen's work
has become a central part of
the repertoire, and his powerful
plays have inspired many
generations of actors.

The Baroque-style building
was designed by Henrik Bull
and is regarded as the country's
most significant expression of
the renaissance of brickwork in
the 19th century. Its Baroque-
like design is typical of theatre
architecture throughout
Europe toward the end of the
19th century. A fire caused
extensive damage to the
building in 1980 and the
subsequent restoration work
took five years to complete.

The ticket for a play also gives
access to one of Norway's finest
art collections. Throughout the
building are paintings by
Erik Werenskiold, Karl Fjell,
Christian Krohg, P S Krøyer
and busts by Gustav Vigeland,
Per Palle Storm and other
Norwegian artists. In front of
the theatre stand sculptures
of two of Norway's most
renowned writers – Henrik Ibsen
and Bjørnstjerne Bjørnson –
each on a pedestal.

The palace's Banqueting Hall with Wergmann's Pompeii-style friezes

❸ Nasjonalgalleriet

The National Gallery houses Norway's largest public collection of paintings, sculptures, drawings and engravings. The main emphasis is on Norwegian art of the 19th and 20th centuries. Visual art up until 1945 is well represented, with particular emphasis on National Romanticism and Impressionism. The Edvard Munch Hall contains a number of the artist's most famous works. Another highlight is the collection of 15th- and 16th-century Russian icons from the Novgorod School. Sculptures by foreign and Norwegian artists can be found in several of the exhibition halls, and there is also a collection of French art from the 19th and 20th centuries. The building, designed by H E and Adolf Schirmer, was completed in 1882.

Façade Detail
The National Gallery is in the Neo-Renaissance style, which was much favoured in the capital in the 1880s.

The Golden Age
Known for his depictions of mythology and religion, Lucas Cranach the Elder's painting of c.1530 explores the Golden Age of classical mythology – an era of peace and prosperity – through an idyllic garden scene.

★ The Scream
Skrik (The Scream), painted by Edvard Munch in 1893, is one of the most frequently depicted works of art in the world. A breakthrough for Expressionism, it was stolen from the gallery in 2004 but found in 2006.

Gallery Guide

On the ground floor there is a shop, a reading room, an auditorium and temporary exhibitions. The first floor showcases Norwegian art and a number of European paintings, as well as engravings, drawings and a selection of antique sculptures.

Main entrance

KEY

① **Reading room**, with the collection of engravings and hand drawings.

② **Studio**

Larvik by Moonlight
A leading figure in Norwegian landscape painting, J C Dahl captures the dramatic interaction of moonlight and water in this 1839 work.

Portrait of Mme Zborowska
This portrait by Amadeo Modigliani was painted in 1918. It is typical of the Italian artist's linear style with flat areas of colour. Modigliani is known for having created Subjective Expressionism.

VISITORS' CHECKLIST

Practical Information
Universitetsgaten 13.
Map 3 D3. **Tel** 21 98 20 00.
Open 10am–6pm Tue, Wed & Fri, 10am–7pm Thu, 11am–5pm Sat & Sun. **Closed** Mon, public hols.
by arrangement. (free Sun).
W nasjonalmuseet.no

Transport
National-theatret. 11, 13, 17, 18, 19. 30, 31, 32, 34, 45, 81, 83.

The Repentant Peter
El Greco's portrayal of the apostle, Peter, is thought to have been painted between 1610 and 1614. The intensity of the painting and the daring choice of colour in the cape is typical of the artist.

2nd Floor

1st Floor

★ Winter Night in the Mountains
Harald Sohlberg's *Vinternatt i Rondane*, 1914, is a major work of Norwegian Neo-Romanticism. It broke with the naturalistic tradition of landscape painting in Nordic art in the early 20th century.

Ground Floor

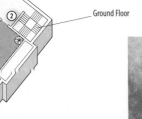

Mount Stetind in the Fog
Peder Balke's *Stetind i Tåke* 1864, is one of the most important works of the National Romantic movement. Balke was a pupil of the landscape artist J C Dahl (1788–1857).

Key to Floorplan
- Norwegian painting and sculpture
- Antique sculpture
- Auditorium
- Scandinavian painting and sculpture
- Older European painting
- 19th- and 20th-century European painting and sculpture
- Exhibition of engravings and hand drawings
- Temporary exhibitions
- Non-exhibition space

❹ Historisk Museum

The Historisk Museum is part of the Museum of Cultural History, University of Oslo, which houses the Oldsaksamlingen (National Antiquities Collection), Etnografisk Museum (Ethnographic Museum) and Myntkabinettet (Collection of Coins and Medals). They document Norwegian and international history from the first settlements to the present day. Rare objects from Viking and medieval times are on show and medieval religious art is particularly well represented. There is also a rich collection from the Arctic cultures. The building was designed by Henrik Bull (1864–1953) and completed in 1902.

Inuit Mask
The mask from East Greenland represents a *tupilak* – a figure which is animated through magic rituals and which brings ill fortune to its victim.

★ Fish Skin Coat
This coat has been made out of fish skin by the Nanai people in sub-Arctic Siberia. The skins of large fish are dried and then beaten before being stitched together.

Lecture hall

★ Portal from Ål Kirke
This intricately carved stave church doorway dating from 1150 is one of the few wooden objects from the early Middle Ages to be found in Europe. Some of the paint on the portal remains.

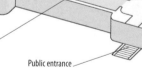

Public entrance

Viking Swords
Delicate inlays of silver and brass threads create the geometric patterns on these swords, which were discovered in Viking burial mounds.

A Buckle Fit for Beowulf
This impressive belt buckle from the early 7th century is believed to have once belonged to a powerful chieftain. It is the work of a master craftsman and is made of silver, gold and bronze, with polished garnets and engraved figures. It is part of the famous Åker Find displayed in the Treasure Room.

Gallery Guide

The Historisk Museum covers four floors. The National Antiquities Collection is on the ground floor. The first floor is shared by the Collection of Coins and Medals, and by the Ethnographic Museum, which also occupies the second and third floors. The collections are well arranged in airy rooms. Many of the exhibits are accompanied by information in Norwegian, English and German.

❼ Theatercaféen

Stortingsgaten 24–26. **Map** 3 D3.
Tel 22 82 40 50. T Nationaltheatret.
🚋 13, 15, 19. 🚌 30, 31, 32, 45, 81, 83.
Open 11am–11pm Mon–Sat, 3–10pm Sun. **Closed** Jul. W hotel-continental.no/theatercafeen

In Oslo, friends often meet for a meal at the classy Theatercaféen, a restaurant conveniently situated just across the street from the Nationaltheatret.

Ever since it opened in 1900, it has been a focal point for Norway's most celebrated artists, authors and actors, including Knut Hamsun, Edvard Munch, Herman Wildenvey and Johanne Dybwad, many of whose portraits line the walls. While most of these names belong to a bygone era, Theatercaféen still attracts many well-known contemporary figures to its tables.

The restaurant has its own classical pianist, who plays on the balcony.

❽ Det Norske Teatret

Kristian IVs Gate 8. **Map** 3 D3.
Tel 22 47 38 00. T Nationaltheatret.
🚌 30, 31, 32, 45, 81, 83. 🚋 13, 19.
Box Office: **Open** 10am–5pm Mon, 11am–6pm Tue–Fri. 🖥
W detnorsketeatret.no

Norway's "second National Theatre", Det Norske Teatret, opened in 1913, but was forever on the move until finally in September 1985 it was able to welcome audiences to its own new, ultra-modern home.

The theatre has two stages, Hovedscenen with 757 seats and Biscenen with 200 seats. There are rehearsal rooms, beautifully decorated foyers and a bistro. Hovedscenen is fitted with advanced technical equipment and movable units, so stage layouts and sets can be changed quickly.

Det Norske Teatret is the main venue for works in the *nynorsk* language *(see p22)*. The principal repertoire features Norwegian/Nordic drama, but both modern and classical plays are performed on a regular basis.

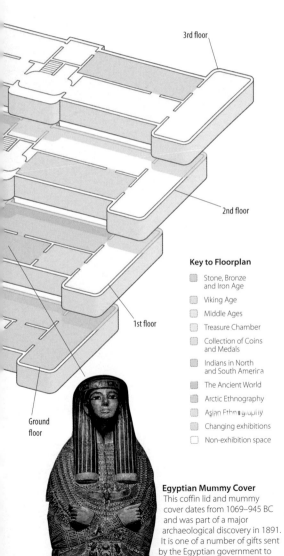

3rd floor

2nd floor

1st floor

Ground floor

Key to Floorplan

☐ Stone, Bronze and Iron Age
☐ Viking Age
☐ Middle Ages
☐ Treasure Chamber
☐ Collection of Coins and Medals
☐ Indians in North and South America
☐ The Ancient World
☐ Arctic Ethnography
☐ Asian Ethnography
☐ Changing exhibitions
☐ Non-exhibition space

Egyptian Mummy Cover

This coffin lid and mummy cover dates from 1069–945 BC and was part of a major archaeological discovery in 1891. It is one of a number of gifts sent by the Egyptian government to King Oscar II in 1894.

❾ Rådhuset

In 1918 the competition to design a new City Hall was won by Arnstein Arneberg and Magnus Poulsson. The building was opened in 1950 to mark the city's 900th anniversary, but it has taken many years for the people of Oslo to come to terms with this Modernist landmark in dark brown brick. The City Hall is the administrative centre of Oslo and contains the richly adorned ceremonial hall known as Rådhushallen in which the Nobel Peace Prize is presented in December each year. Prominent Norwegian artists were invited to decorate the interior, including Henrik Sørensen, whose painting, *Work, Art and Celebration*, fills an entire wall.

Rådhuset from the north, showing the main entrance and courtyard

★ Rådhus Hall
The ceremonial main hall covers 1,519 sq m (16,350 sq ft) of floor space. Henrik Sørensen's oil painting on the rear wall is the largest in Europe.

★ Feast Gallery
Axel Julius Revold's fresco depicts the industrial and consumer society of the 1950s. It focuses on agriculture, shipbuilding, fishing and factories.

KEY

① **The Munch Hall**

② **Crown Princess Märtha Square** is a garden and pedestrian area.

③ **Handmade bricks** known as "monkstone" were used in the construction.

④ **The Eastern Tower** is 66 m (217 ft) tall.

Entrance

St Hallvard
St Hallvard is the patron saint of Oslo. In an attempt to save a woman from robbers he was killed and thrown in the fjord with a millstone around his neck. He floated to the surface and was hailed a martyr.

For hotels and restaurants in this area see pp230–33 and pp238–47

★ Bystyre Hall
The Hall of the City Council (Bystyresalen) lies at the heart of Rådhuset. The council's 59 representatives have regular meetings here.

⑩ Nobel Peace Center

Vestbanebygningen, Rådhusplassen. **Map** 2 C3. **Tel** 48 30 10 00. 🚇 Nationaltheatret. 🚋 12. **Open** 10am–6pm daily. 🔲 📷 🔲 **nobelpeacecenter.org**

Oslo's old railway station of Vestbanen, near the town hall, houses the Nobel Peace Center. Designed by British architect David Adjaye, the centre is not a museum in the traditional sense. Its mission is to present the work of past and present Nobel Peace Prize winners and to provide a forum for discussion on the topics of war, peace and resolution of conflict.

As well as a rich and varied programme of lectures, exhibitions, seminars and talks, the Center offers visitors a documentation base, areas for refreshments and a bookshop. It aims to become a meeting place where reflection, discussion and involvement are encouraged.

⑪ Aker Brygge

Map 2 C4. **Tel** 22 83 80 46. 🚇 Nationaltheatret. 🚋 12. 🔲 **akerbrygge.no**

In 1982 the long-established shipyard, Akers Mekaniske Verksted, closed down, freeing up a potentially attractive area on Oslo's harbourfront. Aker Brygge has been transformed to provide a major shopping and entertainment centre with residential apartments and the city's biggest concentration of restaurants. Many of the old shipyard warehouses have been restored. Bold new architecture blends with the old and has attracted international acclaim as a successful example of inner-city redevelopment.

Aker Brygge is a delightful setting in which to enjoy a beer or a glass of wine at the quayside, or to splash out on a sumptuous dinner in a good restaurant. From here there is a panoramic view across the water to the fortress of Akershus (see pp72–3).

Albertine
The tragic character of Albertine was created by Christian Krohg in his written and painted works. Albertine was later recaptured by Alfred Seland in this relief sculpture on the eastern façade of the Rådhuset.

Banqueting Hall
The venue for grand dinners, the Banqueting Hall (Bankettsalen) is a light and airy room that is richly decorated and embellished with royal portraits.

Sculptures by Turid Eng (1984) at the entrance to Oslo Konserthus

Edvard Munch. They span Munch's output from his early work, *The Sick Room*, to the later *Dance of Life*. In addition to Munch, Scandinavian art is well-represented with works by Kai Fjell, Jakob Weidemann and Per Krohg.

The other two collections feature paintings by Amaldus Nielsen (1838–1932) and Ludvig O Ravensberg (1871–1958).

Nielsen was a landscape painter who immortalized the southern Norwegian coast in his work. Ravensberg was known for his naive portrayals of Roman ruins of old Oslo. He was strongly influenced by Munch, who was his relative.

The museum is due to move to a new building in Bjørvika in 2018 *(see p97)*.

⑫ Oslo Konserthus

Munkedamsveien 14. **Map** 2 C3.
Tel 23 11 31 00. Ⓣ Nationaltheatret.
🚋 13, 19. 🚌 30, 31, 32, 45, 81, 83.
Box office: **Open** 11am–5pm Mon–Fri, 11am–2pm Sat, and 2 hrs before a performance. **Closed** July. ♿
🅦 oslokonserthus.no

Oslo's Concert Hall, situated in the area of Vika, has been a leading venue for Norwegian cultural and musical life since its opening in 1977. The world's top artists and orchestras regularly perform here.

In the 1960s, the Swedish architect, Gösta Åberg, won the competition to design the new building. The exterior is clad in polished granite; inside the floors and walls are of white marble. The hall has been specially designed to stage orchestral works, with a podium large enough to accommodate 120 musicians. It can be transformed into a theatre for shows and musical productions with seating for an audience of 1,400.

The concert hall is the home of Oslo-Filharmonien (the Oslo Symphony Orchestra). The orchestra plays a central role in the musical life of the city. It is also regarded as one of the world's leading symphony ensembles, and its recordings have attracted international acclaim.

More than 300 events are held annually at the Konserthus, with audiences totalling more than 200,000 over the year.

⑬ Stenersenmuseet

Munkedamsveien 15. **Map** 2 C3.
Tel 23 49 36 00. Ⓣ Nationaltheatret.
🚋 13, 19. 🚌 30, 31, 32, 45, 81, 83.
Open 11am–4pm Tue, Wed & Fri, 11am–7pm Thu, 11am–5pm Sat & Sun. 🎨 📷 2:30pm Sun. ♿ 🎁 🏛
🅦 stenersen.museum.no

The Stenersenmuseet is named after the author, art collector and patron of the arts, Rolf Stenersen. In 1936, he donated his collection to Oslo City Council. The paintings remained in store until 1994, when Stenersenmuseet was completed. It is located in Konserthusterrassen (beneath the Konserthus).

The Stenersen bequest is one of three collections on show in the museum. It includes paintings and a large number of graphics and drawings by

⑭ Ibsenmuseet

Arbins Gate 1. **Map** 2 C3. **Tel** 22 12 35 50. Ⓣ Nationaltheatret. 🚋 13, 19.
🚌 30, 31, 32, 45, 81, 83. **Open** guided tours only. 🎨 📷 every hour; 15 May– 14 Sep: 11am–5pm Tue–Sun; 15 Sep–14 May: 11am–4pm Tue–Sun, 11am–6pm Thu. ♿ 🎁 💻 🏛

Henrik Ibsen, Norway's revered playwright, produced the major part of his work while living in Munich (1864–92).

After his return to Oslo, in 1895, Ibsen and his wife took an apartment in Arbiens Gate, on the first floor on the corner facing Drammensveien. This was where he wrote his last

Høstens promenade, Ludvig O Ravensberg, Stenersenmuseet

The Baldishol Tapestry, one of the most prized exhibits in the Kunstindustrimuseet

plays, *John Gabriel Borkman* (1896) and *When We Dead Awaken* (1899). It was in this home that he suffered a stroke, which prevented him from writing, and he subsequently died in 1906, aged 78 years.

Great attention has been paid to the restoration and redecoration of the couple's large apartment. Even the colour scheme resembles that of Ibsen's day and his study contains the original furniture.

Every day he would set off from here to walk to the Grand Café in Karl Johans Gate where he held court until ill-health confined him to the apartment.

The museum is open for guided tours and lectures.

⑮ Kunstindustri-museet

St Olavs Gate 1. **Map** 3 E2.
Tel 22 03 65 40. 🚇 Stortinget, National theatret. 🚊 11, 17, 18.
🚌 60, and a short walk to 30, 31, 32, 45, 81, 83. **Open** 11am–5pm Tue, Wed & Fri, 11am–7pm Thu, noon–4pm Sat & Sun. **Closed** Mon & public hols. 🎫 📷 ♿ 🚻 📖
🌐 nasjonalmuseet.no

The Museum of Decorative Arts and Design (Kunstindustrimuseet) is one of the oldest museums in Europe. It was established in 1876, and contains a fine collection of Norwegian and foreign crafts, fashion and design products from the 17th century to the present day.

The museum holds Norway's biggest collection of tapestries from the 16th and 17th centuries, including the national treasure, the Baldishol Tapestry, dating from the 12th century. This is the only surviving Nordic tapestry that uses the Gobelin technique from the Middle Ages, and is one of the few remaining European tapestries to exhibit Roman characteristics. The tapestry was found when Baldishol Church was demolished in 1879.

The museum also contains collections of silver, glassware, ceramics and furniture. On show in the Royal Costume Gallery are clothes from the Norwegian monarchy. In the Department of East Asian Art there is an imperial Ming vase dating from the 15th century.

Since 1904 the museum has shared an imposing building with the National College of Art and Design. Their joint library is open to the public.

⑯ Oslo Reptilpark

St Olavs Gate 2. **Map** 3 F2.
🚇 Stortinget, Nationaltheateret
🚌 37 to Nordahl Brunsgate.
Open Apr-Aug: 10am–6pm daily.
Sep–Mar: 10am–6pm Tue–Sun.
📷 📷 ♿ 🚻 🌐 reptilpark.no

This small but friendly park located opposite the Kunstindustrimuseet is very popular for families with children. More than 100 animals of a range of different species are exhibited here, including a boa constrictor, grass snakes, caiman, geckos, chameleons, varans and other lizards, tarantulas, black widows (the world's most venomous spider), piranhas and saltwater fish.

Tuesdays are particularly popular, since visitors can witness "feeding time" at 5pm.

Special group rates are available for both adults and children, with some discounts applying to as few as five people, enquire at the ticket office for more information. Children under two are admitted free.

Henrik Ibsen

Described as the father of modern drama, Henrik Ibsen (1828–1906) is Norway's most famous writer. He left a remarkable legacy of plays that revolutionized modern theatre and are still performed worldwide. They included *Peer Gynt*, for which Edvard Grieg composed the music, *A Doll's House*, *Hedda Gabler*, *Ghosts*,

Portrait of Henrik Ibsen, dramatist

The Wild Duck and *An Enemy of the People*. Ibsen was born in Skien (*see p152*) in southern Norway. He began writing while working as a chemist's assistant, but his first play, *Catilina*, was rejected. Undeterred, he took a job as a journalist in Bergen and later became director and playwright at Ole Bull's Theatre. From 1857–1863 he was director of the Norwegian Theatre in Oslo, but the theatre went bankrupt and he moved abroad. Over the next 30 years he wrote numerous dramas, concentrating on social issues and the pettiness of Norwegian society. They earned him literary fame and in 1892 he returned to Olso a national hero.

CENTRAL OSLO EAST

The city originated more than 1,000 years ago in what is now eastern Oslo. The first market was situated in Bjørvika, which became a commercial port, although this area has now been transformed by the striking modern Opera House and waterfront promenade.

In 1624, the old city of Oslo was almost entirely destroyed by fire. The new city spread for the first time to the west of the Akershus fortress. Under the auspices of Christian IV,

the area of Kvadraturen (Quadrangle) developed to the north of the fortress. The king renamed the new city Christiania in 1624. Many of its historic buildings are to be found in Kvadraturen itself, alongside places of interest such as the Norwegian Resistance Museum, the Museum of Contemporary Art and the Theatre Museum. Parts of the eastern area have a multi-cultural population and are characterized by a cosmopolitan mix of restaurants and ethnic shops.

Sights at a Glance

Castles and Museums

1. Akershus Festning pp70–71
2. Norges Hjemmefrontmuseum
3. Høymagasinet
4. Norsk Arkitekturmuseum
5. Old Town Hall
7. Museet for Samtidskunst pp74–5
9. Forsvarsmuseet
12. Filmmuseet

Public Buildings

8. Den Gamle Logen
11. Børsen
14. Stortinget
16. Regjeringskvartalet

Theatre and Opera

10. The Opera House
15. Oslo Nye Teater
18. Oslo Spektrum

Churches and Squares

6. Christiania Torv
13. Oslo Domkirke
17. Youngstorget

See also Street Finder map 3

0 metres   300

0 yards   300

Street-by-Street: Kvadraturen

Oslo has been ravaged by fire on a number of occasions, the worst of which was in 1624, when almost the entire city was destroyed. The king, Christian IV, decided to build a new city to be known as Christiania. Development started at the foot of the Akershus fortress. The area, Kvadraturen (the Quadrangle), took the form of a rectangular grid. Although few of the original buildings remain, Kvadraturen is still characterized by its historic architecture. It has old market squares and museums, picturesque sights and traditional eating-places. The fortress bordering the harbour is the focal point. From the ramparts there is a splendid view across southern Oslo and the inner reaches of Oslofjorden.

⑤ Old Town Hall
Dating from 1641, the Old Town Hall shows models of buildings, and portraits from 1624–1850.

To Stortinget

CHRISTIANIA TORV

AKERSGATA

RÅDHUSGATA

To Rådhus- plassen

AKE

⑥ Christiania Torv
The city's first market square, Christiania Torv, has been renovated and is now home to several eateries. The fountain, *Christian IV's Glove*, is by Wenche Gulbransen (1997).

Key

— Suggested route

③ Høymagasinet
Originally a hay barn, the half-timbered Høymagasinet dates from 1845. It houses models illustrating the history of the city's buildings.

0 metres   100
0 yards   100

② Hjemmefrontmuseet
Norway's Resistance Museum is situated at the top of the Akershus fortress. It provides a comprehensive picture of the years of German occupation in 1940–45.

Christian Radich, 1937, is often moored at Akershus. The sailing ship achieved worldwide fame for its part in the film *Windjammer* (1957).

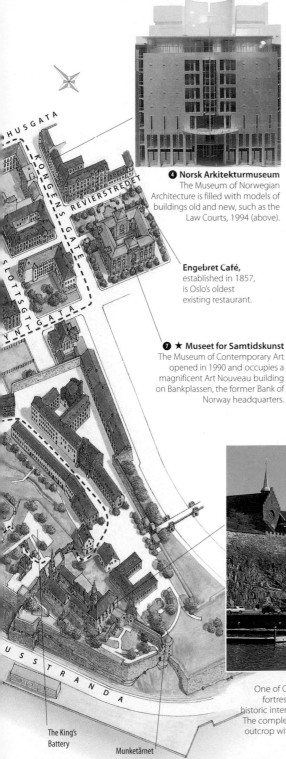

Locator Map
See Street Finder map 3

❹ Norsk Arkitekturmuseum
The Museum of Norwegian
Architecture is filled with models of
buildings old and new, such as the
Law Courts, 1994 (above).

Engebret Café,
established in 1857,
is Oslo's oldest
existing restaurant.

❼ ★ Museet for Samtidskunst
The Museum of Contemporary Art
opened in 1990 and occupies a
magnificent Art Nouveau building
on Bankplassen, the former Bank of
Norway headquarters.

❶ ★ Akershus Festning
One of Oslo's top attractions is the Akershus
fortress. Begun in 1299, its stout walls and
historic interiors bear the scars of many a battle.
The complex is strategically situated on a rocky
outcrop with excellent views over Oslofjorden.

The King's
Battery

Munketårnet

❶ Akershus Festning

For 700 years the Akershus fortress has been standing guard over Oslo to ward off all attempts to invade the city from the sea. The slott (castle) occupies a spectacular setting on a hill at the head of Oslofjorden. King Håkon V began building in 1299, since when the fortifications have undergone numerous improvements and reconstructions. One of the fortress's greatest moments was to resist the siege of the Swedish king, Karl XII, in 1716. In the 19th century, the castle's defensive role declined in significance and it became an administrative centre for the armed forces. Today, Akershus Festning contains historic buildings, museums and defence installations. It is also the government's main venue for state functions.

★ Olav's Hall
The North Hall was renovated in 1976 and named after King Olav V (1903–91).

The Romeriks Hall
The fireplace (1634–42) with the coat-of-arms of Governor-General Christopher Urne and his wife was found in another building in 1900 and restored to the castle.

Scribes Rooms
The rooms known as Skrivestuene were named after a timber-framed building called the Scribes Rooms House that once stood on this site. It was used by court administrators.

KEY

① North Wing

② Romeriks Tower

③ **Remains of Vågehalsen**, the medieval tower which once divided the courtyard.

④ **The Blue Tower (Blåtårnet)**

⑤ **The tapestry**, *Rideskolen*, was woven by E Leyniers, c.1650, to a design by J Jordaiens

⑥ **South Wing**

⑦ **The Virgin Tower (Jomfrutårnet)**

⑧ **The cellars** were used as dungeons from 1500–1700. One of the dungeons was known as The Witch Hole. Later, prisoners were locked up in the fortress.

Akershus Slott in 1699
By Jacob Croning, who was attached to the court of the Danish-Norwegian Christian V, this painting was the result of a request by the king for Croning to paint Norwegian scenes.

★ **Courtyard**
In the Middle Ages, the Courtyard (Borggården) was divided by a large tower, Vågehalsen, which was destroyed by fire in 1527. A Renaissance courtyard was created and the two towers, Romerikstårnet and Blåtårnet, were erected.

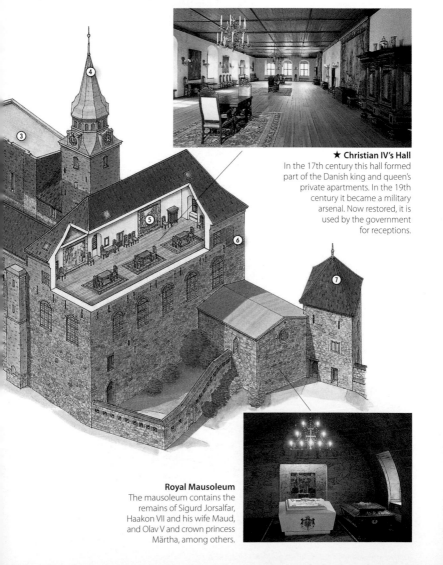

★ **Christian IV's Hall**
In the 17th century this hall formed part of the Danish king and queen's private apartments. In the 19th century it became a military arsenal. Now restored, it is used by the government for receptions.

Royal Mausoleum
The mausoleum contains the remains of Sigurd Jorsalfar, Haakon VII and his wife Maud, and Olav V and crown princess Märtha, among others.

❷ Norges Hjemme-frontmuseum

Akershus fortress area. **Map** 3 D4.
Tel 23 09 32 80. Ⓣ Stortinget.
🚊 10, 12 and a short walk from
13, 19. 🚌 60 and a short walk from
30, 31, 32, 45, 81, 83. **Open** 1 Jun–
31 Aug: 10am–5pm Mon–Sat,
11am–5pm Sun; 1 Sep– 31 May:
10am–4pm Mon–Fri, 11am–4pm
Sat–Sun. **Closed** public hols. 🎫 📷
W visitoslo.com

On 9 April 1940, German forces
occupied Norway. While the
Norwegians made a valiant
attempt at halting their advance,
the country succumbed 62 days
later. For the next five years
the Norwegian Resistance
conducted a heroic campaign
against the occupying German
army, and their exploits are
well-documented in Norway's
Resistance Museum. Taped
speeches and film clips recreate
the World War II years, and bring
to life the comprehensive
collection of documents, posters
and memorabilia from that time.
   The museum is situated in
a 200-m (656-ft) long, 17th-
century stone vault in
Bindingsverkshuset (Half-
Timbered House) at the top
of Akershus Festning. It was
opened on 8 May 1970, which
was the 25th anniversary of
the liberation. Alongside the
museum, there is a memorial
to the Norwegians who were
shot here during the war.
   The museum has a small
bookshop that offers a fine
collection of reference books
on the Norweigian war effort.

Model of old Christiania in Høymagasinet

❸ Høymagasinet

Akershus fortress area. **Map** 3 D4.
Tel 22 33 31 47. Ⓣ Stortinget. 🚊 13
(Christiania Torv); 12, 13, 19 (Wessels
Plass). 🚌 60 (Akershusstranda). **Open**
Jun–Aug: noon–5pm Sat & Sun. 🎫 ♿

A former hay barn at Akershus
Festning is the location for
Høymagasinet, a museum
devoted to the history of
Christiania from 1624 to 1840.
   The year 1624 marked the
devastating fire that left most
of the old city of Oslo in ashes.
The Danish-Norwegian king,
Christian IV, decided to rebuild
the city further west and named
it Christiania. During the first 100
years reconstruction was slow,
but it gathered speed in the
18th century. The history of the

city over 200 years is illustrated
with the help of models and
a variety of other displays, in
addition to a 25-minute long
multi-media programme.
   The museum also offers
visitors short, guided walks
through the streets of
Kvadraturen *(see pp68–9)*,
the original Christiania.

❹ Norsk Arkitektur-museum

Kongens Gate 2. **Map** 3 E4.
Tel 21 98 21 80. Ⓣ Stortinget.
🚊 12, 15, 19. 🚌 60 and a short
walk from 30, 31, 32, 45, 81, 83.
Open 11am–5pm Tue, Wed & Fri.
11am–7pm Thu, noon–5pm Sat &
Sun. **Closed** public hols.
♿ 🚫 📷 **W** nasjonalmuseet.no

Founded in 1975, the Museum
of Norwegian Architecture
features drawings, photographs
and models covering 1,000
years of the nation's building
history. The museum also
arranges touring exhibitions
of present and past architectural projects.
   Norsk Arkitekturmuseum is
located in old Christiania, in
a building from the reign of
Christian IV. The oldest part
of the house dates from 1830.
It was renovated to become
the home of the Museum of
Architecture in 2008.

Norway's Resistance Museum depiction of the battles of April 1940

For hotels and restaurants in this area see pp230–33 and pp238–47

❺ Old Town Hall

Christiania Torv 1. **Map** 3 D4. **Tel** 22 42 65 09. Ⓣ Stortinget. 🚋 12, 13, 19. 🚌 60 and a short walk from 30, 31, 32, 45, 81, 83. **Open** Jun, Jul & Aug: 11am–4pm Tue–Sun. **Closed** public hols. 🎫 every hour. ♿ ✉ 📷

The city's oldest town hall, Gamle Rådhus, is a good starting point for a visit to Oslo. Since its founding in 1641, the building has been used as a fire station, a church and even a prison. Today, it houses a small museum and one of the city's oldest restaurants.

The exhibition, on the first and second floors, gives an excellent overview of the city's history, showing models of buildings and illustrations of the old town of Christiania. It also explores the city's urban development and changes in building traditions and living conditions. Highlights from Oslo's theatre history are also displayed.

The restaurant on the ground floor has been in operation since 1856, a fact that is echoed in its charming, historic decor and traditional Norwegian cuisine.

Christiania Torv, featuring some of Oslo's best-preserved buildings

Charming interior of the restaurant at the Gamle Rådhus

❻ Christiania Torv

Map 3 D4. Ⓣ Stortinget. 🚋 12, 13, 19.

The square is old, but the name is rather new. It was decided in 1958 that this part of Oslo's original market square *(torv)* should be called Christiania, after the old name for Oslo. For many years the square was plagued by heavy traffic. It underwent extensive renovation in the 1990s when traffic was diverted through a tunnel. Now free from vehicles, Christiania Torv is once more a pleasant place to visit. In 1997, a fountain created by the artist Wenche Gulbransen was erected in the square.

Around the square are several popular restaurants and historic buildings, among them the Old Town Hall and the Garnison Hospital, the oldest building in the capital and home to the Oslo Artists' Association.

❼ Museet for Samtidskunst

See pp74–5.

❽ Den Gamle Logen

Grev Wedels Plass 2. **Map** 3 D4. **Tel** 22 33 44 70. Ⓣ Jernbanetorget. 🚋 12, 13, 19. 🚌 30, 31, 32, 41, 45, 60, 81, 83. 🌐 **gamlelogen.no**

If walls could talk those of Den Gamle Logen (The Old Lodge) would have a fascinating story to tell about the history of Oslo. The city council held its meetings here from the end of the 19th century until 1947. The lodge was also used as a court room during the legal proceedings against Vidkun Quisling *(see p45)*, who was sentenced to death for treason at the end of World War II.

Constructed by Freemasons in the 19th century, the design of the Old Lodge is based on drawings by Christian H Malling and Jens S Seidelin. It was opened in 1839.

The vast Neo-Classical banqueting hall is the central feature. Noted for its excellent acoustics, it was for a long time the city's foremost concert hall. But after World War II, the lodge was taken over by the Oslo Port Labour Office and the banqueting hall became a canteen.

It reverted to its original use as a concert venue in the 1980s when Oslo Summer Opera moved in. The Old Lodge has since undergone extensive restoration and once again its beautiful rooms are being used for banquets and musical events. In the entrance there is a statue of Edvard Grieg, created by Marit Wiklund in 1993.

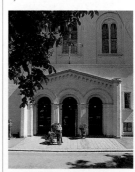
Den Gamle Logen concert hall at Grev Wedels Plass

● Museet for Samtidskunst

The Museum of Contemporary Art is home to Norway's greatest collection of Norwegian and international modern art from the post-World War II period until today. Previously a department of the National Gallery, its opening in 1990 was heralded as a national event. It is now firmly established on the Norwegian arts scene and regularly hosts major international exhibitions. The permanent collection is so large that only part of it is on show at any one time. The building in which the museum is housed – the former head office of the Central Bank of Norway – is an example of Art Nouveau architecture from 1906. It is constructed in Norwegian granite and marble. The richly decorated Banking Hall provides an exciting contrast between old and new.

Winter Sun
Gunnar S Gundersen's *Winter Sun* (1966) may be seen as an abstract impression of a landscape.

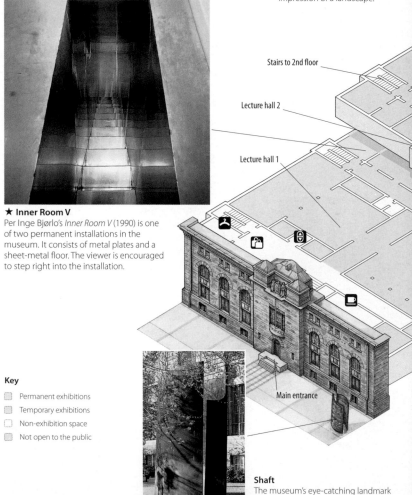

★ Inner Room V
Per Inge Bjørlo's *Inner Room V* (1990) is one of two permanent installations in the museum. It consists of metal plates and a sheet-metal floor. The viewer is encouraged to step right into the installation.

Stairs to 2nd floor

Lecture hall 2

Lecture hall 1

Main entrance

Key
- ▢ Permanent exhibitions
- ▢ Temporary exhibitions
- ▢ Non-exhibition space
- ▢ Not open to the public

Shaft
The museum's eye-catching landmark is Richard Serra's sculpture, *Shaft* (1988). It stands at the entrance on Bankplassen.

★ The Rubbish Man
Ukrainian artist Ilya Kabakov's installation (1983–95) is a "museum" of rubbish dedicated to the Man Who Never Threw Anything Away. Viewers can enter the room to experience the collector's mania and his passion for order.

VISITORS' CHECKLIST

Practical Information
4 Bankplassen. **Map** 3 D4.
Tel 21 98 20 00. **Open** 11am–5pm Tue, Wed, Fri, 11am–7pm Thu, noon–5pm Sat & Sun.
Closed public hols.
w nasjonalmuseet.no

Transport
T Stortinget. 12, 13, 19.
60.

Tilted Form No. 3
Part of a series of six gouaches, *Tilted Form No. 3* (1987) is by the American Sol LeWitt, with variations on the same motif – the cube. This form of seriality is typical of the artist.

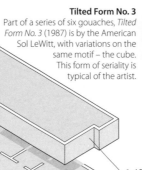

2nd floor

Skylight Hall

1st floor

Stairs to 1st floor

Ground floor

Banking Hall
The splendid Banking Hall (Banksalen) provides a challenging contrast to the contemporary art now adorning its halls.

Gallery Guide
The museum has three floors. The ground floor has temporary exhibitions in addition to one of the museum's two permanent installations. There is also a bookshop and a café. The first floor holds temporary exhibitions and the second permanent installation. The second floor is closed to the public.

Without Title
Per Maning is known for his photographic portraits of animals, mainly dogs, seals and monkeys. This portrait shows a cow with its eyes closed (1990), against a typical Norwegian landscape.

Battle scene tableau on display at Forsvarsmuseet

❾ Forsvarsmuseet

Akershus Festning, Building 62.
Map 3 D5. **Tel** 23 09 35 82. 🚌 10, 12, 13, 15, 19. 🚌 60. **Open** May–Aug: 10am–5pm Mon–Fri, 11am–5pm Sat & Sun; Sep–Apr: 11am–4pm Tue–Fri, 11am–5pm Sat & Sun. **Closed** public hols. 🛇 ♿ ♺ 🎥 📷
W **visitoslo.com**

The history of the Norwegian armed forces, from Viking times to the present day, is represented in Forsvarsmuseet (the Armed Forces Museum) at Akershus Slott. Two large brick buildings from the 1860s, once used as military arsenals, provide an appropriate historical setting.

Of the military items on display, there is a collection from the time of the union with Denmark in the 16th century, and the subsequent Nordic wars, through to the struggle for independence during the union with Sweden. The exhibits are arranged in time blocks, and include a number of life-like models and objects, such as a German tank and a V-1 bomb from World War II, and dioramas. There are also temporary exhibitions.

❿ The Opera House

Kirsten Flagstads Plass 1. **Map** 3 E4.
Tel 21 42 21 21. 🚇 Bjørvika.
🚌 34, 70, 504. **Open** 10am–11pm Mon–Fri, 11am–11pm Sat & Sun.
♿ 📷 daily (Fri, Sat, Sun in English).
W **operaen.no**

Inaugurated in 2008, the Opera House is the home of the Norwegian National Opera and Ballet. Right on the waterfront at Bjørvika, much of the building is positioned in or under the sea. A defining feature of the design is its sloping roof, which is covered in white marble and granite. This creates the illusion of glistening ice, like a glacier rising from the edge of the Oslofjord.

Builders in Norway are not held to European Union safety codes, so visitors can stroll up the incline onto the roof and stand directly over the main theatre, where they can enjoy views of Oslo and the fjord.

With 1,100 rooms, the Opera House has a total area of about 38,500 sq m (415,000 sq ft). It has three main performance spaces for opera, ballet and concerts, though concerts are also held in the foyer and on the roof. The main auditorium seats up to 1,369 people.

The principal entrance is through a crevasse beneath the lowest portion of the sloping roof. The interior, which is mostly wood, creates a stark contrast to the glacial exterior, and the sense of height is breathtaking. Clusters of slim white columns angle up, branching towards the vaulted

ceiling, and light floods in through windows that soar as high as 15 m (49 ft).

At the heart of the theatre is the majestic *Wave Wall*, made from strips of golden oak. Designed by Norwegian boat builders, the wall curves around the auditorium and flows seamlessly into timber stairways leading into the upper levels.

She Lies, a floating sculpture made of steel and glass panels, is permanently installed on a concrete platform in the adjacent fjord. In the winter, the fjord freezes, and visitors can walk across the ice to explore the sculpture.

The opera house presents both classic and contemporary pieces. In addition to its two resident companies, its programme includes work by visiting groups such as the Stockholm Opera and the Alvin Ailey American Dance Theater. It also plays host to music festivals including the Oslo Chamber Music Festival and the Oslo World Music Festival.

Børsen (the Stock Exchange) featuring a Neo-Classical exterior

⓫ Børsen

Tollbugata 2. **Map** 3 E4. **Tel** 22 34 17 00. 🚇 Jernbanetorget. 🚌 11, 13, 19. 🚌 30, 31, 32, 45, 60, 81, 83. **Open** by arrangement. 📷 special tours can be arranged. W **oslobors.no**

One of the oldest institutional buildings in Oslo is Børsen (the Stock Exchange). Long before the construction of the royal palace and the parliament building, it was decided that the trading of commodities should take place on a site of its own. As a result, Børsen was opened in 1828, the first of Oslo's grand buildings.

The Opera House, with its steep sloping roof

For hotels and restaurants in this area see pp230–33 and pp238–47

The lavish interior of the Oslo Domkirke

Designed by the architect Christian H Grosch, the Neo-Classical façade with its Doric columns contrasts strongly with the more modern buildings nearby. The two side wings and a southern wing were added in 1910.

Originally, there was an enclosed courtyard containing a statue of Mercury. The statue was moved outside when the courtyard was redesigned to house the new Stock Exchange hall in 1988.

The entrance hall is dominated by Gerhard Munthe's mural painting from 1912, *Handelen og Sjøfarten* (*Trade and Shipping*).

Børsen also has its own library, reading room and antique trade museum, as well as a portrait gallery.

⑫ Filmmuseet

Dronningens Gate 16. **Map** 3 E4. **Tel** 22 47 45 00. ⓣ Jernbanetorget, Stortinget. 🚊 11, 17, 18. 🚌 31, 30, 34. **Open** 10:30am–5pm Mon–Fri, noon–5pm Sat, 1–9pm Sun. 🎬 9am–4pm Tue–Fri (book in advance) ♿ 🏛 ☑ nfi.no/filmkunnskap/filmmuseet

The Filmmuseet is located in Filmens Hus (the House of Film), home to the Norwegian Film Institute. The museum's collection tells the story of the Norwegian film industry, from silent films to digital technology. Film memorabilia, including photographs, costumes and technical equipment, such as laterna magicas, are on display. Also on show are some of the original puppets that were used in Ivo Caprino's (1920–2001) animated films in the 1950s and 1960s.

The Filmmuseet has its own cinema, Kinematografteatret, which shows both archive films and new Norwegian short films.

There is also a café and a shop on site that sells a variety of imported, classic and Norwegian films .

⑬ Oslo Domkirke

Stortorget 1. **Map** 3 E3. **Tel** 23 62 90 10. ⓣ Jernbanetorget, Stortinget. 🚊 11, 17, 18. 🚌 37. **Open** daily. 🛐 11am & 7pm Sun, noon Wed in English, German or French. ♿ ☑ oslodomkirke.no

Oslo Domkirke (cathedral) is the principal church for the diocese of Oslo. The foundation stone was laid in 1694, and the church was built in several stages. The altarpiece and pulpit date from 1699; the interior was completed in the 1720s. Since then there has been a series of reconstructions and renovations. In the mid-1850s the Baroque interior was remodelled in Neo-Gothic style. In the course of a subsequent restoration, 100 years later, the baptismal font, altarpiece and pulpit were changed back to the pre-1850 style. When the sacristy was renovated in 1963, rich decorations from the 18th century were discovered.

Among the adornments of the cathedral are stained glass windows by Emanuel Vigeland, a silver sculpture with a Lord's Supper motif by Arrigo Minerbi and bronze doors by Dagfin Werenskiold. The modern painted ceiling, depicting scenes from the Bible, was created by Hugo Lous Mohr between 1936 and 1950. In the course of this work, the original ceiling paintings were destroyed, an act which has since attracted much criticism.

The cathedral has 900 seats and was the venue for the wedding ceremony of Crown Prince Haakon and Mette-Marit in 2001.

In its tower hangs the great bell, weighing 1,600 kg (3,527 lb), and three smaller bells. The great bell has been recast six times.

Below the ground floor of the cathedral is a crypt.

Stortinget, home of the Norwegian parliament, centrally situated just off Karl Johans Gate

⑭ Stortinget

Karl Johans Gate 22. **Map** 3 D3. **Tel** 23 31 30 50. Ⓣ Stortinget. 🚋 13, 19. 🚌 30, 31, 32, 41, 45, 81, 83. **Open** guided tours only. 🎫 Sat: 10am Nor, Eng & Ger, 11:30am Nor & Ger, 1pm Nor, Eng & Ger; 1 Jul–20 Aug Mon–Fri: 10am Nor & Eng, 11:30am Nor & Ger, 1pm Nor, Eng & Ger. ♿ Ⓦ **stortinget.no**

Norway's National Assembly has its seat in the grand Stortinget (Norwegian Parliament building). The building was designed by the Swedish architect, Emil Victor Langlet, after a long and bitter debate and a series of different proposals. The foundation stone was laid on 10 October 1861. Construction took five years and in March 1866 the assembly met for the first time in its own building.

Stortinget is built of yellow brick on a reddish granite base. The style is a blend of Norwegian and Italian building traditions. It has been expanded and partly reconstructed on several occasions. The new wing toward Akersgata was added in the 1950s.

The assembly chamber, which seats the 165 members of parliament, resembles an amphitheatre, with the speaker's chair positioned below Oscar Wergeland's painting of the 1814 Eidsvoll assembly, which ratified the Norwegian constitution (see p42). The painting dates from

1885, and depicts some of the 112 men who helped to shape Norway's constitution.

The building has been richly embellished by Norwegian artists, including the painter Else Hagen who decorated the stairwell. A tapestry, *Solens Gang*, by Karen Holtsmark, hangs in the central hall. The sculptures in the stair hall are by Nils Flakstad.

⑮ Oslo Nye Teater

Rosenkrantzgate 10. **Map** 3 D3. **Tel** 22 34 86 00. Ⓣ Stortinget. 🚋 13, 19. 🚌 30, 31, 32, 45, 81, 83. Box Office: **Open** 11am–6pm Mon & Sat, 9am–8pm Tue–Fri.

There are three theatres in what is known as Oslo Nye Teater (the Oslo New Theatre): Hovedscenen (Main Theatre) in Rosenkrantzgate; Dukketeateret

Oslo Nye Teater, a modern and lively city centre theatre

(Puppet Theatre) in Frognerparken; and Centralteateret in Akersgata.

Hovedscenen was established in the 1920s with the aim of providing a stage for new Norwegian and foreign drama. However, the repertoire was for many years dominated by comedy with leading revue artists. There has also been a move toward creating a more urbane and modern theatre with a bolder, fresher approach and an emphasis on younger actors who are just beginning to establish themselves.

⑯ Regjeringskvartalet

Einar Gerhardsenspl 1. **Map** 3 E3. **Tel** 22 24 90 90. Ⓣ Stortinget. 🚋 11, 17, 18. 🚌 33, 37, 46. Ⓦ **regjeringen.no**

The large complex on Akersgata housing the various government departments is known as Regjeringskvartalet (the Government Quarter). It is dominated by a tall H-block in which the prime minister has a suite of offices on the top floors.

Regjeringskvartalet was developed in five stages during the years 1958–96. The architect for the four first stages was Erling Viksjø. Torstein Ramberg designed the fifth stage.

The complex has been the subject of great controversy.

In order to clear the ground, the historic, conservation-worthy Empirekvartalet (Empire Quarter) was torn down. This led to an intense debate about conservation in the 1950s. Today's politicians would probably not have authorized the demolition of such a distinctive area.

The 12-floor, concrete H-block was completed in 1958. A further two floors were added in 1990.

The building features decorative art by Kai Fjell, Tore Haaland, Inger Sitter, Odd Tandberg, Erling Viksjø, Carl Nesjar and Pablo Picasso. Nesjar and the Spanish master collaborated to transfer three drawings by Picasso on to the concrete façade on the Akersgata frontage.

Youngstorget with its market, opera house and trades union offices

Bust of E Gerhardsen, Prime Minister 1945–65, Regjeringskvartalet

⑰ Youngstorget

Map 3 E3. 🇹 Jernbanetorget. 🚋 11, 12, 13, 17. 🚌 30, 31, 32, 34, 38, 56.

Many of the Labour movement's most important institutions have their headquarters around Youngstorget, among them the Norwegian Labour Party and the Norwegian Trades Union Federation, *Landsorganisationen*. Other political parties such as *Fremskrittspartiet* (Progress Party) and *Venstre* (Liberals), also have offices in the area.

Youngstorget was laid out in 1846, and was for many years a cattle and vegetable market, as well as a place for political demonstrations. Today, local farmers continue to sell fresh produce including fruit, vegetables, honey, eggs and other foodstuffs, and there are also clothes and exotic

handicrafts on sale. In the summertime concerts and performances are held here, as well as events for both children and adults.

The square is named after the merchant Jørgen Young, who originally owned the area. In 1990 it underwent substantial renovation. A copy of the original fountain from 1880 was installed and the market kiosks from 1876 were restored. There are shops, workshops and various places to eat and drink in the bazaar halls at the back of the market square, as well as in the market itself. The large building behind the bazaar halls is the old police station.

⑱ Oslo Spektrum

Sonja Henies Plass 2. **Map** 3 F3. **Tel** 22 05 29 00. 🇹 Jernbanetorget. 🚋 12, 13, 18, 19. 🚌 30, 31, 32, 34, 38, 41, 45, 46. Box Office: **Open** 9am–4pm Mon–Fri. ♿ 📷 by arrangement.
🌐 oslospektrum.no

The 10,800 capacity Oslo Spektrum is the main venue for large-scale sporting and cultural events and trade fairs. Designed by Lars Haukland, the complex was completed in 1991. It was planned and constructed as part of a scheme to revitalise the Grønland/Vaterland area of Oslo, and has created a bridge between the city centre and the eastern part of the city.

A number of major events such as the Norwegian Military Tattoo (September) and the Nobel Peace Prize concert (December) are held here, along with shows such as Disney on Ice. International pop stars, including Josh Groban, Elton John, Judas Priest and Rhianna, regularly perform at the stadium. It is also the venue for national handball matches. Tickets can be purchased online or through the box office.

The façade is clad with a massive mosaic designed by Rolf Nesch and crafted by artist Guttorm Guttormsgaard and ceramicist Søren Ubsisch. Made up from 40,000 glazed bricks, it features an eye-catching mix of abstract shapes interspersed with human figures. The choice of materials and architectural expression earned widespread praise.

Oslo Spektrum, the city's main venue for sport, culture and trade fairs

BYGDØY

Situated on the innermost reaches of Oslofjorden, Bygdøy is just a short distance from the city centre. Bygdøy means "the inhabited island", and it was an island until the end of the 19th century when the sound between Frognerkilen and Bestumkilen was filled in. It is one of the city's most exclusive residential areas and a popular tourist destination.

Bygdøy is home to a select group of museums which collectively reflect Norway's cultural history and national life, its seafaring traditions and intrepid voyages of discovery. A signposted walking route links the museums.

Kongsgården covers half the island and is run as an independent farm. The area's connections with royalty go back to the 16th century when the Danish-Norwegian kings came here to hunt. Much of Bygdøy is still forested. There are groves, meadows and parkland, and a wealth of different plant species.

Several of Oslo's most popular bathing beaches, including Huk and Paradisbukta, which means "Paradise Bay", are on Bygdøy.

Sights at a Glance

Museums
2 *Norsk Folkemuseum pp86–7*
3 *Vikingskipshuset pp88–9*
4 Kon-Tiki Museet
5 Norsk Maritimt Museum
6 Frammuseet

Interesting Buildings
1 Dronningen
9 Bygdø Kongsgård
10 Oscarshall Slott

Nature Reserve
8 Hukodden

Churches
7 Sjømannskirken

See also Street Finder map 1

BYGDØY

CHRISTIAN FREDRIKS VEI

BYGDØYVEIEN

STRØMSBORGVEIEN

MUSEUMSVEIEN

OSCARSHALLVEIEN

DRONNINGHAVNVEIEN

MELLBYEDALEN

HUK TERRASSE

HUK AVENY

MUSEUMSVN

FREDRIKSBORG

FREDRIK CHRISTIAN BENNECHES VEI

Frogner-kilen

Langviksbukta

Bygdøynes

BYGDØY KAPELLVEI

BYGDØY TERRASSE

JORDANS VEI

HJAMAR

HUK AVENY

LANGVIKSVEIEN

CONRAD HELMENS VEI

FREDRIKSBORGVEIEN

BYGDØYNESVEIEN LØCHENVEIEN

BYGDØYNESVEIEN

HERBERNVEIEN

ADMIRAL BØRRESENS VEI

GRAAH-BAKKEN

HUK AVENY

GRANDEVEIEN

SCHIELDERUPS VEI

TSNOK VEI

THEODOR LØVSTADS VEI

J MALLINGS VEI

HARALD NORMAN VEI

BYGDØYLUND

DAMMANS VEI

SCHIØTTS VEI

Lille Herbern

Store Herbern

0 metres   500
0 yards   500

For keys to symbols *see back flap*

Street-by-Street: Around Bygdøynes

A visit to Oslo would not be complete without a trip to Bygdøy and the peninsula of Bygdøynes. This is where locals and tourists alike go to enjoy the beautiful outdoors and to explore some of the most remarkable museums in Europe. Viking ships, polar expeditions and daring voyages across the Pacific Ocean on rafts such as the *Kon-Tiki* form the focal points for three of the collections. Stave churches and rural buildings have been reassembled to create the open-air Norsk Folkemuseum. Bygdøy is easily accessible by car, bus and ferry *(see p81)*.

❷ ★ Norsk Folkemuseum
Set in an idyllic landscape, the 21 features 150 reconstructed townhouses, farm buildings and churches from Norway's past. Inside there are exhibitions of folk art and costumes.

Gamlebyen at the Norsk Folkemuseum is a collection of old, restored townhouses.

Key

— Suggested route

| 0 metres | 150 |
| 0 yards | 150 |

❸ ★ Vikingskipshuset
Three splendid Viking vessels steal the show at the Viking Ship Museum. These and other relics provide an insight into life more than 1,000 years ago.

Stately private homes and embassies are situated in the area along Bydøynesveien.

❶ Dronningen
Former restaurant Dronningen, now the headquarters of the sailing club, Kongelig Norsk Seilforning, forms a prominent landmark of Functionalist-style architecture on the fjord's shoreline.

Locator Map
See Street Finder map 1

❹ ★ Kon-Tiki Museet
The main attractions at the Kon-Tiki Museum are the balsa wood raft, *Kon-Tiki* (1947), and the reed boat, *Ra II* (1970). Thor Heyerdahl won worldwide acclaim when he set sail across the oceans in these craft.

Ferry to Rådhusplassen via Bygdøynes

Gjøa, the first ship to cross the Northwest Passage (1903–06).

Ferry to Rådhusplassen

❻ Frammuseet
The museum is dedicated to the polar ship *Fram* (1892) and the expeditions made by Fridtjof Nansen and Roald Amundsen to the Arctic and Antarctic. Their heroic exploits are captured in the various displays.

Boat Hall

BYGDØYNESVEIEN

HERBERNVEIEN

❺ Norsk Maritimt Museum
Norway's proud seafaring history is showcased in an award-winning building from 1960 filled with artifacts and model ships. The Boat Hall contains a variety of craft.

Dronningen, an architectural landmark on the Frognerkilen waterfront

❶ Dronningen

Huk Aveny 1. **Map** 1 C3. **Tel** 23 27 56 00. 🚌 91 (Apr–Oct). ⛴ 30 (a short distance away). **Open** 9am–4pm Mon–Fri. **Closed** Jul. 🆆 knw.no

Before and after World War II, Dronningen ("the Queen") was one of Oslo's most popular summer restaurants. The building, constructed in 1930, was one of the first to be designed in the Functionalist style in Norway. It is situated on Dronningskjæret in Frognerkilen. However, in 1983 it was converted to offices. The Royal Norwegian Yacht Club and the Norwegian Students' Rowing Club are based here.

Dronningen ("the Queen") was often associated with Kongen ("the King"), a restaurant and summer variety theatre on the opposite side of Frognerkilen. In 1986 it, too, was converted to offices.

Frognerkilen is a major sailing centre dotted with large yachting marinas.

❷ Norsk Folkemuseum

See pp86–7.

❸ Vikingskipshuset

See pp88–9.

❹ Kon-Tiki Museet

Bygdøynesveien 36. **Map** 1 C4. **Tel** 23 08 67 67. 🚌 91 (Apr–Oct). ⛴ 30. **Open** Jan–Feb & Nov–Dec: 10am–4pm daily; Mar–Apr & Sep–Oct: 10am–5pm daily; Jun–Aug: 9:30am–6pm daily. **Closed** public hols. ♿ 🅿 🅐 🆆 kon-tiki.no

The world watched with interest when Thor Heyerdahl (1914–2002) and his five-man crew sailed across the Pacific in the fragile balsa-wood raft, *Kon-Tiki*, in 1947. Over the course of 101 days the raft covered 8,000 km (4,970 miles) from Peru to Polynesia. The voyage proved that it would have been possible for South Americans to have reached Polynesia in bygone days on balsa rafts. The raft is the main attraction in the Kon-Tiki Museet. A number of objects connected with the voyage are also on show.

Polynesian mask, Kon-Tiki Museet

Text and montages in both Norwegian and English give a graphic account of how those on board must have felt to have been so close to marine life that it was possible to catch sharks with their bare hands. They describe how on one occasion they felt a massive whale shark pushing against the raft.

Heyerdahl embarked on a new expedition in 1970. He sailed a papyrus boat, *Ra II*, across the Atlantic from Morocco to Barbados to prove a theory that it was possible for West African explorers to have landed in the West Indies before Columbus. *Ra I* had broken up well into the voyage due to a design fault, but *Ra II* survived and is on display in the museum.

Seven years later, Heyerdahl steered the reed boat, *Tigris*, across the Indian Ocean to prove that the ancient civilizations of the Indus valley and Egypt had contact with each other.

The museum's exhibits include a large number of archaeological finds from Heyerdahl's expeditions to places such as Easter Island and Peru.

Its 8,000-volume library, based around Heyerdahl's donated private library, contains the world's largest collection of literature about Polynesia.

The balsa-wood raft, *Kon-Tiki*, in the Kon-Tiki Museet on Bygdøy

❺ Norsk Maritimt Museum

Bygdøynesveien 37. **Map** 1 C4. **Tel** 24 11 41 50. 🚌 91 (Apr–Oct). 🚢 30. **Open** mid-May–Aug: 10am–5pm daily; Sep–mid-May: 10am–3pm Tue–Fri, 10am–4pm Sat & Sun. **Closed** some public hols. 🅿️ 📷 ♿ ✏️ 🏛️ 🌐 **marmuseum.no**

The most southerly of the museums on the idyllic Bygdøy peninsula is Norsk Maritimt Museum (the Norwegian Maritime Museum). It is located on the shore near the Frammuseet and Kon-Tiki Museet, and has its own quay and a marvellous view over Oslo's harbour and its approach from the fjord.

Norwegian maritime traditions, including the fishing industry, shipbuilding, shipping and marine archaeology, form the focal point of the collection. Norway's 1,500-year-old tradition of boat-building is a key part of its coastal culture.

The museum traces the development of shipping from the Middle Ages to present-day supertankers. The main theme linking the exhibits is man's use of the sea through the ages and how people have faced up to the challenges and dangers of this mighty element.

From the museum's main entrance, visitors enter the Central Hall containing a model of the Norwegian Navy's steam frigate, *Kong Sverre*, one of three of the largest and most powerful warships ever to be built in Nordic lands. Christian Krohg's painting, *Leiv Eiriksson Discovers America (see pp38–9)*, hangs on one of the walls. The exhibition halls feature an abundance of model ships through the ages in addition to relics from various maritime activities.

In the Boat Hall traditional fishing craft and working vessels are on show, and there a display on the diversity of stal culture. The schooner, *en*, is often moored at the de when it is not at sea as

Boat Hall of the Norsk Maritimt Museum, Frammuseet and the polar vessel *Gjøa*

a training ship for young people. Also standing outside the museum is the *Krigseiler-monument*, which commemorates sailors killed in World War II *(see p81)*.

The museum is the centre for a marine archaeological department, which protects finds discovered along the Norwegian coast.

The well-stocked museum library contains a collection of drawings, marine literature, archives and photographs.

Figurehead in the Maritimt Museum

❻ Frammuseet

Bygdøynesveien 36. **Map** 1 C4. **Tel** 23 28 29 50. 🚌 91 (Apr–Oct). 🚢 30. **Open** Mar–Apr: 10am–4pm daily; May: 10am–5pm daily; Jun–Aug: 9am–6pm daily; Sep: 10am–5pm daily; Oct: 10am–4pm daily; Nov–Dec: 10am–3pm Mon–Fri, 10am–4pm Sat & Sun. **Closed** public hols. 🅿️ 📷 ♿ partial. 🏛️ 🌐 **frammuseum.no**

No other sailing vessel has been further north or south in the world than the polar ship *Fram*. It was used for three Arctic expeditions by the explorers Fridtjof Nansen (1893–96), Otto Sverdrup (1898–1902) and Roald Amundsen (1910–12). On the third expedition, in 1911, Amundsen became the first person to raise a flag on the South Pole. The schooner was

built by the Scottish-born naval architect Colin Archer, and was specially constructed to prevent it from being crushed by pack ice. On its first commission with Nansen's expedition to the North Pole, it was frozen in at 78° 50'N. The vessel's rounded form allowed it to be pressed up on to the ice, where it remained undamaged until the ice thawed.

Fram also proved itself to be extremely seaworthy in the stormy Antarctic Ocean on Amundsen's historic expedition to the South Pole.

The museum opened in 1936 with the restored ship as its centrepiece. Expedition equipment, paintings, busts and photographs of the polar explorers are on show. The exhibitions have a representative selection of animals from the Polar region, like polar bears, penguins and moscus ox. Outside the museum is Amundsen's first polar exploration vessel, *Gjøa*.

The deck of the polar exploration vessel *Fram* at the Frammuseet

Norsk Folkemuseum

More than 150 buildings from all over Norway have been assembled in Europe's original and largest open-air museum, the Norsk Folkemuseum on Bygdøy. It was established by Hans Aall in 1894 at a time of widespread nationalist enthusiasm. The recreated farms evoke the pattern of everyday life in the valley, fjord and fishing communities of bygone times. Town buildings from all parts of the country have been reconstructed to create Gamlebyen (the Old Town). Traditional folk costumes are on show and Norwegian folk art, with its rich tradition of woodcarving, is well represented. An annual highlight is Julemarkedet (the Christmas market) in December.

★ **Gol Stave Church**
Adorned with paintings and carvings, the Gol stave church was built in Hallingdal c.1200. It was relocated here and restored in 1885. It is one of 30 preserved stave churches in Norway.

Hardangertunet
A rural courtyard in miniature has been created using houses from farms in Hardanger, Vestlandet.

Hallingdalstunet
This is an example of a rectangular courtyard commonly found in Hallingdal. The oldest building is the Hemsedal storehouse (1650–1700). The goatshed from Hol dates from the 18th century.

KEY

① **King Oscar II's collection** of buildings (see p91) became part of the Folkemuseum in 1907.

② **Open-air theatre**

③ **Arkadia Café**

④ **Museum shop**

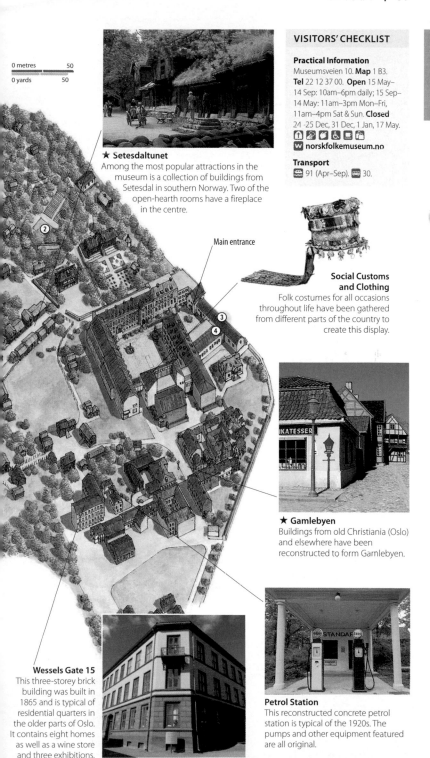

0 metres 50
0 yards 50

★ **Setesdaltunet**
Among the most popular attractions in the museum is a collection of buildings from Setesdal in southern Norway. Two of the open-hearth rooms have a fireplace in the centre.

Main entrance

Social Customs and Clothing
Folk costumes for all occasions throughout life have been gathered from different parts of the country to create this display.

★ **Gamlebyen**
Buildings from old Christiania (Oslo) and elsewhere have been reconstructed to form Gamlebyen.

Wessels Gate 15
This three-storey brick building was built in 1865 and is typical of residential quarters in the older parts of Oslo. It contains eight homes as well as a wine store and three exhibitions.

Petrol Station
This reconstructed concrete petrol station is typical of the 1920s. The pumps and other equipment featured are all original.

❸ Vikingskipshuset

Three of the world's best-preserved Viking ships from the
9th century can be seen in Vikingskipshuset (the Viking Ship
Museum), which forms part of the Museum of Cultural
History, University of Oslo. Found in three large burial mounds
on farmland, the ships are considered to be among Norway's
greatest cultural treasures. The Oseberg and Gokstad vessels
were discovered in Vestfold, and the Tune ship at Haugen in
Tune, Østfold. They were used to transport the bodies of high-
ranking chieftains on their last journey to the kingdom of
the dead. Jewellery, weapons and implements were stolen
by grave robbers but some pieces can still be seen here.
The museum was designed by Arnstein Arneberg to create
a light, airy setting for the ships.

Exterior view of the steep-pitched
Vikingskipshuset

★ **Oseberg Ship**
In 1904 archaeologists opened the
grave where the Oseberg ship was
found along with the remains of
two women and a large number
of artifacts. About 90 per cent of
the 22-m (72-ft) long ship is
of original wood.

Entrance hall

Main entrance

Gallery Guide

*The main attractions are arranged in the form of a cross.
Nearest to the entrance hall stands the Oseberg ship and
on the far side is the Oseberg Collection. The Gokstad ship
stands alone in the left wing. The least well-preserved find,
the Tune ship, is housed in the right wing. In the gallery
above the entrance, there are rotating exhibits. To the left
of the entrance is the museum shop.*

Key to Floorplan

- Oseberg Ship
- Gokstad Ship
- Tune Ship
- Oseberg Collection
- Non-exhibition space

★ **Gokstad Ship**
The excavation of the 24-m (79-ft)
long Gokstad ship took place in
1880. The remains of a 60-year-old
man, a sledge, three small boats, a
gangplank and 64 shields were
uncovered. The vessel has 16 pieces of
planking on each side compared to the
Oseberg's 12 pieces.

★ **Oseberg Wagon**
The richly carved Oseberg wagon is the only one known to exist from the Viking period in Norway. It was probably used by women of high status. Similar wagons have been found in Denmark and Germany.

VISITORS' CHECKLIST

Practical Information
Huk Aveny 35. **Map** 1 A3.
Tel 22 13 52 80.
Open May–Sep: 9am–6pm daily; Oct–Apr: 10am–4pm daily.
Closed public hols. 🎫
🎥 by prior arrangement. 🦽 📷
W khm.uio.no

Transport
🚌 91 (May–Sep). 🚌 30.

Animal Head
This animal-head post and four similar ones were found in the Oseberg ship. It is not known what they were used for. This one is in the shape of a predator's head with a gaping mouth, and is an example of the Viking wood-carvers' skills.

Burial Chamber
On display in the Tune wing, the Gokstad ship dates from around 900 and was found in a burial mound on the Gokstad farm in Sandefjord. It was made of oak and had been rowed with 16 oars. Above the ship's stern lay the remains of a burial chamber.

The Oseberg Collection features the remarkable equipment buried with the two women, including a wagon, sledges, iron-clad chests and caskets.

Excavating the Ships

Unearthing the 1,000-year-old Viking ships from the burial mounds proved a difficult task. The Oseberg ship was buried in blue clay and covered with stones beneath a 6-m (20-ft) high burial mound. The grave was almost hermetically sealed. Ground movement had partly compressed the ship and caused it to break up. The Gokstad ship was also buried in blue clay but the forces of nature had allowed it to lie in peace, and the ship and its contents were well preserved. Robbers had plundered some of the grave furnishings.

Excavation of the Oseberg ship in 1904

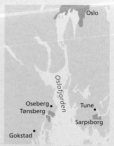

The Viking ship burial sites around Oslofjorden

Sjømannskirken, a church dedicated to the welfare of sailors

❼ Sjømannskirken

Admiral Børresens Vei 4. **Map** 1 B4.
Tel 22 43 82 90. 🚌 91 to Bygdøynes
(Apr–Oct). **Open** noon–5pm Fri–Sun.
🚌 30. ✝ 11am Sun.
Ⓦ sjomannskirken.no

In 1954 Oslo Sjømannsmisjon
(the Seamen's Mission) acquired
a beautiful building on Bygdøy as
a centre to help sailors and those
working in Oslo harbour. The
house was originally a private
residence, built by Arnstein
Arneberg (who designed the
Viking Ship Museum) in 1915.
It was consecrated as a church,
and a large assembly hall and a
sacristy were added in 1962.
Until then, the Seamen's Mission
had operated in very basic
conditions; preachers used to
conduct their sermons standing
on fishing crates.

In 1985, the church was taken
over by Den Indre Sjømannsmisjon (Internal Seamen's
Mission). It contains a memorial,
which was erected in 1966 to
commemorate Norwegian
sailors who died at sea.

❽ Hukodden

Map 1 A5. 🚌 91 to Bygdøynes (Apr–
Oct). 🚌 30. 🚲

Most of Bygdøy's south side
facing the fjord is public land
with tranquil walkways along
the shore and through the
woods. On the southernmost
tip of the peninsula lies
Hukodden beach, teeming
with bathers on fine summer
days. It is easily accessible from
the city by boat or bus. Despite
its proximity to the city, the
water quality is good for
bathing. A beach restaurant
is open in season.

From the furthest point on
Huk there is a splendid view
over Oslofjord, from Dyna
lighthouse to Nesoddlandet in
the south and to the islands in
the west. The waterway is busy
with ships and pleasure craft.

In the park area there are two
modern sculptures, *Large Arch*,
by Henry Moore, dating from
1969, and *Ikaros*, 1965, by Anne
Sofie Døhlen. On a spit of land
to the north of Huk there is a

naturist beach, and beyond is
the popular bathing spot of
Paradisbukta (Paradise Bay).

❾ Bygdø Kongsgård

Map 1 A2. **Tel** 22 12 37 00. 🚌 91 to
Dronningen, then by bus. 🚌 30.
Residence: **Closed** to the public.
Tracks: **Open** for walking. 🎞 of the
farm by prior arrangement.
Ⓦ norskfolkemuseum.no

King Olav V (1957–91) used
the royal estate of Bygdø
Kongsgård as a summer
residence for many years. He
treasured the tranquillity and
idyllic surroundings of the
4th-century royal farm.

King Håkon V Magnusson
had acquired the farm and
given it to Queen Eufemia in
1305. It became a monastic
estate in 1352, but was taken
over by the crown in 1532.
At the time of the Reformation
in 1536 it became a royal
ladegård (working estate).

King Karl Johan bought it
from the state in 1837. Included
in the deal was the main
building erected in the 1730s.
It was in the garden room here
that King Christian Frederik
received his farewell deputation
on 10 October 1814. He had
expected to become king of
Norway but was forced to make
way for Karl Johan *(see p42)*.

Oscar II took an interest in
the estate, and in 1881 he set
up an open-air museum of old
Norwegian wooden houses in
the grounds. This collection

The furthest point of Hukodden offering panoramic views over the inner Oslofjord

later became the foundation of the Norsk Folkemuseum *(see pp86–7)*. King Oscar also built the Kongvillaene in Swiss Alps chalet style for employees of the court. Today only one of these villas remains, Villa Gjøa.

The main building, a stately wooden mansion painted in brilliant white, makes a lovely sight in summer when surrounded by green foliage.

Bygdø Kongsgård covers a large area of northwestern Bygdøy. It comprises 200 hectares (500 acres) of forest and agricultural land. The area facing the sea is known as Kongeskogen (King's Wood). Here there are 9.5 km (6 miles) of public walking tracks. The grounds around the main house are part of the Norsk Folke-museum, which now runs the farm. The manor house is used and cared for by the royal family.

The dining room in Oscarshall Slott with friezes by Adolf Tidemand

Bygdø Kongsgård, the former summer residence of King Olav V

❿ Oscarshall Slott

Oscarshallveien. **Map** 1 B2. **Tel** 22 56 15 39. 🚌 30. **Open** May–Sep: 11am–5pm Sat & Sun; mid-Jun–Aug: 11am–5pm Wed–Mon. 🐾 🛈 ♿ 🌐 royalcourt.no

King Oscar I of Sweden and Norway (1799–1859) built a pleasure palace on a headland in Frognerkilen between 1847 and 1852, at the height of the era of National Romanticism. He named it Oscarshall and it became a favourite party venue for the kings of the Bernadotte dynasty. In 1863 the palace was sold to the state, and since then it has been at the disposal of the ruling monarch. It was never intended to be a residence, but rather a showcase for the architecture, handicrafts, applied art and fine art of the time, and for many years it was open to the public.

After the dissolution of the union in 1905 *(see p43)*, Oscarshall was closed, and large parts of its artistic decoration were placed in the Norsk Folke-museum. In 1929, plans were made to refurbish the palace as a residence for the crown prince, but they were later abandoned. Instead, the building was extensively restored and re-opened to the public.

Oscarshall is built in the style of an English castle. For inspiration, the architect, J H Nebelong, drew on Norman castle design and looked at the design of oriental white buildings with terraces and fountains. A Classical influence is evident in the proportions of the palace and in the strictly geometric shape of the rooms.

The drawing room is the largest room in Oscarshall with elegant windows and glazed doors opening on to the park. The entrance hall was inspired by a chapel from the Middle Ages with a circular stained-glass window on one of the end walls. The dining room is noted for its decorations by Adolph Tidemand (1814–76), a popular artist famous for his portrayals of everyday life in Norway. The king invited him to decorate the dining room with a series of 10 paintings inlaid in friezes around the upper walls. The pictures depict peasant life from childhood to old age.

The king's living room contains Gothic-style carved and moulded decorations and paintings based on the old Norwegian sagas.

Oscarshall Slott, Oscar I's 19th-century pleasure palace

FURTHER AFIELD

Many of Oslo's attractions are to be found just outside the city centre, often in rural surroundings. They are easily accessible by public transport, and several are close enough to one another that they can be visited in a single day.

Vigelandsparken *(see pp94–5)* is the showcase for the sculptures of Gustav Vigeland and nearby a museum is dedicated to his work. Edvard Munch's paintings can be seen in the Munch-museet, and an innovative collection of art by children has been assembled at the Barnekunstmuseum. Holmenkollen is the site of the famous ski jump. It is in areas such as Holmenkollen, Sørkedalen and Kjelsås, with their forests, lakes and wildlife, that it is possible to appreciate why the inhabitants of Oslo treasure the countryside on their doorstep. In summer it is never too far to go swimming, and in winter there are many ski tracks and slopes. Some areas, despite being near the centre, are so uncrowded that occasionally a solitary elk might be seen.

Sights at a Glance

Museums and Galleries
1 Vigelandsparken pp94–5
2 Oslo Museum
3 Vigelandsmuseet
4 Tjuvholmen and Astrup Fearnley Museet
6 Munch-museet

7 Botanisk Hage and Museum
8 Geologisk Museum
9 Zoologisk Museum
11 Det Internasjonale Barnekunstmuseet
12 Norsk Teknisk Museum
13 Emanuel Vigeland Museum
16 Bogstad Herregård

Historic Districts
5 Gamlebyen
10 Grünerløkka

Recreation Areas
14 Holmenkollen
15 Frognerseteren

Key
- Central Oslo sightseeing areas
- Greater Oslo
- Motorway
- Major road
- Minor road
- Railway
- Tunnel

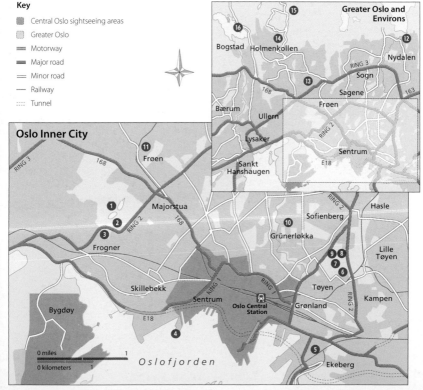

◄ Holmenkollen Ski Jump with the inner Oslofjord in the background

For keys to symbols *see back flap*

❶ Vigelandsparken

Oslo's largest park is named after the sculptor, Gustav Vigeland, whose 212 sculptures depicting humanity in all its forms are artfully positioned along the central axis. The focal point is the soaring Monolith on a stepped plinth surrounded by groups of figures. Vigeland started work on the park in 1924. By 1950, seven years after his death, most of the pieces were in place. The sculptures were modelled in full size in clay by Vigeland himself, but the carving in stone and casting in bronze were carried out by others. The interplay between the sculptures, the green areas and the architecture is a breathtaking sight.

Wheel of Life

The *Wheel of Life* (Livshjulet), which sums up the park's dramatic theme, was modelled in 1934. The wheel is a symbol of eternity and consists of a garland of men, women and children holding onto each other in an eternal cycle.

★ Monolith

The 17-m (56-ft) tall *Monolith* is the highest point in the park. It comprises 121 human figures, supporting and holding onto each other. On the plinth at the base of the column there are 36 groups of granite figures depicting the cycles of life and relationships.

KEY

① **Vigelandsmuseet** *(see p96)*, just outside the park, houses the artist's studio and an exhibition of his earlier works.

② **Sundial** (Soluret), stands on a granite plinth decorated with the signs of the zodiac.

③ **Bronze statuette**, Pike og øgle (Girl and the Lizard), 1938

④ **Frogner ponds**

⑤ **Kafé Vigeland and Visitors' Centre**

⑥ **Oslo Bymuseum** *(see p96)*

0 metres	100
0 yards	100

Triangle

The group of figures known as *Triangle* was one of the last pieces to be placed in Vigelandsparken. It was erected in 1993.

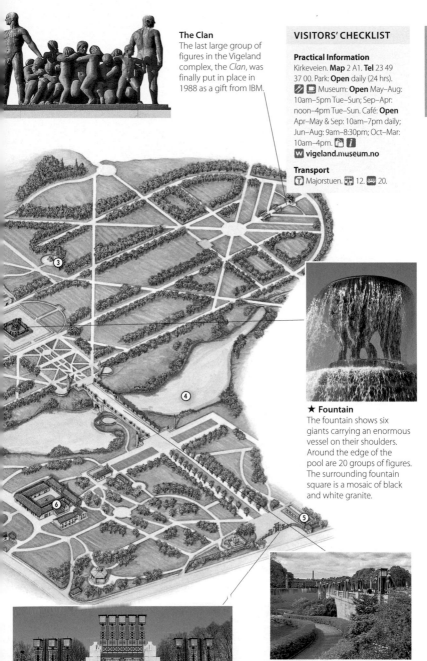

The Clan
The last large group of figures in the Vigeland complex, the *Clan*, was finally put in place in 1988 as a gift from IBM.

VISITORS' CHECKLIST

Practical Information
Kirkeveien. **Map** 2 A1. **Tel** 23 49 37 00. Park: **Open** daily (24 hrs).
🎿 💻 Museum: **Open** May–Aug: 10am–5pm Tue–Sun; Sep–Apr: noon–4pm Tue–Sun. Café: **Open** Apr–May & Sep: 10am–7pm daily; Jun–Aug: 9am–8:30pm; Oct–Mar: 10am–4pm. 📷 ℹ️
🅦 vigeland.museum.no

Transport
🚇 Majorstuen. 🚋 12. 🚌 20.

★ **Fountain**
The fountain shows six giants carrying an enormous vessel on their shoulders. Around the edge of the pool are 20 groups of figures. The surrounding fountain square is a mosaic of black and white granite.

★ **Bridge**
The granite bridge is lined with 58 bronze sculptures, modelled in the years 1925–33, and depicting the various stages of life. The lizard groups on each corner symbolize mankind's fight against evil.

Main Entrance
The monumental entrance consists of five wrought-iron main gates and two smaller pedestrian gates leading through to the sculptures.

❷ Oslo Museum

Frognerveien 67. **Tel** 23 28 41 70.
🚋 12. 🚌 20. **Open** 11am–5pm
Tue–Sun. **Closed** occasional public
hols and 1–15 Jan. 🎫 ♿ 🚫 📷 📷
W oslomuseum.no

The Oslo Museum is housed in
the Frogner Hovedgård, a well-
preserved 18th-century manor
house located in Gustav
Vigelands park (see pp94–5). This
museum of cultural history has
one of the largest collections of
paintings in Norway. The history
of Oslo is illustrated by thematic
exhibitions on the development
of the city and its cultural
and commercial activities. A
15-minute presentation entitled
"Oslo During the Past 1,000 Years"
offers an informative overview.

Also within the museum is the
Teatermuseet, which explores
Oslo's dramatic arts from the early
19th century onwards. Theatre,
ballet, opera, music revues and
the circus are all represented
through paintings, photographs,
posters, cartoons and costumes,
along with other memorabilia.

With its origin in the Middle
Ages, the former farm is in
traditional style, with three
buildings laid out around a
square yard behind the museum.

❸ Vigelandsmuseet

Nobelsgate 32. **Tel** 23 49 37 00. 🚋 12.
🚌 20. **Open** May–Aug: 10am–5pm
Tue–Sun; Sep–Apr: noon–4pm Tue–
Sun. **Closed** some public hols.
🎨 ♿ 📷 **W** vigeland.museum.no

A major part of Gustav Vigeland's
(1869–1943) artistic output can
be seen in Vigelandsmuseet,

Vigelandsmuseet, showcasing the work of the sculptor, Gustav Vigeland

located just outside the vast
Vigelandsparken (see pp94–5).

The collection contains 2,700
sculptures in plaster, bronze,
granite and marble; 12,000
drawings and around 400 wood-
cuts and carvings. The original
models for the Vigeland Park
sculptures, as well as casts for
busts and other monuments,
are on display. Old photographs
show the making of the
sculpture park. The museum is
the result of a contract drawn
up in 1921 between the artist
and Oslo City Council. Vigeland
donated all his existing and
future works to the city. In return,
the council built him a studio,
which was later converted into
a museum to exhibit his work.

Built in the 1920s, the studio-
turned-museum is considered
to be one of the finest examples
of Norwegian Neo-Classicism.
Vigeland himself chose the
interior colour scheme.

Moving through the rooms, it
is possible to follow the artist's
development from his 1890s'
expressive and thin-figure style
to the heavier expression of the
years between the two world
wars. The artist's living quarters
are also on view.

After Vigeland's death in 1943,
his ashes were placed in the
tower at his request.

❹ Tjuvholmen and Astrup Fearnley Museet

Strandpromenaden 2 , Tjuvholmen
Waterfront/Akerbygee. **Map** 2 C4/B4.
Tel 22 93 60 60. 🚇 Nasjonal Theatret.
🚋 12, 19. 🚌 21, 30, 31, 32, 54.
Open Jun–Aug: 10am–7pm daily
(to 10pm Thu, Sat & Sun); Sep–May:
noon–5pm Tue, Wed & Fri, noon–7pm
Thu, 11am–5pm Sat & Sun.
W afmuseet.no

Tjuvholmen, meaning "Thief
Island", was once Oslo's most
dangerous corner. In 2012, a
team of acclaimed architects,
including Niels Torp and Renzo
Piano, redesigned the inner city
waterfront, which is now home
to hotels, restaurants and the
Astrup Fearnley Museum. Two
striking buildings house temporary exhibitions and display
Norwegian and international
art from the post-World War II
period to the present day.

The exhibitions include
works by Francis Bacon, Lucian
Freud and R B Kitaj, who are all
key figures in the School of
London. Other international
names include Anselm Kiefer,
Gerhard Richter, Cindy Sherman,
Jeff Koons and Damien Hirst.
Norwegian art is represented
with works by Knut Rose, Bjørn
Carlsen, Olav Christopher
Jenssen, Kjell Torriset and
Odd Nerdrum.

A middle-class home dated around 1900 in Oslo Museum

❺ Gamlebyen

2 km (1 mile) E of town centre.
18, 19. 34, 70.

In the Middle Ages, the town of Oslo was centred on Gamlebyen (the Old Town). From the 12th century until the great fire of 1624, nearly all development in this area lay between Ekebergåsen, Bjørvika, Grønland and Galgeberg. Many of the medieval ruins have been preserved, including those of Mariakirken (Maria Church), Kongsgården (the Royal Manor) and Clemenskirken (Clemens Church). Excavations have revealed the remains of timber townhouses, and a medieval park has been re-created next to the ruins of St Hallvard Cathedral. Other reminders of the Middle Ages include Oslo Ladegård og Bispegården (Oslo Manor and the Bishops' Residence).

East of the Gamlebyen is the historic **Ekebergparken**, which dates from 1800. It now has a sculpture garden with works by Renoir, Rodin, Dalí and more. A gondola runs from the waterfront area at Bjørvika to Ekeberg.

Ekebergparken
E of Gamlebyen. Ⓣ Oslo S (then tram or bus). 18, 19. 34, 74.
W ekebergparken.com

Munch-museet containing Edvard Munch's extensive artistic output

❻ Munch-museet

Tøyengata 53. **Tel** 23 49 35 00
Ⓣ Tøyen/Munchmuseet. 20, 60.
Open Jun–Aug: 10am–9pm Mon–Fri, 11am–5pm Sat, 11am–9pm Sun; Sep–May: 10am–9pm Tue–Thu, 10am–4pm Fri, 11am–5pm Sat, 11am–9pm Sun.
Closed 1 Jan, 1 May, 17 May, 24 & 25 Dec.
W munchmuseet.no

The largest collection of work by Edvard Munch (1863–1944) is housed in Oslo's Munch-museet. Prior to his death, Edvard Munch bequeathed all the paintings in his possession to the City of Oslo. The Munch-museet opened in 1963, a century after Munch's birth. Designed by Gunnar Fougner and Einar Myklebust, the museum is situated next to Tøyenparken on Oslo's east side, where the artist grew up.

The collection is extensive, comprising 1,100 paintings, 4,500 drawings and 17,000 prints. It contains the main works from every period of the artist's productive life, including versions of *The Scream*, the worrying *Anxiety* (1894), the serene but melancholic *Young Woman on the Shore* (1896) and the sensuously claustrophobic *Kiss* (1897).

Some of Munch's major works may be on loan to museums elsewhere, and not all pieces are displayed at the same time. However, with 1,888 sq m (20,322 sq ft) of exhibition space and such a rich collection to draw on, the museum is never without material to provide a detailed account of the artist's life and work. Special exhibitions presenting new perspectives on his art are shown regularly. The museum's programme also comprises film screenings, concerts, guided tours and lectures.

Other examples of Munch's work can be seen in the Nasjonalgalleriet *(see pp56–7)*, Henie Onstad Kunstsenter *(see p124)* and Bergen's Rasmus Meyers Samlinger *(see p177)*.

Plans are currently under way to move the Munch-museet, along with the Stenersenmuseet *(see p62)*, into a new building located next to the Opera House *(see p76)* in the Bjørvika neighbourhood. The building is due to be completed in 2019. Visitors can see how the paintings are being prepared for moving.

Edvard Munch

Norway's most renowned visual artist and one of the forerunners of Expressionism, Edvard Munch (1863–1944) made his debut at the Autumn Exhibition in Oslo when he was just 20 years old. He painted a number of masterpieces shortly after his debut, including *The Sick Child*, connected to a personal experience – his sister's death from tuberculosis when she was 14 years old. After studies in Norway he moved to Paris in 1889, and later to Berlin, where he further developed his highly individual style with themes of love and death in the *Frieze of Life* series.

Spiritual experiences and angst characterize his work, as is evident in his best-known painting, *The Scream* (1894), in which a desperate figure can be seen screaming on a bridge. The agitated style of his works reveals a troubled life: in 1908 he suffered a mental breakdown, and a year later, he returned to Norway. By then he was accepted as a major artist and was commissioned to do works for public buildings, including the Aula of Oslo University *(see p54)*.

Munch's self-portrait, *The Night Wanderer*

Floral splendour in the Botanisk Hage at Tøyen in Oslo

❼ Botanisk Hage and Museum

Sars' Gate 1. **Tel** 22 85 16 30. Ⓣ Tøyen/Munch-museet. 🚋 17. 🚌 20, 31, 32, 60. Museum and greenhouses: **Open** 11am–4pm Tue–Sun. Botanisk Hage: **Open** 7am–9pm Mon–Fri; 10am–9pm Sat & Sun. **Closed** some public hols. 🖼 🚫 ♿ 🅿 🖥 📷 🖵 **nhm.uio.no**

Right across from Munchmuseet is the Botanisk Hage, Norway's largest botanical garden. It is a popular excursion for Oslo's residents, who come both to admire the thousands of Norwegian and foreign plants and to escape from the hustle and bustle of the city.

One of the highlights is the Alpine Garden, with a waterfall and 1,450 species of mountain flora from Norway and abroad. In the Systematic Garden plants are grouped according to family and genus. The Medicinal and Herbal Garden contains medicinal plants, spices and cash crops. For those in wheelchairs or with impaired vision, the Aromatic Garden is a special attraction. Here, fragrant plants grow in raised beds and are accompanied by texts in Braille. In the Victoria House and Palm House are plants from tropical and temperate regions, including rare orchids, carnivorous pitcher plants, cacti, cocoa trees, fig trees and palms.

The Botanisk Hage is part of the Natural History Museum and since 1814 has formed the basis for research and education in botany at the University of Oslo.

In the middle of the Botanical Garden is a manor house, Tøyen Hovedgård, dating from 1780. The old greenhouses and three museum buildings form an attractive planted enclosure.

An extensive herbarium containing 1.7 million examples of herbs, both medicinal and poisonous, provides an important resource for the documentation and research of Norwegian flora.

❽ Geologisk Museum

Sars' Gate 1. **Tel** 22 85 16 30. Ⓣ Tøyen/Munch-museet. 🚌 20, 31, 32, 60. **Open** 11am–4pm Tue–Sun. **Closed** some public hols. 🖼 🚫 ♿ 🖥 📷 🖵 **nhm.uio.no**

A circular showcase of gemstones is the first eye-catching exhibit on entering the Geologisk Museum. The gems are mainly Norwegian in origin. The ground floor of the museum is devoted to a presentation of the geological processes at work in the Earth, including the formation of volcanoes, mountain ranges and rocks.

Norway as an oil-producing nation is the subject of a separate exhibition.

In an intriguing display about Oslofeltet (the Oslo Field), remarkable fossil-bearing rocks are on show alongside other geological items that would normally lie hidden deep below the crust of the earth or in the murky depths of the North Sea. Exhibits include fossils such as weird-looking trilobites, brachiopods, cuttlefish and various microscopic creatures.

❾ Zoologisk Museum

Sars' Gate 1. **Tel** 22 85 16 30. Ⓣ Tøyen/Munchmuséet. 🚋 17. 🚌 20, 31, 32, 60. **Open** 11am–4pm Tue–Sun. **Closed** some public hols. 🖼 🚫 ♿ 📷 🖵 **nhm.uio.no**

The Norwegian Hall of the Zoologisk Museum features displays of stuffed native animals in recreations of their various habitats, including fish and marine and freshwater creatures, mammals and birds. Ptarmigan and reindeer can be observed against a mountain backdrop; cranes and black grouse are on show, and the pre-mating antics of the wood grouse are demonstrated. There are beaver dams and a display of the bird colonies that nest on the sea-cliffs.

In the Svalbard Hall exhibits feature Arctic animals, such as polar bears and seals. The

Arctic animals on display at the Zoologisk Museum

Animal Geography Hall presents large and small creatures in different world zones, such as penguins in Antarctica, and lions, hippopotamuses and crocodiles in the tropical regions. Also, there are several butterfly montages.

In the Systematic Hall there are detailed displays of Norway's animal life, from single-celled amoebas to the largest mammals. A "sound bar" provides recordings of animal noises from the wild.

Grünerløkka, a renovated and old popular working class district

❿ Grünerløkka

1 km (half a mile) N of the centre. 🚌 30, 58. 🚋 11, 12, 13.

The former working class district of Grünerløkka has undergone something of a renaissance in recent decades. It is made up largely of apartment blocks dating from the end of the 19th century, which were under threat of demolition. But repeated proposals to clear the area and build afresh have finally been shelved and instead the old housing stock has been restored. Small and inadequate apartments have been combined, and units have become larger and fewer, but the neighbourhood still retains the character of old Oslo. As a result, people from all walks of life have been attracted to Grünerløkka and the area has become particularly popular among young people.

With the influx of this vibrant community, a large number of cosmopolitan shops, cafés and restaurants thrive here, including the popular Mathallen (see p240).

Collections in the Norsk Teknisk Museum appealing to all ages

⓫ Det Internasjonale Barnekunstmuseet

Lille Frøens Vei 4. **Tel** 22 46 85 73. 🚇 Frøen. 🚌 46. **Open** Jul–mid-Aug: 11am–4pm Tue–Thu; Sep–Jun: 9:30am–2pm Tue, Wed & Thu, 11am–4pm Sun. **Closed** public hols. 🅿 🅲 🆉 🅵

Children's art from 150 countries has been assembled in Barnekunstmuseet (the International Museum of Children's Art). Exhibits include paintings, sculptures, ceramics, collages and textiles by children from around the world.

The museum was set up in 1968 in collaboration with the SOS Children's Villages, an international organization for children in need.

Although the museum is designed to give space specifically to children's opinions and things that are dear to them, the works have been selected on the basis of quality, just as they would be in an adults' museum.

Visiting children can express themselves actively in a variety of ways, in the Music and Dance Room, the Doll Room and the Painting and Drawing Studio. Videos and films on children's art are shown on various weekdays and workshops held.

Barnekunstmuseet, a lively forum for children's art

⓬ Norsk Teknisk Museum

Kjelsåsveien 143. **Tel** 22 79 60 00. 🚋 11, 12 to Kjelsås. 🚌 54. 🚉 to Kjelsås. **Open** 20 Jun–20 Aug: 10am–6pm daily; 21 Aug–19 Jun: 10am–4pm Tue–Fri, 11am–6pm Sat & Sun. **Closed** some public hols. 🅿 🅲 🅴 🅵 🆆 tekniskmuseum.no

Technology past and present is the subject of Norsk Teknisk Museum (the Norwegian Museum of Science and Technology), founded in 1914 in Kjelsås. Exhibits include Norway's first steam engine, its first car, imported in 1895, and its first aeroplane, in addition to early sewing machines, vacuum cleaners and other everyday objects.

The ground floor is dedicated to industry. The first floor covers transport and communications, telecom technology and information technology. Here it is possible to follow the development of steam power and the transition to mass production. Tele-communication is traced from the first warnings sent via beacons to the development of the telegraph and telephones, mobile phones and the Internet.

An exhibition illustrates oil and gas exploration in the North Sea, and shows how the raw material is pumped to the surface, transported and refined. In an unusual display titled *The Forest as a Resource*, the importance of cellulose in revolutionizing the production of paper 150 years ago is also highlighted.

There are educational exhibits and a science centre, Teknoteket, with hands-on activities. A variety of family events take place at weekends.

Emanuel Vigeland Museum, featuring the artist's work and mausoleum

⑬ Emanuel Vigeland Museum

Grimelundsveien 8, 5 km (3 miles) N of centre. **Tel** 22 14 57 88. Ⓣ Slemdal. 🚌 46. **Open** noon–5pm Sun (to 4pm Sep–May). 📷

On the western side of Oslo lies one of the most unusual museums in Norway. It is dedicated to the artist Emanuel Vigeland, younger brother of Gustav, the sculptor who created Vigelandsparken *(see pp94–5)*.

Emanuel Vigeland (1875–1948) pioneered fresco painting in Norway. He also perfected the art of medieval stained glass techniques.

The museum building was originally Vigeland's studio; on his death it became his mausoleum and was opened to the public in 1959. On show is his lifework, *Vita*, a series of fresco paintings from 1927–47, in addition to portraits, drawings and sculptures. The frescoes have to be viewed in somewhat subdued lighting, because in the 1940s the subjects in *Vita* were considered too daring for public taste, and it was thought that strong lighting would make them even more provocative. Today, few people would regard Vigeland's work as indecent.

Another oddity is the unusually low-ceilinged entrance area. This has been attributed to the artist's desire for humility in the face of the art one is coming to view.

Examples of Vigeland's stained glass can be seen in the windows of Oslo Domkirke *(see p77)*.

⑭ Holmenkollen

6 km (4 miles) N of centre. **Tel** 91 67 19 47. Ⓣ Holmenkollen. 🚫 💻 Skimuseet & Ski Jump: **Open** Jan–Apr & Oct–Dec: 10am–4pm daily; May & Sep: 10am–5pm daily; Jun–Aug: 9am–8pm daily. 📷 by arrangement. 🌐 **holmenkollen.com**

Ski-jumping is guaranteed to attract the crowds in Norway, and the impressive ski jump at Holmenkollen, which was rebuilt in 2011, is no exception. The venue for the annual Holmenkollen Races and ski-jumping events is Norway's biggest tourist attraction, drawing more than 1 million visitors a year. The races have been held here since 1892 when the ski jump was created from branches covered in snow. Crown Prince Olav participated in the jumping competitions in both 1923 and 1924. The ski jump, which has been remodelled 15 times and was completely rebuilt for the FIS Nordic World Ski Championships in 2011, is regarded by some as the most important arena for Nordic skiing. The world championships have been held here on four occasions, as were many of the skiing events for the 1952 Winter Olympics. The most recent World Championships, in 2011, included 21 competitions within cross-country and ski-jumping along with a variety of cultural events. The complex has also become the main arena for the Biathlon, involving cross-country skiing and marksmanship.

The public can visit both the ski jump and the jump tower all year round. The tower, in particular, offers a splendid view over Oslo and the inner Oslofjord, with an outdoor viewing platform, as well as panoramic views from the snack bar below. In summer, a zipline allows intrepid visitors to travel from the top to the bottom of the jump tower for a fee.

The Skimuseet, at the base of the ski jump, opened in 1923. It focuses on more than 4,000 years of skiing history *(see pp30–31*. Displays illustrate various types of skis from different eras and regions of Norway, and follow the development of each of the skiing disciplines. The Olympics in Oslo in 1952 and Lillehammer in 1994 are also covered. In addition, Norway's prominent role in polar history receives special attention and the now antique-looking equipment used by Nansen and Amundsen can be admired.

The large area outside the museum has a waterfall and spectacular views.

The striking profile of the rebuilt Holmenkollen ski jump

The wooden lodge at Frognerseteren on a winter's daye

⓯ Frognerseteren

7 km (4 miles) N of centre. Restaurant:
Tel 22 92 40 40. Ⓣ Frognerseteren.
▨ 🖥 🆆 **frognerseteren.no**

Only a short walk from the station that bears its name is Frognerseteren, a favourite excursion spot. Originally it was a pasture, which was first inhabited in the 1790s.

Just 15-minutes from the city centre, Frognerseteren is the last station on the Holmenkollen Tunnelbane line. It is a popular starting point for walks in the Nordmarka woods throughout the year, giving access to the network of footpaths and ski trails.

The road northward from Holmenkollen to Frogner-seteren was opened in 1890 in the presence of Oscar II and the German Emperor Wilhelm II. It was named Keiser Wilhelms Vei. After World War II it was renamed Holmenkollveien.

The wooden lodge at Forgnerseteren is one of Oslo's most unusual buildings. Designed by the architect Holm Munthe (1848–98) and built by the municipality, it was completed in 1892. The structure is built in the traditional Scandinavian "dragon style", so called because of the carvings of dragon heads located at the peak of the gables.

The terrace, with its spectacular panoramic view over Oslo, the fjord and surrounding areas, is 435 m (1,427 ft) above sea level. Below the lodge is a stone monument commemorating the 1814 Constitutional Assembly, plus a number of houses with grass-topped roofs.

The building also houses two eateries: Restaurant Finstua and Kafe Seterstua. Guests at the restaurant can sample traditional Norwegian food (including reindeer). The café offers hot and cold dishes from self-service counters, as well as delicious homemade treats from the Frognerseteren pastry shop.

Prime minister Peder Anker (1749–1824) and his family

⓰ Bogstad Herregård

Sørkedalen 826, 8 km (5 miles) NW of centre. **Tel** 22 06 52 00. 🚌 41.
Open mid-May–end Sep, only for guided tours. 🅿 📷 1pm, 2pm Tue–Sun. 🛗 🖥 ☕ (café and shop open noon–4pm Tue–Sun year-round).
🆆 **bogstad.no**

On a promontory on the eastern side of Bogstad Lake in Søkerdalen lies Bogstad Herregård, a farming estate which dates from the Middle Ages.

Bogstad originally belonged to the Cistercian Monastery on Hovedøya, an island situated in the innermost part of Oslofjorden. It then passed to the crown before being sold to the alderman, Morten Lauritzen.

The present manor house was erected in the late 18th century by Peder Anker (1749–1824) who later became prime minister. Most of the contents and the large art collection date from that time. The estate then passed to Baron Herman Wedel Jarlsberg. Oslo Municipality took over its forests and arable land in 1954 when the building, complete with contents, and the surrounding parkland became part of Norsk Folkemuseum (see pp86–7).

The manor house is open to the public during the summer months, and in December it is the venue for various Christmas events.

In 1978 the wagonhouse and woodshed next to the driveway from Sørkedalsveien burned down and were later replaced by reproductions. Extensive restoration took place in 1999, when the barn was converted to provide banqueting facilities.

The park surrounding Bogstad Herregård was established around 1785 by the Norwegian garden designer Johan Grauer. For inspiration, Peder Anker had sent Grauer to England to study English landscape design. Grauer's park layout was one of the first Norwegian examples of the English landscape style.

Bogstad Herregård, a farming estate dating back to the Middle Ages

SHOPPING IN OSLO

While Norway is undoubtedly one of the most expensive places in Europe to shop, you can find some wonderful, high-quality items to take back with you. The high prices become a bit more palatable once you consider the 25 per cent discount (15 per cent for food) offered by the country's tax-free-for-tourists scheme *(see p250)*. Moreover, if you shop smartly and have time to look around you should be able to find a bargain or two. The most popular items to buy are souvenirs such as Viking- or troll-related items, traditional sweaters and cheese slicers, *rosemaling* ("rose paintings"), finely painted wooden plates, dolls in traditional *bunads* (costumes) and native Sámi (Lapp) items.

Designer boutiques in the Aker Brygge shopping mall

Where to Shop

Karl Johans Gate *(see p52)* is Oslo's main pedestrian thoroughfare, with a mix of major chains and smaller outlets. **Stortorvet** *(see p67)* and the market place at **Strøget** have more of the same, while just south, **Aker Brygge** *(see p61)* is good for designer shops. **Bogstadveien**, towards Majorstua, also has small designer boutiques. **Grønland** is good for inexpensive fabrics and fancy jewellery, while **Grünerløkka** *(see p99)* is the best area for Norwegian fashion designers.

Souvenirs

For Scandinavian souvenir items, head to **Husfliden**, which sells a wide range of traditional handcrafted items, including slippers, folk costumes and rose paintings. **Norway Shop**, near the city hall, is another good venue for Viking-themed items that include jewellery, drinking horns and Sámi goods.

Wool Sweaters

The Norwegian wool sweater personifies Scandinavian workmanship and attention to detail. Those made by Dahl and Nordstrikk are of high quality. **Oslo Sweater Shop** carries over 5,000 sweaters, as well as knitted jackets, caps and socks. Another good option for woven and knitted garments is **Oleana**.

Antiques, Art and Markets

For antiques, try **Blomqvist Kunsthandel**, which has art, crystal and other fine items for sale and auction. **Far & Sønn**

Traditional Scandinavian souvenirs on sale in the city

Brukt Antikkmarked has cheaper items, including old furniture.

For the best selection of Norwegian art, you can buy works straight off the walls at **Kunstnernes Hus**, a local exhibition space. **Abel Kunst** sells an impressive selection of contemporary painting and sculptures.

The city's weekend flea markets are another great place to seek out bargains for antiques, clothes, arts and crafts. **Vestkanttorget** (Sat 10am–5pm), near Vigeland Park is filled with bric-a-brac, while **Birkelunden** (Sun noon–6pm) in Grünerløkka is good for vintage clothing.

Shopping Centres and Department Stores

Though tourist-related shopping in Oslo is best at small handicrafts stores, there are a number of shopping malls for more general items. **Byporten Shopping**, opposite Oslo Central Station, contains more than 70 shops that sell a number of well-known brands. **Oslo City** is one of the capital's largest department stores, with many specialty Nordic items. **Aker Brygge** is another popular shopping mall in the city, while **Paléet** has dozens of exclusive shops that sell clothing, art and cosmetics.

Clothing and Fashion

Norwegian fashion designers to look out for include Kristian Aadnevik and Laura Armonaite. **MA Fashion** is one of the best places for modern designs, while **Norway Designs** stocks designer clothing and

Examples of world-renowned Norwegian glassware

accessories. **Skapeverket** offers clothing and accessories by up-and-coming Norwegian designers. Given the high price of new clothes in Norway, it makes sense to scour Oslo's used clothing boutiques. The Markveien branch of **Fretex** sells trendy second-hand clothes.

Books and Music

The city's best bookshops are **Norli**, **Tanum Libris** and **Ark Bokhandel**, all with good selections of all the major European languages. **Bjørn**

Ringstrøms Antikvariat is a huge used bookseller.

With regard to music shops, **Platekompaniet** is the best of the chain stores. For more eccentric tastes, **Big Dipper** is the city's largest indie music store, with much of its music on vinyl, while **Bare Jazz** sells a good selection of jazz CDs in a café setting.

Glassware

Norway is well-known for its glassware; **Glasmagasinet** is the country's largest shop,

and **Norway Designs** also carries an impressive inventory of glass-ware, ceramics and pottery.

Jewellery, Gold and Silver

For antique jewellery and second-hand gold and silver items, **Esaias Solberg** is the city's oldest and best shop, selling earrings, necklaces, watches and houseware items. **David-Andersen** is also a good place for jewellery, particularly enamelled pieces.

Karl Johans Gate shopping area in central Oslo

DIRECTORY

Souvenirs

Husfliden
GlasMagasinet, Stortorvet.
Tel 22 42 10 75.

Norway Shop
Fr. Nansens Plass 2.
Tel 22 33 41 97.

Wool Sweaters

Oleana
Stortingsgata.
Tel 22 33 31 63.

Oslo Sweater Shop
Biskop Gunnerus
Gate 3.
Tel 22 42 42 25.

Antiques, Art and Markets

Abel Kunst
Kristian's IV's Gate 15.
Tel 22 20 25 02.

Birkelunden
Birkelunden.

**Blomqvist
Kunsthandel**

Tordenskiolds.
Tel 22 70 87 70.

Far & Sonn Brukt Antikkmarked
3 Sanner Gate.
Tel 22 35 05 36.

Kunstnernes Hus
Wergelandsveien 17.
Tel 22 85 34 10.

Vestkanttorget
Amaldus Nilsens Plass.

Shopping Centres and Department Stores

Aker Brygge
Stranden 3B.
Tel 22 83 26 80.

Byporten Shopping
Jernbanetorget 6.
Tel 23 36 21 60.

Oslo City
Stenersgate 1.
Tel 81 54 40 33.

Paléet
Karl Johans Gate 37–43.
Tel 23 08 08 11.

Clothing and Fashion

Fretex
Markveien 51.
Tel 22 35 59 16.

MA Fashion
Hegdehaugsveien 27.
Tel 20 60 72 90.

Norway Designs
Stortingsgaten 28.
Tel 23 11 45 10.

Skapeverket
Markveien 60,
Grünerløkka.
Tel 22 38 50 70.

Books and Music

Ark Bokhandel
Grensen 17.
Tel 22 99 07 50.

Bare Jazz
Grensen 8.
Tel 22 33 20 80.

Big Dipper
Møllergata 1.
Tel 22 20 14 41.

Bjørn Ringstrøms Antikvariat
Ullesvålsveien 1.
Tel 22 20 78 05.

Norli
Universitetsgata 20–24.
Tel 22 00 43 00.

Platekompaniet
Bodstadveien 40.
Tel 22 46 03 55.

Tanum Libris
Karl Johans Gate 37–41.
Tel 22 47 87 30.

Jewellery, Gold and Silver

David-Andersen
Karl Johan's Gate 20.
Tel 24 14 88 00.

Esaias Solberg
Kerkeristen.
Tel 22 86 24 80.

ENTERTAINMENT IN OSLO

When it comes to entertainment, Oslo can certainly give its Scandinavian brethren in Stockholm and Copenhagen a run for their money. It is a hip getaway destination with loads of cultural and artistic goings-on, several well-attended festivals and a thriving café and nightlife scene to boot. In terms of nightlife, the city is home to over a hundred bars and clubs, many of them in the centre and several dozen of which keep their doors open until 3am. Be sure to pick up a copy of *What's On in Oslo*, available from most hotels and tourist information offices, and *Streetwise*, a free listings brochure covering bars and clubs in the city. Tickets to all theatre, ballet, opera, concert and festival events can be purchased at Billettsentralen or at any post office.

Theatre and Cultural Events

Oslo is, naturally, the perfect place to catch the works of Henrik Ibsen, Norway's greatest playwright. Ibsen productions are best seen in the **Nationaltheatret** – it was built in 1899 exclusively for performances of his plays – though other modern works are also put on. Tickets generally start at 190 Nkr. The theatre organizes a special Ibsen festival every other year. In the same location, the **Amfiscene** has (cheaper) avant-garde performances. Ibsenmuseet (the Ibsen Museum, *see pp62–3*) is just a short walk from the Nationaltheatret, and offers a programme of talks presented by literary experts and theatre professionals.

Other theatre venues include **Det Norske Teatret** and **Oslo Nye Teater** and, for young, new writing, **Den Åpne Teater**. One of Oslo's more unusual venues is the **MS Innvik**, a large ship moored in Bjørvika that organizes regular bespoke theatre shows. **Chat Noir** is the oldest revue theatre in Scandinavia and great for comedy, cabaret and vaudeville-type musical events. The chapel at the **Akershus Castle and Fortress** has theatre and concerts in summer; a Chamber Music festival is also held here in August.

Parkteatret is a smart cultural centre offering weekly music, films and theatre performances. One of the largest cultural events is the annual December gala evening at **Oslo Spektrum**, held in connection with the Nobel Peace Prize ceremony.

Classical Music, Opera and Ballet

Oslo Konserthus is the home of the nation's largest symphony orchestra, the Oslo Philharmonic. Concerts are generally held on Thursdays and Fridays in the spring and autumn, with tickets starting at around 200 Nkr. **Chateau Neuf** and **Sentrum Scene** are

The Nationaltheatret, the city's principal stage-production venue

popular entertainment theatres in Oslo, staging musicals, farces, comedies and cabarets. **Rockefeller Music Hall** also puts on a wide range of musical events.

Chamber music is increasing in popularity in Norway. In October, Oslo's **Ultima Contemporary Music Festival** features opera, ballet, classical and folk music performances at a variety of spots throughout the city. **Oslo Kirkemusikk-festival** (the Oslo Festival of Church Music) draws thousands of people to the capital's churches in March. The Opera House (*see p76*) is home to **Den Norske Opera** (the Norwegian National Opera). The Opera features many of the world's best-known works in its repertoire, and also presents three or four newly commissioned works every season. In total, they put on 20 different operas and operettas each year, as well as hosting the many

A church music ensemble at the Oslo Kirkemusikkfestival

A band plays at the Oslo Spektrum, the city's largest popular music venue

modern dance performances by the **Nasjonalballetten** (the National Ballet), Norway's only classical ballet company. Both the opera and ballet seasons generally operate during the winter months, and tickets usually start at around 170 Nkr, though you can occasionally get cheaper day-of tickets. An interesting alternative venue is the **Underwater Pub**, which is a unique way to see opera stars in the making – local opera students perform their latest librettos here on Tuesdays and Thursdays.

Folk Dancing

Norway has a strong tradition of folk dancing. There are regular international and Norwegian traditional dance performances at **Dansens Hus** throughout the year. During the summer you can catch twice-weekly performances of folk dancing at the **Oslo Konserthus** (see Classical Music, above). The **Norsk Folkemuseum** on Bygdøy has its own folk dancing group that put on shows in an open-air theatre several nights a week between July and August. Admission to the museum also includes entry to dance performances. Both Crown Prince Haakon and Princess Märtha Louise have participated keenly in folk dancing at the Folkemuseum.

Cinema and Film

Most non-Scandinavian films are screened in their original language with Norwegian subtitles. **Oslo Kino Klingenberg** is one of the city's largest cinemas, while **Saga Kino** shows a wide range of films across six screens; both generally show the latest Hollywood blockbusters.

If your preference is for arthouse films, classic features, interesting documentaries and "alternative" movies just off the festival circuit, then **Filmens Hus** is the place to go.

Cinema tickets generally go for around 100 Nkr, and are usually cheaper for matinee performances. You can call 82 05 00 01 or look at www.oslokino.no to find out what features are playing at any of the city's cinemas.

Rock and Blues

Most live music in Oslo happens during the weekend, though sometimes there are shows on Wednesday and Thursday nights. Big-name international bands mainly perform at **Oslo Spektrum** (see Theatres, opposite), as well as at the country's biggest rock festival, Norwegian Wood, held outside of Oslo in the early summer. Øyafestivalen, a rock festival held in Middelalder-parken in downtown Oslo in mid-August, features international groups as well as popular Scandinavian bands.

For live rock music in the city centre, your best bet is **Last Train**, a popular venue; bands feature every night except Sunday. Another good bet is **Café Mono**, a dimly-lit place that's good for rock and punk music most nights from Sunday to Thursday. Nearby, **Blitz** and **Elm Street Rock Café** have live rock several evenings a week.

Elsewhere, **Sawol** is a good spot to catch both established and up-and-coming Norwegian rock 'n' roll bands, while **Revolver** is a trendy place that has live rock gigs by local and international bands, as well as DJ sets, in its basement most nights of the week. **Sound of Mu** is a British-run bar that has live music, much of it from Oslo's underground music scene, from Tuesday through to Sunday.

Traditional dancing at the Norsk Folkemuseum

Jazz

Scandinavians are well known for their love of jazz music and Norway has provided noted musicians such as Jan Garbarek, Terje Rypdal, Nils Petter Molvær and Sidsel Endresen. Oslo has a large number of jazz cafés and clubs, most of which usually charge a cover of 60–70 Nkr when there is a live group performing. One of the best jazz venues in Oslo is **Blå**, a mellow joint that regularly features both established and up-and-coming musicians. Other good jazz bars include **Herr Nilsens Pub**, with live music from Thursday to Saturday, and **Café Con Bar**, where trios and quartets play late on Sundays. **Bare Jazz** is a favourite for music scene insiders and has live concerts once a week, while **Bar Boca**, a tiny 1950s-style bar, occasionally puts on live jazz on Thursdays. In August, the Oslo Jazz Festival hosts the biggest names in world jazz.

Contemporary interior of The Sense Cocktailbar & Lounge

Bars and Cafes

Most bars and clubs in Oslo are open until 3am, though some close at 1am during the week. The Akerselva river is the rough dividing line between the upscale bars and clubs in the west and the more alternative, student-type venues in the east. In general, the areas around Majorstuen, Vika and Frogner have the most fashionable bars; Karl Johan's Gate and Aker Brygge are mainstream; Grünerløkka has hip lounges;

The popular waterside location of Aker Brygge's bars

and Grønland is a student area.

In the centre, the **Skybar** is located atop the Radisson SAS Hotel, and is where Oslo's elite come for the great views. The bars around Aker Brygge include **Bar 1**, which serves several hundred types of cognacs and whiskeys.

Behind the train station **Stargate** and **Choice** are fun, grungy bars, though **Fru Hagen** is a bit classier. Nearby, **Oslomekaniskeverksted** is a bar popular with young professionals. For something more alternative, head to Grünerløkka and its after-hours bars. **Parkteatret** is one of the area's best-loved spots as it puts on regular concerts and theatre performances. **Tea Lounge** is an airy spot with plush seating and a huge cocktails list. Just down the road is **Kaos**, a lounge bar with a terrace in the back that has great dancing; **SüdØst**, with its basement nightclub; and **Aku-Aku**, a jovial tiki bar adorned with original slats from Thor Heyerdahl's ocean expedition (see p83).

The Sense Cocktailbar & Lounge, near the Nationaltheatret (see p55), is well-known for its superb cocktails, great atmosphere and varied music programme, featuring both DJs and live bands.

Clubs

Oslo's club scene is lively, but can be expensive, as many venues charge upwards of 100 Nkr entry. At many of the more fashionable spots, there is often a dress code of dark clothing and dark shoes, so it's best to not show up in trainers and jeans. **Blå** (see Jazz, above), in Grünerløkka, is a large space that is one of Oslo's most popular venues to listen and dance to a range of live and DJ music. In the centre, expect long queues at **Pi** and **The Villa** are good hotspots for techno and electronica; keep an eye out for discount student nights at each.

Popular with the chic crowd on weekends is **Badstugata**, while the retro-styled **Robinet** has a hedonistic feel. More mainstream options include **Soliis Bar & Lounge**; **Yatzi**, with three floors comprising a live jazz club, dance club and pop bar; and **Nivou**, Oslo's largest night club. A longstanding favourite for electronic music is **Sikamikanico**.

Revellers strut their stuff in one of Oslo's nightclubs

DIRECTORY

Theatres

Akershus Castle and Fortress
Akerhus Festning.
Tel 23 09 39 17.

Amfiscene
Johanne Dybwadsplass 1.
Tel 81 50 08 11.

Chat Noir
Klingenberggata 5.
Tel 22 83 22 02.

Den Åpne Teater
Tøyenbekken 34.
Tel 22 05 28 00.

Det Norske Teatret
Kristian IV Gate 8.
Tel 22 42 43 44.

Ibsenmuseet
Henrik Ibsens Gate 26.
Tel 22 12 35 50.

MS Innvik
Hollendergata 8.
Tel 22 41 95 00.

Nationaltheatret
Johanne Dybwadsplass 1.
Tel 81 50 08 11.

Oslo Nye Teater
Rosenkrantz Gate 10.
Tel 22 34 86 00.

Oslo Spektrum
Sonja Henies Plass 2.
Tel 22 05 29 00.

Parkteatret
Olaf Ryes Plass 11.
Tel 22 35 63 00..

Classical Music, Opera and Ballet

Chateau Neuf
Slemdalsveien 15.
Tel 22 96 15 00.

Oslo Konserthus
Munkedamsveien 14.
Tel 23 11 31 00.

Den Norske Opera / Nasjonalballetten
Kirsten Flagstads Pass 1.
Tel 21 42 21 21.

Oslo Kirkemusikkfestival
Øvre Slottsgate 3.
Tel 22 41 81 13.

Rockefeller Music Hall
Torggata 16.
Tel 22 20 32 32

Sentrum Scene
Torggata 16.
Tel 22 20 32 32.

Ultima Contemporary Music Festival
Kongensgate 4.
Tel 22 40 18 90.

Underwater Pub
Dalsbergstien 4.
Tel 22 46 05 26.

Folk Dancing

Dansens Hus
Møllerveien 2.
Tel 23 70 94 00.

Norsk Folkemuseum
Museumsveien 10.
Tel 22 12 37 00.

Cinemas

Filmens Hus
Dronningens Gate 16.
Tel 22 47 45 00.

Oslo Kino Klingenberg
Olav V's Gate 4.
Tel 99 43 20 00.

Saga Kino
Stortingsgata 28.
Tel 99 43 20 00.

Rock and Blues

Blå
Pilestredet 30C.
Tel 22 11 23 49.

Café Mono
Pløensgate 4.
Tel 22 41 41 66.

Elm Street Rock Café
Dronningens Gate 32.
Tel 22 42 14 27.

Last Train
Karl Johans Gate 45.
Tel 22 41 52 93.

Revolver
Møllergata 32.
Tel 22 20 22 32.

Sawol
Grønland 18.
Tel 45 20 43 81.

Sound of Mu
Markveien 58.

Jazz

Bar Boca
Thorvald Meyers Gate 30.
Tel 22 04 10 80.

Bare Jazz
Grensen 8.
Tel 22 33 20 80.

Blå
Brenneriveien 9C.
Tel 40 00 42 77.

Café Con Bar
Brugata 11.
Tel 22 05 02 00.

Herr Nilsens Pub
CJ Hambros plass 5.
Tel 22 33 54 05.

Bars and Cafes

Aku-Aku
Thorvald Meyers Gate 32.
Tel 41 17 69 66.

Bar 1
Holmens Gate 3.
Tel 22 83 00 02.

Choice
Grønlandsleiret 38.
Tel 22 12 23 00.

Fru Hagen
Thorvald Meyers Gate 40.
Tel 22 35 67 87.

Kaos
Thorvald Meyers Gate 56.
Tel 22 04 69 90.

Oslomekanlskeverk-sted
Tøynebekken 34.
Tel 45 23 75 34.

Parkteatret
Olav Ryes Plass 11.
Tel 22 35 63 00.

Sense Cocktailbar & Lounge
Henrik Ibsens Gate 4.
Tel 90 74 07 89.

Skybar
Sonja Henies Plass 3.
Tel 22 05 80 00.

Stargate
Grønlandsleiveret 2.
Tel 22 12 23 00.

SüdØst
Trondheimsveien 5.
Tel 22 35 30 70.

Tea Lounge
Thorvald Meyers Gate 33B.
Tel 22 37 07 05.

Clubs

Badstugata
Badstugata 1.
Tel 22 20 82 55.

Nivou
Møllergata 12.
Tel 22 41 41 00.

Pi
Storgata 24.

Robinet
Mariboes Gate 7.

Sikamikanico
Stortorvet 10.
Tel 22 41 44 09.

Soliis Bar & Lounge
Henrik Ibsens Gate 90.
Tel 21 89 90 20.

The Villa
Møllergata 23.
Tel 93 25 57 45.

Yatzi
Nedre Slottsgate 2.
Tel 93 45 45 44.

OSLO STREET FINDER

The map below shows the areas of Oslo covered by the *Street Finder*. The map references given in the guide for the capital's sights, restaurants, hotels and shops refer to the maps in the *Street Finder*. The first number of the map reference tells you which map to turn to. The letter and number that follow refer to the grid reference on that map.

All the major sights are marked and should be easy to find. The symbols listed in the key below indicate other important points plotted on the maps, such as post offices, Tunnelbane (metro) stations, bus and ferry terminals, car parks and churches. On page 89 there is a small-scale map of Greater Oslo and Environs.

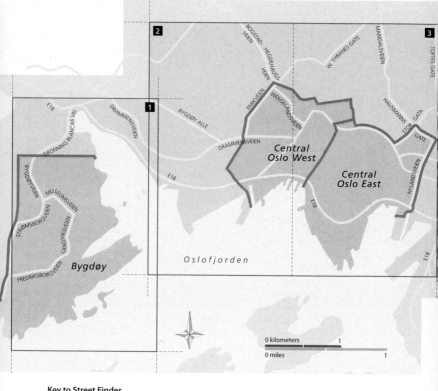

Key to Street Finder

- Major sight
- Place of interest
- Other building
- Train station
- Tunnelbane station
- Ferry stop
- Main ferry terminal
- Bus station

- Tourist information
- Hospital
- Church
- Synagogue
- Railway line
- Pedestrian street
- Tunnel

Scale of Maps 1–3

| 0 metres | 250 |
| 0 yards | 250 |

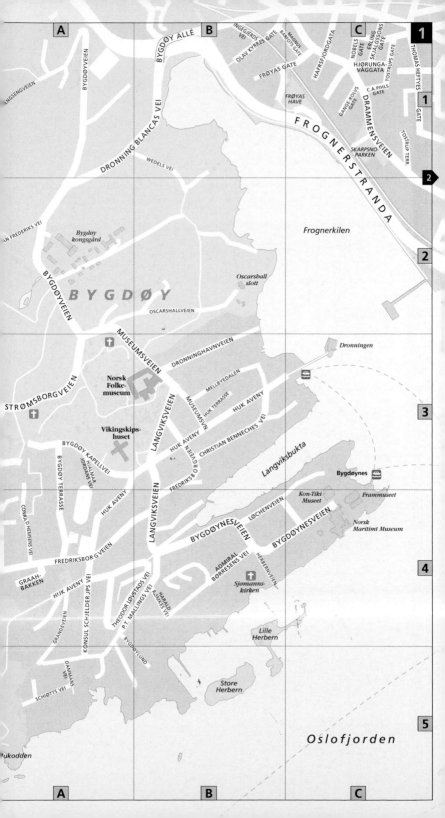

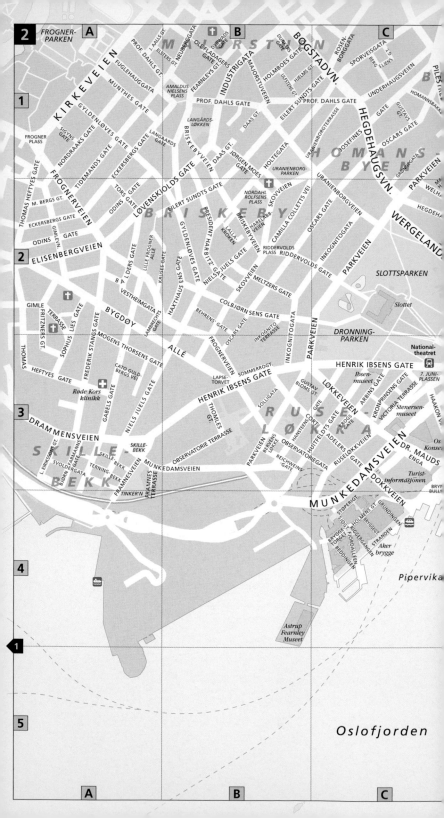

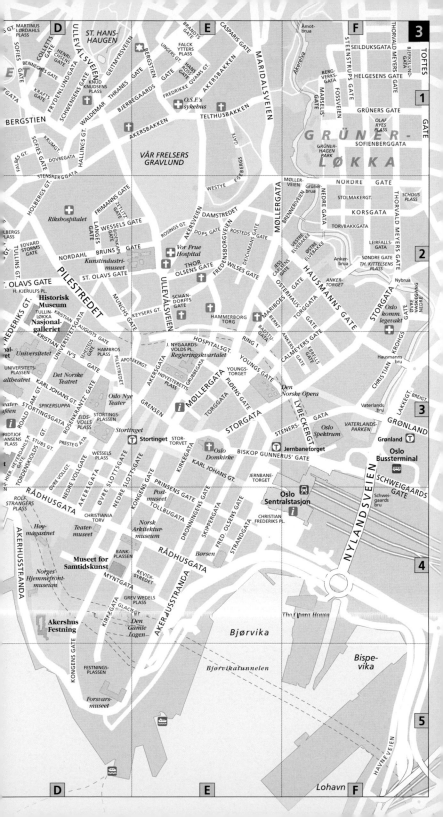

Street Finder Index

Grass-roofed huts in a beautiful location in Jotunheimen National Park, Oppland ▶

NORWAY
AREA BY AREA

AROUND OSLOFJORDEN

The oldest settlements in the area surrounding Oslofjorden date from the Stone Age and Bronze Age, and it was here on the eastern and western shores that three of the best preserved Viking ships were unearthed. Although the land around the fjord close to Oslo is built-up, further south it is a haven of serene villages with quaint clapboard houses, quiet islands and boats galore.

The sight of Oslofjorden on a summer's day teeming with ferries, cruise boats, yachts and leisure craft is breathtaking. The 100-km (60-miles) long fjord extends deep inland from the Skagerrak to the port of Oslo. It narrows around Drøbak before opening out closer to the capital. The counties of Akershus and Østfold lie to the east, and Buskerud and Vestfold to the west.

More than one million people live around the shore in some of the oldest towns and villages in the country. Many of these settlements have a long history of trading and seafaring. The entire region bears evidence of its proximity to the capital. The infrastructure is well developed, road connections are good and Europe's longest road tunnel beneath the sea, 7.2 km (4 miles) long, links Frogn on the east with Hurum on the west.

Many people who work in Oslo commute from their homes around the fjord.

The Oslofjorden area offers a combination of an ancient cultural heritage alongside modern industry and commerce. Away from the industrial areas, the coast is peppered with islands large and small, inlets and coves, holiday resorts and marinas, and clusters of painted summer cabins. There are castles and Viking burial mounds to explore, and colourful timber-built villages to relax in with museums and art galleries. Boating, fishing, swimming and walking are among the many pursuits on offer.

Summers are usually warm in this region. Stavern *(see p129)* holds the record for 200 days of sunshine a year. The winters are seldom severe, and the amount of snow varies from place to place according to how high up or how far inland it is situated.

Badeparken at Drøbak, one of the most visited beaches on the eastern side of Oslofjorden

◄ Cafés and restaurants on the waterfront, Tønsberg Brygge

Exploring Oslofjorden

Oslofjorden, from its innermost reaches to the skerries out near Færder Lighthouse, is surrounded by idyllic towns and villages. Bustling harbours are guarded by sturdy fortresses and at Borre National Park the burial mounds of ancient kings have been discovered. One of the most rewarding ways to explore Oslofjorden at close quarters is by sailing boat or motorboat. It is easy to take a trip on a sightseeing boat or simply cross the fjord by ferry. For those travelling by car, it is worth turning off to explore along the minor roads that lead to beaches, quays and waterside hamlets.

Stavern with its many historic buildings from the 18th century, when the town was a naval base

0 kilometres   20
0 miles   10

Hønefoss

OSLO

HENIE ONSTAD **8**
KUNSTSENTER

OSLO

Bærum

Asker

Oppega

Røyken

TUSENFRYD

Drammen

23

DRØBAK **6**

Eikeren

Svelvik

Kongsberg

Sande

Tofte

Sundbyfoss

32

Holmestrand

Son

40   312   35

HORTEN **9**

5 MO

Svarstad

BORRE
NATIONAL PARK **10**

Rygge

VESTFOLD

Andebu

311

Råd

Tønsberg

40

E18

Nøtterøy

308

HANKØ

SANDEFJORD **12**

304

11 TØNSBERG TO
VERDENS ENDE

Kristiansand

303

Tjøme

13 LARVIK

Verdens
Ende

301   **14** STAVERN

Skagerrak

Key

- ▬▬ Highway
- ▬ Major road
- ▭▭ Minor road
- ▭▭ Main railway
- — Minor railway
- ▬ International border
- ▬ County border

Sights at a Glance

1. Halden
2. Sarpsborg
3. *Fredrikstad pp122–3*
4. Hankø
5. Moss
6. Drøbak
7. Tusenfryd
8. Henie Onstad Kunstsenter
9. Horten
10. Borre National Park
12. Sandefjord
13. Larvik
14. Stavern

Tour

11. Tønsberg–Verdens Ende

The yachting town of Tønsberg, gateway to the many island retreats around Oslofjorden

Getting Around

Oslofjorden can be reached by international flights to Gardermoen and Torp airports, by ship and ferry to Oslo and Kristiansand, and by train, bus and car from the Continent via Sweden. The E6 runs along the eastern side of the fjord from the Swedish border in the south. On the western shore, the E18 leads toward Kristiansand. It is possible to cross Oslofjorden by the underwater tunnel between Hurum on the western side and Drøbak on the eastern. There are ferry crossings between Moss and Horten.

Granite islands large and small making up Hvaler archipelago at the entrance to the fjord

For hotels and restaurants in this area see pp230–33 and pp238–47

❶ Halden

County of Østfold. 🏙 29,000. 🚉 🚌
ℹ️ Torget 2, 69 19 09 80. 🎭 Food
and Wooden Boat Festival (4th
weekend Jun). 🌐 **visithalden.com**

The town of Halden is the
gateway to Norway for those
arriving from Sweden to the
southern regions. It is set back
on Iddefjorden between a
beautiful archipelago on one
side and forests and lakes on
the other. The town developed
in the 16th and 17th centuries
as an outpost on the border
with Sweden. It has many well-
preserved old buildings, and
clusters of Neo-Classical houses.

Halden's crowning glory is
Frederiksten Festning, an
imposing fortress straddling the
ridge above the town, complete
with ramparts and powder
houses and a warren of
passageways. The first
fortifications were built around
1643–5, and it was here, in 1718,
that the Swedish king, Karl XII,
was shot during his second
attempt to attack the fortress.

The fortress comprises the
citadel, beyond which lies
Borgerskansen and three
outlying forts facing south and
east: Gyldenløve, Stortårnet
and Overberget. The fortress
museums contain extensive
collections of war history and
civil memorabilia. There is a
pharmacy from the 1870s, and
the old bakery and brewery
in the inner fort.

The canal, Haldenkanalen, is
part of Haldenvassdraget, which
flows through a series of large
lakes. Boats can navigate the

Historic Sarpsborg's busy commercial centre

75-km (46-mile) stretch
between Tistedal and Skulerud
through three groups of
locks. The 26.6-m (87-ft) high
Brekke Locks, comprising four
chambers, are the highest
locks in northern Europe.

The M/S *Turisten* operates
between Tistedal and Strømsfoss and Strømsfoss and Ørje
in summer.

🏰 Frederiksten Festning
1 km (half a mile) S of the centre.
Tel 69 19 09 80. Fortress: **Open** all
year. Museum: **Open** 18 May–31 Aug:
daily; Sep: Sun. 🎫 📷 ♿ ✏️ 🖥 🏛

❷ Sarpsborg

County of Østfold. 🏙 52,000. 🚉 🚌
ℹ️ Torget 5, 69 13 00 70. 🎭 Gleng
Music Festival (May/Jun), Olav's
Festival (end Aug).

King Olav the Holy founded
Sarpsborg in 1016, making it
Norway's third oldest town.
In fact, its history can be traced
back 7,000 years through the

discovery of burial mounds,
primitive fortifications, stone
monuments and rock carvings.
At nearby Tune, the Viking ship,
Tuneskipet, from around AD 900
was unearthed *(see p89)*.

The Glomma river and the
waterfall, Sarpsfossen, formed
the backbone of the com-
mercial development of the
town. The rivers were used for
floating timber to the sawmills.
The harbour became the
country's second largest port
for timber in the 19th century
and the timber industry is still
important to the town today.

Borgarsyssel Museum was
opened in 1929 in the area
where Olav the Holy had his
castle. The ruins can be seen,
as can those of a church,
Nikolaskirken, from 1115.
Medieval stonework from
the region is exhibited in
Steinhoggerhallen. In the
museum's main building,
the Østfoldgalleriet contains
collections of folk art, arts and
crafts and industrial products
such as Rococo-style glazed
earthenware from Herrebøe.
Outside there is a monastic
garden with herbs.

The open-air section features
a collection of historic houses.
Among them is a workmen's
dwelling house, St Olavs Vold,
from the 1840s. It is made up
of 20 apartments each with
one room and a kitchen.

🏛 Borgarsyssel Museum
Gamlebygaten 8. **Tel** 69 11 56 50.
Open Jun–Aug: daily; Sep–Apr: Tue–
Fri. **Closed** public hols. 🎫 📷 🏛
🌐 ostfoldmuseene.no

Fredriksten Festning providing a dramatic backdrop to Halden

For hotels and restaurants in this area see pp230–33 and pp238–47

❸ Fredrikstad

See pp122–3.

❹ Hankø

County of Østfold. 302 from Fredrikstad to Vikane.
i Turistinformasjonen, Fredrikstad, 69 30 46 00.

The picturesque island of Hankø lies to the west of Fredrikstad toward the outer part of Oslofjorden. It became especially popular as a holiday resort in the 1950s and 1960s when King Olav had a summer residence, Bloksberg, here.

Although Hankø presents a bare rock face to the fjord, its sheltered eastern side is forested, providing a much favoured harbour and anchorage. The Norwegian Association of Yachting was founded here in 1882, since then the island has been a venue for national regattas, sailing races and world championship events. In July, over 200 boats compete in the hugely popular Hankø Regatta.

Rowing has also had a long tradition on Hankø. The Fredrikstad Rowing Club was established here around 1870.

Galleri F15 occupying the manor house of Alby on Jeløy, near Moss

❺ Moss

County of Østfold. 28,000.
i Skogaten 52, 69 24 15 20.
Momentum Art Festival (end Aug–Oct). **W** visitmoss.no

An important industrial and trading centre for the County of Østfold, Moss is also known for its art galleries and streets lined with sculptures. Its harbour has long been a junction for boat traffic on Oslofjorden and today car ferries continually ply between Moss and Horten.

The Town and Industry Museum, **Moss by- og Industrimuseum**, charts Moss's industrial development.

Konventionsgården was built in 1778 and is the main building of Moss Jernverk (Moss Ironworks), which was constructed in the mid-18th century. It was here that the Moss Convention was signed in 1814 to ratify the union between Norway and Sweden rather than Denmark.

Moss is protected to the west by the island of Jeløy, once a peninsula connected to the mainland in the southeast. A canal, dug between Mossesundet and Værlebukta, cut Jeløy from the mainland, but did not deter a rash of house-building here in the 1960s. The manor house on the Alby Gods estate on Jeløy is the location for an art gallery, **Galleri F15**. The elegant Refsnes Gods is now a hotel *(see p231)*.

North of Moss is the idyllic harbour village of **Son**, a popular excursion spot. The buildings in the centre of Son recall a time in the 18th century when the timber trade, shipping and commerce, spinning and the production of spirits were thriving industries.

Son has charming little streets, an eco museum, a museum harbour, coastal cultural activities, exhibitions and many cosy places to eat.

🏛 **Moss by- og Industrimuseum**
Fossen 21–23. **Tel** 69 24 83 60.
Open Tue–Fri & Sun. **Closed** public hols.

🏛 **Galleri F15**
Alby Gård 4 km (2 miles) W of Moss.
Tel 69 27 10 33. **Open** Tue–Sun.
Closed some public hols.

Hankø, a favourite haunt for yachting enthusiasts

➌ Street-by-Street: Fredrikstad

When Sarpsborg was burned down in 1567 during the Nordic Seven-Year War, Frederik II gave permission for the inhabitants to move to a spot closer to the mouth of the Glomma river, which would be better placed for trading, shipping and fishing. And so Fredrikstad was established. It became a fortress town in 1663, and Gamlebyen (the Old Town) developed within the bastion walls. Cobbled streets, art galleries, a renowned handicrafts centre, shops and restaurants make Gamlebyen an attractive place. A bridge, built in 1957, leads to the modern industrial and commercial town and the busy town centre.

Old Town Hall
Fredrikstad's first aldermen had their seat in the Old Town Hall (Gamle Rådhus), built in 1784. The lay preacher, Hans Nielsen, was imprisoned here for five weeks in 1797.

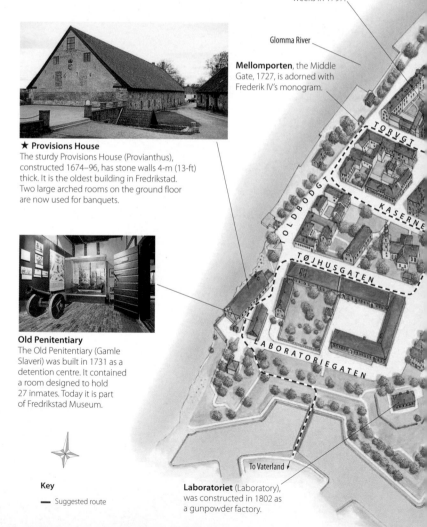

★ Provisions House
The sturdy Provisions House (Provianthus), constructed 1674–96, has stone walls 4-m (13-ft) thick. It is the oldest building in Fredrikstad. Two large arched rooms on the ground floor are now used for banquets.

Old Penitentiary
The Old Penitentiary (Gamle Slaveri) was built in 1731 as a detention centre. It contained a room designed to hold 27 inmates. Today it is part of Fredrikstad Museum.

Glomma River

Mellomporten, the Middle Gate, 1727, is adorned with Frederik IV's monogram.

TORVGT

TOLDBODGT

KASERNE

TØJHUSGATEN

LABORATORIEGATEN

To Vaterland

Key

— Suggested route

Laboratoriet (Laboratory), was constructed in 1802 as a gunpowder factory.

★ **Kongens Torv**
The King's Square has a statue of Frederik II, who founded the town in 1567. It marks the centre of the town and was where criminals were put in the stocks.

To Fredrikstad centre

Rampart Gate
The Rampart Gate (Voldporten) was built in 1695. Above the gateway is Christian V's monogram and his motto, *Pietate et justitia* (Piety and Justice).

0 metres   100
0 yards   100

Drawbridge
The drawbridge was raised between last post and reveille. If the mounted postman arrived after it was raised, his sack was sent across the moat on a line.

Drøbak, south of Oslo, at Oslofjorden's narrowest point

❻ Drøbak

County of Akershus. 🏠 14,000. 🚌 summer. 🛈 Havnegaten 4, 64 93 50 87. 🎭 Oscarsborg plays (Jul). 🌐 visitdrobak.no

Half an hour's drive south of Oslo on the eastern side of Oslofjorden is the attractive wooden village of Drøbak. Originally it was a pilot station and served as Oslo's winterport when the fjord closer to the capital was ice bound. Today the village, with its narrow 18th- and 19th-century streets, is a popular place to live and a favourite summer holiday spot. From here, the 7.2-km (4.5-mile) Oslofjord Tunnel, opened in 2000, runs deep under the fjord to its western shore.

Drøbak has Norway's largest permanent year-round Christmas exhibition with Julehus (Christmas House) and Julenissens Postkontor (a post office, run by Father Christmas's pixie-like helper). The main square, Torget, and the adjoining streets have shops, art galleries and places to eat. Badeparken, a park area with a beach, is close by.

At the small harbour, the sea-water aquarium, **Saltvanns-akvariet**, displays local species of fish and other marine life. Next to it, **Drøbak Båtforenings Maritime Samlinger** (the Maritime Collection), focuses on the area's coastal heritage.

Close to the centre, on Seiersten, is **Follo Museum**

with a collection of 200–300-year-old buildings.

On an island just west of Drøbak lies **Oscarsborg Festning**. The fortress is best known for its role in the sinking of the German warship, *Blücher*, on 9 April 1940. Torpedoes fired from here hit the vessel as it made its way toward Oslo with the first occupational forces on board. This delayed the occupation and gave the king time to flee. In summer, plays are staged at the fortress.

🏛 Drøbak Båtforenings Maritime Samlinger
Kroketønna 4. **Tel** 64 93 50 87. **Open** Jun–Aug: daily. 🐾

🏛 Follo Museum
Belsjøveien 17. **Tel** 64 93 99 90. 🚌 504. **Open** Jun–mid-Sep: Tue–Fri & Sun; mid-Sep–May: Wed–Fri & Sun. **Closed** some public hols. 🐾 ◻ ◻ ◻ ◻

🏰 Oscarsborg Festning
Kaholmene. **Tel** 81 55 19 00. 🚢 from Sjøtorget to Drøbak. **Open** Jun–Aug: daily. 🐾 ◻

❼ Tusenfryd

County of Akershus. **Tel** 64 97 64 97. 🚌 special bus from Oslo Bussterminal every half hour 10am–1pm. **Open** May–Aug: daily. 🐾 ◻ ◻ ◻ ◻

Norway's largest amusement park, Tusenfryd, is situated in a rural location 20 km (12 miles) south of Oslo at the intersection of the E6 and the E18 motorways.

The park's main attraction is Thundercoaster, the biggest wooden roller-coaster in Northern Europe. It thrills visitors with drops of 32 m (105 ft).

There are numerous rides, places to eat, shops and entertainments in addition to an area for water activities. Nearly half a million guests visit Tusenfryd every year.

One of many rides at Tusenfryd amusement park

❽ Henie Onstad Kunstsenter

County of Akershus. **Tel** 67 80 48 80. 🚌 151, 152 from Oslo. **Open** 11am–7pm Tue–Fri, 11am–5pm Sat & Sun. 🐾 ◻ ◻ ◻ ◻ ◻ ◻ 🌐 hok.no

The remarkable centre for modern art, Henie Onstad Kunstsenter, was a gift to the nation from the three-times

Henie Onstad Kunstsenter, a fine collection of modern art

Olympic gold medal-winning skater, Sonja Henie (1928, 1932, 1936), and her husband, Niels Onstad. It houses the couple's art collection, including works by Matisse, Bonnard, Picasso and Miró, as well as Expressionist and abstract painters from the post-war period such as Estève and Soulages.

The trophy collection from Sonja Henie's exceptional sporting career is also on show. Alongside are the medals and cups she received for her outstanding performances in figure skating at the Olympic Games and in no fewer than 10 world championships.

The museum has a library, auditorium, a children's workshop, shop, café and an excellent restaurant.

Model of a three-masted ship at Marinemuseet, Horten

♥ Horten

County of Vestfold. 🔺 17,000. 🚌 to Skoppum 10 km (6 miles) W of town. 🛈 ✉ *i* Tollbugata 1A, 33 03 17 08. 🌐 **visithorten.com**

A bronze statue known as Hortenspiken (the Girl from Horten) welcomes visitors approaching the town from the north. The boat she is holding hints that this is a harbour town popular with pleasure boat owners. Horten developed

Borre National Park with its many burial mounds from the Viking age

around the 19th-century naval base of Karljohansvern, with its shipyard and harbour. In the well-preserved garrison buildings is **Marinemuseet**. Established in 1853, it is the oldest naval museum in the world. The museum contains an extensive collection of model ships, artifacts and exhibits relating to naval history. The world's first torpedo boat, *Rap*, 1872, is on display outside. A recent acquisition is the submarine, KNM *Utstein*, 1965, which is open to the public.

Next door is **Norsk Museum for Fotografi** (the Norwegian Museum of Photography). Cameras, photographs and other items are used to illustrate the development of the art.

Horten town centre, with its timber houses, retains much of its 19th-century character. In summer, the streets are decorated with flowers, and speed restrictions force cars to drive slowly. Outdoor cafés add to the charming atmosphere. But the town's main claim to fame is Storgaten, said to be Norway's longest shopping street.

Figurehead, Marinemuseet

🏛 Marinemuseet
Karljohansvern, 1 km (half a mile) E of the centre. **Tel** 33 03 33 97.
Open May–Sep: daily; Oct–Apr: Sun.
Closed public hols. 📷 ♿ 🏛

🏛 Norsk Museum for Fotografi
Karljohansvern, 1 km (half a mile) E of the centre. **Tel** 33 03 16 30.
Open noon–5pm Tue–Sun. 🌿 📷 ♿ 🖥 🏛

⓾ Borre National Park

County of Vestfold. **Tel** 33 07 18 50. 🚌 01 from Horten. Park: **Open** all year. Midgard Historical Centre: **Open** 11am–6pm daily. **Closed** public hols; Sep–May: Mon. 🌿 📷 ♿ 🖥 🏛

The site of the most extensive collection of kings' graves in Scandinavia, Borre has seven large and 21 smaller burial mounds. Excavations at the end of the 1980s revealed that the oldest of the mounds dates from AD 600, i.e. before the Viking age, and it is likely that some of the mounds contain kings of the Ynglinge dynasty who had settled in Vestfold after fleeing from Sweden. The burial ground was used for another 300 years.

A remarkable selection of craftwork has been unearthed. Given the name Borrestilen, the pieces feature intricate animal and knot ornaments, which were often used to decorate harnesses. The finds also confirm that the mounds might have contained ships similar to the Gokstad and Oseberg ships discovered around Oslofjorden (*see pp88–9*).

Borre was Norway's first national park. The grassy mounds are set among woodlands in a well-tended area at the water's edge. Each season offers outdoor events with a historic theme, such as Viking Age Markets. The Historical Centre has displays of finds from the area.

The harbour at Drøbak on Oslofjorden, south of Oslo ▶

⓫ A Trip from Tønsberg to Verdens Ende

The shortest route between Tønsberg and the southernmost tip of Tjøme, otherwise known as World's End, is just 30 km (19 miles), but plenty of time is needed to explore this stunning archipelago, especially on the eastern side. The tour passes through a string of attractive holiday resorts. There are pretty coves, narrow sounds, old skipper's houses and quaint boathouses. Bridges connect the larger islands and the sea is never far away for a refreshing swim.

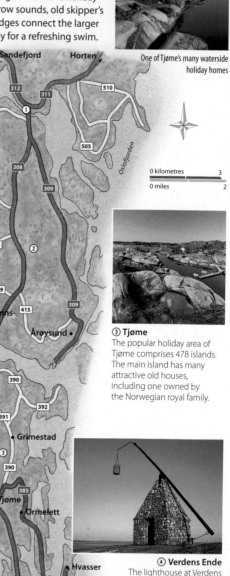

One of Tjøme's many waterside holiday homes

① Tønsberg
Founded in 871, Tønsberg was a prosperous trading centre in the Middle Ages. The 19th-century tower, Slottsfjelltarnet, was built on the ruins of an ancient castle.

② Nøtterøy
Between Tønsberg and Tjøme lies the archipelago of Nøtterøy comprising 175 islands. Nøtterøy has a number of ancient monuments, including a beautiful 12th-century church.

③ Tjøme
The popular holiday area of Tjøme comprises 478 islands. The main island has many attractive old houses, including one owned by the Norwegian royal family.

④ Verdens Ende
The lighthouse at Verdens Ende, standing on the southernmost tip of Tjøme, is distinguished by its pivoting fire basket.

Key

▬ Tour route

= Other routes

Sandefjord

Horten

312 311 510

①

505

Ostofjorden

428 308

309

0 kilometres   3

0 miles   2

410

②

Snipetorp

409

Kjøpmanns-skjær 415

309

Arøysund

390

392

391

Grimestad

③

308 390

385

Tjøme

Ormelett

Hvasser

380

308

④

Tips for Drivers

Starting point: Tønsberg is the starting point for driving to the islands of Nøtterøy and Tjøme.
Length: about 20 km (12 miles).
Places to eat: there are many places to eat en route, including a restaurant at Verdens Ende.

Sandefjord's whaling monument by Knut Steen, 1969

⑫ Sandefjord

County of Vestfold. 🏔 43,000. ✈ 🚂
🚌 ⛴ 🛈 Thor Dahls Gate 1, 33 46 05
90. 🎭 Midsummer Boat Procession
(23 Jun), Summer Show on Rika (Jul),
Classical Music on a Summer Night
(1st and 2nd week Jul), Christmas
Market (last week Nov).

The present town of Sandefjord is
relatively new, but archaeological
finds from the Bronze and Viking
Ages, such as the Viking ship
unearthed at Gokstadhaugen
in 1880 *(see pp88–9)*, point to
a long history of trading and
seafaring. The harbour on the
fjord was known around 1200.
In 1800, Sandefjord was burned
to the ground and rebuilt.

Until the early 20th century,
the spa, **Kurbadet** (1837), was
renowned for its health-giving
mud bath. It has been restored
and is now a protected building,
although the mud bath is no more.

Whaling was a dominant
industry at Sandefjord for many
years until it was halted in 1968.
Hvalfangstmuseet (the Whaling
Museum) shows the
development of the industry
from the primitive methods
of catching whales to the
introduction of factory ships.
There is a special section on
Arctic and Antarctic animal life.

The whaling monument
on Strandpromenaden was
designed by Knut Steen.

🏛 **Kurbadet**
Thor Dahls Gate. **Tel** 33 46 58 57.
Open for cultural events and guided
tours only. 🎥 by prior arrangement.

🏛 **Hvalfangstmuseet**
Museumsgate 39. **Tel** 94 79 33 41.
Open daily. **Closed** some public hols.
🐾 🎥 ♿ 📷 📁

⑬ Larvik

County of Vestfold. 🏔 42,000. ✈ 🚂
🚌 ⛴ 🛈 Feyersgate 7, 33 17 10 00.
🎭 Herregårdsspille plays (mid-Jul),
Jazz concerts (Fri in summer).
🌐 **visitlarvik.no**

Larvik came into its own in
the 17th century, when Ulrik
Frederik Gyldenløve was
appointed count of Larvik
and the county of Laurvigen.
In 1671 the town achieved
market town status.

The count's residence,
Herregården, was built in 1677
and is one of Norway's finest
secular Baroque buildings. In
1835 the estate was acquired by
the Treschow family who have
played a prominent role in
Larvik's economic life since
then, mostly in the forestry
industry alongside the Fritzøes.
The **Larvik Museum**, in a manor
house south of the town, charts
their business dealings from
1600 onwards.

Larvik Sjøfartsmuseum
(Maritime Museum) focuses
on the nautical history of Larvik,
particularly the age of sailing
ships. Models by the famous
boat-builder, Colin Archer, are
on display and there is an
exhibition on Thor Heyerdahl.
Larvik is also known for being

the location of Norway's only
mineral water spring.

🏛 **Herregården**
Herregårdssletta 6. **Tel** 48 10 66 00.
Open end Jun–mid-Aug: Tue–Sun;
mid-Aug–Sep & May–end Jun: Sun.
Closed public hols. 🐾 🎥

🏛 **Larvik Museum**
Nedre Fritzøe Gate 2. **Tel** 48 10 66 00.
Open end Jun–mid Aug: Tue–Sun;
mid-Aug–end Jun: Sun **Closed** public
hols. 🐾 🎥 ♿ 📷 📁

🏛 **Larvik Sjøfartsmuseum**
Kirkestredet 5. **Tel** 98 23 12 90.
Open end Jun–mid-Aug: Tue–Sun;
mid-Aug–Sep & May–end Jun: Sun.
Closed public hols. 🐾 🎥 ♿

⑭ Stavern

County of Vestfold. 🏔 2,000. 🚂 to
Larvik. ⛴ 🛈 summer: Skippergaten
6, 33 19 73 00; winter: Larvik, 33 13 91
00. 🎭 Stavern Festival (Jun/Jul).
🌐 **visitlarvik.no**

A quaint mixture of old and
new, Stavern is a charming
place beloved by holiday-
makers. In summer the
population more than doubles,
due partly to the town's record
of more than 200 days of
sunshine a year.

From the mid-1750s until
1864, Stavern was Norway's
main naval base with a shipyard,
Fredriksvern. A gunpowder
tower and commandant's
house remain on Citadelløya
(Citadel Island), today a refuge
for artists. The town is made up
of wooden buildings, most of
them brightly painted in a
colour known as "Stavern
yellow". Minnehallen, a monument with a plaque containing
the names of seamen killed
during World Wars I and II,
is a fitting memorial to those
who lost their lives.

Herregården, Larvik, an example of Norwegian Baroque

EASTERN NORWAY

The three counties, Hedmark, Oppland and Buskerud, together make up one-fifth of Norway's total land area. Mountains, valleys and lakes dominate the landscape, except for Buskerud which has a coastal strip to the far south. This is a region that has attracted artists and inspired writers such as Bjørnstjerne Bjørnson and Henrik Ibsen. It has a special appeal for climbers and hikers.

Stretching through the heart of Eastern Norway like the five fingers on a hand are the long, thin valleys of Østerdalen, Gudbrandsdalen, Valdres, Hallingdal and Numedal. Great rivers such as Norway's longest, the Glåma (or Glomma), cut deep swathes through the landscape. The Glåma is 601 km (374 miles) in length and sweeps through Østerdalen from Riasten in Sør-Trøndelag to Fredrikstad. Lakes such as Mjøsa, measuring 107 km (66 miles) from its northern end near Lillehammer to Vorma in the south, make their mark on the landscape. Mountain villages cling to steep valley sides, topped by highland plateaux.

At the head of the valleys are vast towering mountain chains, which are highest in the north and west. Highland pastures and sparse forests gradually give way to bare rock and plateaux and peaks that are forever snow-covered. Climatically,

the valleys have cold winters and warm summers, with a significant disparity between day and night temperatures.

Toward the south of the region, in the rural areas of Solør-Odal, Romerike, Ringerike and Hedmark, the fertile agricultural land is among the best in the whole of Norway. Extensive forests cover the landscape at relatively moderate altitudes.

The opportunity for outdoor activities in the area is legion. Hiking trails are well-marked. Cycle routes are signposted and there are facilities for canoeing and other water sports. A network of mountain huts provides comfortable accommodation.

In late summer there is often an abundance of mushrooms and wild berries in the forests. In autumn, the mountains put on a magnificent show of colours before the winter brings snow and the chance to ski.

Cattle grazing in an enclosed pasture at Ringebu, Gudbrandsdalen

◀ Lom Stavkirke in the Gudbrandsdalen valley, Eastern Norway

Exploring Eastern Norway

The mountains of Eastern Norway offer exceptional opportunities for mountaineering, from the easy alpine pastures in Alvdal to the demanding peaks of the national parks in the northwest. The best way to experience the peaceful forests which characterize the most easterly parts of Norway is to follow a section of Finnskogleden, a 240-km (150-mile) long trail through Finnskogene (the Finn Forest) on the border with Sweden. However, Eastern Norway is more than just forests and mountains. The valleys and lowlands have a charm of their own, with interesting towns and attractions. Many areas offer good fishing, too.

0 kilometres 50

0 miles 25

Peer Gynt memorial stone at Sødorp old cemetery, Vinstra

Sights at a Glance

1 Kongsvinger
2 Elverum
3 Trysil
4 Østerdalen and Rendalen
5 Mjøsa
6 Hamar
7 Lillehammer pp140–41
8 Aulestad
9 Ringebu
10 Vinstra
11 Otta
12 Rondane National Park
13 Dovrefjell
14 Lom
15 Jotunheimen pp144–5
16 Elveseter
17 Valdres and Fagernes
18 Geilo
19 Hallingdal
20 Numedal
21 Kongsberg
22 Drammen

Key

━━━ Highway

━━━ Major road

┉┉┉ Minor road

╍╍╍ Main railway

──── Minor railway

▬▬▬ International border

━━━ County border

△ Summit

For additional map symbols *see back flap*

The valleys and majestic mountains of Ottadalen, reflected in Lake Vågåvatnet

Ringebu Stavkirke, a 13th-century wooden church in Gudbrandsdalen

Getting Around

The valleys of eastern Norway are in themselves important arteries. Østerdalen and Gudbrandsdalen have main roads (RV3 and E6) and railway lines running south to north. In Hallingdal the road runs east to west (RV7). Often, it is worth exploring some of the more interesting alternative routes. The mountain passes between the valleys are never far apart. Airports include Gardermoen on the E6 to the south of the region and Røros to the north.

For hotels and restaurants in this area see pp230–33 and pp238–47

❶ Kongsvinger

County of Hedmark. 🏠 17,500. 🚉
🚌 𝒊 Glommengata 33, 90 06 64 86.
🎭 Kongsvinger Market (1st week
May & last week Sep).

The fortress town of
Kongsvinger, situated on the
Glåma River, was established
during the Hannibal Feud
in 1644 when a fortification
was built here which grew to
become a solid fortress.
Øvrebyen (the Upper Town) was
situated near the castle ramparts.

With the arrival of the railway
in the 1860s, Kongsvinger
became a market town.
New building was concentrated
around the train station.
Later, the quarter between
the station and Øvrebyen
developed into the town
centre, and a bridge and
town hall were built. In 1965
the town was designated as
a "Development Centre" which
led to industrial expansion.

Kongsvinger Festning
(Fortress) is an irregular star-
shaped castle with 16 batteries,
fine old buildings and a
museum of the armed forces.
From the castle ramparts there
is a splendid view over the town
and river toward Sweden.

The forests between Glåma
and the Swedish border were
settled by Finnish immigrants
in the 17th century. **Finnetunet**,
a museum of Finnish culture at
Svullrya, in Grue Finnskog, is
made up of 13 buildings, the
oldest dating from the end
of the 18th century. It gives a
picture of farming culture and
the daily life of the people of
Finnskogene (Finn Forest).

Houses at the Glomdalsmuseet, Elverum, recalling a bygone era

A hiking track, Finnskogleden,
heads north through the forests
from Finnetunet.

🏠 **Kongsvinger Festning**
1 km (half a mile) N of town centre.
Tel 91 14 69 51. Castle area: **Open**
daily. Museum: **Open** Jun–Aug: daily.

🏠 **Finnetunet**
40 km (25 miles) NE of Kongsvinger.
Tel 62 94 56 90. **Open** Jun–Aug: daily.
🖼 ✅ 🏠

❷ Elverum

County of Hedmark. 🏠 19,500. 🚉
🚌 𝒊 Solørvegen 151, 62 40 90 45.
🎭 Grundsetmart'n (Mar), Elverum
Football Tournament (Jun), Culture
Festival (Aug), Nordic Hunting and
Fishing Days (Aug). 🌐 visiter.no

On 9 April 1940, the day of
the German invasion, the
Norwegian Parliament
approved the Elverum Mandate,
giving the fleeing Norwegian
government considerable
powers for the remainder of
World War II. The following day
King Haakon rejected Germany's

demand for a new Norwegian
government. On 11 April,
Elverum was bombed; 54
people died. At the high school,
a monument by Ørnulf Bast
commemorates the king's stand.

The city quickly rose from the
ashes after the war to become
an administrative, commercial,
educational and military centre.

The quarter on the eastern
side of the Glåma River is known
as Leiret, and evolved from the
buildings below the old
fortification, Christiansfjell.
Grundsetmart'n, a winter
market that between 1740 and
1900 was the most important in
Scandinavia, is still held here.

Glomdalsmuseet, Norway's
third-largest open-air museum,
is a comprehensive collection of
91 buildings from the mountain
villages and rural lowland
communities and contains
some 30,000 exhibits.

Connected by a bridge
across the Glåma is **Norsk
Skogbruksmuseum** (the
Norwegian Forestry Museum),
founded in 1954. This is the
only museum in the country
specializing in forestry, hunting
and fishing. The open-air
section features different
types of buildings, from
lumberjack cottages to fishing
huts and boathouses.

🏛 **Glomdalsmuseet**
Museumsveien 15. **Tel** 62 41 91 00.
Open Jun–Aug: daily; Sep–May: Sun
only. 🖼 ✅ ♿ 🍴 🏠

🏛 **Norsk Skogsbruksmuseum**
Solørveien 151. **Tel** 62 40 90 00. **Open**
daily. **Closed** some public hols. 🖼 ✅
♿ 🍴 🖥 🏠 🌐 skogmus.no

Kongsvinger Festning and the panoramic view toward Sweden

❸ Trysil

County of Hedmark. ⛰ 7,000. 🚌
ℹ Storvegen 3, 62 45 10 00. 🎿 Trysil Ski Season Finale (end Apr), Swingin' Trysil Blues, Jazz and Rock Festival (end Jun), Sund Market (Sep). 🌐 trysil.com

In the past, the road through the forest from Elverum to Trysil was known as "the seven-mile forest". The trip used to be very slow for drivers with heavy loads, but today the roads are good and the journey quick. Trysil is a typical woodland valley with spruce and pine forests and marshland topped by mountainous terrain.

The valley follows the Trysil River from the lake of Femunden to the Swedish border. Femunden is Norway's third-largest lake, stretching 60 km (37 miles) north. Ferries operate in summer. The administrative centre is at Innbygda.

The mountain of **Trysilfjellet** (1,137 m/3,730 ft) is the site for Norway's biggest alpine skiing centre. Sports fishing is good in the Trysilelva and "little" Ljøra.

In the eastern wilderness is **Femundsmarka National Park**, where the Svukuriset tourist lodge is located, and **Gutulia National Park** with its 300–400-year-old primeval forests.

Snowboarder on Trysilfjellet

❹ Østerdalen and Rendalen

County of Hedmark. ⛰ 28,000. 🚐
🚌 ℹ Alvdal Tourist Information, Aukrustsentret 2560, 62 48 89 99.

The two valleys of Østerdalen and Rendalen run parallel in a south-north direction. The RV3 road through Østerdalen follows the Glåma, Norway's longest river, past several places of interest. **Rena**, the next town north of Elverum, had a ferry crossing already in the Middle Ages, as well as accommodation for pilgrims on their way to the cathedral of Nidarosdomen (see p203). Today, Rena is a skiing centre and the starting point for the Birkebeiner race (see p140). A further 55 km (34 miles) upriver, **Koppang** has a folk museum with buildings from the region. North of Atna, the road runs through virtually uninhabited forest, passing **Jutulhogget**, a precipitously deep gorge. Further north, in the small town of **Alvdal**, the Husantunet is a folk museum with 17 houses from around 1600, while **Aukrustsenteret** has paintings and drawings featuring colourful characters from the books of author and illustrator Kjell Aukrust. Alvdal is the starting point for family-friendly mountain walks and also of Norway's second-highest turistvei (tourist road), which runs to the top of the

Jutulhogget, a gorge more than 100m (328 ft) deep

1,666-m (5,466-ft) high **Tronfjellet** mountain.

At Tynset, the RV30 leads northeast to the old mining centre of **Tolga** and the village of **Os**, close to the county boundary with Trøndelag.

Rendalen valley can be reached by taking the RV30 south from Tynset through **Tylldalen**, where the harvest-related feast day of Olsok (St Olav's Day) is celebrated on 29 July. Alternatively, a road from Hanestad, south of Alvdal, leads to the valley across the mountain passes, ending at the church of **Øvre Rendal** at Bergset, which dates from 1759. Its vicarage has a museum dedicated to Jacob B Bull, who wrote about daily life in the region. From here, there is a mountain road to the fishing village of **Fiskevollen** on Sølensjøen lake, and the 1,755-m (5,758-ft) high mountain of Rendalsølen.

The RV30 runs from Bergset south along the valley toward **Otnes** by **Lomnessjøen** lake, a particularly beautiful part of Rendalen. Rushing south from the lake, the Åkrestrømmen is renowned for its abundance of Common white fish (Coregonus lavaretus). From here the RV217 leads to two other famous fishing spots – **Galten** and **Isterfossen** – 45 km (28 miles) to the northeast.

Åkrestrømmen ends in Stors-jøen ("Big Lake") from where the river Rena runs south to join the Glåma at Rena.

🏛 **Aukrustsenteret**
Alvdal centre. **Tel** 62 48 78 77. **Open** May–mid-Oct: daily, mid-Oct–Apr: by arrangement. 🖼 📷 ♿ 🖥 📹

An old farm wall providing a sheltered resting place for skiers

❺ Mjøsa

Counties of Hedmark & Oppland.
ℹ Grønnegata 52, Hamar, 40 03 20 32;
Lillehammer, 61 28 98 00.

Norway's largest lake, Mjøsa, is
117 km (72 miles) long and lies
at the heart of an agricultural
area. Many of the farms in
Hedemarken, Helgøya and
Totenlandet have been
settlements since Viking
times. They are bordered by
forests and mountains,
including Skreiafjellene
(700 m/2,296 ft). Three towns,
Lillehammer *(see pp140–41)*,
Hamar and Gjøvik are spread
around the lakeshore.

Before the arrival of cars and
trains, Mjøsa was an important
communications centre, even
in winter when horses and
sledges would cross the frozen
lake. The completion of the
railway to Eidsvoll in 1854 led
to the arrival of a paddle
steamer, *Skibladner*, known as
"The White Swan of Mjøsa".
Built in Sweden, it was
transported to Mjøsa in pieces
and reassembled. Today the
world's oldest paddle steamer
is still in regular service.

Helgøya, "the holy island",
situated in the widest part of
the lake, was the site of
medieval mansions for bishops
and the aristocracy, and a seat
for the king. Among the farming
estates are Hovinsholm and
Baldishol, where the Baldishol
Tapestry (1200) was found *(see
p63)*. Further north, between
Brumunddal and Moelv, lies
Rudshøgda, the childhood
home of the writer and singer,
Alf Prøysen.

Hamar's ruined 16th-century cathedral
encased in a glass dome

❻ Hamar

County of Hedmark. 🏘 28,000. 🚉
🚌 **ℹ** summer: Grønnegata 52, 40 03
20 32. 🎪 Hamar Market (Aug/Sep).

Hamar is the largest town on
Lake Mjøsa. It was a Norse market
town from 1049 until 1567 when
a fire destroyed the cathedral. In
1849 Hamar achieved town status.

The remains of the cathedral,
Domkirkeruinerna, are
protected by a glass dome.
Built in 1100, the cathedral was
noted for its triple nave, but
after the fire and subsequent
pillaging, only crumbling
columns and arches give an
idea of its original appearance.

Hedmarksmuseet is a folk
museum comprising more than
50 traditional buildings and a
monastery herb garden. Just
2 km (1 mile) away is the **Norsk
Utvandrermuseum**,
(Norwegian Emigrant Museum),
with a section devoted to those
who emigrated to North
America. The Railway Museum,
Jernbanemuseet, features a
narrow-gauge railway (the
Tertitbanen), engines and
railway carriages.

Looking like an upturned boat,
Hamar Olympic Hall was built
as a skating rink for the 1994
Winter Olympics. Akersvika,
to the south of the town, hosts
a bird sanctuary.

🏛 Domkirkeruinerna
Strandvegen 100. **Tel** 62 54 27 00. **Open**
mid-May–Aug: daily; Sep–mid-May:
by arrangement. 🅿 🎫 ♿ 🖥 📷

🏛 Hedmarksmuseet
Strandvegen 100. **Tel** 62 54 27 00.
Open mid-May–Aug: daily; Sep–mid-
May: by appointment. 🅿 🎫 🖥 📷

🏛 Jernbanemuseet
Strandveien 163. **Tel** 62 51 31 60.
Open daily. **Closed** public hols; Sep–
May: Mon. 🅿 🖥 📷

🏛 Norsk Utvandrermuseum
Åkershagan. **Tel** 62 57 48 50. **Open** Jun–
Aug: daily; Sep–May: Tue–Thu. **Closed**
some pub hols. 🅿 🎫 ♿ 🖥 📷

❼ Lillehammer

See pp140–41.

Aulestad, the home of Bjørnstjerne
Bjørnson in Østre Gausdal

❽ Aulestad

County of Oppland. 🏘 400. 🚌
ℹ Lillehammer, 61 28 98 00.
🎪 Aulestad Festival (May).

The writer Bjørnstjerne Bjørnson
(1832–1910) bought the farm
of Aulestad, in Østre Gausdal,
18 km (11 miles) northwest
of Lillehammer, in 1874.
The following year, he moved
here with his wife, Karoline.

As well as writing Norway's
national anthem, stories,
poems and plays, Bjørnson
was an outstanding orator
and a key politician. He was
awarded the Nobel Prize for
literature in 1903.

The paddle steamer, *Skibladner*, plying Lake Mjøsa since 1856

The countryside near Ringebu looking toward Lågen river

The author's home, known as **Dikterhjemmet på Aulestad**, remains as it was when he lived here. It contains a varied selection of Bjørnson memorabilia and the couple's fine collections of sculptures and paintings, photographs and manuscripts. The property was bought by the state in 1922.

Dikterhjemmet på Aulestad
RV255, 11 km (7 miles) NW of Lillehammer. **Tel** 61 28 89 00. **Open** mid-May–Sep: daily.

❾ Ringebu

County of Oppland. 4,600. Ringebu Skysstasjon (Train Station), 61 28 47 00. Alpine World Cup (lst week Mar).

Situated on the river Gudbrandsdalslågen, the village of Ringebu is known for its stave church. The **Ringebu Stavkirke** dates from the 13th century. It was extended between 1630 and 1631 by the builder Werner Olsen, who rebuilt several stave churches in the Gudbrandsdalen valley. The doorway with dragon motifs is from the original stave church, while the altarpiece and pulpit are Baroque.

Environs
The long valley of **Gudbrandsdalen**, running from north of Lillehammer up past Dovrefjell (see p142), cuts through a beautiful landscape, with many roads providing access into the mountains. It is at its widest in the district

of **Fron**, where it has been compared to Germany's Mosel valley. The octagonal church of Sør-Fron, in Louis XVI style, dates from the 18th century. The area is also known for its distinctive brunost goat cheese.

Ringebu Stavkirke
1 km (half a mile) S of town centre. **Tel** 61 28 43 50. **Open** May–Aug: daily; Sep–Apr: by prior arrangement. May–Aug.

❿ Vinstra

County of Oppland. 6,000. Vinstra Skysstasjon (Train Station), 61 29 53 70. Titano Festival (Jul), Peer Gynt-Festival (Aug).

At Vinstra, the **Peer Gynt-samlingen** contains considerable material on both

the historical and the literary figure of Peer Gynt.

The 65-km (40-mile) long Peer Gyntveien (Peer Gynt Road) is a mountain toll road running west of the Gudbrandsdalen valley from Tretten to Vinstra. Offering splendid views, it passes a number of hotels and mountain lodges, among them Skeikampen, Gausdal, Gålå, Wadahl and Fefor. The highest point on the road is at 1,053 m (3,455 ft). At Gålå there is the open-air theatre, Gålåvatnet Friluftsteater, which stages a musical interpretation of Ibsen's original Peer Gynt every year in early August.

Peer Gynt-samlingen
Vinstra, town centre south. **Tel** 61 29 20 04. **Open** end Jun–mid-Aug: daily.

Peer Gynt

Henrik Ibsen's dramatic poem, Peer Gynt, was written in 1867 and is regarded as the most important of all Norwegian literary works. Ibsen had hiked in the area north of Vinstra in 1862 and the farm, Hågå, where his supposed model, the hunter and habitual liar Peder Laurtisen, lived in the 17th century is situated next to the Peer Gynt Road on the northeastern side of the valley – an attraction in itself. Ibsen's play starts with Peer telling his mother, Åse, about the buck ride along Gjendineggen.

Åse berates him for running around in the mountains rather than courting the heiress at the farm of Hægstad. So Peer goes there, but instead meets Solveig, who says she will wait for the adventurer "both winter and spring" and who becomes his redeemer.

The "Peer Gynt" farm at Hågå, northeast of Vinstra

❼ Lillehammer

The skier in the city's coat of arms signifies that Lillehammer has long been a popular winter sports centre. In 1994 it came to worldwide attention as the venue for the XVII Winter Olympic Games, but its skiing traditions go back to 1206 when the royal infant, Håkon Håkonsson, was carried to safety across the mountains by skiers *(see pp30–31)*. The annual Birkebeiner Race is run on skis from Rena in Østerdalen to Lillehammer in memory of the rescue. Tourists and painters alike have also been attracted to Lillehammer by the beautiful scenery and the quality of the light. The city's other claim to fame, the Maihaugen outdoor museum, is the legacy of Anders Sandvig, a dentist with a passion for antiques and old buildings, who settled here in 1885.

Historic vehicle in the Norsk Kjøretøyhistorisk Museum

The museum of Maihaugen depicting life in rural communities

🏛 Maihaugen
Maihaugveien 1. **Tel** 61 28 89 00. **Open** 1 Jun–30 Sep: daily; 1 Oct– 16 May: Tue–Sun. **Closed** public hols. 🅿 🅲 🅱 🖉 🖳 🖨 🅰 **W** maihaugen.no

In 1887 Anders Sandvig established one of the biggest museums of farming culture in Norway, De Sandvigske Samlinger in Maihaugen.

Sandvig was a dentist who, during his travels in Gudbrandsdalen, started collecting both objects and houses. What began as a hobby grew to include 200 historical buildings reflecting the building techniques and everyday lives of local people. The museum, which includes a farming estate, a mountain farm, a crofter's holding and a summer pasture hamlet, aims to show a living environment with animals and people going about their normal activities. One of Norway's oldest stave churches, Garmokirken, can be seen here.

Maihaugen also houses the Post Museum (Postmuseet), with its collection of objects connected to the history of the post office over the centuries.

🏛 Lillehammer Kunstmuseum
Stortorget 2. **Tel** 61 05 44 60. **Open** Jul–Aug: daily; Sep–Jun: Tue–Sun. **Closed** some public hols. 🅿 🅲 🅱 🖳 🅰

It was the 19th-century artist, Fredrik Collett, who first became fascinated by the light and motifs at Lillehammer. Erik Werenskiold, Frits Thaulow and Henrik Sørensen were among the many artists to follow in his footsteps.

Their work forms the basis of the superb collection of Norwegian painting, sculpture and graphic design on show at the museum, which also includes a selection of pieces by Munch, Christian Krohg and Adolf Tidemand.

The building itself is strikingly modern and also features a stone and water garden of stark beauty.

🏛 Norsk Kjøretøyhistorisk Museum
Lilletorget 1. **Tel** 61 25 61 65. **Open** daily. 🅿 🅰 **W** lillehammer.com

The Norsk Kjøretøyhistorisk Museum (Museum of Historic Vehicles) has around 100 vehicles, including cars, motorcycles, horse-drawn carriages and old pedal cycles such as the velocipede (the so-called "Veltepetter").

For train enthusiasts, there is an electric locomotive from 1909, and a superb large model railway.

🏛 Bjerkebæk
Nordseterveien 23. **Tel** 61 25 22 57. **Open** Jun–Sep: daily. **Closed** public hols. 🅿 🅲 🖳 🅰 **W** maihaugen.no

Lillehammer's most notable resident was the author and Nobel Prize-winner, Sigrid Undset, who settled here in 1921. She lived in splendid isolation in this house with its magnificent garden protected by a hedge. The house itself had been moved from Gudbrandsdalen and re-erected here.

Undset's great work about the medieval heroine, Kristin Lavransdatter, was published at the time she moved to Lillehammer. Her historical oeuvre about Olav Audunssøn in Hestviken was to follow.

🏛 Norges Olympiske Museum
Håkonshall, Olympiaparken. **Tel** 61 05 76 50. **Open** Jun–Aug: daily; Sep–May: Tue–Sun. **Closed** some public hols. 🅰 🅲 🅱 🅰 **W** maihaugen.no

Norges Olympiske Museum (the Olympic Museum) offers an opportunity to experience the atmosphere of the 1994 Winter Olympic Games, when 1,737 participants from 67 countries came to Lillehammer.

Innovative techniques are used to convey the history of the Olympics, going back to the Greek summer and winter games of 776 BC, and to glimpse the societies in which the games took place.

Pierre de Coubertin's re-creation of the games in

Athens in 1886 is shown, as are the first Winter Olympics, held in Chamonix in 1924.

🏟 Lillehammer Olympiapark

1 km (half a mile) E of town centre. **Tel** 61 05 42 00. **Open** daily year-round. 🌐 olympiaparken.no

The investment for the 1994 Winter Olympics provided Lillehammer with magnificent amenities, including Lysgårdsbakkene Ski Jumping Arena. In winter it is possible to take the chairlift to the top for a fantastic view. Håkons Hall, the

Lillehammer Olympiapark ski jump complex, 1994 Winter Olympics

ice-hockey arena, has facilities for other sports such as handball and golf. It also has a 20-m (66-ft) climbing wall. Birkebeineren Skistadion is the starting point for a floodlit skiing track and cross-country trails.

🎪 Lilleputthammer

Hundervegen, 14 km (9 miles) N of town centre. **Tel** 61 28 55 50. **Open** Jun–Aug: daily. 🏊 ♿ 🖥 📷

The pedestrian part of Storgata in Lillehammer is known as "Gå-gata", the model for the miniature town of Lilleputt-hammer. It is an enjoyable place for children.

🎡 Hunderfossen Adventure Park

Fåberg, 13 km (8 miles) N of town centre. **Tel** 61 27 55 30. **Open** mid-May–Aug: daily. 🏊 ♿ 🖥 📷

🌐 hunderfossen.no

The world's largest troll and a glittering fairytale palace themed on old Norwegian tales welcome the visitor to Hunderfossen. There are some 40 rides and attractions for both children and adults, including a swimming pool, car circuit, whitewater rafting and a high-ropes course.

VISITORS' CHECKLIST

Practical Information
County of Oppland.
🗺 184,000. 🚉 Jernbanetorget 2, 61 28 98 00. 🎿 Winter Festival (Feb), Birkebeiner Race (Mar), Blues Festival (Apr), Literature Festival (May), Lillehammer Festival (Jun), Dølajazz (Sep).
🌐 lillehammer.com

Transport
🚍 🚌

Water ride at Hunderfossen Adventure Park

Nearby, the **Hafjell Alpine Centre**, with 25 km (16 miles) of graded slopes, is the largest skiing complex in the area. There is a 710-m (2,330-ft) long artificially frozen bobsleigh run with 16 bends, or if ice is in short supply, there is a "wheeled bob" instead.

Lillehammer Town Centre

① Maihaugen
② Lillehammer Kunstmuseum
③ Norsk Kjøretøyhistorisk Museum
④ Bjerkebæk
⑤ Norges Olympiske Museum

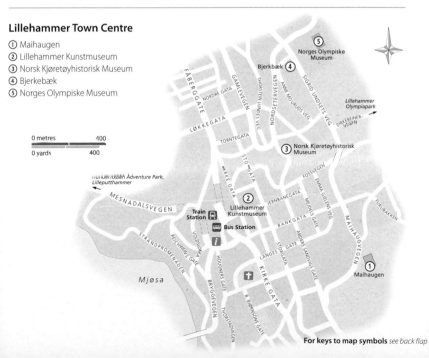

0 metres   400
0 yards   400

For keys to map symbols *see back flap*

Rondane National Park, a much loved recreational area at all times of the year

⑪ Otta

County of Oppland. 🏔 4,000. 🚌 🚙
ℹ Ola Dahl's Gate 1, 61 23 66 50. 🎿
Dance Festival (mid-Jul), Kristin Festival
(1st week Jul), Sjoa Kajak Festival (3rd
week Jul), Otta Market (1st week Oct).

Since the arrival of the railway
in 1896, Otta has been a
tourist hub, because of its
proximity to the national
parks of Rondane, Dovre and
Jotunheimen. Otta lies at the
junction of the Otta and Lågen
rivers. It is the regional centre
for North Gudbrandsdalen
and a main terminus for buses
to and from the adjoining
valleys and mountain areas.
Historically, Otta is known for
the Battle of Kringen in 1612,
when an army of local farmers
destroyed a Scottish army of
mercenaries on their way to
fight in the Kalmar War.

At Selsverket there is a
summer toll road to Mysuseter
and Rondane.

⑫ Rondane National Park

County of Oppland. ℹ Otta Tourist
Information, 61 24 14 44.
🌐 **visitrondane.com**

Established in 1962, Rondane
was Norway's first national park.
It has a well-developed network
of routes with several tourist
lodges, including Rondvassbu
and Bjørnhollia.

The landscape is split by
deep gorges: Ilmanndalen runs
in an east/west direction;

Rondvatnet/Rondvassdalen and
Langglupdalen run south to
north. There are 10 peaks in
excess of 2,000 m (6,562 ft) and
even the lowest areas are
around 900 m (2,953 ft) above
sea level. Rondeslottet ("Ronde
Castle") is the highest mountain
here, reaching 2,178 m (7,145 ft).

Rondane has both gentle,
rounded mountains and wild,
practically inaccessible parts
with deep, north-facing glacial
cirques. Among the geological
oddities from the last Ice Age
are strange hollows of dead ice
(a glacial deposit left behind
after the glacier melted). Large
numbers of wild reindeer
populate the mountains.

The rural centre of **Folldal**
grew up around an 18th-
century community that mined
deposits of copper-rich pyrite.
The mines were later moved
to Hjerkinn at Dovre. Original
houses from Folldal and

Dovre have been preserved
in a rural museum.

The valley of Einunndalen,
extending north from Folldal,
is used as a summer pasture.

⑬ Dovrefjell

County of Oppland. ℹ in Dombås,
61 24 14 44.

The mountain plateau of
Dovrefjell marks the conceptual
divide between Norway "north
of the mountains" and Norway
"south of the mountains". In
1814, Dovrefjell was used to
signify the unity of the nation
when the men at Eidsvoll (see
p42) sang Enige og tro til Dovre
faller ("In harmony and faith till
Dovre falls").

Kongeveien, the King's Road
from the south, crossed the
plateau. Mountain huts built
nearly 900 years ago have saved
the lives of many a traveller in

The mighty Snøhetta rising majestically over the Dovrefjell plateau

these parts. The Dovrebane railway was completed in 1921.

Wild reindeer and musk oxen inhabit the region and rare species of birds, such as short-eared owl, cuckoo and hen harrier, live on the moorlands of Fokstumyrene.

Dovrefjell National Park was established in 1974. It surrounds Norway's fourth tallest mountain, the 2,286-m (7,500-ft) high Snøhetta ("Snow Cap"). Hjerkinn is the highest point on both the road and the railway. Here, Eysteins Kirke was consecrated in 1969 in memory of King Eystein (c.1100) who built the mountain huts. This is also the starting point of the infamously steep road, *Vårstigen*, to Kongsvoll in the county of Trøndelag (*see p190*).

Lom Stavkirke constructed in the early Middle Ages

⓮ Lom

County of Oppland. 🗺 2,600. 🚉 to Otta. 🚌 ℹ️ Norsk Fjellmuseum, 61 21 29 90. 🎿 Flåklypa Veteran Car Rally (May). 🌐 **visitlom.com**

The rural centre of Lom, on the banks of the Otta river, is a gateway to the valley of Bøverdalen, the Jotunheimen mountain range and Sognefjellet mountain. The stave church here, **Lom Stavkirke**, was built in 1000 and retains its original deep foundations. It acquired its cruciform shape around 1600. Details such as the dragon heads on the gables have much in common with the churches seen around Sognefjorden (*see pp184–5*). **Norsk Fjellmuseum** (the Norwegian Mountain

Fossheim Steinsenter, with an 8-m (26-ft) tall model of a rock crystal

Museum), opened in 1994, is a good source of practical information on the mountain wilderness and it has videos showing mountain routes. This is in addition to its natural history exhibits. The Fossheim Hotel – a piece of cultural history in itself – houses **Fossheim Steinsenter** (the Fossheim Stone Centre) comprising a geological museum and a silversmith workshop.

East from Lom, at a crossing on the Otta river, is Vågå, which is also known for having a stave church (1130). Vågå is the burial site of the reindeer hunter Jo Gjende. Its other claim to fame is Jutulporten, a giant "door" in the mountainside that appears in Norwegian legend.

🏛 **Lom Stavkirke**
Lom. **Tel** 97 07 53 97. **Open** mid-May–mid-Sep: daily. 🎫 📷 📅

🏛 **Norsk Fjellmuseum**
Lom. **Tel** 61 21 16 00.
Open May–Sep: daily; Oct–Apr: Mon–Fri. 🅿️ 🎫 📷 ♿ 📅

🏛 **Fossheim Steinsenter**
Lom. **Tel** 61 21 14 60. **Open** daily. **Closed** some public hols. 🎫 🖥 📅

⓯ Jotunheimen
See pp145–6.

⓰ Elveseter
Bøverdalen, 25 km (16 miles) SW of Lom. **Tel** 61 21 99 00. **Open** 1 Jun–mid-Sep. 🌐 **elveseter.no**

Lying in Bøverdalen valley and in the shadow of Galdhøpiggen (2,469 m/ 8,100 ft), Norway's highest mountain, is the farming estate of Elveseter, which has accommodated visitors since 1880. It has since been rebuilt as a dedicated tourist hotel in the architectural style of the valley. The oldest house, Midgard, dates from 1640. Nearby stands Sagasøylen, a 33-m (108-ft) tall monument decorated with motifs from Norwegian history and crowned by Harald Finehair on horseback.

From here, the scenic RV 55, Sognefjellsveien, continues to Skjolden in Sogn. The road was maintained by farmers from Lom and Sogn from around 1400 so that people from northern Gudbrandsdal could reach Bergen in order to trade their goods. According to a traffic survey dating from 1878, 16,525 people and 2,658 horses travelled across the mountain in that year.

The current road was built in 1938. Its highest point is 1,440 m (4,724 ft) above sea level. On the way to Skjolden on Sognefjorden it runs past the Sognefjell tourist hut, and Turtagrø hotel, a centre for climbers since 1888.

Elveseter, a farmhouse turned hotel in deepest Jotunheimen

⓯ Jotunheimen

Before 1820 the Jotunheimen mountain range was known only to local hunters, fishermen and herdsmen. It was not until the late 19th century that tourists began to discover this wild and mighty mountain region in the heart of the county of Oppland. The National Park was established in 1980. Norway's highest peaks – over 2,300 m (7,546 ft) – are located in Jotunheimen, interspersed between large glaciers, lakes and valleys. A well-developed network of footpaths crosses the mountains, linking 30 mountain huts. Some of these are run by the Norwegian tourist authorities (DNT) and some are privately owned.

Bøverdalen
From Bøverdalen valley a toll road winds up to Juvasshytta (1,841 m/ 6,040 ft). From here there is a relatively easy walk to the top of Galdhøpiggen.

Galdhøpiggen
Even in summer it is possible to ski in the vicinity of Galdhøpiggen, Norway's highest mountain at 2,469 m (8,100 ft). The snow is always good on the glacier.

Leirvassbu
The hut is 1,400 m (4,593 ft) above sea level, at the head of Leirdalen, with splendid views of peaks and glaciers.

Sogndal

Skogadalsbøen

Ingjerdbu

0 Kilometres   10
0 miles   5

Key
— Major road
— Minor road
--- National park boundary
--- Hiking trail
🏠 Mountain hut

Store Skagastølstind
"Storen", 2,403 m (7,884 ft), is Norway's third highest peak and a mountain climbers' dream. It was first scaled by William C Slingsby in 1876.

For hotels and restaurants in this area see pp230–33 and pp238–47

Fishing

Trout fishing can be good in the rivers and lakes of Jotunheimen. Many walkers take their own fishing equipment with them. Huts and hotels have information about licences, and the chances of a bite.

Svellnosbreen

The glacier above Spiterstulen has deep crevices, dramatic ice formations and tunnels. Ropes and the services of a glacier guide are essential.

Besseggen

The high route across the Besseggen ridge between Gjendesheim and Memurubu is one of the most popular in Jotunheimen. The ridge rises above the green waters of Gjende and the deep blue Lake Bessvatnet.

Gjende

The fabled Lake Gjende, coloured green by glacial water, is considered the soul of Jotunheimen. It is 18 km (11 miles) long, and stretches between two of the most popular lodges, Gjendesheim and Gjendebu.

⓱ Valdres and Fagernes

County of Oppland. 🚠 2,000
(Fagernes). 🚆 🚌 ℹ️ Jernbaneveien
7, Fagernes, 61 35 94 10. 🎪 Valdres
Festival (Jul), Folk Music Festival (Jul).
🌐 visitvaldres.no

North Aurdal is the biggest
community in Valdres, attracting
a large number of visitors year-
round. Around 150 years ago it
was little more than a farming
community, but that changed
with the arrival of the railway in
1906. Then long-distance buses
made their appearance and in
1987 Leirin airport was built, the
highest airport in Norway at
820 m (2,690 ft). Despite the
closure of the railway in 1988,
the area is easily accessible.

The main valley through
Valdres follows the river Begna
to Aurdal and Fagernes, where
the valley divides into Vestre and
Østre Slidre. The mountain resort
of **Beitostølen**, with its health
and sports centre for disabled
people, is at Øystre Slidre.

The Slidre valleys are home
to several stave churches,
including Hegge in Øystre Slidre
and Lomen, Høre and Øye in
Vestre Slidre. Long, narrow lakes
and stretches of river
characterize the region.

Valdres Folkemuseum is
situated on Fagernes, a
peninsula in Strandafjorden.
It has 100 buildings, some
20,000 artifacts, a separate high
mountain section and a
regional costume exhibition.

🏛 **Valdres Folkemuseum**
Tyinvegen 27. **Tel** 61 35 99 00. **Open**
Jun–Aug: daily; Sep–May: Mon–Fri.
🎨 🎫 ♿ 🚫 📷

Villandstua, Hallingdal Folkemuseum, featuring traditional rose-painting

⓲ Geilo

County of Buskerud. 🚠 2,500. 🚆 🚍
🚌 ℹ️ Vesleslåttveien 13, 32 09 59 00.
⛷ End of skiing season (4th week Apr).
🌐 geilo.no

Thanks to its proximity to
Hardangervidda *(see pp162–3)*
and the mountain of
Hallingskarvet (1,933 m/ 6,342 ft),
Geilo has become one of
Norway's most popular tourist
destinations, conveniently
located midway between
Oslo and Bergen. There are
opportunities for hiking, cycling
and fishing, and a great
selection of accommodation,
from wooden cabins to elegant
hotels, and many places to eat.

Geilo has also gained a
reputation as a winter sports
centre, with 33 alpine pistes,
17 ski lifts, three snowboard
parks and 500 km (311 miles)
of prepared tracks up in the
mountains. The highest alpine
piste is at 1,178 m (3,865 ft) with
good snow conditions from
November until May.

⓳ Hallingdal

County of Buskerud. 🚠 4,200. ℹ️
Stasjonsgata 7, Nesbyen, 32 07 01 70.

The long narrow valley of
Hallingdal, with mountains
rising steeply on both sides,
widens out beyond Gol to form
an agricultural landscape.

Nesbyen, one of the
populated areas along the way,
is known for its extreme
temperatures: the lowest
recorded was –38° C, and the
highest +35.6° C (a Norwegian
record). The open-air **Hallingdal
Folkemuseum** in Nesbyen
comprises 20 old houses,
among them Stavaloftet which
dates from around 1300,
and the extravagantly rose-
painted Villandstua.

Hallingdal's magnificent
mountain regions, including
Norefjell and Hallingskarvet,
have made it popular with
outdoor people. The valley of
Hemsedal, on the road to
Lærdal, has a ski centre, which
is one of Scandinavia's finest.

🏛 **Hallingdal Folkemuseum**
Møllevegen 18, Nesbyen. **Tel** 32 07 14
85. **Open** Apr–May & Sep–Oct: Sun;
Jun–Aug: daily. **Closed** public hols.
🎨 🎫 📧 📷

⓴ Numedal

County of Buskerud. 🚠 7,500. 🚌
ℹ️ Stormogen in Uvdal, 32 74 39 00.
🌐 visitnumedal.com

The landscape of Numedal is
dominated by the 18-km
(11-miles) long Norefjorden.
Rødberg is the site of a huge
power station powered by

Østre Slidre, looking toward Beitostølen and Jotunheimen

the Numedal river. It flows from its source high on Hardangervidda (see pp162–3) to a dam at Tunhovdfjorden. An animal park, **Langedrag Naturpark**, features species adapted to mountain life, such as polar foxes, wolves and Norwegian Fjord Horses.

From Rødberg the valley leads into Uvdal and the pass at **Vasstulan** (1,100 m/3,609 ft). Footpaths from here link into the network of mountain huts on Hardangervidda. The richly decorated **Uvdal Stavkirke** (stave church) dates from 1175.

On the eastern side of Norefjorden the road passes some weather-worn houses and a stave church (1600).

🔲 **Langedrag Naturpark**
30 km (19 miles) NW of Nesbyen.
Tel 32 74 25 50. **Open** daily. **Closed** some public hols. 🔲 🔲 🔲 🔲 🔲

🔲 **Uvdal Stavkirke**
Kirkebygda, Uvdal. **Tel** 32 74 39 00.
Open mid-Jun–Aug: daily. 🔲 🔲 🔲

The 12th-century Uvdal Stavkirke, on the site of an even older church

🟤 Kongsberg

County of Buskerud. 🔲 23,000. 🔲 🔲 🔲 Schwabes Gate 2, N3611, 32 29 90 50. 🔲 Kongsberg Market (4th week Feb), Kongsberg Jazz Festival (1st week Jul), Silver Festival (Aug).

Silver mining was for 335 years the main focus of activity at Kongsberg until the Sølvverket (Silverworks) were closed in 1957. It was also the site of the royal mint.

The town was laid out by Christian IV in 1624, and developed rapidly. The large Baroque church, **Kongsberg Kirke**, was opened in 1761.

Ore-wagon at Bergverksmuseum (Mining Museum) in Kongsberg

Its lavish interior features wood carvings, faux marble work and an altar with biblical motifs. The organ (1760–65), by Gottfried Heinrich Gloger, is considered a masterpiece. The remarkable chandeliers were made at Nøstetangen Glassworks.

Kongsberg is the location for the Norwegian Mining Museum, **Norsk Bergverksmuseum**, which contains the Royal Mint Museum and the Sølvverket collections. The former technical school, **Bergseminaret**, is a splendid wooden building dating from 1783. To the west at Saggrenda it is possible to ride on a train deep into **Kongens Gruve** (King's Mine).

🏛 **Norsk Bergverksmuseum**
Hyttegata 3. **Tel** 91 91 32 00.
Open daily. **Closed** public hols.
🔲 🔲 by arrangement. 🔲 🔲 🔲
🔲 **norsk-bergverksmuseum.no**

🏛 **Kongens Gruve**
8 km (5 miles) W of town centre.
Tel 32 72 32 00. **Open** 18 May–Aug: daily; Sep: Sun; other times by arrangement. 🔲 🔲 🔲 🔲 🔲

🟤 Drammen

County of Buskerud. 🔲 60,000. 🔲 🔲 🔲 Engene 1, 03008. 🔲 River Festival (Aug). 🔲 **drammen.kommune.no**

The river port of Drammen has Norway's largest harbour for the import of cars. Its location on the navigable Drammenselva has been the source of its prosperity. It was mentioned as early as the 13th century as a loading place and port for timber and when the Kongsberg silver mine opened, Drammen became the port for the Silverworks.

In the early days there were two towns, Bragernes and Strømsø, on either side of the river estuary. They were merged into one in 1811.

Drammens Museum, at the manor house of Marienlyst Herregård, has collections of city and farming culture.

The art gallery, **Drammens Kunstforening**, has Norwegian 19th- and 20th-century paintings and a large collection of Italian art from the 17th and 18th centuries.

The Drammenselva river is one of the best in the country for salmon fishing. For panoramic views, take the road via the Spiraltunellen to the summit of Bragernesåsen.

🏛 **Drammens Museum**
Konnerudgatan 7. **Tel** 32 20 09 30.
Open 11am–3pm Mon–Fri (to 8pm Tue), 11am–5pm Sat & Sun. 🔲 🔲 🔲 partly. 🔲 🔲 🔲

🏛 **Drammens Kunstforening**
Konnerudgatan 7. **Tel** 91 11 92 75.
Open Tue–Sun. **Closed** public hols.
🔲 🔲 🔲

The old manor house of Marienlyst, home to Drammens Museum

SØRLANDET AND TELEMARK

Telemark and the area known as Sørlandet (the "southern lands") create a gentle transition between the eastern and western parts of southern Norway. High mountain plateaus form a dramatic backdrop to the forests and pastures of the lowlands with their river valleys and lakes. Painted harbour-front houses, sandy beaches and tiny islands draw holiday-makers to the south coast.

The county of Telemark is dominated by the mountain plateau of Hardangervidda *(see pp162–3)*, topped by the 1,883-m (6,178-ft) high peak of Gaustadtoppen to the northeast. Valleys criss-cross the landscape and a multitude of lakes – many rich in fish – shine like jewels. Rivers such as the Bjoreia plunge from the plateau, providing power for hydro-electricity. The Skienvass-draget underwent a major makeover in the 19th century to create the Telemark Canal *(see p152)*. An important working waterway in its time, it is now popular for boating.

The beautiful and varied scenery has influenced local culture and the temperament of the people. There are few places in the country with such a rich and diverse folklore. Many Norwegian fairytales and folk songs were written, and folk music composed, in the region. Building skills have been preserved and you can literally smell the sunburnt, tarred timber of centuries-old cabins and log barns. The 13th-century Heddal Stavkirke (stave church) is like a cathedral in wood *(see p161)*.

Sørlandet (made up of the counties of Vest-Agder and Aust-Agder) has a coastline 250 km (155 miles) long as the crow flies, from Langesunds-fjorden in the east to Flekkefjord in the west. However, the fjords, islands and skerries make the coastline many times longer. This is an area much loved by visitors, with its white-painted villages and towns, bobbing boats and busy quays. The archipelago is a haven for fishing and swimming, and the pleasant, though sometimes old-fashioned towns, make Sørlandet a paradise for holiday-makers. Lindesnes lighthouse casts its beam from Norway's most southerly point *(see p155)*.

Mountain trekking on horseback, a popular way of exploring Hardangervidda

◀ Kilden Performing Arts Centre, Kristiansand

Exploring Sørlandet and Telemark

Sørlandskysten (the southern coast) is known as the sunny side of Norway. It is a summer paradise for holiday-makers. White-painted towns huddle within easy reach of each other; harbours reminiscent of the busy seafaring days of old dot the coast. Boats take visitors around Skjærgårdsparken (meaning, literally, "archipelago park"), which stretches from Risør in the northeast to Lindesnes in the southwest, and the area is great for fishing and beach picnics. Inland in Telemark and Sørlandet there are mountains and hidden valleys with historic stave churches. Indeed, a large part of the mountain plateau of Hardangervidda is in Telemark. To the east of the region boats ply the Telemark Canal toward the mountain passes bordering the west coast, Vestlandet.

Grimstad, one of Sørlandet's many "white towns" attracting holiday-makers throughout the summer season

Getting Around

The main roads through the region from east to west are the E18, E39 and RV42 in the south and the E134 in the north. They are connected to roads running north and south through the valleys, which give access to the rural byways in the south. The railway line, Sørlandsbanen, winds inland, often crossing valleys. The region is well served by bus and express coach routes. The main airport is Kjevik, near Kristiansand, which has direct flights to London. There are airfields at Notodden and Skien. Kristiansand has ferry connections with Denmark.

Key

▬▬ Highway
— Major road
····· Minor road
╌╍╌ Main railway
— Minor railway
▬▬ County border
△ Summit

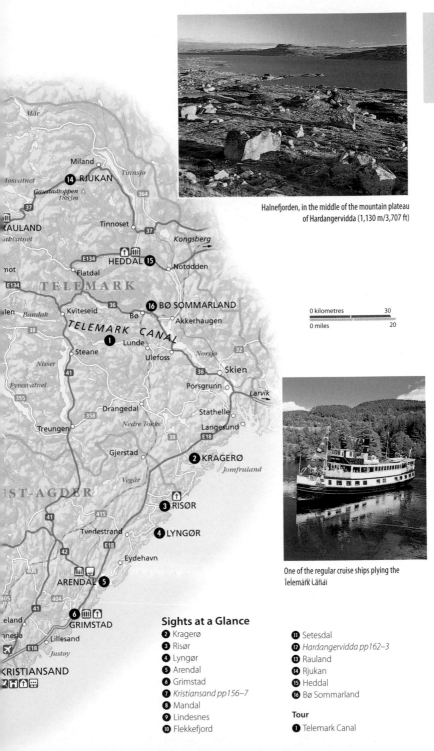

Halnefjorden, in the middle of the mountain plateau of Hardangervidda (1,130 m/3,707 ft)

One of the regular cruise ships plying the Telemark Canal

Sights at a Glance

2 Kragerø
3 Risør
4 Lyngør
5 Arendal
6 Grimstad
7 *Kristiansand pp156–7*
8 Mandal
9 Lindesnes
10 Flekkefjord

11 Setesdal
12 *Hardangervidda pp162–3*
13 Rauland
14 Rjukan
15 Heddal
16 Bø Sommarland

Tour
1 Telemark Canal

For hotels and restaurants in this area see pp230–33 and pp238–47

❶ Tour along the Telemark Canal

In 1861, during the heyday of waterways transport, Telemark's greatest river, Skienvassdraget, was transformed into the Skien-Nordsjø Canal. Thirty years later, the Nordsjø-Bandak Canal to Dalen was completed, creating the 105-km (65-mile) long Telemark Canal. Eight locks were built to lift boats 72 m (236 ft) above sea level. At the time it was hailed as the "eighth wonder of the world". In 1994, the canal received the Europa Nostra Gold Medal for restoration and conservation. Today, it has become one of the biggest attractions in the county.

Cabin-cruiser navigating the Telemark Canal

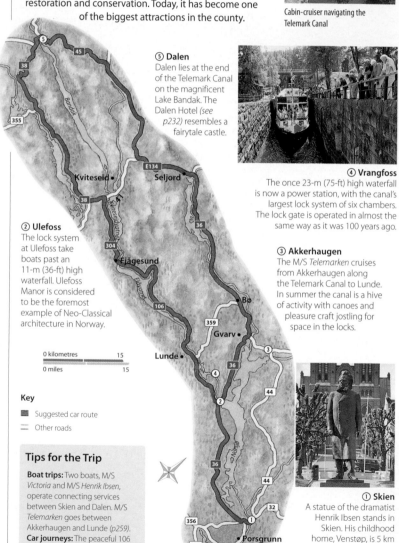

⑤ Dalen
Dalen lies at the end of the Telemark Canal on the magnificent Lake Bandak. The Dalen Hotel (see p232) resembles a fairytale castle.

④ Vrangfoss
The once 23-m (75-ft) high waterfall is now a power station, with the canal's largest lock system of six chambers. The lock gate is operated in almost the same way as it was 100 years ago.

② Ulefoss
The lock system at Ulefoss take boats past an 11-m (36-ft) high waterfall. Ulefoss Manor is considered to be the foremost example of Neo-Classical architecture in Norway.

③ Akkerhaugen
The M/S Telemarken cruises from Akkerhaugen along the Telemark Canal to Lunde. In summer the canal is a hive of activity with canoes and pleasure craft jostling for space in the locks.

0 kilometres   15
0 miles   15

Key

▬ Suggested car route

═ Other roads

Tips for the Trip

Boat trips: Two boats, M/S Victoria and M/S Henrik Ibsen, operate connecting services between Skien and Dalen. M/S Telemarken goes between Akkerhaugen and Lunde (p259).
Car journeys: The peaceful 106 road meanders along the canal, past the lake, Flåvatnet.

① Skien
A statue of the dramatist Henrik Ibsen stands in Skien. His childhood home, Venstøp, is 5 km (3 miles) from the town centre and forms part of the Telemark Museum.

❷ Kragerø

County of Telemark. 🚗 11,000. 🚂 to Neslandsvatn. 🚌 ℹ️ Torvgata 1, 35 98 23 88. 🎿 Summer Ski Festival (4th week Jun), Easter Bathing (Easter Eve), Kragerø Festival (3rd week Jun).
🌐 visitkragero.no

A popular holiday resort since the 1920s, Kragerø is surrounded by a magnificent archipelago of small islands divided by narrow, twisting waterways. The picturesque little town was the home of the artist Theodor Kittelsen (1857–1914), best known for his fine illustrations of Asbjørnsen & Moe's collection of Norwegian folk tales. Some of these can be seen in his house-museum.

The morainic island of **Jomfruland**, the outermost in the Kragerø archipelago, has a distinctive flora and bird life, an old brick lighthouse from 1839 and a newer one from 1939. The island can be reached by local ferry from Kragerø.

❸ Risør

County of Aust-Agder. 🚗 7,000. 🚂 to Gjerstad, then bus. 🚌 ℹ️ Kragsgate 3, 37 15 22 70. 🎿 Festival of Chamber Music (4th week Jun), Arts and Crafts Market (2nd week Jul), Wooden Boat Festival (1st week Aug).
🌐 visitnorway.com

Protected from the sea by just a few islets, Risør is known as the "White Town of Skagerrak". It is the row of dazzling white merchants' and ship owners' houses on Solsiden ("the sunny side") by the harbour, as well as the cottages nestling on

White-painted merchants' houses overlooking Risør harbour

Lyngør, the "Venice of the Norwegian coast" with its narrow waterways

Innsiden ("the inside") that have given the town its nickname. Despite several fires, the town has preserved much of its 19th-century layout.

Risør had its heyday toward the end of the sailing ship era, from around 1870. The traditions live on, as proved by the Wooden Boat Festival held here every August. Magnificent vessels fill the harbour and boat builders can be seen at their craft.

The wooden church at Risør, **Den Hellige Ånds Kirke**, was built in 1647 with Baroque details and a 17th- to 18th-century interior. The deactivated Stangholmen Fyr lighthouse, dating from 1885, features a summer restaurant and bar offering glorious views, as well as temporary exhibitions in its lamp room.

🏠 Den Hellige Ånds Kirke
Prestegata 6. **Tel** 37 15 00 12. **Open** Jul: daily; other times by arrangement. 📷 by prior arrangement. ♿

❹ Lyngør

County of Aust-Agder. 🚗 130. 🚂 to Vegårshei, then bus. 🚌 to Gjeving, then taxi boat. 🚌 summer only. ℹ️ Wrold Wroldsens Gt 2 (Tvedestrand), 37 16 40 30. 🎿 Coastal Culture Week (mid-Jul), Tvedestrand Regatta (mid-Jul), Skjærgård's Music and Mission Festival (1st week Jul).

A former winner of the "best preserved village in Europe" award, Lyngør is one of the idyllic islands in Skjaergårds-parken (Archipelago Park) which covers most of the coast of Aust-Agder county. Accessible only by boat taxi from Gjerving on the mainland, the island has no roads for motor vehicles and is a peaceful haven.

Lyngør has fine historic buildings near the old pilot and customs station. Narrow footpaths wind past painted houses with white picket fences and fragrant gardens. The forests that once covered the islands are long gone, but there is an abundance of flowers, initially brought here as seeds in the ballast of sailing ships.

In 1812, Lyngør was the scene of a bloody sea battle when the Danish-Norwegian frigate, *Najaden*, was sunk by the English vessel, *Dictator*. The population sought refuge in Krigerhola, a pothole near the sea. A cultural history museum is connected to the restaurant, *Den Blå Grotte*.

The islands share an early 13th-century church at Dybvåg on the mainland.

Arendal town hall, 1813, Norway's second largest wooden building

❺ Arendal

County of Aust-Agder. 39,000.
Kristiansand. Sam Eydes
Plass, 37 00 55 44. International
Market (1st week Jul), Arendal Jazz
and Blues Festival (4th week Jul), APL
Offshore Race (1st week Aug).
W arendal.com

Sørlandet's oldest town,
Arendal, dates back to 1723.
It was built originally on seven
islands. The buildings on the
peninsula of Tyholmen next
to the busy visitors' moorings,
Pollen, were saved from fire
around 1800. They have since
been carefully preserved and
were awarded the Europa Nostra
conservation medal in 1992.

The town hall, **Rådhuset**, is an
architectural gem, built in Neo-
Classical style in the early 19th
century. At that time, Arendal
was the biggest shipping town
in the country, with a merchant
fleet larger than that of Denmark.

Aust-Agder Museet has
archaeological and seafaring
exhibits. In the harbour of
Merdøy (half-an-hour by boat
from Langbrygga) the former
captain's home of Merdøgård
is open to the public.

From Tvedestrand, there are
boat trips on the M/S *Søgne*
to the islands beyond.

🏛 Rådhuset
Rådhusgaten 10. **Tel** 37 01 30 00.
Open for pre-booked tours only.
by prior arrangement.

🏛 Aust-Agder Museet
Parkveien 16. **Tel** 37 07 35 00.
Open Mon–Fri & Sun. **Closed** public
holidays.

❻ Grimstad

County of Aust-Agder. 18,000.
Kristiansand. Storgata 1a,
37 25 01 68. Short Film Festival
(mid–Jun), St Hans Festival (21–24
Jun). W grimstad.net

The old centre of Grimstad dates
from the days of sailing ships,
with narrow streets winding
between the hills. **Grimstad
Bymuseum**, featuring arts and
crafts and a maritime section,
is situated in the town centre
together with the pharmacy
from 1837 where Henrik Ibsen
was an apprentice and where
he wrote his first plays.

Northeast of the town is
Fjære Kirke, a church with a
memorial stone to Terje Vigen,
about whom Ibsen wrote. This
brave seaman came rowing
from Denmark to Grimstad
with two tons of barley in the
year of starvation, 1809.

Nørholm, on the south-
western outskirts, was the
home of Nobel prize-winning

Grimstad Bymuseum with a bust of Henrik
Ibsen in the foreground

novelist Knut Hamsun. The
coast toward Kristiansand is
renowned for its holiday
resorts and has often been
featured in paintings, poetry
and literature.

Lillesand is a charming
skerries town, with an elegant
town hall and white-washed
wooden houses. Sightseeing
boats depart from the town for
Blindleia, a 12-km (7-mile) long
series of inlets, which are busy
with small craft in summer.

The beauty spots of **Justøy**
island and **Gamle Hellesund**
in Høvåg are close by. There is
a Bronze-Age settlement at
Høvåg. A coastal ferry calls at
one idyllic place after another,
including **Brekkstø**, an artists'
community on Justøy, a much
loved holiday spot.

🏛 Grimstad Bymuseum
Henrik Ibsens Gate 14. **Tel** 37 04 04 90.
Open May–mid-Sep: daily; mid-Sep–
Apr: by arrangement. by
arrangement. W gbm.no

❼ Kristiansand

See pp156–7.

Mandal, characterized by narrow streets
and wooden houses

❽ Mandal

County of Vest-Agder. 14,000.
Kristiansand. to Marnardal
or Kristiansand, then bus.
Bryggegata 10, 38 27 83 00.
Shellfish Festival (2nd week Aug).
W lindesnesregionen.com

Mandal owes its fortunes to the
timber trade in the 18th century.
But its boom years were short-
lived and with the transition
from sail to steam, around 1900,
one in four inhabitants departed
for America. Yet, despite mass

emigration, floods and fires, the town has retained more of its former characteristics than many others in Sørlandet. **Mandal Bymuseum**, located in an old merchant's house, has a large art collection, a ship gallery and a fishing museum. The town church dates from 1821 and is one of the bigger in the country.

The coastal road to Mandal passes near the harbour of Ny-Hellesund, where the writer Vilhelm Krag (1871–1933) lived. This was also where Amaldus Nielsen painted his famous picture *Morning at Ny-Hellesund* (1885, Nasjonalgalleriet, Oslo).

Norway's finest beach is nearby, the eggshell-white **Sjøsanden**. This is where the salmon river, Mandalselven, flows into the sea.

🏛 **Mandal Bymuseum**
Store Elvegata 5. **Tel** 38 25 60 23.
Open end Jun–mid-Aug: daily; mid-Aug–end Jun: Sun. 🖼

❾ Lindesnes

County of Vest-Agder, 35 km (22 miles) W of Mandal. 🚹 Lindesnes Informasjonssenter, 38 27 83 00. 🎪 Foghorn Day (last Sun Jul). Lighthouse: **Tel** 38 25 54 20. **Open** May–Sep: daily; Oct–Apr: Sat & Sun. 🖼 🖼 ☐ 🏛 🖥 lindesnesregionen.com

The southernmost point on the mainland of Norway is the Lindesnes peninsula, 2,518 km (1,565 miles) from the North

Traditional boat moored in Flekkefjord's Dutch Town

Cape in the far north. Here stands Lindesnes lighthouse, built in 1915 on the site of Norway's first lighthouse, which was lit in 1655.

The peninsula marks a distinctive change in the landscape between the small fjords and gently rounded islands to the east and the longer fjords to the west with more barren islets and wilder looking mountains.

The Skagerrak and North Sea meet at this point, some days with great force. This can be the roughest place on the south coast, but at other times the water can look quite benign and inviting.

Two small harbours on the southeastern side of the peninsula, **Lillehavn** and **Vågehavn**, enable sailors to shelter and weather the worst of the storms.

❿ Flekkefjord

County of Vest-Agder. 🚌 8,500. 🚉 to station of Sira, 20 km (12 miles) N of town centre. 🚌 🚹 Elvegata 9, 38 32 69 95. 🎪 Salmon Festival (4th week Jul), Gyland Grand Prix (1st week Aug). 🖥 visitsydvest.no

The port of Flekkefjord is the biggest fishing and fish farming town on the Skagerrak coast. The Dutch were early trading partners, hence Hollenderbyen (the Dutch Town), dating from 1700. The town museum, **Flekkefjord Bymuseum**, housed in a 1720s patrician building, recreates old shipping scenes.

At the mouth of the fjord is the island of **Hidra**, which can be reached by car ferry from the mainland. It is known for its scenic harbours – Kirkehan, Rasvåg and Eie – and vibrant island community, which has preserved much of its charm from its days as a sailing and fishing centre.

To the west of Flekkefjord is the fishing village of Åna-Sira, which marks the border between Sørlandet and Vestlandet. Nearby, the **Sira-Kvina Kraftselskap** arranges tours of its power station, one of seven on the Sira-Kvina waterway.

🏛 **Flekkefjord Bymuseum**
Dr Krafts Gate 15. **Tel** 38 32 26 59.
Open Jun–Aug: daily; other times by prior arrangement. 🖼 🖼 🖼 partly.

🏛 **Sira-Kvina Kraftselskap**
60 km (37 miles) N of Flekkefjord. **Tel** 38 37 80 00. **Open** end Jun–mid-Aug: daily (guided tours only). 🖼 🖼 🖼

Lindesnes lighthouse standing at the southernmost point of Norway

❼ Kristiansand

The capital of Sørlandet, Kristiansand, was founded by Christian IV in 1641. It immediately obtained market town status and certain trading privileges. The layout followed a strict grid pattern and, as a result, the town centre became known as Kvadraturen ("the quad"). Kristiansand expanded in 1922 and again in 1965. Now the fifth largest town in Norway, it is a delightful mixture of old and new. In addition to the town itself, the municipality incorporates the surrounding hills, forests and moors, small quiet lakes and farmland, as well as a stretch of coastline.

Restored house in the popular neighbourhood of Posebyen

🏛 Posebyen

NE part of town centre. 🚪 Jun–Aug: Sat.

In Kristiansand's early days as a fortress and garrison town, the soldiers lived in private houses in what has become the best preserved part of the old town. The name Posebyen stems from the French *reposer*, meaning to rest (French was the military language of the time).

The small, pretty houses in this area of town, complete with courtyards, stables and wagon sheds, wash-houses and outbuildings, have survived several fires and the threat of demolition. Nowadays Posebyen is a fashionable place to live, and the historic houses are maintained in good order by the inhabitants.

🏰 Christiansholm Festning

Østre Strandgate. **Tel** 38 07 51 50. **Open** Jun–Jul: daily; Sep–May: by prior arrangement. 📷 by arrangement. ♿

One of the main reasons why Christian IV wanted a town on the south coast was to strengthen the Danish-Norwegian union militarily in the frequent wars against neighbouring countries. In 1628 there was a blockhouse at the mouth of the fjord, and around 1640 a permanent fortification was established.

The solid Christiansholm Festning, on Østre Havn (the Eastern Harbour), was erected in the years after 1667. The town became a garrison, and the fortress was long regarded as the most important in the country after Akershus and Bergenhus. The fortress was the scene of a battle in 1807, when it was used to drive off the English warship, *Spencer*. Today, it is a public area.

🏰 Domkirken

Tel 38 10 69 00. **Open** Jun–Aug: Mon–Fri and during services, Jul also Sat. 🏰 Sun. 📷 ♿

Kristiansand became a diocese in 1682 when the bishopric was moved here from Stavanger. The Neo-Gothic cathedral, Domkirken, is the fourth to be built on the site. It was completed in 1885, after a fire five years earlier, and can hold 2,000 people. The organ in the east gallery dates from 1967 and has 50 pipes. A painting on the altarpiece by Eilif Petersson shows Jesus in Emmaus.

🏛 Gimle Gård

Gimleveien 23. **Tel** 38 10 26 80. **Open** 20 Jun–20 Aug: daily; 21 Aug– 19 Jun: Sun. **Closed** public hols. 📷 📷

The manor house of Gimle Gård was built for the wealthy ship-owner Bernt Holm around 1800, in the Neo-Classical style popular at the time. It has a colonnaded loggia, and the interior contains many fine pieces of Empire-style furniture as well as additions from the end of the 19th century.

On the walls are 17th- and 18th-century paintings from Denmark, Germany, Italy and the Netherlands, most of which were part of Holm's private collection.

Gimle Gård, a 19th-century manor house with a distinctive colonnade

Turned into a museum in 1985, Gimle Gård provides visitors with an excellent glimpse of life of the Norwegian bourgeoisie during the Napoleonic era, from the stately salons to the basement kitchen.

🏛 Vest-Agder Fylkesmuseum
Vigeveien 22. **Tel** 38 12 03 50. **Open** 20 Jun–20 Aug: daily; 21 Aug–19 Jun: Sun. **Closed** some public hols.
🖼 🧺 🖥 🏠

Established in 1903, the open-air Vest-Agder Fylkesmuseum features wooden buildings from around the county, arranged according to origin. The Agdertunet and Setesdalstunet have farmyards, storehouses on stilts and bath houses, while Bygaden consists of 19th-century town houses, shops and workshops from Kristiansand.

In the museum's main building there is an exhibition of traditional folk costumes and examples of the typical rustic decorations known as *rosemalt*, featured on pottery, tools, furniture and walls.

Animals drawing the crowds at Kristiansand Dyrepark

Not far from the museum, **Oddernes Kirke** is one of the oldest churches in the country, dating from 1040.

🦁 Kristiansand Dyrepark
10 km (6 miles) E of town centre. **Tel** 38 04 97 00. **Open** daily. **Closed** some public hols. 🚗 ♿ 🚻 🖥 🏠

Wolves, lynx, elk, capercaillies and eagle owls are among the Nordic species that can be seen at the park. From further afield, there are giraffes, apes, alligators and boa constrictors. Other attractions include a bobsleigh track and water chutes.

VISITORS' CHECKLIST

Practical Information
County of Vest-Agder. 🚹 75,000.
🛈 Rådhus Gate 6, 38 12 13 14.
🎭 International Church Music Festival (mid-Jun), Water Festival (2nd wk Jun), Quart Music Festival (1st wk Jul), Dark Season Festival (1st wk Nov). 🆆 **visitkrs.no**

Transport
✈ 🚉 🚌 ⛴

🏛 Setesdalsbanen Museumsjernbane
Grovane Stasjon, Vennesla, 17 km (11 miles) N of town centre. **Tel** 38 15 64 82. **Open** 16 Jun–1 Sep: departures 11:30am and 2pm Sun; Jul: departures also at 11:30am, 2pm, 6pm Tue–Fri (and 12 noon Thu). 🚗 🏠

Steam trains are running once again on part of the narrow-gauge Setesdalsbanen line between Grovane and Røyknes. The original railway from Kristiansand opened in 1896. It was closed in 1962. There are guided tours of the engine shed and workshops.

Kristiansand Town Centre

① Posebyen
② Christiansholm Festning
③ Domkirken
④ Gimle Gård

0 metres 300
0 yards 300

For keys to map symbols *see back flap*

Typical interior from one of the many old mountain farms in Rauland

⓫ Setesdal

County of Aust-Agder, Municipality of Valle. 1,500. Valle Sentrum, 37 93 75 00.

The biggest of the Agder valleys is Setesdal. The steep Setesdalsheiene, 1,000-m (3,280-ft) high spurs of the Hardangervidda plateau, form towering walls on each side of the River Otra, which flows from the Bykleheiene hills.

Setesdal has maintained its distinctive rural culture, which manifests itself particularly in folk music, silversmithing, folk costumes and architecture. The museum, **Setesdalsmuseet**, in Valle, has a medieval open-hearth house and Rygnestadloftet, a small barn from around 1590. Not far from the museum, the fine Hylestad stave church once stood. Objects from the church (demolished in 1668) are sometimes displayed in the museum, although its portal with motifs from the *Volsunga* saga is now in the Historisk Museum in Oslo.

At **Setesdal Mineralpark** in Hornnes, rare minerals such as beryl, aquamarine and amazonite can be seen in large halls hollowed out inside the mountain.

🏛 Setesdalsmuseet
Rysstad on RV9. **Tel** 37 93 63 03.
Open 20 Jun–1 Sep: daily; Sep–19 Jun: Mon–Fri. **Closed** public hols.
by arrangement.

🏛 Setesdal Mineralpark
10 km (6 miles) S of Evje. **Tel** 37 93 13 10. **Open** May–Sep: daily.

⓬ Hardangervidda

See pp162–3.

⓭ Rauland

County of Telemark. 1,300.
Raulandshuset, 35 06 26 30.
Winter Folk Music Contest (Feb), Arts and Crafts Days (2nd week Jun).
W rauland.org

The mountainous area around the beautiful lake of Totakvatnet is known for its well-preserved buildings and its culture. Many artists had strong ties with the lake-side village of Rauland, and their sculptures, paintings and drawings are on display at **Rauland Kunstmuseum**, including works by Dyre Vaa (1903–80). Just east of here is an abundance of historic buildings,

such as the old farmhouses near **Krossen**, and those at **Austbøgrenda**, one of which has wood-carvings from the 1820s. Other collections of wooden buildings, including an 1820s sawmill, are at Lognvik farm by lake Lognvikvatnet.

At the westernmost end of Totakvatnet, in Arabygdi, is the **Myllarheimen** cottage where the fiddler virtuoso Tarjei Agundson (1801–72) lived. In summer, folk music is sometimes performed.

🏛 Rauland Kunstmuseum
1 km (half a mile) W of Rauland centre.
Tel 35 07 32 66. **Open** 20 Jun–Sep: daily; other times by arrangement.

⓮ Rjukan

County of Telemark. 4,000.
Torget 2, 35 08 05 50. Rjukan Rock Festival (end May), Women's Mountain Hike (1st week Sep).
W visitrjukan.com

Rjukan's international claim to fame was as the site of the hydrogen factory that was blown up in 1943 in a daring act of heroism by Norwegian Resistance fighters *(see box)*. Before that, however, the small rural community played a key role in Norway's industrial development when a power station was built here in 1911. Fuelled by the 105-m (344-ft)

The Heroes of Telemark

On the night of 27–28 February 1943, at the height of World War II, there was a powerful explosion in the hydrogen factory at Rjukan. A by-product of the production here was heavy water, which the Allies knew was an important resource for the nuclear research being undertaken by Germany, and the possible production of nuclear bombs.

The sabotage had been meticulously prepared with the help of Allied paratroopers. Nine men from the Norwegian "Kompani Linge" descended from Hardangervidda through deep snow, crossed the precipitous gorge and laid the explosives which destroyed the plant. The heroic operation, code-named "Gunnerside", was one of the most effective acts of resistance to take place during the war.

Kirk Douglas in the film *The Heroes of Telemark*, 1965

high waterfall, Rjukanfossen, the power station, a hydrogen factory and a chemical plant helped the village expand into a model industrial community, with everything provided by the company, Norsk Hydro.

A new power station was built in 1971. The old one is now a museum, **Norsk Industriarbeidermuseum**, which tells the story both of the thrilling sabotage and of Norway's industrial past.

On the opposite side of the valley is the cable car, **Krossobanen**, erected by Norsk Hydro in 1928 to enable the residents of the shaded valley to glimpse the sun in winter. It rises to 886 m (2,907 ft) and is an excellent starting point for walking trips on Hardangervidda. Beside Rjukanfossen is the **Krokan Tourist Hut**, opened in 1868 when the untamed waterfall was a popular destination for tourists and painters. Today, because of the power station, the waterfall can be seen at full force only occasionally.

Gaustadtoppen, a peak 1,883 m (6,178 ft) high, can be reached via a well-marked path from the Stavro car park. The walk to the summit takes about two hours.

🏛 Norsk Industriarbeidermuseum
7 km (4 miles) W of town centre. **Tel** 35 09 90 00. **Open** Nov–Mar: Tue–Fri; Apr & Oct: Tue–Sat; May–Sep: daily. 🅿🕐🦽🖥📷

⛷ Krossobanen
1 km (half a mile) W of town centre. **Tel** 35 09 00 27 (bookings). **Open** daily. 🅿

The Rambergstugo house dating from 1784 at Heddal Bygdetun

⓯ Heddal

County of Telemark, Municipality of Notodden. 🚹 12,000 (Notodden). 🚌 🚆 ℹ Teatergaten 3, 35 01 50 00. 🎫 Notodden Blues Festival (1st week Aug). 🌐 **visitnorway.com**

The main attraction in the village of Heddal is **Heddal Stavkirke**, erected in 1242. With its three spires and 64 different roof surfaces, this "wooden cathedral" is the largest of the preserved medieval churches in Norway. It has three naves, a portico and an apse. Notable internal features include the richly carved bishop's chair, the altarpiece and the late 17th-century wall paintings.

Heddal Stavkirke is still the main church in the district. The vicarage barn beside the church houses various exhibitions and a restaurant.

Among the buildings on display at nearby **Heddal Bygdetun** is Rambergstugo, a house decorated in 1784 in the rustic style known as "rose painting", by the well-known painter, Olav Hansson.

The Norsk Hydro company was established in Notodden

in 1905. The company museum, **Bedrifts-historisk Samling**, shows its first years of operation, and looks at the lives of the railway navvies.

⛪ Heddal Stavkirke
Heddalsvegen 412. **Tel** 35 02 04 00. **Open** end May–beg Sep: daily; other times by arrangement. 🕐🖥📷

🏛 Heddal Bygdetun
6 km (4 miles) W of Notodden. **Tel** 35 02 08 40. **Open** mid-Jun–mid-Aug: daily. 🕐🖥📷

🏛 Bedriftshistorisk Samling
Notodden town centre. **Tel** 35 09 39 99. **Open** 15 Jun–18 Aug: daily; Jan–14 Jun & 19 Aug–31 Dec: by arrangement. 🕐🖥📷📷

Bø Sommarland, a paradise for water enthusiasts large and small

⓰ Bø Sommarland

County of Telemark. **Tel** 35 06 16 00. 🌐 **Open** Jun–Aug: daily. 🕐🦽♿ 🖥📷🌐 **sommarland.no**

Norway's biggest waterpark, Bø Sommarland, offers more than 100 activities of different kinds and appealing to different ages. There are paddling pools and safe water activities for youngsters. For older children, the range of attractions includes a water carousel, water slides, rafting and an artificial wave pool.

For those seeking bigger thrills, there are diving towers, a water rollercoaster, surf waves to ride, and the heart-stopping free-fall slide, Magasuget.

Dry land attractions include a fairground and several places to eat. The park lies just north of the small town of Bø.

...n's Vemork power station, scene of a daring sabotage in 1943

For hotels and restaurants in this area see pp230–33 and pp238–47

⑫ Hardangervidda

Europe's largest high mountain plateau stands well above the tree line at 1,100–1,400 m (3,608–4,593 ft), punctuated with prominent peaks such as Hårteigen and the glacier of Hardangerjøkulen. A national park covers part of the region. Many rivers have their sources in the mountain lakes, the best known being Numedalslågen and Telemarksvassdraget in the east, and Bjoreia with the waterfall Vøringsfossen (see p173) in the west. Ancient tracks and well-trodden paths bear witness to the passage of people across the mountains in times past. Hunters stalked reindeer and fishermen still come to catch trout. Today, though, it is the *hytte*-to-*hytte* (hut-to-hut) hikers who make up the majority of visitors to Hardangervidda.

Vøringsfossen
The River Bjoreia plunges vertically 145 m (476 ft) down from the plateau into the valley of Måbødalen.

Trout Fishing
Hardangervidda is one of Norway's best areas for trout fishing. Information about fishing licences can be obtained in advance from tourist offices and huts.

Hårteigen
The strange shape of Hårteigen rises from the plateau. The gneissic outcrop is the remains of an ancient mountain ridge.

Bergen

Eidfjord

Fos

Kinsarvik

Viveli

Stavali

Hadlaskar

Torehytten

Tyssevassbu

Litlos

Odda

Hellevassbu

Middalsbu

Haugesund

E134

0 Kilometres 20
0 miles 10

Key

■ Major road
═ Minor road
--- National park boundaries
-- Hiking route
🏠 Mountain hut

Glacier Buttercup
Hardangervidda is the habitat for a rich variety of flowers, including the hardy glacier buttercup, *Ranunculus glacie*

Hardangerjøkulen

The 6th largest glacier in Norway, Hardangerjøkulen is also the most accessible. It attracts visitors all year round, not least in May when many combine a spot of spring skiing with a visit to Hardangerfjord where fruit trees are in blossom.

VISITORS' CHECKLIST

Practical Information
Counties of Telemark, Buskerud and Hordaland.
ℹ Hardangervidda Natursenter in Eidfjord, 53 67 40 00.
Open Apr–Oct: daily; other times by prior arrangement.
🌐 **hardangervidda.org**

Mountain Huts
Some mountain huts are only a short distance from the road, such as this one near Ustetind, while others can only be reached after a few hours by footpath.

Hiking
The terrain on Hardangervidda is generally easy-going, providing good walking for hikers of all levels.

Haukeligrend

Wild Reindeer
Hardangervidda's population of around 17,000 wild reindeer is the biggest in Europe. Ancient animal burial sites and other hunting evidence indicate that reindeer have been living on the plateau for many thousands of years.

VESTLANDET

The long, thin westerly region bordering the North Sea from Stavanger to Kristiansund is known as Vestlandet. This is the land of the fjords, where fingers of deep blue and green water penetrate far inland from the island-studded coast, cutting spectacularly through the awesome mountains. Picturesque villages edge the shoreline, linked by ferries, tunnels and precipitous winding roads.

Vestlandet comprises four counties which together cover about 15 per cent of Norway: Rogaland, Hordaland, Sogn and Fjordane, and Møre and Romsdal. In the far south in Rogaland are the agricultural plains of Jæren and the towns of Egersund, Sandnes and Stavanger. The Jæren coast features pebbly beaches and broad sandy bays suitable for swimming and other water activities.

Further inland is the rocky heathland of Høg-Jæren, after which the landscape rises steeply to the dramatic Ryfylkefjellene mountains.

North of Stavanger is the fourth longest fjord in Vestlandet, Boknafjorden. One of its arms is the wild Lysefjorden beneath the famous Preikestolen (Pulpit Rock), which can be reached on foot, or seen from a ferry on the fjord below.

Bergen, the second biggest town in Norway is, along with Stavanger and Ålesund, a good starting point for trips to Sunnfjord and Nordfjord. Known as the "enchanting fjords", they are famous for their impressive mountains, waterfalls and glaciers, and idyllic beaches. This region of Hardanger and Sogn is renowned for its stave churches, historical sites and museums. Extending into the sea, the Stad peninsula marks the point where the North Sea meets the Norwegian Sea.

The county of Møre and Romsdal has equally stunning fjords and mountains. Especially noteworthy are Geirangerfjorden and Romsdalsfjorden with its spectacular panorama of towering peaks.

Vestlandet offers excellent opportunities for mountain hiking in both easy and more challenging terrains. For the angler, there is superb sea fishing and salmon and trout fishing in the lakes and rivers. The island of Runde is rich in bird-life.

Historic Bryggen, the wharf area of Bergen, a distinctive feature of the city

Lyserfjorden, overlooked by the towering Preikestolen (Pulpit Rock)

Exploring Vestlandet

Vestlandet is renowned for its fjords and each town eagerly extols the virtues of its own particular stretch of deep clear water cutting through the mountain ranges: Bergen has named itself "the gateway to the fjords"; Molde sings the praises of its "Molde panorama" over Romsdalsfjorden and the surrounding peaks; Stavanger boasts "the shortest road to Lysefjorden". The smaller fjords such as Sunnfjord, Nordfjord, Geirangerfjorden and Sunndalsfjorden are equally as beautiful as their larger counterparts and all have villages and towns of interest huddled at the water's edge. Buildings from the past, museums and galleries are to be found in many of the larger towns. Around Sognefjorden are fine examples of Norway's stave churches, including those at Urnes and Borgund.

The Norwegian Fjord horse, typical of the region of Vestlandet

Key

═══ Highway

─── Major road

═══ Minor road

┠┈┈┥ Tunnel

━━ Main railway

─── Minor railway

━━ County border

△ Summit

0 kilometres   50

0 miles   25

Bergen harbour and the mountain of Fløyfjellet

For additional map symbols *see back flap*

Låtefoss, south of Odda in Hardanger, one of Vestlandet's spectacular waterfalls

Getting Around

It is easy to get to Vestlandet. There are international flights to the large towns, and domestic flights to a number of smaller centres. Car ferries from Great Britain and the Continent have regular services to Bergen and Stavanger. Cruise ships ply the fjords in summer. There is a railway line to Stavanger, Bergen and Åndalsnes from Oslo. For those travelling by car or bus from Eastern Norway, there are several main roads over the mountains. The road network through Vestlandet and out to the islands is well developed with spectacular bridges and tunnels. Where there are no bridges, ferries are usually close at hand. Express boats link many towns and villages, and a large number of car ferries cross the fjords or call in at the islands along the coast. The coastal express, Hurtigruten *(see p215)*, to Northern Norway has its most southerly port-of-call at Bergen.

Stryn on inner Nordfjord, surrounded by mountains and glaciers

Sights at a Glance

1. *Stavanger pp168–9*
2. Egersund
3. Lysefjorden
4. Suldal
5. Utstein Kloster
6. Karmøy
7. Haugesund
8. Baroniet Rosendal
9. Hardangerfjorden
10. Sørfjorden
11. Eidfjord
12. Ulvik
13. Voss
14. *Bergen pp174–81*
15. *Sognefjorden pp184–6*
16. *Borgund Stavkirke p187*
17. Urnes Stavkirke
18. Jostedalsbreen
19. Førde and Jølster
20. Nordfjord
21. Selje and Stad
22. Geirangerfjorden
23. Ålesund
24. Åndalsnes
25. Molde
26. Kristiansund

For hotels and restaurants in this area see pp230–33 and pp238–47

❶ Stavanger

Sardines and oil have been the mainstay of Stavanger's economic development. Before the cathedral was built around 1125, Stavanger was little more than a fishing village. It was not granted status as a market town until 1425. From the 19th century onwards, an influx of herring in the waters offshore gave rise to the town's lucrative fishing and canning industry. Then, in the 1960s, oil was discovered off the coast, boosting the town's prosperity. Today, Stavanger is the fourth-largest city in Norway with some 110,000 inhabitants. It is situated between the flat countryside of Jæren to the south and, to the north, Boknafjorden, the southernmost of the west coast fjords.

Gamle Stavanger, with its winding streets of immaculately preserved timber houses

🏛 Gamle Stavanger
Stavanger town centre. 📷 Jun–Aug, visit the tourist office to book.

To the west and southwest of Vågen harbour is Gamle ("Old") Stavanger, a residential and commercial quarter characterized by its wooden houses and narrow cobbled streets. Between Øvre Strandgate and Nedre Strandgate, there are complete terraces of well-preserved, 19th-century whitewashed timber houses with small front gardens and picket fences. Once the homes of seafarers and local workers, the 156 protected houses are lovingly cared for by their modern-day owners.

🏛 Norsk Hermetikkmuseum
Øvre Strandgate 88A. **Tel** 51 84 27 00. **Open** mid-Jun–mid-Aug: daily; mid-Aug– mid-Jun: Tue–Sun. **Closed** public hols, Dec. 📷 📷 📷 📷

The canning museum, Norsk Hermetikkmuseum, is situated in picturesque Gamle Stavanger. Housed in an old cannery, it provides an overview of an industry that in its heyday was of greater importance to the town, relatively speaking, than the oil industry is today. In the 1920s there were 70 canneries in Stavanger. Visitors are offered a glimpse of the pioneering time around 1850 when innovations such as "tinned suppers" made their first appearance, followed by developments in technology and the launching of tinned sardines on the world market in the early 20th century.

🏛 Stavanger Sjøfartsmuseum
Nedre Strandgate 17–19. **Tel** 51 84 27 00. **Open** Sun. **Closed** public hols. 📷 📷 📷 📷 📷
🌐 **stavanger.museum.no**

The sailing vessel *Anna of Sand* was launched in 1848 and is Norway's oldest sailing ship still in use. Between voyages, it can be seen here at the Sjøfartsmuseum (the Maritime Museum), which also owns the pleasure yacht *Wyvern*, built in 1897 by Colin Archer (who built the polar vessel *Fram* for the explorer Fridtjof Nansen). The museum, located in two converted warehouses next to the harbour, focuses on the maritime history of south-western Norway.

🏛 Valbergtårnet
Valberget 2. **Tel** 51 53 12 19. **Open** Mon–Sat: daily. **Closed** public hols. 📷 📷 by arrangement. 📷

The fire lookout tower on the hill of Valberget, designed by C H Grosch, was ready in 1852. Stavanger has suffered many big fires over the years – one, in 1684, was so catastrophic that the possibility of abandoning the town altogether was considered. That didn't happen and today the tower provides a splendid view of the town, the harbour and Boknafjorden.

🏛 Norsk Oljemuseum
Kjerringholmen. **Tel** 51 93 93 00. **Open** daily. **Closed** some public hols. 📷 📷 Sun. 📷 📷 📷

Oil and gas production in the North Sea has created an economic boom in Stavanger, with the consequence that the town is the most cosmopolitan in the country. The ultra-modern Norsk Oljemuseum (Petroleum Museum), designed by architects Lunde and Løvseth, offers a graphic account of life at work and play on a drilling platform with a top-to-bottom presentation of an oil rig.

Models of the equipment used are on display, including drilling bits, diving bells and a 28-person survival capsule. Tableaux illustrate how oil and gas were created, the history of the industry, and the technology used to extract and distribute the oil and gas.

The Norsk Oljemuseum, featuring the history of Norway's oil industry

For hotels and restaurants in this area see pp230–33 and pp238–47

Stavanger's historic Domkirken, dating from around 1100

🏛 **Domkirken**

Haakon VII's Gate 7. **Tel** 51 53 96 50.
Open Jun–Aug: 11am–7pm daily;
Sep–May: 11am–4pm Mon–Sat; Sun:
check times for services. ♿

Reinald, the first bishop of Stavanger, was an Englishman from Winchester, where St Swithun had been a bishop in the 9th century. During the reign of King Sigurd Jorsalfar, Reinald was given the means to construct a cathedral. The imposing Romanesque nave was completed around 1100, and dedicated to St Swithun, who thus became the patron saint of Stavanger.

After a fire in 1272, the cathedral was rebuilt with a magnificent Gothic choir which it still has today. About the same time, the Gothic eastern façade and the Bishop's Chapel were added. The two pyramid-shaped towers on the eastern façade date from 1746. The Baroque pulpit with its biblical motifs was, according to legend, created by the Scottish immigrant Anders (Andrew) Smith in 1658. The stained-glass paintings behind the altar are by Victor Sparre and were installed in 1957.

Along with Nidarosdomen in Trondheim (see p203), this is a remarkable example of a medieval cathedral.

🏛 **Stavanger Museum**

Muségaten 16. **Tel** 51 84 27 00. **Open** 15 Jun–15 Aug: daily; 1 Sep–14 Jun: 11am–4pm Tue–Sun. **Closed** Dec, some public hols. ♿🖼📷📷

Four museums on different sites make up Stavanger Museum. The main building houses a zoological exhibition and the old canning factory, located on Ovre Strandgt 88, has been restored to recreate a factory environment from the 1920s. Nedre Strandgt 17 & 19 are the only former retail stores in the town that are perfectly preserved, and are now the home of the Maritime Museum.

Bronze lur from Hafrsfjord

VISITORS' CHECKLIST

Practical Information
County of Rogaland. 🗺 117,000.
ℹ️ Domkirkeplassen, 51 85 92 00.
🎷 May Jazz (May), Fishing Festival (early Jun), Glamat Food Festival (end July), Chamber Music Festival (Aug).
🌐 **regionstavanger.com**

Transport
✈ 12 km (7 miles) SW of the centre. 🚆 🚌 Jernbaneveien 3.
🚌 Østre Havn.

🏛 **Museum of Archaeology**

Peder Klows Gate 30A. **Tel** 51 83 10 00.
Open Sep–May: 11am–8pm Tue, 11am–3pm Wed–Sat, 11am–4pm Sun; Jun–Aug: 10am–5pm Mon–Fri, 11am–5pm Sat & Sun. 📷📷📷

This museum focuses on ancient man and his environment, from prehistoric times to the Middle Ages. Artifacts from Rogaland include excavated settlements, rock carvings and rune stones. The collection includes two 3,000-year-old, 1.5-m (5-ft) long, bronze lurs, wind instruments discovered in Hafrsfjord.

Stavanger Town Centre

① Gamle Stavanger
② Norsk Hermetikkmuseum
③ Stavanger Sjøfartsmuseum
④ Valbergtårnet
⑤ Norsk Oljemuseum
⑥ Domkirken
⑦ Stavanger Museum

0 metres 300
0 yards 300

Wide horizons and a small place of worship on the Jæren plains

❷ Egersund

County of Rogaland. 🚶 14,000. 🚉
🚌 ⛴ 𝒾 Jernbaneveien 18, 51 49
27 44. 🎏 Lighthouse Festival (early
May), Opening of Summer-Egersund
(early Jun), Egersund Festival (1st wk
Jul). 🅦 reisemal-sydvest.no

When the sea is rough,
Egersund is the only good
natural harbour along the
Jæren coast to provide shelter.
It is Norway's largest fishing
harbour, but picturesque old
white wooden houses still perch
on the steep rocks around the
wharves. The cruciform church
dates from 1620.

The cultural history museum,
Dalane Folkemuseum, is
located at Slettebø, once the
residence of a high-ranking
civil servant. Handicrafts, old
farming tools and industrial
equipment are on display.

Environs
At Eide, glazed earthenware –
once a major local industry – is
exhibited in a former faience
factory (part of the Dalane
Folkemuseum). Northwest of
Egersund is a waterfall, **Fotland-
sfossen**, with salmon steps.

The agricultural and industrial
region of **Jæren** is flat for
Norway. There are some sandy
beaches, but no islands to
protect the shore. The towering
Eigerøy lighthouse presides
over the coast.

🏛 **Dalane Folkemuseum**
2 km (1 mile) N of town centre.
Tel 51 46 14 10. **Open** mid-Jun–
mid-Aug: daily; other times by prior
arrangement. 🚗

❸ Lysefjorden

County of Rogaland. 🚌 ⛴ car ferry
Stavanger–Lysebotn, 4 hrs. 𝒾 Turistinformasjonen, Stavanger, 51 85 92 00.

The breathtaking Lysefjorden
cuts through the mountains like
the blow of an axe. Only in a
few places is the starkness of
the mountain sides interrupted
by some sparse greenery and a
solitary farm. About 12 km
(7 miles) from its mouth is
the spectacular **Preikestolen**
(Pulpit Rock),
an overhanging
platform. Dropping
597 m (1,959 ft) to
the fjord, it is a popular
site for base jumping
(parachuting from a fixed
object). For those less
adventurous, the view from
the top, reached by footpath,
is dizzying enough.

At the inner end of the fjord,
the **Lyseveien** road features
27 hairpin bends with views of
Kjerag peak, 1,000 m (3,281 ft)

Dramatic Preikestolen (Pulpit Rock)
towering over Lysefjorden

above the water. South of
Lysefjorden is Frafjorden and
the 92-m (302-ft) high waterfall
of **Månafossen**.

❹ Suldal

County of Rogaland. 🚶 4,000. ⛴
𝒾 Turistinformasjonen, Sand, 52 79
05 60. 🎏 Ryfylke Festival (Jun),
St Olaf Celebration (4th week Aug).
🅦 suldal-turistkontor.no

The famous salmon river,
Suldalslågen, flows into
Sandsfjorden through the town
of Sand. Here, beside a waterfall
is **Laksestudioet** (the Salmon
Studio), where a glass wall
enables visitors to watch the
salmon and trout as they
negotiate the cascade on their
journey up river. There is also
an exhibition on the history
of salmon fishing. The heritage
of the English "salmon lords"
can be seen throughout
Suldal valley in the grand
manor houses that they
had constructed along
the river toward the end of
the 19th century. At the
**Kolbeinstveit
Museum**, further
up the river, is a
collection of old
wooden cottages, smoke
houses, mills, storage houses
on stilts, and the Guggendal loft
and storehouse, dating from
1250. From here, a road inland
leads to **Kvilldal Kraftstasjon**,
Norway's largest power station.

At the eastern end of the
river, steep mountains on
each side of the water form
the mighty **Suldalsporten**
(Suldal gateway), creating a
narrow sound before leading
into the lake, Suldalsvattnet,
from where the river springs.

Laksestudioet in Suldal

🎣 **Laksestudioet**
Sand town centre. **Tel** 52 79 05 60.
Open 15 Jun–31 Aug: daily; other
times by prior arrangement. 🚗 📷

🏛 **Kolbeinstveit Museum**
17 km (11 miles) E of Sand. **Tel** 52 79
29 50. **Open** end Jun– mid-Aug: Tue–
Sun. 🚗 📷

🏛 **Kvilldal Kraftstasjon**
Soldalsosen. **Open** by prior
arrangement. 🚗 📷 call Suldal
Tourist Office, 52 79 05 60. ♿

❺ Utstein Kloster

County of Rogaland. **Tel** 51 72 47 05.
Open May–mid-Sep: Tue–Sun (Jul
also Mon). **Closed** some public hols.

On the island of Mosterøy,
northwest of Stavanger, is the
12th-century monastery, Utstein
Kloster. It stands on what was
originally a royal estate from the
time of King Harald Hårfagre.
Around 1265, it was presented to
the Augustinians and remained
in their ownership until the
Reformation, when it became
the property of Norwegian and
Danish aristocrats.

   The monastery, surrounded
by a large estate of 139 farms,
has been well preserved despite
fires and attacks. In 1935 the
buildings were taken over by
the state and restored as a
national monument.

❻ Karmøy

County of Rogaland. 🌄 39,400. ✈
🚌 ⛴ ℹ Turistinformasjonen,
Stratsråd Vinjes Gate 25, 52 01 08 20.
🎪 Viking Festival (Jun), Skude Festival
(1st week Jul), Fisheries Festival (4th
week Jul). 🖥 **visitkarmoy.no**

The 30-km (19-mile) long island
of Karmøy lies like a shield
against the sea (the Old Norse
word *karmr* means protection).
On the inside is the Karmsundet,
a shipping channel that was
part of the ancient *Nordvegen*
(Northern passage), from which
the word *Norge* (Norway) is
derived. By the bridge to the
island, stone megaliths known
as the Five Wayward Virgins
guard the sound. It is said that
they were raised over the five

Haugesund, looking out across Karmsundet

sons of a monarch who fought
the king of Avaldsnes, where
there was a royal estate (870–
1450). The area's many burial
mounds are proof that
Avaldsnes was an important
prehistoric centre.

   Olavskirken (St Olav's Church)
was built at Avaldsnes by King
Håkon around 1250. Next to the
church leans the Virgin Mary's
Sewing Needle, a 7.5-m (25-ft)
high stone pillar. The nearby
island of **Bukkøya** hosts a
reconstructed Viking estate. Iron
Age stone pillars can be seen
at Åkrahavn on the western
side of Karmøy.

   On Karmøy's southern tip
lies the whitewashed town of
Skudeneshavn with a museum
at **Mælandsgården**. Karmøy's
main town is Kopervik.

🏛 Mælandsgården
Skudeneshavn. **Tel** 52 84 54 60. **Open**
20 May–20 Aug: Mon–Fri & Sun; other
times by prior arrangement. 🎨 🎞

❼ Haugesund

County of Rogaland. 🌄 31,000. ✈
Karmøy, 13 km (8 miles) S of town
centre. 🚌 ⛴ Hurtigbåtterminalen.
ℹ Strandgt 171, 52 01 08 30.
🎪 Sildajazz (Aug), Norwegian Film
Festival (Aug), Harbour Festival (Aug).
🖥 **visithaugesund.no**

The three seagulls in the town's
coat of arms are a symbol of
Haugesund's seaside location,
and its fishing and shipping
industries, which have aided the
town's development. This is a
young town, but the area has
important historical connections.
To the north is the burial mound
of **Haraldshaugen**, where King
Harald Hårfagre was buried
around 940. Norway's National
Monument (Norges Riks-
monument) was erected on this
site in 1872 to commemorate
1,000 years of a united Norway.

   Haugesund has museums, a
gallery and a town hall, which
is richly adorned with works
of art. It is a popular town for
congresses and festivals.

   Out to sea in the west, and
with a good boat connection,
is the island of **Utsira**, renowned
for its rich bird life.

🏠 Haraldshaugen
3 km (2 miles) N of Haugesund town
centre. 🚌

🏝 Utsira
1 hr 20 min W of Haugesund by boat.
🏛 Municipality of Utsira, 52 75 01 00.
🌄 230. ⛴ timetable, 47 88 01 44
(Turistinformasjonen, Haugesund).

…eneshavn, a pretty coastal settlement on Karmøy

The Rosendal estate in Hardanger, Norway's only barony

❽ Baroniet Rosendal

County of Hordaland. **Tel** 53 48 29 99.
🚌 from Bergen, Haugesund and
Odda. **Open** guided tours May–Aug:
daily; Sep–May: by prior arrangement.
🅿️ 🚻 🎟️ 🖼️ 🎁 **W** baroniet.no

In 1658 a big wedding was
celebrated at Kvinherad
between Karen Mowatt and
the Danish aristocrat Ludvig
Rosenkrantz. The groom was
the highest ranking admini-
strator in the then fiefdom of
Stavanger and war commis-
sioner for Norway. The bride
was one of Norway's richest
heiresses at the time. Among
the many wedding gifts was the
estate of Hatteberg, where the
couple built a small Renaissance
palace, Rosendal, in 1665.

The estate became a barony
in 1678. In 1745 it was sold
to Edvard Londeman of
Rosencrone and remained in
the family until it was given
to Oslo University in 1927.

The magnificent garden,
dating from the 1660s, was
extended in the 19th century to

The library in the baronial palace on the
Rosendal estate

include a landscaped park with
Gothic towers, fairy-tale houses
and walls. At the same time the
palace interior was modernized.
It contains a number of
artworks, among them Meissen
porcelain, a French Gobelin
(1660) and Norwegian paintings
in the National Romantic style.

Nearby is **Kvinherad Kirke**, a
fine Gothic church with Baroque
interiors (1250).

❾ Hardanger-fjorden

County of Hordaland. 🚌 🛈 Ulvik
Tourist Information, 56 52 63 60.
W hardangerfjord.com

Hardangerfjord stretches 180
km (112 miles) from the island
of Bømlo in the North Sea to
Odda. The main fjord extends to
Utne, at the tip of the Folgefonn
peninsula, where it forks into a
number of tributaries. The
largest of these are Sørfjorden,
Eidfjorden and Ulvikfjorden.

The glacier, **Folgefonna**, lies
1,600 m (5,249 ft) above the
fjord with arms extending down
to 500 m (1,640 ft). One of these,
Bondhusbreen, resembles an
almost vertical, frozen waterfall
tumbling toward Mauranger,
with the Furebergsfossen
waterfall nearby. On the
western side of the Folgefonn
peninsula are Jondal and
Utne. Jondal has a ferry quay
and museum, **Det Gamle
Lensmannshuset** (the Old

Sheriff's House). Utne is home to
the cultural heritage museum,
Hardanger Folkemuseum,
which gives an idea of how life
was lived in the region in the
18th and 19th centuries.

Nordheimsund and Øystese
are tucked in a bay on the
northwestern side of the fjord,
near the suspension bridge
across Fyksesundet. Both are
popular tourist resorts. At
Øystese there is a museum
featuring the work of the
sculptor Ingebrigt Vik.

🏛️ **Det Gamle Lensmannshuset**
Viketunet, Jondal, RV550. **Tel** 53 66 95
00. 🚻 **Open** by prior arrangement.
🅿️ 🎟️ 🖳

🏛️ **Hardanger Folkemuseum**
Utne. **Tel** 53 67 00 40. **Open** daily.
🅿️ 🎟️ 🖳 🛖

Captivating scenery around the
meandering Hardangerfjorden

❿ Sørfjorden

County of Hordaland. 🚌 🛈 Odda
Tourist Information, 53 65 40 05.

The longest arm of
Hardangerfjorden is Sørfjorden,
which runs along the eastern
side of the Folgefonn peninsula.
On its western side, below the
1,510-m (4,954-ft) high peak
of Aganuten, is the cultural
heritage site of **Agatunet**, with
32 medieval timber houses, and
Lagmannsstova, a court house
with a basement prison, dating
from 1300.

In the region of **Ullensvang**,
where the fjord villages of
Lofthus and Kinsarvik are found,
Sørfjorden is at its most scenic,
especially in spring when more
than 200,000 fruit trees bloom
on the slopes. Nearly one-fifth
of all fruit trees in Norway grow
here. The district has always
been a centre of prosperity.
This is where the monks fro

the Lysekloster monastery near Bergen grew fruit in the Middle Ages. They educated the farmers, as did the clergyman Niels Hertzberg (d.1841).

The Gothic-style Ullensvang church dates from the early Middle Ages. Its stone walls are 1.4-m (5-ft) thick. In the garden of Hotel Ullensvang is Edvard Grieg's composing hut, where he wrote *Spring* and parts of *Peer Gynt*.

Around the industrial town of **Odda** are a number of beautiful waterfalls, including Låtefoss, with a fall of 165 m (541 ft), and the 612-m (2,008-ft) high Langfoss.

🏛 **Agatunet**
25 km (16 miles) N of Odda. **Tel** 53 66 22 14. **Open** mid-May– mid-Aug: daily; other times by arrangement.

⓫ Eidfjord

County of Hordaland. 🏔 1,000. 🚌
ℹ Ostangvegen 1, 53 67 34 00.
🔲 visiteidfjord.no

The scenery around Eidfjord is dramatic. Almost vertical valleys have been scoured out by glaciers and rivers. The Bjoreia river flows through the valley of Måbødalen to **Vøringsfossen**, a dramatic waterfall that plunges 145 m (476 ft) into a formidable gorge extending down toward upper Eidfjord.

The main road through the valley passes through a series of unexciting tunnels, while cyclists and pedestrians can travel on the old road cut into the gorge. A footpath up **Måbøgaldane**

comprises 1,500 steps and 125 bends. A bridleway leads to Vøringsfossen.

Hardangervidda Natursenter, a nature centre containing information about the Hardanger mountain plateau, is at Sæbø.

🏛 **Hardangervidda Natursenter**
7 km (4 miles) E of Eidfjord. **Tel** 53 66 59 00. **Open** Apr–Oct: daily; other times by prior arrangement.

Hotel in the lush fjord landscape of Ulvik

⓬ Ulvik

County of Hordaland. 🏔 1,200. 🚌
🚢 summer only. ℹ Ulvik town centre, 56 52 63 60. 🎣 Fish Festival (Jul), Poetry Festival (Sep), Norwegian Cultural Traditions (mid-Sep), Accordion Festival (Oct). 🔲 visitulvik.com

The village of Ulvik sits at a softly curving bow at the inner end of a small fjord. It is almost as if the glacier made a special effort to leave a particularly rich type of soil here; terraced farms rise from the fjord with their lush green fields and abundant

orchards. A 19th-century church stands on the site of a 13th-century stave church. Its altarpiece dates from the Middle Ages.

The area is ideal for hiking and winter sports. The impressive waterfall of **Røykjafossen** is at Osa, about 10 km (6 miles) from Ulvik.

⓭ Voss

County of Hordaland. 🏔 14,000.
🚉 🚌 ℹ Vangsgata 20, 40 61 77 00.
🎵 Vossajazz (weekend before Easter), Extreme Sport Festival (4th week Jun), Traditional Food Festival (1st week Oct), Osa Festival (mid-Oct).
🔲 visitvoss.no

Isolated until the arrival of the railway in 1883, Voss is today the largest winter sports resort in Western Norway. It has chair lifts, ski lifts and a cable car, **Hangursbanen**, which rises 660 m (2,165 ft) into the mountains. The beautiful landscape attracts visitors all year round.

The resort's cultural heritage museum, **Voss Folkemuseum**, focuses on items of historical interest found in Finnesloftet, a building thought to date from around 1250. The museum incorporates the farmstead of Mølstertunet, complete with 16 well-preserved, 400-year-old buildings.

Voss Kirke (1270) is a Gothic-style church with fine interiors.

🏛 **Voss Folkemuseum**
Mølsterveien 143. **Tel** 56 51 15 11.
Open May–Sep: daily; Oct–Apr: Mon-Fri & Sun. **Closed** public holidays.

Traditional farmhouses in the Voss region

⑭ Bergen

Granted town status by King Olav Kyrre in 1070, Bergen was at the time the largest town in the country and the capital of Norgesveldet, a region that included Iceland, Greenland and parts of Scotland. Even after Oslo became capital of Norway in 1299, Bergen continued to grow as a trading centre, especially for the export of dried fish during the era of the Hanseatic League trading company. Following a period of decline in the 15th century, the town entered a new era of prosperity as a centre for shipping. Bergen is a World Heritage City, and in spite of its size, still has all the charm and atmosphere of a small town.

Vågen harbour, with the Bryggen area on the right

Exploring Bryggen Area

The area north of Vågen harbour, between the Bryggen quay and Øvregaten, a street lined with Hanseatic buildings, has some of Bergen's most important sights. Old and new architecture provide an exciting backdrop to the hustle and bustle of the streets and the quays busy with ships loading and unloading their goods.

🏛 Norges Fiskerimuseum

Sandviksboder 23. **Tel** 55 69 96 01. **Open** Jun–Aug: daily; Sep–May: Sun–Fri. 🅿 🅲 🕭 🖳 🎦

Situated on the waterfront, Norges Fiskerimuseum (the Norwegian Fishing Museum) provides a comprehensive insight into Norway's long-established fishing industry, including the management of its resources. Fishing boats and equipment through the ages are on show. Other displays cover various types of fishing, such as herring and cod fishing, fish farming, whaling and sealing. Historical films are also screened, along with a slideshow.

🏛 Håkonshallen and Rosenkrantztårnet

Bergenhus Festning. **Tel** 55 31 60 67. Håkonshallen: **Open** daily. Rosenkrantztårnet: **Open** 15 May–Aug: daily; Sep–14 May: Sun. **Closed** public holidays. 🅿 🅲

Håkonshallen is a Gothic ceremonial hall built by King Håkon Håkonsson for the coronation and wedding in 1261 of his son, Magnus Lagabøter. It is thought to be the largest secular medieval building remaining in Norway. It was built of local stone

Rosenkrantztårnet, a fortified residence built in 1560

with architectural details in soapstone. Originally, the ceremonial hall was situated on the top floor. The middle storey comprised living and working areas and the cellar was used for provisions. In 1683 the hall was redesigned to store corn. The building was later restored and decorated with paintings by Gerhard Munthe, but in World War II it suffered extensive damage. The restoration work that followed created a grand venue for official functions.

The Rosenkrantz Tower is, along with Håkonshallen, part of the old fortifications of Bergenhus (Bergen Castle). The main building dates from the same period as Håkonshallen. The present tower was built in 1560 by the governor of Bergen Castle, Erik Rosenkrantz, as a defence post and residence.

🏛 Mariakirken

Dreggen. **Tel** 55 31 59 60. **Closed** closed for renovation until 2015. 🅿

Part of the chancel in Mariakirken (St Mary's Church) dates from the 11th century, around the time when Bergen was granted town status by King Olav Kyrre. As such it is the city's oldest surviving church.

In Hanseatic times the German merchants used it as their special church and richly embellished it. There is a splendid Baroque pulpit dating from 1677, decorated with constellations and Christian virtues such as Faith, Hope, Love, Chastity, Truth and Temperance.

🏛 Bryggens Museum

Dreggsalmenning 3. **Tel** 55 58 80 10. **Open** daily. **Closed** some public holidays. 🅿 🅲 by arrangement. 🕭 🖳 🎦

The excavations that were begun after a catastrophic fire on Bryggen in 1955 were the largest of their kind in northern Europe. Bryggens Museum is based on the archaeological findings and provides a picture of everyday life in a medieval town. It features a wealth of well-presented material, both graphic and written, including runic inscriptions from the 14th century.

The old wharf, Bryggen, with the Hanseatiske Museum on the right

🏛 Bryggen
North side of Vågen harbour.
Jun–Aug, 55 55 20 00.
The old timber warehouses
on the northern side of the
harbour were originally known
as Tyskebryggen (the German
Quay), because for 400 years, until
1754, they were at the hub of
Hanseatic trade in Norway. Long
before the German Hansa traders,
this part of the town had been
a trading centre for fish and fish
products. On many occasions
over the centuries the medieval
gabled houses facing the harbour
have been ravaged by fires. The
last, in 1955, left only 10 gables
standing. Today, Bryggen is a
centre for artists and a popular
restaurant area. It is included in
UNESCO's World Heritage List.

🏛 Hanseatiske Museum
Finnegårdsgaten 1A. **Tel** 55 54 46 90.
Open daily. **Closed** 1 Jan, 17 May, 24,
25 & 31 Dec. summer.
Established in 1872, the
Hanseatisk Museum is located
in one of Bryggen's expansive
German merchant's houses
dating from the end of the
Hanseatic era. A number of
traders were housed here, next
to rooms for drying fish, offices
and storerooms. The early
18th-century interiors give a
good impression of how they
lived and worked.

A separate section of the
museum features four assembly
rooms used for eating,
entertainment, learning, and
for keeping warm in winter.

Bergen Town Centre
1. Norges Fiskerimuseum
2. Håkonshallen and Rosenkrantztårnet
3. Mariakirken
4. Bryggens Museum
5. Bryggen
6. Hanseatiske Museum
7. Korskirken
8. Domkirken
9. Buekorpsmuseet
10. Akvariet
11. Kulturhuset USF
12. Den Nationale Scene
13. Vestlandske Kunstindustri- museum
14. Bergen Kunstmuseum
15. Bergens Kunsthall
16. Grieghallen
17. Bergen Museum: De Kulturhistoriske Samlinger
18. Bergen Museum: De Naturhistoriske Samlinger
19. Bergens Sjøfartsmuseum

| 0 metres | | 400 |
| 0 yards | | 400 |

For keys to symbols *see back flap*

Exploring Bergen Town Centre

Bergen has at its heart the peaceful haven of Lille Lungegårdsvann, a lake surrounded by parkland and trees and, in summer, a colourful show of rhododendrons. On its western side is Festplassen, the city's festival square with its music pavilion. Festplassen opens into the boulevard, Ole Bulls Plass, that leads to Den Nationale Scene (the National Theatre). A few blocks to the north of Festplassen is the famous Fisketorget (the Fish Market). Bergen's most important art galleries are situated on the south side of the lake.

The fish market taking place on Torget, Monday to Saturday

Buekorps boys parading in Bergen town centre

🏛 Korskirken

Korskirkealmenningen. **Tel** 55 59 32 70. **Open** Mon–Sat. 🏛 noon Wed.

To the east of Torget and the innermost part of Vågen is Korskirken (the Church of the Cross). It was erected around 1100, originally as a three-aisled Romanesque long church. A south wing was added in 1615 and a north wing in 1623, thus creating its characteristic cruciform plan. A beautiful Renaissance portal with Christian IV's monogram graces the northern end.

🏛 Domkirken

Kong Oscars Gate 22. **Tel** 55 31 58 75. **Open** daily. 🏛 11am Sun; Jun–Aug: 9:30am Sun in English.

Bergen's cathedral was originally a parish church, Olavskirken, dating from the latter half of the 12th century. When a Franciscan monastery was established in Bergen around 1250, the church was taken over by the monks. As with so many other buildings

in Bergen, Olavskirken was ravaged by fire. On one occasion it was restored by Geble Pederssøn, who in 1537 became Norway's first Lutheran bishop. He built a new tower and installed the clock above the western entrance. The multi-sided Gothic choir with its high windows has remained untouched. The church's large Rieger organ has 61 stops.

The poet Ludvig Holberg, considered the founder of modern Norwegian literature, was a pupil at the nearby Latin School from 1698 to 1702.

🏛 Buekorpsmuseet

Murhvelvingen. **Tel** 55 90 45 30. **Open** Sat & Sun. **Closed** mid-Jul–mid-Aug.

The 400-year-old Muren (Wall Gate), originally the private home of a high-ranking official Erik Rosenkrantz, houses the Buekorpsmuseet. The Buekorps (literally "Bow Corps") are boys' brigades. They originated in the 1850s in Bergen, and have

become a very special part of the town's traditions.

At one time the various Buekorps were rivals, but today their drills and marches are more lighthearted. Their longbows, banners and historic photographs are on display in the museum.

🐟 Akvariet

Nordnesbakken 4. **Tel** 55 55 71 71. **Open** daily. **Closed** 17 May, 24, 25 Dec. 🐟 📷 🚻 📱

The aquarium is one of Bergen's most popular attractions. It contains Europe's largest collection of sea and freshwater fish and invertebrates. Inside, there are nine large and 40 smaller tanks. In addition, there are two pools with sea birds, seals and penguins. One section is dedicated to the development of marine life.

Every day 3 million litres (666,000 gals) of seawater are pumped up from the depths of Byfjorden through 8,000 m (26,246 ft) of plastic pipes.

Young spectator at the penguin pool in Akvariet (the Aquarium)

🏛 Kulturhuset USF

Georgernes Verft 12. **Tel** 55 30 74 10. **Open** daily. 🚻 📱

The former United Sardines Factories (USF) have been renovated to house the USF Cultural Centre, a large

Den Nationale Scene (the National Theatre), an imposing landmark in the heart of Bergen

contemporary arts complex featuring music, films, theatre, dance, visual arts and handicrafts. It is rare in Norway to find such a varied artistic programme under one roof.

🎭 Den Nationale Scene

Engen 1. **Tel** 55 54 97 00. Box office: **Open** Mon–Sat. 🚻 📖

The first Norwegian National Theatre has its roots in Det Norske Theater in Bergen, founded in 1850 by the violinist Ole Bull. Henrik Ibsen was a director here for six years from 1851, followed by Bjørnstjerne Bjørnson from 1857 to 1859.

Since 1909 the theatre has been housed in a splendid Art Nouveau building. The original theatre called, "the Theatre in Engen", was destroyed by bombs in 1944. Den Nationale Scene has played a significant role in Norwegian theatre history, both with its repertory and its plays.

🏛 Vestlandske Kunstindustrimuseum

Nordahl Bruns Gate 9. **Tel** 55 33 66 33. **Open** 15 May–15 Sep: daily; 16 Sep–14 May: Tue–Sun. **Closed** public hols. 🖼 ⬜ 🚻 ✏ 📷

Also known as Permanentum, the West Norway Museum of Decorative Art features a collection of Norwegian and foreign treasures. It includes local goldsmith art and Buddhist/Chinese art from the Sung, Ning and Ching dynasties. Also on show is a violin made by Gaspar de Salo in 1562, which belonged to the musician Ole

Bull (*see p181*). Contemporary arts and crafts are exhibited too. Part of the museum are the country mansion at Damsgård Hovedgård and the former Alvøen paper factory, situated 5 km (3 miles) and 20 km (12 miles) from Bergen respectively. The factory has been preserved complete with workers' cottages and the owner's mansion, now a museum.

🏛 Bergen Kunstmuseum

Rasmus Meyers Allé 3 & 7, Lars Hilles Gate 10. **Tel** 55 56 80 00. **Open** mid-May–mid Sep: daily; mid-Sep–mid-May: Tue–Sun. **Closed** public hols. 🖼 🚻 ⬜ 🔷 📷 **W kodebergen.no**

The three main collections of Bergen Art Museum are based in two buildings by Lille Lungegårdsvann. Bergen Billed-galleri (the City Art Collection) was established in 1878 and expanded in 2000 with a new building in Lars Hilles Gate.

It is known as Vestlandets Nasjonalgalleri (Vestlandet's National Gallery) and has a fine collection of Norwegian and European visual art from the 19th and 20th centuries. Of great historical interest are J F L Dreier's paintings of old Bergen mainly from the 1830s.

In the same building is the Stenersen Collection. It has works by Munch, Picasso, Miró, Klee and Utrillo, among others, donated by Rolf Stenersen (*see p62*).

The focus of the Rasmus Meyer Collection is on Norwegian and Scandinavian works, 1760–1915, including Edvard Munch, J C Dahl, Adolf Tidemand, Harriet Backer and Christian Krohg. They were donated to Bergen by the art collector Rasmus Meyer, who died in 1916.

Note the decorative Rococo interiors with ceilings painted by Mathias Blumenthal.

Scene from Bergen's Inner Harbour, J C Dahl (1834), Bergen Kunstmuseum

🏛 Bergen Kunsthall

Rasmus Meyers Allé 5. **Tel** 55 55 93 10.
Open Tue–Sun. **Closed** some public
hols. 🎨 ♿ 📷 📹 **kunsthall.no**

The Bergen Art Association was
established in 1838. It holds
nine or ten exhibitions of
contemporary art every year at
Bergens Kunstforening, of which
the prestigious Festspillutstilling
(May–August) is the most
important. The building was
designed by the architect Ole
Landmark (1885–1970).

🎵 Grieghallen

Edvard Griegs Plass 1. **Tel** 55 21 61 50.
Box office: **Open** Mon–Sat and before
events. ♿ 📷 🎨

Bergen's modern concert hall,
Grieghallen, was opened in
1978. Designed by the Danish
architect Knud Munk, it is the
country's largest auditorium
with 1,500 seats. A smaller hall
accommodates 600 people.
Grieghallen is also used for
opera, ballet, theatrical
productions and congresses.
It is the central venue for events
during the Bergen International
Festival (Festspillene). The
festival has been held every year
in May and June since 1953,
attracting artists from all
over the world.

Bergen Filharmoniske Orkester
(the Bergen Philharmonic
Orchestra), also known as
Harmonien, holds concerts
every Thursday at Grieghallen
from September to May. The
orchestra was founded in 1765.

Whales skeletons in Bergen Museum's De Naturhistoriske Samlinger

🏛 Bergen Museum: De Naturhistoriske Samlinger

Muséplass 3. **Tel** 55 58 29 20.
Open Tue–Sat. **Closed** public hols.
🎨 📷 ♿

Comprehensive botanic,
geological and zoological
collections as well as a botanical
garden and plant house make
up Bergen Museum's De
Naturhistoriske Samlinger (the
Natural History Collection).
Both the natural history and the
cultural history collections were
founded by the president of the
Norwegian Parliament, W F K
Christie, in 1825. The natural
history collection is housed in
an imposing hillside building
on Nygårdshøyden dating from
1866 and 1898. It was designed
by J H Nebelong and H J Sparre.

The zoological section shows
stuffed animals, birds and fish
from all over the world,
including an exhibition titled
"Wild Life in Africa".

The geological section
features an eye-catching
mineral collection with fine
samples from the Bergen region
and further afield. The life of
our early ancestors is exposed
in "The Evolution of Man". Other
exhibits focus on "Oil Geology"
and "The Green Evolution – the
Development of the Planet".

The botanical gardens, known
as Muséhagen, are a mass of
blooms in the summer months.
In the greenhouses tropical

Grieghallen (1978), venue for the annual Bergen International Festival

For hotels and restaurants in this area see pp230–33 and pp238–47

plants can be seen all year round. Muséhagen was established in 1897 and over the years it has amassed 3,000 different species. The selection of plants is particularly large and varied. When the gardens outgrew their original site new gardens and an arboretum were created at Milde about 20 km (12 miles) south of the town centre.

The extensive research carried out by Bergen Museum's natural and cultural history departments paved the way for the establishment of Bergen University, which today has more than 17,000 students, seven faculties and 90 institutes.

Romanesque bench from Rennebu church, De Kulturhistoriske Samlinger

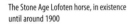

The Stone Age Lofoten horse, in existence until around 1900

⬚ Bergen Museum: De Kulturhistoriske Samlinger

Håkon Sheteligs Plass 10. **Tel** 55 58 31 40. **Open** Tue–Sun. **Closed** public hols. 🅿 ♿ 🆆 visitbergen.com

Situated opposite the Natural History Museum, on the other side of Muséhagen, is the Cultural History Collection of Bergen Museum, De Kulturhistoriske Samlinger.

The collection occupies a large building designed by Egill Reimers in 1927.

Innovative displays focus on Norwegian culture and folk art as well as some exhibits from foreign cultures.

The unusual archaeological collection is based on finds from the counties of Hordaland, Sogn and Fjordane, and Sunnmøre in Western Norway. Exhibits are shown in themed displays such as "The Stone Age" and "The Viking Age". "Legacy from Europe" depicts the cultural exchange between Norway and the rest of Europe.

The colourful motifs of Norwegian folk art are explored in the "Roses and Heroes" exhibition, while beautiful local folk costumes *(see pp28–9)* are part of the "Rural Textiles" collection.

"Ibsen in Bergen" describes Henrik Ibsen's inspirational work at Det Norske Theatre (the National Theatre) in Bergen from 1851–7.

Anthropological exhibitions include "Between Coral Reef and Rain Forest", "Indians, Inuit and Aleut: the Original Americans" and "Eternal Life: Egyptian Mummies".

The museum is noted for its collection of ecclesiastical art, including Russian icons.

⬚ Bergens Sjøfartsmuseum

Håkon Sheteligs Plass 15. **Tel** 55 54 96 00. **Open** Jun–Aug: daily; Sep–May: Mon–Fri, Sun. 🅿 ♿ 🆆 bsj.uib.no

The story of Norwegian shipping from early times can be explored in Bergens Sjøfartsmuseum (Maritime Museum), with special emphasis on Vestlandet. The ground floor covers the era up to 1900; the first floor focuses on the 20th century and the age of steam and motor craft, to the present day.

There is an extensive model collection of Viking ships and various working boats, including the deckhouse of the training ship *Statsraad Lemkuhl*. "Coastal and Fjord Boats" describes life aboard for the crew and passengers of the vessels working up and down the coast.

The Maritime Museum was founded in 1921. It is housed in a striking stone building, with an atrium in the centre, designed by Per Grieg and completed in 1962.

In summer children of all ages congregate in the atrium to play with remote-controlled model boats. On the "promenade deck" visitors are invited to relax in deckchairs and look out over one of Bergen's busiest harbours.

Bergens Sjøfartsmuseum, left, and De Kulturhistoriske Samlinger

Bergen Further Afield

When the old town of Bergen was combined for administrative purposes with a number of outlying districts in 1972, it increased in size tenfold. The "new" Bergen now includes fjords and mountains, lakes and plateaus, forests and fields, valleys and rivers, and a wealth of architectural treasures.

The funicular railway Fløybanen, with panoramic views of Bergen

🏛 Gamle Bergen

Elsesro, 5 km (3 miles) N of town centre. **Museum Tel** 55 39 43 00. **Open** 12 May–1 Sep: daily. 🏛 ⬜ 🅿 ⬜

An open-air museum, Gamle Bergen was founded in 1949 on the old patrician site of Elsesro in Sandviken. The buildings, furniture, domestic utensils, clothes and everyday items on show provide a graphic illustration of life in Bergen in the 18th and 19th centuries. Workshop interiors and shops give an idea of the living conditions of the different social classes, such as sailors and high-ranking officials, artisans and labourers. Around the houses are streets and paths, squares and alleys designed to imitate the style of the times.

≋ Fløyen

Vestrelidsalmenningen 23. Kabelbanen: **Tel** 55 33 68 00. **Open** daily. 🅿 📷

The mountain of Fløyfjellet, commonly known as Fløyen, is named after the weather-vane at its summit. This has stood here for centuries, showing wind strength and direction for the benefit of sailors entering and leaving the harbour below. It has been blown down, burnt down, even torn down, but each time it has been rebuilt.

A funicular, opened in 1918, carries passengers 320 m (1,050 ft) to the summit from the city centre near Fisketorget. At the top there are wonderful panoramic views and numerous paths for walking.

Fløyen is one of seven peaks around Bergen. Another is

Fantoft stave church, rebuilt after a serious fire in 1992

Ulrikken (642 m/2,106 ft), celebrated in Bergen's anthem by Johan Nordahl Brun.

🏛 Fantoft Stavkirke

Fantoftveien 46, 5 km (3 miles) S of town centre. **Tel** 55 28 07 10. **Open** mid-May–mid-Sep: daily. 📷

Fantoft Stavkirke (stave church) was originally built in Fortun in Sogn county around 1150. It was moved to Fantoft in 1882 where it was embellished with dragon finials and high-pitched roofs. In June 1992 the church was destroyed by fire, but was rebuilt within three years.

It was not uncommon for Norway's wooden stave churches to be relocated. Often they were transported by sea as it was more practical than using country roads. Vang Stavkirke in Valdres, for example, was sold to the king of Prussia. In 1842 it was driven across Filefjell mountain to Sogn from where it was shipped to Germany.

🏛 Gamlehaugen

Gamlehaugveien 10, 5 km (3 miles) S of town centre. **Tel** 55 92 51 20. **Open** Jun–Aug: Mon–Fri. **Closed** when King is in residence.

The King of Norway's official residence in Bergen is Gamlehaugen in Fjøsanger, just south of the city. It was built in 1901 by Professor Jens Zetlitz Kielland for the shipping magnate, Christian Michelsen, and is situated on a hill overlooking the land-locked fjord of Nordåsvannet.

Michelson was Norway's first prime minister after the break up of the union with Sweden in 1905. On his death the property was purchased by the state. It features Swiss chalet-style woodcarvings and contains mostly Norwegian paintings

Gamle Bergen, an open-air museum depicting life in old Bergen

from the late 1800s. English-style landscaped gardens surround the house.

🏛 Troldhaugen

Troldhaugveien 65, 8 km (5 miles) S of town centre. **Tel** 55 92 29 92. **Open** Jan–Mar: Mon–Fri; Apr–Nov: daily. **Closed** Dec. 🌿 🚻 🚾 ♿ 🚽 🖼 🏛

Troldhaugen, the former home of the composer Edvard Grieg and his wife Nina, is beautifully situated on a promontory on Nordåsvannet. According to local legend, it was a haunt for trolls, hence the name Troldhaugen, meaning "Hill of Trolls".

The couple lived here for 22 years from 1885 until Grieg's death in 1907. Designed by Schak Bull, the interior walls are bare timber in keeping with Norwegian building traditions. The house remains as it was in 1907, complete with Grieg's Steinway piano, a gift on the occasion of the couple's silver wedding anniversary in 1892, and other mementos.

The small Composer's Cabin, where several of Grieg's influential compositions came to fruition, was built in 1892. There is also a museum and a 200-seat concert hall, Troldsalen, which is used for musical recitals. Hidden in a cave facing the lake are the graves of Grieg and his wife.

Edvard and Nina Grieg's home, Troldhaugen, in Fana

🏛 Lysøen

25 km (16 miles) S of town centre. **Tel** 56 30 90 77. **Open** mid-May–Aug: daily; Sep: Sun; groups by arrangement. 🌿 🚻 ♿ 🚽 🏛

Ole Bull was one of the greatest violin virtuosos of his time, and in Norway he is regarded as a

Interior of Lysøen, violinist Ole Bull's idiosyncratic summer residence

national hero. He was born in Bergen in 1810 and died at his summer island retreat, Lysøen, in 1880. The extraordinary house, his "little Alhambra", was built in 1872 and extended in 1905.

Bull designed his summer residence himself with the help of the architect C F von der Lippe. The house is inspired by a diversity of classical and medieval styles. Built in Norwegian pine, it features a tower with a Russian Orthodox onion dome and a Moorish door, and is exotically decorated both inside and out.

Lysøen is a testament to its capricious creator. In 1973 Bull's great-granddaughter, Sylvia Bull Curtis, donated the property to the Society for the Preservation of Norwegian Ancient Monuments. The island can be explored through its many footpaths.

🏛 Bergens Tekniske Museum

Thormøhlens Gate 23. **Tel** 55 96 11 60. **Open** Sun and, by arrangement, Mon–Fri. 🌿 ♿

The old Trikkehallen (tram hall) in Møhlenpris houses Bergens Tekniske Museum (Technical Museum). Its exhibitions on energy, industry, communications and science appeal to all ages.

There are displays of technical appliances ranging from vehicles and washing machines to fire-fighting equipment and military materials. Here it is possible to find vintage cars, motorcycles, buses, a working smithy, a printing-press and an early steam-engine and carriages. The museum also has model boats and a model railway.

Edvard Grieg

Edvard Grieg (1843–1907) was Norway's foremost composer, pianist and conductor. He was born in Bergen in 1843. At the age of 15, on the advice of the violinist Ole Bull, he enrolled at the Leipzig Conservatory to study music. Later, in Copenhagen, he came into contact with influential composers of the time, such as Niels Gade. Grieg's aim was to create a Norwegian style of music for which he sought inspiration in folk music. Among his most well-known works is the music for Ibsen's *Peer Gynt*. In 1867 he married his cousin, the soprano singer Nina Hagerup.

Edvard Grieg
1843–1907

⑮ Sognefjorden

The longest fjord in Norway, Sognefjorden extends for 206 km (128 miles) from the archipelago in the west to Skjolden below Jotunheimen in the east. It reaches a maximum depth of 1,308 m (4,291 ft). While the outer section maintains a fairly straight line from the west to the small town of Balestrand, the inner section branches in all directions. Five large arms subdivide into long fjord fingers and it is these innermost sections that have the most to offer the visitor. Each one is well-known for its beauty: Fjærlandsfjorden, Sogndalsfjorden and Lustrafjorden to the north, Årdalsfjorden to the east, and Lærdalsfjorden, Aurlandsfjorden and Nærøyfjorden to the south. They encompass some of the finest natural scenery to be found anywhere in the world.

Kvinnefossen
The River Kvinna plunges 120 m (394 ft) down toward Sognefjorden – a beautiful sight when the river is full.

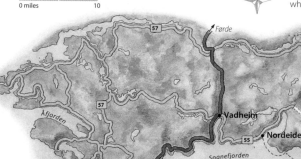

Map locations: Førde, 57, 13, 57, Vadheim, Nordeide, 55, Dragsvik, Balestrand, Vangsn, Åfjorden, Sognefjorden, Rysjedals-vika, Lavik, Ortnevik, 55, Rutledal, Sognefjorden, Oppedal, 57, E39, 13

0 kilometres 20
0 miles 10

Balestrand
At the scenic resort of Balestrand, surrounded by a landscape changing from benign to harsh, is the Kviknes Hotel, a grand timber structure dating from 1877 *(see p186)*.

KEY

① **Urnes stave church** is on the World Heritage List of sites worthy of preservation *(see p188)*.

② **Borgund** (1150) is the only stave church to have remained unaltered since the Middle Ages *(see p187)*.

③ **Undredal stave church** *(p186)*.

Vik
There are two churches near the village of Vik: Hopperstad stave church (1130) and a Romanesque stone church from the Middle Ages. At the ferry landing stage stands a 26.5-m (87-ft) high statue of the mythical hero, Fridtjov, a gift from Kaiser Wilhelm II.

Sogndal

Sogndalsfjorden is surrounded by orchards, which look spectacular in spring. At Sogndalsfjøra, a local trade centre and traffic junction, the main road through the village is appropriately named Gravensteinsgata after an apple *(see p186)*.

VISITORS' CHECKLIST

Practical Information
County of Sogn and Fjordane.
🏠 6,600. ℹ Kulturhuset,
Sogndal, 99 23 15 00. 🎭 Balejazz
(2nd week May), Cheese Festival
in Vik (mid-Jun), Jotunheimen
Cycle Race (mid-Jul).
W sognefjord.no

Transport
🚌 🚉 ⛴

Norsk Villakssenter

On the banks of Lærdalselva – a famous salmon river – is the Norwegian Wild Salmon Centre *(see p186)*.

Key

━━ Major road
━━ Minor road
--- Ferry route
═══ Tunnel

Flåmsbanen

The spectacular trip on the Flåmsbanen railway line offers stunning views of mountains, waterfalls, picturesque hamlets and curious-looking rock formations on the short but steep route between Flåm and Myrdal *(see p186)*.

Aurland and Aurlandsdalen

Aurlandsvangen is the starting point for excursions on the fjord and into the mountains – by car, boat, train, and on foot *(see p186)*.

Exploring Sognefjorden

The first tourists came to Sognefjorden more than 150 years ago. In those days travel was exclusively by cruise ship. Today, a number of ferries, the Hurtigruten cruises *(see p275)*, local buses and the E16 and 55 roads enable an ever-increasing number of visitors to enjoy the area.

Vassbygdvatnet, a picturesque lake in the Aurland valley

Balestrand

It is the scenery above all that makes Balestrand such a popular destination on Sognefjorden. Wide and fertile strips along the shore are set against a backdrop of mighty peaks and glaciers.

The view from Balholm in the centre of town takes in the entire fjord and it is this that has attracted tourists from all over the world, laying the foundations for the early development of hotels and communications. The chalet-style Kviknes Hotel *(see p233)*, built in 1877, has a hall with dragon carvings and a large art collection.

There are two Viking burial mounds at Balholm, dating from AD 800. One mound has a statue of Bele, a legendary king in Nordic mythology who was the father of Ingeborg, Fridtjof's beloved.

Sogndal

In the orchard-dotted area of Sogndal, the village of **Kaupanger** features a stave church dating from the 12th century. Nearby is the open-air Sogn Folkemuseum, with 32 historic buildings.

At the innermost tip of the fjord is the fast-flowing River **Årøyelva**, renowned for physically demanding salmon fishing (record catch: a fish weighing 34 kg/75 lb). The path

of the salmon is blocked by Helvetesfossen (Hell's waterfall), and the fishing spots below are wryly named "the platforms of despair".

Lærdal

The small centre features a collection of beautiful timber buildings from the 18th and 19th centuries. On the banks of the river Laerdalselva, the **Norsk Villakssenter** (Norwegian Wild Salmon Centre) has an observatory for viewing the salmon. The only way to get from Laerdal to Aurland used to be either by a long detour via ferry, or the so-called Snøveien ("snow road") over the mountains. Open in summer only, it is lined by snow drifts even then. Since November 2000, however, a 24.5-km-

(15-mile-) long tunnel cuts across deep under the mountain, linking the E16 near Laerdalsøyri with Aurlandsvangen and Flåm.

🏛 **Norsk Villakssenter**
Lærdal. **Tel** 57 66 67 71.
Open May–Sep: daily. 🎦 ♿ 🏠 ⚡

Aurland

The charming little town of **Aurlandsvangen** retains some of its original buildings, among them the guesthouse Åbelheim (1770). The 13th-century stone church contains stained-glass panels by Emanuel Vigeland. This is a good starting point for the hiking routes in the Aurland valley. Across the Aurland fjord, the 601 road leads to **Undredal**, Norway's smallest stave church.

Further west, on the E16, is **Gudvangen**, from where a ferry plies the dramatically narrow Naerøyfjord before continuing to Kaupanger on the other side of Sognefjord.

Flåmsbanen

One of the world's most breathtaking railway journeys is the Flåmsbanen. It is just over 20 km (12 miles) long, but has an impressive height difference of 864 m (2,835 ft) between Myrdal on the mountain plateau and Flåm by the shore of Aurlandsfjord.

The railway was opened in 1942. There are 20 tunnels on the line and nine stops, each with a different panorama, including the awe-inspiring waterfall of Kjosfossen. The 50-minute journey can be taken as part of the "Norway in a Nutshell" tour *(see p274)*.

Lærdalsøyri with its wharfside buildings bordering Sognefjorden

⑯ Borgund Stavkirke

Borgund Stavkirke at Lærdal is the only stave church to have remained unchanged since the Middle Ages. Dedicated to the apostle St Andrew, it dates from around 1150 and is built entirely of wood. The interior is very simple: there are no pews or decorations, and the lighting is limited to a few small openings high up on the walls. The exterior is richly decorated with carvings, dragon-like animals in life and death struggles, dragonheads and runic inscriptions. There is a free-standing belfry with a medieval bell. The pulpit dates from the 16th century.

VISITORS' CHECKLIST

Practical Information
County of Sogn and Fjordane,
30 km (19 miles) E of Lærdalsøyri.
Tel 57 66 81 09. **Open** 1 May–10
Jun, 21 Aug–30 Sep: 10am–5pm
daily; 11 Jun–20 Aug: 8am–8pm
daily. **Closed** Oct–Apr.

w stavechurch.com

Transport
🚌 from Lærdal.

Dragonheads
The tower has a three-tiered roof. The first tier is decorated with dragonheads on the gables similar to those on the main roof.

The windows were originally simply circular openings in the outer walls.

Nave
Twelve posts (staves) around the central part of the nave support the roof. Disappearing into the semi-darkness of the roof, they give an increased sense of height.

The roofs are clad in pine shingles.

Crosses decorate the gables above the doorways and apse tower.

Altar with an altar-piece dating from 1654.

West Door
The exterior of the church is richly adorned. The decorations on the Romanesque west door show vine-like ornamentation and dragon battles.

Crosses of St Andrew border the central nave.

Roof Construction
Seen from below, the roof is composed of an intricate framework using numerous rafters and joists.

Urnes Stavkirke occupying a lofty location above Lustrafjorden

⓱ Urnes Stavkirke

County of Sogn and Fjordane.
17 km (11 miles) NE of Sogndal.
Tel 57 67 88 89. 🚌 🚢 15 min walk
from ferry. **Open** May–Sep: daily.
🏞 📷 🏊

The queen of Norway's stave churches, Urnes is also the oldest. It appears on UNESCO's list of World Heritage sites along with Røros, the Alta rock carvings and Bryggen in Bergen. Built around 1130–50, it contains beams from an 11th-century church that stood on the same site.

The most notable feature of the church is the north portal. This, too, dates from an earlier building and its carvings depict the conflict between good and evil in the form of animals engaged in battle with snakes. Such animal ornamentation is known as the "Urnes Style".

Two candlesticks on the altar in metal and enamel date from the 12th century and were made in Limoges in France.

Also situated in the district of Luster is Sogn's most beautiful stone church, Dale Kirke, built in 1250.

⓲ Jostedalsbreen

County of Sogn and Fjordane. 🚌
ℹ️ Jostedalen Tourist Information,
57 68 32 50; Jostedalsbreen National
Park Centre, Oppstryn, 57 87 72 00.
🅆 **jostedal.com**

The largest glacial area in continental Europe, Jostedalsbreen is 100 km (62 miles) long and 15 km (9 miles) wide. Together with Jostefonn, which used to be joined to it, it covers

486 sq km (188 sq miles). Its highest point is Lodalskåpa (2,083 m/6,834 ft).

The ice cap sends fingers into the valleys below. In the 18th century a number of these glacial spurs extended so low they destroyed cultivated fields, but since then they have receded.

The starting points for glacier tours include Jostedalen (Nigardsbreen and Bergsethbreen glaciers), Stryn (Briksdalsbreen glacier) and Fjærland (Bøyabreen and Supphellebreen glaciers).

On the innermost reaches of the sparkling green Fjærlandsfjorden is **Norsk Bremuseum** (the Norwegian Glacier Museum), an award-winning "activity museum" devoted to snow, ice, glaciers, glacier hiking and climbing. A panoramic film presentation takes the viewer on a virtual glacier experience.

🏛 Norsk Bremuseum
Fjærland. **Tel** 57 69 32 88. **Open** Apr–
Oct: daily; other times by prior
arrangement. 🏞 🦽 🛢 🏠
🅆 **bre-museum.no**

⓳ Førde and Jølster

County of Sogn and Fjordane.
🚠 10,800. 🚏 🚌 ℹ️ Langebruveien
20, 57 72 19 51. 🎭 International Folk
Music Festival (1st week Jul).
🅆 **sunnfjord.no**

The town of Førde lies at the heart of the county of Sogn and Fjordane. It has a cultural centre, **Førdehuset**, housing an arts centre and gallery, library,

cinema and theatre. The **Sunnfjord Museum**, comprising 25 buildings from around 1850, is also in Førde.

East of the town, in Vassenden, there is another cultural heritage museum, **Jølstramuseet**, with houses from the 17th century. Nearby is the tranquil rural museum **Astruptunet**, where the painter Nikolai Astrup once lived (1880–1928).

This area is renowned for fishing. The Jølstra river has a salmon ladder dating from 1871. The river flows from Jølstravatnet lake, which teems with large trout. There is good fishing in Gularvassdraget.

🏛 Sunnfjord Museum
9 km (6 miles) E of Førde. **Tel** 57 72 12
20. **Open** Jun–Aug: daily; Sep–May:
Mon–Fri. **Closed** public hols. 🏞
📷 by arrangement. 🦽 🛢 🏠

🏛 Jølstramuseet
20 km (12 miles) E of Førde. **Tel** 57 72
71 85. **Open** 15 Jun–15 Aug: Sat &
Sun; other times by arrangement.
🏞 📷 🏠

🏛 Astruptunet
26 km (16 miles) E of Førde. **Tel** 57 72
67 82. **Open** late May–mid-Aug: daily;
mid-Aug–Sep: Thu, Sat & Sun. 🏞 📷
🦽 🏊 🛢 🏠

⓴ Nordfjord

County of Sogn and Fjordane.
🚏 Sandane. 🚌 🚢 ℹ️ Stryn Tourist
Information, 57 87 40 40. 🎭 Summer
Skiing Festival in Stryn (Jun); Fish
Festival in Stryn (Jul). 🅆 **nordfjord.no**

The northernmost fjord in Sogn and Fjordane county is Nordfjord. Measuring 110 km

Astruptunet, home of the painter and graphic artist Nikolai Astrup

For hotels and restaurants in this area see pp230–33 and pp238–47

The hamlet of Ervik on Stad peninsula

(68 miles) in length, Nordfjord extends from Måløy in the west inland to Stryn near the border with eastern Norway.

The area around Stryn has been a sought-after destination since 1850 when the first English outdoor enthusiasts arrived. Opportunities abound for mountaineering, glacier hiking, skiing and fishing.

There are several glacier spurs from Jostedalsbreen. Briksdalsbreen can be reached by horse and carriage from Briksdal (tickets, Stryn tourist office); the one on Strynfjell is accessible by chairlift from Stryn Summer Ski Centre.

Loen, on Lovatnet lake, was devastated in 1905 when part of the mountain, Ramnefjellet, fell into the lake causing an enormous wave. It killed 63 people and destroyed houses.

From Stryn there are two roads around Nordfjorden. The northernmost (RV15) runs along Hornindalsvatnet, Europe's deepest lake, to **Nordfjordeid**, a centre for the breeding and rearing of Norwegian Fjord Horses. The southernmost (RV60, E39) passes through Innvik, Utvik and Byrkjelo to Sandane. The **Nordfjord Folkemuseum** in Sandane comprises 40 18th- and 19th-century houses.

Ⅲ Nordfjord Folkemuseum
Sandane. **Tel** 57 88 45 40. **Open** 1 May–30 Jun: Mon–Fri; 1 Jul–15 Aug: daily; 16 Aug–12 Sep: Mon–Fri; 13 Sep–30 Apr: by prior arrangement. **Closed** public hols. ⬛️ summer only.

㉑ Selje and Stad

County of Sogn and Fjordane.
⛰️ 3,100. 🚌 🚢 ℹ️ Selje Tourist Information, 57 85 66 06.

From Måløy on the outer reaches of Nordfjorden it is not far to the Stad peninsula and **Vestkapp**, one of Norway's westernmost points. Here stands "Kjerringa", a 460-m (1,509-ft) high rock that plunges steeply into the water. From the top there are panoramic views out to sea. Below, in **Ervik**, a chapel commemorates the loss of the coastal passenger ferry, St Svithun, in World War II.

On the island of Selje are the ruins of a monastery built by Benedictine monks in the 12th century. The monastery is dedicated to St Sunniva, daughter of an Irish king, who fled east to escape betrothal to a heathen chieftain. Her party came ashore on Selje and sought refuge in a cave.

㉒ Geirangerfjorden

County of Møre and Romsdal. 🚌
ℹ️ Geiranger, 70 26 32 14.
🌐 **geiranger.no**

The inner part of Storfjorden divides to form two of Norway's best-known fjords: Tafjorden to the north and Geirangerfjorden to the south.

The 16-km (10-miles) long Geirangerfjorden is the quintessential fjord. A strip of dazzling green water snakes its way to the village of Geiranger, below precipitous mountains with farms perched on the slopes and cascading waterfalls.

The RV63, Grotli-Geiranger-Åndalsnes, is known as the Golden Route. Driving south from Geiranger, the road passes Flydalsjuvet, an overhanging cliff providing a picture-postcard view of the fjord and surrounding mountains. It continues to the mountain hut of Djupvasshytta, from where it is possible to reach the summit of Dalsnibba (1,476 m/4,843 ft).

North from Geiranger, a dramatic part of the Golden Route leads to Norddalfjorden. This is known as Ørnveien (the Eagle's Road) and offers panoramic vistas. A ferry leads across the fjord to Valldal, where the next section, known as Trollstigveien (the Trolls' Path), leads to Åndalsnes (see p186) via some dizzying hairpin bends and great views.

Tafjorden was hit by a tragedy in 1934 when an immense rock from Langhammaren crashed into the fjord, causing a huge wave which killed 40 people in Tafjord.

Geirangerfjorden, known as the pearl of the Norwegian fjords

㉓ Ålesund

Møre and Romsdal. 🗺 42,300. ✈ 🚌
🚢 ℹ Keiser Wilhelms Gate 11, 70 15
76 00. 🎭 Dragon Boat Festival (mid-
Jun), Ålesund Theatre Festival (2nd
week Jul), Ålesund Boat Festival (2nd
week Jul), Norwegian Food Festival
(4th week Aug). 🆆 **visitalesund.com**

The centre of Ålesund was
destroyed in a catastrophic
fire in 1904. Fellow Europeans
came quickly to the rescue
with help and donations and
in just three years the town
was rebuilt almost entirely
in the Art
Nouveau style.
For this reason,
Ålesund occupies
a very special
place in the
architectural
history of Europe.
It spans several
islands linked by
bridges. Today, it
is an important
fishing port, but
Ålesund did not receive town
status until 1848.

Art Nouveau detail,
Ålesund

The area of Borgund, now
part of Ålesund, was a market
town and centre of the
Sunnmøre region from around
1200. From the mountain lodge,
Fjellstua, there is a panoramic
view over the town.

Ålesund Museum has one
section devoted to the town
and another to the Arctic.
Sunnmøre Museum consists
of 40 historic houses and

The Trolltindane, described in legends as a troll wedding procession

boathouses and 30 different
types of fishing boats.

Southwest of Ålesund is
the island of **Runde**. It is
renowned for its nesting cliffs,
which provide a habitat for
around one million seabirds.
There are 100,000 puffins and
50,000 kittiwake pairs, and the
rare northern gannet can also
be seen here.

The Dutch East India vessel
Akerendam went down off
the island in 1725 with a
valuable cargo. Divers have
subsequently recovered a large
haul of gold and silver coins
from the wreck.

🏛 Ålesund Museum
Rønnebergs Gate 16. **Tel** 70 12 31 70.
Open daily. **Closed** some public hols.
🅿

🏛 Sunnmøre Museum
5 km (3 miles) E of town centre.
Tel 70 17 40 00. **Open** mid-May–23
Jun: Mon–Fri & Sun; 24 Jun–Aug: daily;
Sep–mid-May: Mon, Tue, Fri, Sun.
🅿 🎥 summer. 🖥 📷

Runde
30 km (19 miles) SW of town centre.
🚌 to Fosnavåg. 🚢 ℹ 70 01 37 90.

㉔ Åndalsnes

County of Møre and Romsdal.
🗺 7,700. ✈ Molde. 🚉 🚌
ℹ Jernbanegt 1, 71 22 16 22.
🎭 Norwegian Mountain Festival
(mid-Jul), Sinclair Festival (2nd week
Aug). 🆆 **visitandalsnes.com**

Where the Rauma river enters
Romsdalsfjorden lies the resort
of Åndalsnes, terminus of the
Raumabanen railway. On the
eastern side of the valley is
Romsdalshorn (1,554 m/5,098 ft).
Opposite are the ragged peaks
of **Trolltindane** (1,795 m/5,889 ft)
with a sheer vertical cliff to
the valley. This is a popular spot
for mountaineering.

Trollstigveien (the Troll's
Path) is a thrilling drive with
11 breathtaking hairpin bends
between Åndalsnes and
Valldalen to the south. Along
the road there are views of
the waterfalls, Stigfossen and
Tverrdalsfossen. Each summer
a ski race, *Trollstigrennet*, is held
on the Trollstigheimen pass.

㉕ Molde

County of Møre and Romsdal.
🗺 24,000. ✈ 🚉 to Åndalsnes, then
bus. 🚌 🚢 ℹ Torget 4, 71 20 10 00.
🎭 Molde International Jazz Festival
(mid-Jul), Bjørnsson Festival (mid-Aug).
🆆 **visitmolde.com**

Known as the "Town of Roses"
for its rose gardens and lush
vegetation, Molde is an
attractive fjord-side place. The
term "Molde Panorama" is used
to describe the scenery here:

Bird's eye view of Ålesund from Fjellstua

For hotels and restaurants in this area see pp230–33 and pp238–47

from Varden it is possible to see 87 snow-covered peaks on a clear day. In July Molde is the site of a lively jazz festival, attracting top musicians from abroad.

The outdoor museum of timber houses, **Romsdalsmuseet**, also contains a fascinating collection of national costumes.

Fiskerimuseet (the Fisheries Museum), on the island of Hjertøya near Molde, focuses on the cultural history of the coastal population.

While on the Molde peninsula, it is worth visiting both the fishing village of **Bud**, which faces the infamous stretch of sea known as Hustadvika, and the marble cave of **Trollkyrkja** (Troll Church), some 30 km (19 miles) to the north.

On Eresfjorden is a waterfall, **Mardalsfossen**, with the highest unbroken vertical drop in Northern Europe, 297 m (974 ft). It is at its most dramatic from 20 Jun–20 Aug.

Atlanterhavsveien (the Atlantic Road), from Averøy toward Kristiansund, is spectacular. It passes over islets and skerries across 12 low bridges that have been built right out in the sea.

🏛 **Romsdalsmuseet**
Per Adams Vei 4. **Tel** 71 20 24 60. **Open** Jun–mid-Aug: daily. 🅿 🔲 🖥 📷

🏛 **Fiskerimuseet**
Hjertøy (boat from Molde in summer). **Tel** 71 20 24 60. **Open** end-Jun–mid-Aug: daily. 🅿 🔲

㉖ Kristiansund

County of Møre and Romsdal.
🚹 17,000. ✈ 🚌 ⛴ 🛈 Kongens Plass 1, 71 58 54 54. 🎭 Opera Festival (Feb), Children's Festival (Apr), Nordic Light Festival (Apr/May), Music Festival (Jun) 🌐 visitkristiansund.com

From the cairn on the island of Kirkelandet there is a magnificent view over this and the two other islands that comprise Kristiansund.

The sheltered harbour, always busy with boats, gave rise to the coastal settlement of Lille-Fossen, or Fosna. In 1742 when it acquired town status it was

The Atlantic Road, winding its way across islands and sounds

renamed Kristiansund. Between 1830 and 1872 the town developed into the country's biggest exporter of *klippfisk* (salted, dried cod). Kristiansund was almost entirely destroyed by bombs in April 1940. The reconstruction created a new image for the town, with modern buildings such as the town hall and the church in many different colours.

Nordmøre Museum contains a special exhibition of archaeological finds from the Fosna culture, as well as a fisheries exhibition.

North of Kristiansund is the tiny island of **Grip**, inhabited only in summer. All that remains of this former fishing community is a 15th-century stave church in which the population took refuge from the fearsome storms. There is a boat connection in summer.

Long ago Kristiansund could only be reached by boat, but today there is an airport and road connections to the mainland. To the southeast the RV70 passes through a number of tunnels and

over bridges as the landscape becomes more mountainous. **Tingvoll Kirke**, also known as Nordmøre Cathedral, dates from around 1200 and has an exquisite altarpiece and runic inscriptions on the chancel wall.

At Tingvollfjorden the road passes Ålvundeid, where there is a side road to the magnificent **Innerdalen** valley with the Dalatårnet peak and the mountains of Trollheimen. At the end of the fjord is **Sunndalsøra**, where the famous salmon and sea trout river Driva has its mouth.

🏛 **Nordmøre Museum**
2 km (1 mile) N of town centre. **Tel** 71 58 70 00. **Open** Mar–Nov: Tue–Fri & Sun; other times: Tue–Fri. 🅿 🔲 🅰 partly. 🔲 🖥 📷

🏕 **Grip**
14 km (9 miles) N of Kristiansund. 🖥 ⛴ from Kristiansund. 🛈 Turistinformasjonen, Kristiansund, 71 58 54 54.

🏰 **Tingvoll Kirke**
55 km (32 miles) SE of Kristiansund. **Tel** 71 53 03 03. **Open** May–Sep: daily (concert 5pm Sat). 📷

Kristiansund with its colourful houses and imposing church

TRØNDELAG

A journey over Dovrefjell to Trøndelag was a challenge in times gone by. The route from southern to northern Norway across the mountains, undertaken by kings and pilgrims of old, was arduous. Travellers would breathe a sigh of relief after negotiating the notorious Vårstigen (Spring Path) and arriving safely on the Trøndelag side of the fells. Today's roads and railway lines make this an easy trip.

Most of those crossing Dovrefjell, whether royalty, pilgrims or merchants, would have been heading for the city of Trondheim (Nidaros as it was known originally). All roads lead to Trondheim, so it was said. Throughout history Trondheim has been the capital of central Norway, and for a time it was the first capital of the kingdom.

Trondheim was founded by King Olav Tryggvason, who built a house at the mouth of the Nidelv river in 997. However, it was the martyrdom of the future saint, King Olav Haraldsson, at the infamous Battle of Stiklestad in 1030, that led to Kristkirken (the Church of Christ) being built. It became the cathedral, Nidarosdomen, a focal point for pilgrimage in Scandinavia.

South Trøndelag is a mainly agricultural region with coniferous and deciduous forests tailing off into scraggy mountain woodland in the fells. North Trøndelag is dominated by coniferous forests. The style of farm building, especially around Trondheimsfjorden, is unique to the Trøndelag region. The main buildings, *trønderlåner*, are long, narrow, double-storied houses, usually painted white and situated at a high point in the terrain.

The mountainous regions of Børgefjell, Sylene, Rørosvidda, Dovrefjell and the spectacular Trollheimen have much of interest in the way of outdoor activities, hunting and fishing. Many of the rivers offer excellent salmon-fishing from the banks and boats.

The offshore islands, particularly the archipelago of Vikna, are easily accessible. Here, bird-watching and sea fishing are among the attractions.

Sculptures decorating the west front of Nidarosdomen in Trondheim, with Olav the Holy at the centre

◀ Former copper-mining town Røros, now a UNESCO World Heritage site

Exploring Trøndelag

Trøndelag is made up of two counties, Nord-Trøndelag and Sør-Trøndelag, which together comprise 12.7 percent of Norway. In the west, the mainland and the fjords on the Norwegian Sea coast are mostly protected by a wide band of rocky isles. The landscape around Trondheimsfjorden is generally level, fertile farmland. In the east, near Kjølen and the Swedish border, there are large mountain plateaus with high peaks such as the Sylene range. Great tracts of forest cover the central area. For centuries pilgrims have flocked to the cathedral in Trondheim and to Stiklestad, where Olav the Holy died in battle in 1030.

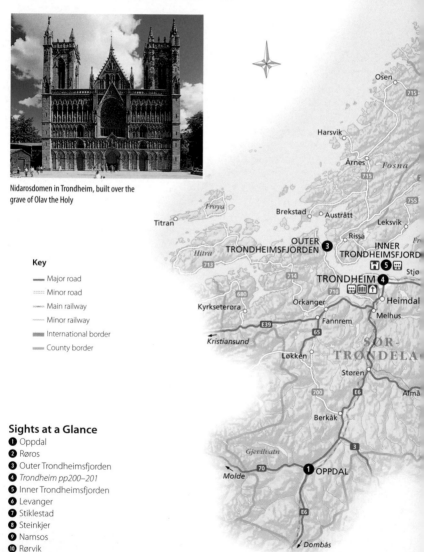

Nidarosdomen in Trondheim, built over the grave of Olav the Holy

Key

— Major road

⋯⋯ Minor road

⋙ Main railway

— Minor railway

▬ International border

— County border

Sights at a Glance

❶ Oppdal

❷ Røros

❸ Outer Trondheimsfjorden

❹ *Trondheim pp200–201*

❺ Inner Trondheimsfjorden

❻ Levanger

❼ Stiklestad

❽ Steinkjer

❾ Namsos

❿ Rørvik

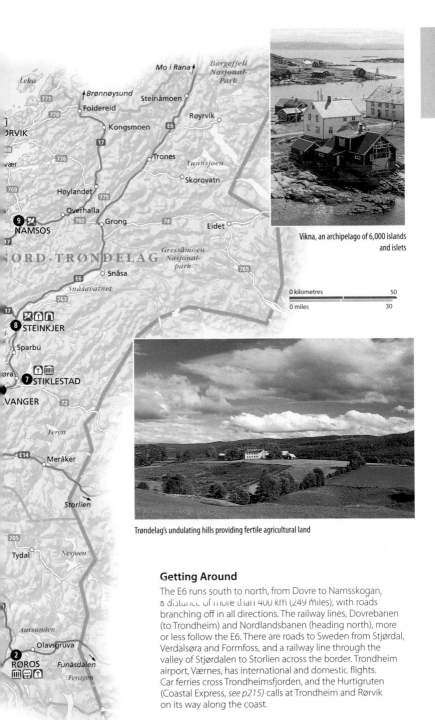

Vikna, an archipelago of 6,000 islands and islets

| 0 kilometres | | 50 |
| 0 miles | | 30 |

Trøndelag's undulating hills providing fertile agricultural land

Getting Around

The E6 runs south to north, from Dovre to Namsskogan, a distance of more than 400 km (249 miles), with roads branching off in all directions. The railway lines, Dovrebanen (to Trondheim) and Nordlandsbanen (heading north), more or less follow the E6. There are roads to Sweden from Stjørdal, Verdalsøra and Formfoss, and a railway line through the valley of Stjørdalen to Storlien across the border. Trondheim airport, Værnes, has international and domestic flights. Car ferries cross Trondheimsfjorden, and the Hurtigruten (Coastal Express, see p215) calls at Trondheim and Rørvik on its way along the coast.

❶ Oppdal

County of Sør-Trøndelag. ⛰ 6,300.
🚉 🚌 𝒊 O. Skasliens Vei 15, 72 40
04 70. 🎿 Oppdal Free-ride Challenge
(Easter), Fell Market (Sep), Vintersleppet
(1st week Dec). 🅦 oppdal.com

Oppdal is a vibrant tourist
centre all year round, but
particularly in winter.

Its excellent winter sports
facilities include 200 km
(124 miles) of ski slopes, a cable
car and ski lifts, ski huts, cafés and
restaurants. The skiing season
starts with the Vintersleppet
festival, while the off-piste Free-
ride Challenge race attracts
daring skiers around Easter.

The town occupies a beautiful
mountain setting. It is an
important junction on the
Dovrebanen railway and has
good road connections.

The open-air **Oppdal
Bygdemuseum** has a fine
collection of old houses of
cultural interest. Outside the
town, at **Vang**, there is a large
Iron Age burial ground.

Oppdal is the starting point
for the journey northward to
Vårstigen (the Spring Path),
the old pilgrims' route *(see p193)*,
through Drivdalen valley and
to Dovrefjell National Park
(see pp142–3).

From Festa bridge in the
west, the toll road heads
north to **Gjevilvasshytta**, an
elegant tourist lodge
incorporating Tingstua, the
old courthouse from Meldal.

🏛 **Oppdal Bygdemuseum**
Museumsveien. **Tel** 72 42 15 50. **Open**
end Jun–mid-Aug: Tue–Sun. 🎫 ♿ 🏠

The 17th-century copper-mining town of Røros, preserved for posterity

❷ Røros

County of Sør-Trøndelag. ⛰ 5,500.
✈ 🚉 🚌 𝒊 Peder Hiorts Gate 2,
72 41 11 65. 🎿 Røros Market (3rd
week Feb), Winter Festival (mid-Mar),
Garpvukku Historical Play (2nd week
Aug). 🅦 rorosinfo.com

Life in Røros revolved around
the copper mine founded in
1644 on a bleak site 600 m
(2,000 ft) above sea level. The
mining town, complete with
its turf-roofed timber cottages,
church and company buildings,
has survived, unscathed by
fire, to become a UNESCO World
Heritage site.

The town's most prominent
landmark is the Baroque church
of Bergstadens Ziir, built in
stone in 1780. Inside there is an
imposing Baroque organ, pulpit
and altar, and pews where the
community were obliged to sit
in strict hierarchical order.

Bergskrivergården, the mining
company director's house, is
situated on Bergmannsgata, the
street that was home to those
who had wealth and status. The
mining museum, **Rørosmuseet**,
housed in the reconstructed
Smeltehytte (the old smelter),
has models of the mines and
smelting processes.

About 13 km (8 miles) east
of Røros is the disused mine
of **Olavsgruva**, featuring
Bergmannshallen, a concert
hall and theatre built inside
the mountain. There are tours
of the old mineshafts.

Røros has been immortalized
in books by Johann Falkeberget
(1879–1967), who lived locally.
His story about a peasant girl
who transported copper ore
was made into a film, *An-Magritt*,
starring Liv Ullmann.

🏛 **Rørosmuseet**
Sleggeveien. **Tel** 72 41 61 55.
Open daily. **Closed** some public hols.
🏠 ♿ 🖥 🏠

🏚 **Olavsgruva**
13 km (8 miles) E of town centre.
Tel 72 40 61 70. **Open** tours only.
🏠 🎫 Sat. 🖥 🏠

Oppdal, a region of farmland and mountains renowned for winter sports

❸ Outer Trondheimsfjorden

County of Sør-Trøndelag.
🛈 Trøndelag Reiseliv, 73 84 24 40.
W trondelag.com

Approaching Trondheimsfjorden from the west, the shipping channel passes to the inside of Hitra, the largest island in southern Norway. The fjord itself begins at the promontory of Agdenes.

To the north of the fjord entrance lies the flat and fertile region of Ørlandet, site of the castle of **Austrått**. The estate was owned by the powerful Rømer family. Inger Ottesdatter Rømer, who died in 1555, is the main protagonist in Ibsen's play *Lady Inger of Østeråt*.

The land then passed by marriage to the Bjelke family. The castle was built in Renaissance style between 1654 and 1656 by Chancellor Ove Bjelke, brother to Jørgen Bjelke, who in 1658 recaptured the county of Trondheim from Sweden.

Austrått appears rather stern and unwelcoming from the outside, with its soapstone doorway and coats of arms. Inside, it is quite the opposite. A brightly painted inner courtyard is embellished with carved pillars in the form of female figures – "the wise and foolish virgins".

West of Trondheim, an arm of the fjord leads to Orkanger near the Thamshavnsjenbanen (Thamshavn railway line). Here,

electric locomotives and three-person carriages from 1908 are on display. Pride of place at **Orkla Industrimuseum** (Orkla Industrial Museum) is given to the lavish train carriage used by the king. The museum also includes a mining museum and the old mines of Gammelgruva.

🏛 **Austrått**
Opphaug. **Tel** 72 52 18 04. **Open** Jun–mid-Aug: daily. 🅿 🅾 🅿 🅿

🏛 **Orkla Industrimuseum**
Løkken Verk (Løkken Mine).
Tel 72 49 91 00. **Open** Jun–Aug: daily; Sep–May: Mon–Fri. **Closed** public hols. 🅿 🅾 🅿 🅿 🅿 **W** oi.no

❹ Trondheim

See pp200–201.

❺ Inner Trondheimsfjorden

County of Nord-Trøndelag.
🛈 Trøndelag Reiseliv, 73 84 24 40.
W trondelag.com

On the inner Trondheimsfjorden, the Byneset peninsula west of Trondheim is the site of Gråkallen, one of the city's main areas for sports and recreation. Off Fosen Quay in Trondheim, **Munkholm** island has served as a fortress, monastery and prison. It is now a popular bathing spot.

The fjord is at its widest east of Trondheim. Here, by Vaernes airport, the reputed salmon river of Størdalselva has its mouth. Inland, along the river is **Hegra Festning.**

The island of Munkeholmen, in Trondheimsfjorden, once a prison

In 1940, General Holtermann and his soldiers – 248 men and one woman – resisted a German attack here for 23 days. Further east at **Reinå**, Engelskstuggu (the English cabin) recalls the early English salmon-fishing pioneers.

On the small island of **Steinvikholm**, off the eastern shore of the fjord, is a castle built by Archbishop Olav Engelbrektsson in 1525. He fled here with the casket of Olav the Holy *(see p204)* during the Reformation. The peninsula of **Frosta** is an old *tingsted* (assembly site). It contains Bronze Age burial mounds and petroglyphs.

🏛 **Hegra Festning**
15 km (9 miles) E of Stjørdal.
Tel Stjørdal Tourist Office, 74 83 45 80. **Open** mid-May–Sep: daily; other times by arrangement. 🅿 🅾 🅿 🅿

❻ Levanger

County of Nord-Trøndelag. 🄫 17,500.
🚉 Værnes, 50 km (31 miles) SW.
🚌 🚍 🛈 Levanger, 74 05 25 00.
🎪 Levanger Market (early Aug).
W levanger.kommune.no

In inner Trondheimsfjorden is Levanger, site of Iron Age rock carvings, burial mounds and graves. South of here, near Ekne, is **Falstad Fangeleir**, a former World War II concentration camp.

Out in the fjord is the island of Ytterøy, beyond which the Indreøy peninsula almost blocks the fjord before its end at Steinkjer *(see p204)*. Strauma on **Indreøy** is an idyllic timber-housed hamlet.

🏛 **Falstad Fangeleir**
20 km (12 miles) S of Levanger. **Tel** 74 02 80 40. **Open** Tue–Sun. 🅿 🅾 🅿

The inner courtyard at Austrått with its "wise and foolish virgins"

Aerial view of homes in the suburbs of Trondheim ▶

❹ Trondheim

According to the Saga writer, Snorre, in 997 King Olav Tryggvason decreed that there should be a town at the mouth of the Nidelva river. The town of Trondheim, then known as Nidaros, quickly became a centre for the Trøndelag region and, for a time, capital of Norway. After King Olav Haraldsson was canonized in 1031, pilgrims flocked to his shrine at the site of Nidaros cathedral. Fire and wars in the 17th century destroyed large parts of the medieval city. The modern town with its grid-like street layout was established after a catastrophic blaze in 1681.

View over Trondheim showing Nidaros cathedral in the background

Exploring Trondheim

Most of Trondheim's sights are within easy walking distance of each other. The town centre, known as Midtbyen, is almost totally surrounded by the fjord and the meandering Nidelva river. The main street, Munkegata, passes right through the heart of the town, from the cathedral of Nidarosdomen in the south to the famous fish market of Ravnkloa in the north.

After the fire in 1681, it was the military engineer Johan Caspar de Cicignon who was mainly responsible for the grid-like layout which exists even today. Yet in the narrow side streets it seems that property owners and chance also had a hand in the layout.

🏛 Erkebispegården

Kongsgårdsgaten 1B. **Tel** 73 53 91 60. **Open** Jun–Aug: daily; Sep–May: Tue–Sun. **Closed** some public hols. 🅿 🎫 ♿ partly. 🖼 📷

Erkebispegården (the Archbishop's Palace) has been a political and spiritual centre of power in Norway since soon after the introduction of Christianity. Part of the north wing of the main house dates from the 12th and 13th centuries, and was built as a fortified bishop's palace. Other parts of the structure were commissioned between 1430 and 1530. After the Reformation, the Archbishop's Palace became the private residence of the feudal overlord. It later served as a military base. In the 19th century it housed the Norwegian crown jewels (now in Nidaros cathedral).

In the museum in the restored south wing there are original sculptures from the cathedral and finds from the palace, among them the archbishop's coin workshop.

There is also an armoury, Rustkammeret, with a large collection of firearms and a section about the Norwegian resistance movement in World War II.

🏛 Trondheim Kunstmuseum

Bispegaten 7. **Tel** 73 53 81 80. **Open** Jun–Aug: daily; Sep–May: Tue–Sun. 🅿 ♿ 📷 📷

Trondheim Kunstmuseum (Museum of Art) is located close to Nidaros cathedral and the Archbishop's Residence. It contains a fine collection of paintings dating back to its precursor, the Trondheim Art Society, founded in 1845.

The most important works in the gallery are Norwegian paintings from the beginning of the 19th century until today, ranging from the Düsseldorf School to the Modernists. There is also a collection of Danish paintings that would be hard to rival outside Denmark, and an international collection of graphic art.

🏛 Nordenfjeldske Kunstindustrimuseum

Munkegaten 5. **Tel** 73 80 89 50. **Open** Jun–Aug: daily; Sep–May: Tue–Sun. **Closed** some public hols. 🅿 📷 ♿ 📷

The red-brick buildings of Katedralskolen (the Cathedral School) and Kunstindustrimuseum (the Museum of Applied Art) sit opposite one another next to the cathedral. The museum's collections include furniture, silver and textiles. In a section titled *Three Women, Three Artists*, works by the tapestry artists Hannah Ryggen and Synnøve Anker, and the glass designer Benny Motzfeld, are on show.

🎭 Trøndelag Teater

Prinsens Gate 22. **Tel** 73 80 50 00. Box Office: **Open** Mon–Sat. ♿ 📷 during performances.

The splendid Trøndelag Teater complex was completed in 1997. It comprises five separate stages, with seating for between 50 and 500 people in each auditorium, and offers a broad repertoire.

Incorporated into the theatre is the main stage from the original theatre, constructed in 1816. Before this time, the theatre-loving citizens used to perform in their own homes. Another piece of the interior, rescued from the old building, is the Art Nouveau café.

🏛 Vitenskapsmuseet

Erling Skakkes Gate 47. **Tel** 73 59 21 45. **Open** daily. 🅿 ♿ 📷 📷 📷

The collections of the Museum of Natural History and Archaeology are housed in

Trøndelag Teater combining five stages in one building

three separate buildings, named after the founders of the Royal Society of Norwegian Science (1706).

The Gerhard Schøning building traces Norway's ecclesiastical history and exhibits church interiors and religious art. The Peter Frederik Suhms building focuses on the Middle Ages.

In the Johan Ernst Gunnerus branch there are the departments of zoology and mineralogy. Special displays cover such subjects as "From the Stone Age to the Vikings" and "The Culture of the Southern Sami".

🏛 Vår Frue Kirke

Kongens Gate 2. **Tel** 73 53 84 80. **Open** Jun–Aug: Wed; other times: Sat.

The words "The holy Mary owns me" are inscribed in Old Norse on the walls of the Vår Frue Kirke (the Church of Our Lady). Built in the late 12th century, it was the only church in Trondheim to survive the Reformation. The church was originally known as Mariakirken (the Church of Mary). It has

Vår Frue Kirke, a 12th-century church near the town square

been extended on several occasions: the tower dates from 1739. The altarpiece came from Nidaros cathedral in 1837.

🏛 Bryggen

Øvre Elvehavn.

The warehouses and wharves at the mouth of the Nidelva river have been the focus of business and trading since early times. On a number of occasions the buildings were ravaged by fire.

Now restored, the colourful buildings line both sides of the river. On the city centre side in Kjøpmannsgata they are in a terraced area from where it was possible to attack the

VISITORS' CHECKLIST

Practical Information
County of Sør-Trøndelag.
🗺 165,000. 🛈 Munkegata 19, 73 80 76 60. 🎭 Festival of St Olav (4th week Jul), Norfishing (2nd week Aug).
🌐 **trondheim.com**

Transport
✈ Vaernes, 50 km (31 miles) E of town centre. 🚉 Brattøra. 🚌 Brattøra. ⛴ Pier 2.

enemy on the river with cannon fire. On the Bakklandet side of the river, they are situated in the streets of Fjordgata and Sandgata. The oldest remaining wharf dates from around 1700.

Warehouses on the Nidelva river, restored after fire and decay

Trondheim Town Centre

① Erkebispegården
② Trondheim Kunstmuseum
③ Nidarosdomen (see p203)
④ Nordenfjeldske Kunstindustrimuseum
⑤ Trøndelag Teater
⑥ Vitenskapsmuseet
⑦ Vår Frue Kirke
⑧ Bryggen
⑨ Stiftsgården
⑩ Sjøfartsmuseet

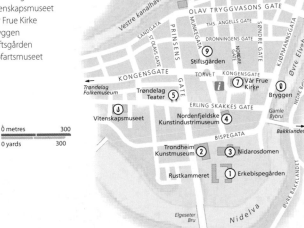

0 metres 300
0 yards 300

For keys to symbols *see back flap*

The Queen's Room in the Royal Residence, Scandinavia's largest timber building

🏛 Royal Residence

Munkegaten 23. **Tel** 73 84 28 50.
Open Jun–Aug: daily for guided
tours only. **Closed** for royal visits.

This royal residence of
Stiftsgården is one of the most
imposing old timber mansions
in Trondheim. It is an important
example of Norwegian wooden
architecture, designed by
General G F von Krogh and
completed in 1778.
The style is Rococo,
with Baroque details.

The original owner
was Cecilie Christine
de Schøller, the widow
of the privy councillor.
Connected to the royal
court in Copenhagen,
she was influenced
by foreign ideas
and was keen to build
a grand mansion in her
attempt to become the "first
lady" of Trondheim.

The building is 58-m (190-ft)
long and has 64 rooms. It was
given the name of "Stiftsgården"
when it was bought by the government in 1800 as a residence
for the chief officer of the
diocese, the *Stiftsamtmannen*.
It became a royal residence
in 1906. The dining room,
with paintings of London and
Venice by J C C Michaelsen,
is especially worth a look.

🏛 Trondheims Sjøfartsmuseum

Fjordgata 6A. **Tel** 73 89 01 10.
Open Jun–Aug: 11am–6pm daily;
Sep–May: 11am–3pm Mon–Fri,
noon–4pm Sat & Sun.

Trondheim Maritime Museum
is housed in a prison building
dating from 1725. It has a

comprehensive collection of
models of sailing ships, figure-
heads and artifacts relating to
maritime life in Trøndelag from
the beginning of the 16th
century. The exhibits include
objects rescued from the frigate
Perlen, which sank in 1781.

🏛 Bakklandet

1 km (half a mile) E of town centre.

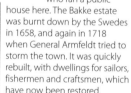

Balustrade detail, Stiftsgården

East of the Nidelva
river lies Bakklandet,
a charming quarter
with narrow, winding
streets dating back
to 1650. The area
originally belonged
to a nunnery. From
1691 it was owned
by Jan Wessel, the
father of the maritime
hero Tordenskiold,
who ran a public
house here. The Bakke estate
was burnt down by the Swedes
in 1658, and again in 1718
when General Armfeldt tried to
storm the town. It was quickly
rebuilt, with dwellings for sailors,
fishermen and craftsmen, which
have now been restored.

From the town centre,
Bakklandet can be reached
using the Old Town Bridge,
Gamle Bybro, which acquired
ts carved gates in 1861. High
above Bakkland is the fortress
of Kristiansten, built by Johan
Caspar de Cicignon in 1682.

🏛 Ringve Museum

Lade Allé 60, 4 km (2 miles) NE of
town centre. **Tel** 73 87 02 80.
Open 18 May–15 Sep: daily; other
times: Sun.

Ringve is Norway's national
museum for music and musical
instruments. It was opened in

1952, after Victoria and Christian
Anker Bachke had designated
in their will their large country
estate and collection of musical
instruments to become a
museum. The instruments had
previously been owned by Jan
Wessel, father of the maritime
hero, Peter Wessel Tordenskiold,
after whom the museum café,
Tordenskiolds Kro, is named.

The exhibition takes visitors
through the stages of musical
history, presenting its masters
and instruments to the
accompaniment of music from
each period.

The Botanical Gardens of
Ringve, surrounding the
mansion, are stocked with 2000
species of plants and trees.

🏛 Trøndelag Folkemuseum

Sverresborg Allé, 4 km (2 miles)
S of town centre. **Tel** 73 89 01 10.
Open daily. **Closed** public hols.
partly.

Featuring more than 60
buildings from Trondheim and
around, Trøndelag Folkemuseum
gives a unique insight into the
building traditions and daily life
of the region. The museum is
located next to the medieval
fortress of King Sverre, with a
splendid view over the town.

The 18th- and 19th-century
Gammelbyen (Old Town) has
been recreated with a dentist's
surgery, a grocery store and a
shop selling old-fashioned
sweets. Look out for Vikastua,
a cottage from Oppdal with an
exceptional rose-painted interior.
The stave church, originating
from Haltdalen, dates from 1170.

Trøndelag Folkemuseum focusing on the traditions of the region

Trondheim: Nidarosdomen

Built on the site of Kristkirken, over the grave of Olav the Holy (*see p204*), the oldest part of Nidaros cathedral dates from around 1320 in Norman, Romanesque and Gothic styles. The cathedral is the largest construction in Norway from the Middle Ages, 102-m (335-ft) long and 50-m (164-ft) wide. Several fires have ravaged it over time and large parts lay in ruins when restoration work began in 1869. A Gothic reconstruction has now been completed. One of the chapels houses the Norwegian crown jewels, including the crowns of the king, queen and prince.

VISITORS' CHECKLIST

Practical Information
Bispegaten 5. **Tel** 73 89 08 00.
Open May–mid-Sep: 9am–3pm
(5:30pm Jun–Jul) Mon–Fri,
9am–2pm Sat, 1–4pm Sun; mid-
Sep–Apr: noon–2:30pm Mon–Fri,
11:30am–2pm Sat, 1–3pm Sun.
🚫 ♿ ✉ ✍ 📷
w nidarosdomen.no

The main tower is 97.8 m (321ft) high.

Nave
Inspired by the architecture of Lincoln Cathedral and Westminster Abbey, the nave is 21 m (69 ft) high.

Rose Window
Gabriel Kielland created many of the cathedral's beautiful Chartres-inspired stained-glass works, including the magnificent rose window.

Northern transept from the 12th century in Romanesque style.

The altar table is in patinated bronze.

Silver Crucifix
The cross, by W Rasmussen, was donated by Norwegians in the USA for the cathedral's 900th anniversary in 1930.

West Front
The middle row of sculptures on the ornate west wall shows, from left to right, the Norwegian saints Archbishop Øystein, St Hallvard, St Sunniva and St Olav (Olav the Holy), and the heavenly virtue: Love.

The church at Stiklestad, built 100 years after the fatal battle

❼ Stiklestad

County of Nord-Trøndelag, 4 km (2 miles) E of Verdal town centre. 🚆 to Verdal, then taxi. 🚌 during Olsok feast. **W** stiklestad.no

Stiklestad is one of the most famous places in Norwegian history. It was here at a battle in 1030 that King Olav Haraldsson, later St Olav, died. The site is marked by the **Stiklestad Nasjonale Kultursenter** (National Cultural Centre). The St Olav Monument is, according to legend, situated exactly where the body of the king was hidden in a shed the night after the battle. His remains were later buried in Nidaros (now Trondheim) (see p203).

Every year, around the time of the St Olav celebrations of *Olsok* (29 July), the play *Spelet*

om Heilag Olav (*The Story of St Olav*), by Olav Gullvåg and Paul Okkenhaug, is performed in the amphitheatre at Stiklestad, attracting an audience of 20,000. At the top of the amphitheatre is a statue by Dyre Vaa depicting Olav the Holy on his horse (see below).

The altarpiece in **Stiklestad Kirke** is said to have been built above the stone against which Olav the Holy died. A church was built on the site shortly after the battle and replaced 100 years later by the present long church.

The tableaux in the church date from the 17th century and resemble a picture book from the Bible. The frescoes in the choir by Alf Rolfsen, showing scenes from the battle, were commissioned for the church's

restoration for the St Olav Jubilee in 1928.

Verdal Museum, near the church, has a typical 19th-century farm from Verdal among its exhibits.

🏛 **Stiklestad Nasjonale Kultursenter**
4 km (2 miles) E of Verdal town centre. **Tel** 74 04 42 00. **Open** daily. **Closed** some public hols.

🏛 **Verdal Museum**
4 km (2 miles) E of Verdal town centre. **Tel** 74 04 42 00. **Open** 10 Jun–10 Aug: daily.

Bølareienen, a 6,000-year-old rock carving of a reindeer

❽ Steinkjer

County of Nord-Trøndelag. 🚹 21,000. 🚆 🚌 ℹ Namdalsveien 11, 74 16 36 17. 🎪 Steinkjer Market (Aug). **W** visitinnherred.com

Archaeological finds indicate that there has been human settlement in the Steinkjer area for 8,000 years. Burial mounds, stone circles and memorial stones have been discovered at Eggekvammen, Tingvoll and Egge, near the Byafossen waterfall. There are petroglyphs from the Stone Age and Bronze Age near Bardal, and there is also a large area of rock carvings near Hammer, 13 km (8 miles) west of Steinkjer town centre. Other finds indicate that there was an important trade and shipping centre at the head of Beitstadfjorden. Snorre writes in his sagas that Olav Tryggvason established a market town here in 997. Steinkjer church stands

St Olav and the Battle of Stiklestad

Olav Haraldsson was declared king of a united Norway at the assembly of Øretinget in 1016. He went on to convert the entire country to Christianity and in so doing made many enemies, particularly among farmers who feared that the king would become too powerful.

Instead, they gave their support to King Canute of Denmark. In 1028, Canute sent 50 ships with an army to invade Norway. Olav was forced to flee.

In 1030, Olav returned to re-conquer his realm. In the Verdalen valley he came face to face with his enemy at Stiklestad and died in the ensuing battle, on 29 July 1030. A year after his death, his undecayed body was exhumed and he was declared a saint. Olav was moved from one church to another until, in 1090, he was laid to rest in Kristkirken, on the site of the future Nidaros cathedral. His shrine became a place of pilgrimage. Many churches have been consecrated in his honour.

Statue of Olav the Holy at Stiklestad

on the hill of Mærehaugen. Before the introduction of Christianity there was a temple to the Norse gods here. This is the third church on the site. The first, from 1150, burnt down, the second was destroyed during a bombing raid in 1940. The new church, designed by Olav Platou (1965), is richly decorated by artists Sivert Donali and Jakob Weidemann.

Steinkjer has good communications: the Nordlandsbanen train line and the E6 pass through the town, and the RV17 leads to the coastal areas of Flatanger and Osen. On the eastern side of Snåsavatnet lake is Bølareienen, a 6,000 year-old life-size rock carving of a reindeer.

Snåsa is the starting point for trips to Gressåmoen National Park, and to the Snåsaheiene hills, noted for their excellent fishing. In the town, **Samien Sitje** is a museum devoted to the southern Sami culture.

Salmon fishing, a popular activity on the Namsen river

🏛 **Samien Sitje**
58 km (36 miles) NE of Steinkjer. **Tel** 74 13 80 00. **Open** 20 Jun–20 Aug: Tue–Fri, Sun; 21 Aug–19 Jun: by prior arrangement. 🚻 🎫 ♿ 📷 🏠

❾ Namsos

County of Nord-Trøndelag. 🚹 12,500. 🚆 🚌 ⛴ ℹ Dampskipskaia, 74 22 66 04. 🎪 Namsos Market (3rd week Aug). 🌐 **en.trondelag.com**

Namsos is situated at the innermost tip of the 35-km (22-miles) long Namsenfjorden, inside the islands of Otterøy and Jøa, featured in the novels of Olav Duun (1876–1939). The town was established in 1845 as a shipping port, particularly for timber. It was twice destroyed by fire, and was razed to the ground by bombs in World War II, but has since been rebuilt.

The Namsen river, the longest in the county of Trøndelag, enters the sea here. It is one of Norway's best salmon rivers.

Popular fishing areas are Sellæg, Grong and Overhalla. Fishing is done from boats known as *harling*, but it is also possible to fish from the bank. The Fiskumfossen waterfall north of Grong has the longest set of salmon steps in northern Europe, at 291 m (955 ft).

The **Namsskogan Familiepark** in Trones features Nordic animals in their natural environment. Further north, a side road leads to Røyrvik, the starting point for a boat connection to the Børgefjell National Park.

🐾 **Namsskogan Familiepark**
70 km (43 miles) N of Namsos. 🚌 from Namsos. **Tel** 74 33 37 00. **Open** Jun–Aug: daily. 🚻 🎫 by arrangement. ♿ 📷 🏠

❿ Rørvik

County of Nord-Trøndelag. 🚹 4,000. 🚌 ⛴ ℹ Vikna, 74 36 16 70. 🎪 Rørvik Festival (4th week Jul), Hurtigruten Day (1st week Jul).

North of Namsos is the archipelago of Vikna, comprising nearly 6,000 islands. Rørvik is one of the main centres of population. At the **Nord-Trøndelags Kystmuseum** (Coastal Museum) 19th-century rowing boats used for fishing, typical of Trøndelag, are on display.

A large part of outer Vikna is a conservation area with an abundance of nesting birds, as well as otters, porpoises and several species of seal.

To the north of Vikna, near the county boundary with Nordland, the mountain of Lekamøya rises from the sea. *Leka-møya* (the Leka Virgin) is the principal character in a Nordland folk tale. The main attractions on Leka are cave paintings in Solsemhulen and a burial mound, Herlagshaugen. The museum of cultural history, **Leka Bygdemuseum**, is located nearby.

🏛 **Nord-Trøndelags Kystmuseum**
Museumsgata 2. **Tel** 74 39 04 41. **Open** daily. 🚻 🎫 📷 🏠

🏛 **Leka Bygdemuseum**
1 km (half a mile) N of Leka. **Tel** Leka, 74 38 70 11. **Open** Jul: daily. 🚻 🎫

A European shag, part of the rich bird life on the Vikna islands

NORTHERN NORWAY AND SVALBARD

The author Knut Hamsun described Northern Norway as "the land hidden behind a hundred miles". Other writers have called it "the land of excitement" or "the land of the high flames". These expressions capture the essence of this northern land – the great distances, the rugged scenery, the dancing Northern Lights of winter and the midnight sun that shines day and night in summer.

Northern Norway consists of three counties – Nordland, Troms and Finnmark – covering about a third of the country. Busy ports such as Bodø, Narvik, Tromsø, Hammerfest and Kirkenes nestle in sheltered coves or straddle islands along the coast. Inland, the national parks are the habitat of bears and wolves, while out to sea, birds flock to the steep nesting cliffs. Lying 640 km (400 miles) north of the mainland are the Arctic Ocean islands of Svalbard (Spitsbergen), almost 60 per cent covered in glaciers.

Nordland's unspoilt Helgaland coast comprises a multitude of islands, sounds, fjords and snow-clad peaks. The mountains of Lofoten rise like a wall from a sea of islets to the north-west. Here, fishing has been the islanders' life-blood.

Further north lies Tromsø, the "Paris of the North" and capital of Northern Norway. Beyond Tromsø the scenery becomes more severe.

Perhaps the ultimate goal of a journey to the top of Norway is to reach Nordkapp (the North Cape). The perpendicular cliffs marking Europe's most northerly point were named by an English sailor, Richard Chancellor, in 1533.

The Finnmark towns of Alta, Kautokeino and Karasjok are rich in Sami culture. Karasjok is home to the Sami Parliament. At Hjemmeluft, magnificent 5,000-year-old rock paintings and carvings have been discovered. There is a distinct Finnish influence in Kirkenes, which is situated close to the borders with Finland and Russia.

Cod hanging up to dry, Lofoten

◄ A small boat approaching Bodø, Nordland's capital

Exploring Northern Norway and Svalbard

The Lofoten Islands, Nordkapp (the North Cape) and Helgelandskysten in particular have attracted tourists over the years. But it is the magnificent scenery of all of Northern Norway and Svalbard (Spitsbergen), combined with the midnight sun in summer and the wide range of outdoor activities on offer, which make this part of Norway so appealing to travellers. People cross the Arctic Circle to fish in the sea and rivers, to join whale and seal safaris, to go bird watching and cave walking, to take trips into the mountains, or simply to enjoy a holiday in a fisherman's cabin on stilts. Far to the north lies Svalbard, with its distinctive Arctic landscape, flora, animal and bird life.

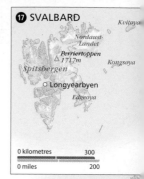

17 SVALBARD

Kvitøya
Nordaust-Landet
Perriertoppen 1717m
Spitsbergen
Kongsøya
Longyearbyen
Edgeøya

0 kilometres 300
0 miles 200

The fishing hamlet of Hamnøy on Vestfjord in the Lofoten Islands

TROMSØ

VESTERÅLEN
Andenes
Andøya
Risøyhamn
Langøya
Hinnøya
Sortland
Lødingen
Austvågøya
Svolvær
LOFOTEN
Vestvågøya
Leknes
Vestfjorden
Moskenesøy
Sørvågen
Værøy
Røst

Fag
SENJA
7
Finnsn
86
Andselv
Setermoen
E6
Harstad
E10
Bjerkvik
E10
NARVIK 6
Ballangen
Kiruna
Storriten 1503m
Bognes
Skutvik
Nordfold
Bonåsjøen
Kjerringøy
E6
BODØ 4
80
Fauske
Saltstraumen
Rognan
830
Sulitjelma
17

NORDLAND

Ørnes
Arjeplog

0 kilometres 100
0 miles 50

Arctic Circle
Snøtinden 1594m
Hestemona
SALTFJELLET-SVARTISEN NATIONAL PARK 3
Storforshei
MO I RANA 2
Korgen
Sandnessjøen 1
Vega
E6
Mosjøen
Oksskolten 1916m
Røssvatnet
HELGELANDSKYSTEN
Hattfjelldal
Brønnøysund Trofors
17
76
Leka
E6
Trondheim

Sperm whale off the island of Andøya in Vesterålen

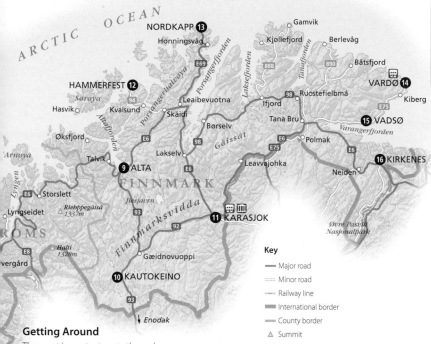

Key

— Major road

···· Minor road

∿∿ Railway line

▬ International border

— County border

△ Summit

Getting Around

The most important route through the three counties is the E6, which extends some 1,600 km (994 miles) from southern Nordland to Kirkenes. Four roads go from the E6 to Sweden: from Trofors, Mo i Rana, Storjord and Narvik. Roads lead to Finland from Skibotn, Kautokeino, Karasjok and Neiden, and to Russia from Kirkenes via Storskog. The Nordlandsbanen railway line ends at Bodø. The Hurtigruten coastal express and a number of local boats serve the coast. There are eight main airports, including Svalbard.

The Northern Lights dancing across the sky on a clear winter's night

Sami handicrafts being sold from a *lavvo* (traditional tent)

Sights at a Glance

1. Helgelandskysten
2. Mo i Rana
3. Saltfjellet-Svartisen National Park
4. Bodø
5. *Lofoten and Vesterålen pp212–14*
6. Narvik
7. Senja
8. Tromsø
9. Alta
10. Kautokeino
11. Karasjok
12. Hammerfest
13. Nordkapp
14. Vardø
15. Vadsø
16. Kirkenes
17. *Svalbard pp224–5*

The 1,065-m (3,494-ft) long Helgeland Bridge, north of Sandessjøen

❶ Helgelandskysten

County of Nordland.
Helgelandsgaten 1, Sandnessjøen, 75 04 25 80.
visithelgeland.com

The shipping channel from Leka northward along the coast of Helgelandskysten passes through a stunning landscape of islands and mountains. Whether seen from aboard the Hurtigruten *(see p203)*, or from the RV17 as it winds along the coast, this region never fails to delight.

Helgelandskysten is also known as the Realm of the Nessekonge, the wealthy merchants who held power both economically and politically over northern Norway until the early 1900s. They made their fortunes trading with passing cargo ships and fishing vessels.

On the island of **Torget**, near Brønnøysund, is the strange-looking mountain Torghatten, which has a 160-m (525-ft) long passage running right through it, formed when the land was lower than it is now.

On the northern side of Vefsfjorden, on the island of **Alsten**, is the Norse homestead of Tjøtta. The estate has several ruined houses and burial mounds from the Viking Age. The island is dominated by the majestic mountain range De Syv Søstre (the Seven Sisters), rising to 1,072 m (3,517 ft). The 12th-century stone church Alstadhaugkirke was where writer Petter Dass (1647–1707) was a clergyman. In the rectory there is a museum devoted to him. Sandnessjøen is the biggest settlement on the island.

Near the mouth of Ranfjorden is the island of **Dønna**, with the aristocratic estate, Dønnes, and a stone church from 1200. Among the other islands, **Lovunden** is known for its large colony of puffins. **Hestemona**, situated on the Arctic Circle, is dominated by the 568-m (1,863-ft) mountain of Hestmannen, named after a giant troll who, according to an early saga, turned to stone. **Rødøy** island marks the furthest point north on the Helgeland coast.

❷ Mo i Rana

County of Nordland. 25,000.
O T Olsens Gate 3, 75 13 92 00. Winter Light Festival (Jan), Sjonstock Rock & Hemnes Jazz Festivals (1st week Aug), Open Air Festival (4th week Aug).
visithelgeland.com

Little is known about the origins of Mo i Rana, today an industrial town, except that it had a church and a Sami market before 1860. The place was bought by L A Meyer, who started a guesthouse and initiated trade with Sweden. Today central Mo is dominated by Meyergården, a hotel and shopping complex.

The museum, Rana Bygdemuseum, features the collections of Hans A Meyer, with sections on geology, mining and rural culture. Friluftsmuseet, an open-air museum, about 9 km (6 miles) from Mo town centre, is part of Rana Bygdemuseum.

Environs

From Mo, the E6 runs southward along Ranfjord, eventually reaching **Mosjøen** (75 km/ 46 miles southwest of Mo) with its beautiful Vefsn Museum, showing works by contemporary Nordland artists. The street Sjøgata is lined with timber buildings and warehouses dating from the early 19th century.

About 20 km (12 miles) north of Mo is **Grønligrotten**, a limestone cave 107-m (351-ft) deep with a gushing stream which re-emerges in nearby Setergrotten. Helmets must be worn in the caves, and a miner's lamp is needed to explore Setergrotten.

The enchanting cave of Grønligrotten with an underground river

For hotels and restaurants in this area see pp230–33 and pp238–47

❸ Saltfjellet-Svartisen National Park

County of Nordland. 🔲 ℹ️ Mo i Rana Tourist Information, 75 13 92 00. 🖼️

Gloriously untouched landscapes typify the national park of Saltfjellet and Svartisen. In the east, toward the Nordlandsbanen railway line, E6 and the Swedish border, the undulating terrain is punctuated by peaks rising to 1,700 m (5,577 ft). Further west there are wide mountain plateaus and forested valleys.

Between here and the coast, the Svartisen ice-cap, Norway's second largest glacier, is made up of two glaciers, Østisen and Vestisen. The glacier has several arms running down toward the surrounding valleys. The southeastern one, Østerdalsisen, is strangely contoured. To reach it, take the 32 km (20-mile) long road from Mo, cross Svartisvannet by ferry (in season), and walk 3 km (2 miles) to the glacier toe.

Polarsirkelsenteret (the Arctic Circle Centre) is located in Saltfjellet, just by the Arctic Circle (84 km/52 miles north of Mo i Rana on the E6). It has a tourist information office, slide shows and a restaurant. Nearby there are three Sami sacrificial stones and a memorial to Yugoslav prisoners of war who were killed while working on the railway during World War II.

🏛️ **Polarsirkelsenteret**
84 km (52 miles) N of Mo i Rana.
Tel 75 12 96 96. **Open** May–15 Sep: daily. **Closed** 17 May. 🖼️ 🚻 ⭐ 🏕️
🌐 polarsirkelsenteret.no

Marking the Arctic Circle at Polarsirkelsenteret on Saltfjellet

Norsk Luftfartsmuseum, a national aviation centre

❹ Bodø

County of Nordland. 🏔️ 42,000. ✈️ 🔲 🚌 🚢 ℹ️ Tollbugata 13, 75 54 80 10. 🎵 Nordland Music Week (4th week Jul). 🌐 visitbodo.com

Nordland's capital, Bodø, occupies a wonderful setting with Saltfjorden and its islands and nesting cliffs to the west, the mountain ranges of Børvasstindene across the fjord to the south and the island of Landegode to the north. The midnight sun can be seen here from 1 June to 12 July.

Domkirken, Bodø's cathedral, is a modern, three-aisle basilica, designed by G Blakstad and H Munthe-Kaas, and consecrated in 1956. The stained-glass painting above the altar is by Aage Storstein.

Norsk Luftfartsmuseum (the Aviation Museum), illustrating Norwegian civil and military history, is one of Bodø's big attractions. Of particular interest are Catalina seaplanes, Mosquito fighter aircraft, the US spy plane U2 and Junkers 52.

Kjerringøy, 40 km (25 miles) north of Bodø, was Nordland's richest trading post in the 19th century. It is now part of Nordland's county museum and has 15 historic buildings complete with interiors. Nyfjøset (New Barn), which has a tourist information office and a café, is a replica of a barn that was demolished in 1892. The main museum building is located near the cathedral.

A past owner of Kjerringøy was Erasmus Zahl (1826–1900), who helped Knut Hamsun when he wanted to become a writer. In his books, Hamsun called the place Sirilund.

Saltstraumen is a natural phenomenon taking place 33 km (21 miles) southeast of Bodø. This is one of the world's strongest tidal currents. The water is forced at speeds of up to 20 knots through a 3-km (2-mile) long, 150-m (492-ft) wide strait. It changes direction every six hours.

At Opplevelsessentret, a multimedia show explains the current. There is also an aquarium and a seal pool.

🏛️ **Norsk Luftfartsmuseum**
Olav V Gata. **Tel** 75 50 78 50.
Open daily. 🖼️ 🖼️ ⭐ 🏕️ 🏕️

Whale Watching

Killer whales can be seen on organized safaris (see p259), especially in Tysfjord – the deepest fjord in northern Norway – particularly between October and January when they arrive in the fjords to feast on herring. The killer whale is a toothed whale of the dolphin family. The female can be up to 7.5 m (25 ft) long, and a fully-grown male can measure up to 9 m (30 ft). The latter has a particularly powerful, triangular dorsal fin. The killer whale is fast, supple and greedy. It feeds on fish, but is also known to eat other sea animals such as whales and seals.

On the island of Andøya there are safaris to see seals and the enormous sperm whales.

A killer whale patrolling in Tysfjorden

❺ Lofoten and Vesterålen

Viewed from Vestfjorden, north of Bodø, the mighty mountains of the Lofoten Islands rise up like a wall in the sea. Lofoten comprises six large and many smaller islands. Corries, hollows and sharp peaks create an exciting backdrop to the fjords, moorlands and farms, small towns and fishing villages. The island of Moskenesøya is southernmost of the larger islands. Between Moskenesøya and the remote Skomvær Island lie 60 km (37 miles) of steep nesting cliffs, called *nyker*. Northeast of Lofoten is Vesterålen, which shares the island of Hadseløya with Lofoten, and also includes three other large islands: Langøya, Andøya and Hinnøya.

Kabelvåg
In the 19th century, Kabelvåg was the most important fishing village in Lofoten. The timber-frame church, known as Lofoten's "cathedral", seats 1,200.

Nusfjord
The well-preserved fishing village of Nusfjord on Flakstadøya *(see p214)*, has many picturesque 19th-century buildings illustrating the development of Lofotfisket (the Lofoten Fisheries).

KEY

① **Skomvær**

② **Moskstraumen** (the Moskenes Current) is an infamous maelstrom, portrayed in the literature of Jules Verne, Edgar Allan Poe, Peder Claussøn Friis and Petter Dass.

③ **Western Flakstadøya** has long, white, sandy beaches and in summer is a good place to swim – even this far north.

④ **Vestvågøy Museum** at Fygle, south of Leknes, tells the story of the life of local fishermen through the ages.

LOFOTEN

Vest- vågøya
Leknes
Stamsund
Flakstad-øya
Ballstad
Moskenesøya
Moskenes

Vestfjorden

Norwegian Sea

Værøy

↓ *Bodø*

Røst

①

↓ *Bodø*

Å
The E10 road ends at the southerly village of Å, site of two fishing museums, Lofoten Tørrfisk-museum and Norsk Fiskeværmuseum.

0 kilometres	50
0 miles	30

Key

— Major road
═══ Minor road
— Hurtigruten route *(see also p215)*
- - - Other ferry

VISITORS' CHECKLIST

Practical Information
Counties of Nordland and Troms.
🚌 56,000. ℹ️ Svolvær, 76 07
05 75. 🎭 Cod Fishing World Cup
(Apr), Codstock Blues Festival
(Whitsun), Lofoten International
Chambers Music Festival
(Feb & Jul). 🔲 **lofoten.info**

Transport
✈️ Leknes; Andenes; Svolvær.
🚌 ⛴️

Andenes
Andenes, on the northern tip of Andøya in Vesterålen, has a
large fishing quarter, a Polar Museum and the world's most
northerly launching pad for rockets and scientific balloons.

Trondenes
The 40.6 cm calibre
Adolf Cannon, a relic
from World War II, is
one of the attractions
at Trondenes
(see p214).

Getting Around
*There are flights from Bodø
to Røst and Leknes and
Svolvar in Lofoten, and to
Andenes in Vesterålen.
Helicopters operate to
the island of Værøy.
Hurtigruten coastal ships
call at Stamsund and
Svolvær. Road bridges
and tunnels, buses, ferries
and express boats connect
the many islands.*

Tjeldsundbrua
The 1,001-m (3,284-ft) long Tjelsund Bridge
extends from the mainland across to
Hinnøya, Norway's biggest and most
populated island. The towers stand 76 m
(249 ft) above the waterline.

Svolvær
Beneath the mountain of Svolværgeita (Svolvær
goat) is Svolvær, the "capital" and transport hub
of Lofoten *(see p214)*.

For additional map symbols *see back flap*

Exploring Lofoten and Vesterålen

The coastline of the Lofoten and Vesterålen islands is dominated by sharp peaks such as Tinden and Reka on the island of Langøya, and Møysalen on Hinnøya. Small towns and fishing villages lie at the water's edge. Some of these settlements are deserted, like Nyksund, others, such as Myre, are thriving. At the northernmost tip of the Vesterålen island of Andøya is the port of Andenes. Svolvær is the most important town on Lofoten.

Jagged mountains forming a backdrop to the skerries in Lofoten

Svolvær

Despite being long regarded as the "capital" of Lofoten, the bustling harbour town of Svolvær only received town status in 1996. Its location on Austvågsøya and good transport links make it an important gateway for tourism on the islands. The town's economy depends on Lofotfisket (the Lofoten Fisheries). In March and April every year the cod arrive in Vestfjorden to spawn and the fishing boats follow.

Other than fishermen and tourists, artists have long been attracted to Svolvær and a centre for North Norwegian artists has been established in the town, **Nordnorsk Kunstnersenter**. NNKS is an artist-run institution and serves as a centre for them to exhibit their art. Works on show change throughout the year.

The 569-m (1,867-ft) peak, **Svolværgeita** (the Svolvær goat), with its two horns, is the town's most distinctive feature. It appears to rise from the town centre and presents a challenge for all climbers.

🏛 **Nordnorsk Kunstnersenter**
Svolvær. **Tel** 76 06 67 70. **Open** mid-Jun–mid-Aug: daily; mid-Aug–mid-Jun: Tue–Sun. **Closed** public hols.
🅿 🖵 🆆 nnus.no

Vestvågøya

From the island of Austvågøya there is a road connection, via Gimsøy and two bridges, to Vestvågøya, where there is an airfield at Leknes and a Hurtigruten coastal express stop at Stamsund. **Stamsund**, like **Ballstad**, is one of the largest and most picturesque fishing villages in west Lofoten. Vestvågøya is also an important agricultural island, which has been farmed since the Stone Age.

Vestvågøy Museum at Fygle has a fine collection, including a fisherman's cabin dating from 1834. The island is rich in Stone and Iron Age monuments and Viking settlements. **Lofotr – Vikingmuseet på Borg** (Viking Museum at Borg), north of Leknes, features a reconstruction of a chieftain homestead

The old trading post of Sund on Moskenesøya

from AD 500–900. It is a lively museum, where Viking banquets and crafts demonstrations are arranged.

🏛 **Vestvågøy Museum**
2 km (1 mile) E of Leknes. **Tel** 76 08 49 00. **Open** Jun–mid-Aug: daily.
🅿 🖵 🅿

🏛 **Lofotr – Vikingmuseet på Borg**
Prestegårdsveien 59, Borg. **Tel** 76 08 49 00. **Open** mid-May–Aug: daily; Sep–mid-May: Wed–Sun. **Closed** public hols. 🅿 🖵 ♿ 🖾 🖵 🅿

Flakstadøya and Moskenesøya

The island of Flakstadøya is best known for the fishing village of **Nusfjord**. It was chosen in 1975 as part of the European Year of Nature Conservation to be a pilot project for the conservation of building traditions in Norway.

On Moskenesøya there is a string of fishing villages, including Reine, set in a wild mountainous landscape. The charming village of **Å** *(see p206)* lies at the southern end of the Lofoten road. **Sund** has a fishing museum and a smithy for artistic metalwork.

Between Moskenesøya and Værøy whirls the current of **Moskstraumen**, the world's biggest maelstrom. When the wind and the current are in the same direction, the roar can be heard 5 km (3 miles) away.

On **Værøy** and **Røst**, Lofoten's southernmost islands, vast numbers of sea birds nest in the strangely shaped cliffs of Trenykene. The fabled lighthouse of **Skomvær** stands alone at the outermost point.

Vesterålen Islands

Hinnøya is Vesterålen's (and Norway's) largest and most populated island. Its main town is **Harstad**, which developed around 1870 as a result of the abundance of herring. The Northern Norway culture festival, is held here each year, around the summer solstice.

On nearby Trondenes stands an early Gothic church. The northernmost island is Andøya, with the fishing community of **Andenes** *(see p213)*.

Hurtigruten: "The World's Most Beautiful Voyage"

It was captain Richard With of the shipping company, Vesteraalske Dampskibsselskab, who initiated the coastal express amid much controversy. Few people believed that it would be possible to operate an express route all year round, least of all during the dark days of winter, since only poor maps existed of the treacherous Norwegian coast. However, a contract was signed between With and the government in May 1893. At the beginning there were weekly sailings and nine ports of call between Trondheim and Hammerfest in summer. In winter the boats stopped at Tromsø. The coastal express soon proved to be a lifeline for the communities along the route. Today, two shipping lines operate 12 ships, with daily south and northbound departures *(see p275)*. The cruise from Bergen to Kirkenes, calling at 34 ports, has been called "the world's most beautiful voyage".

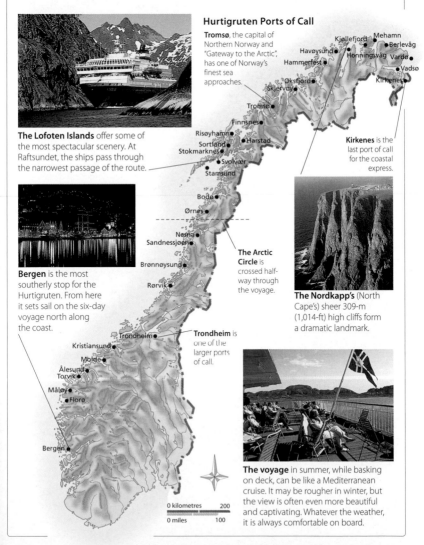

Hurtigruten Ports of Call

Tromsø, the capital of Northern Norway and "Gateway to the Arctic", has one of Norway's finest sea approaches.

The Lofoten Islands offer some of the most spectacular scenery. At Raftsundet, the ships pass through the narrowest passage of the route.

Kirkenes is the last port of call for the coastal express.

Bergen is the most southerly stop for the Hurtigruten. From here it sets sail on the six-day voyage north along the coast.

The Arctic Circle is crossed halfway through the voyage.

The Nordkapp's (North Cape's) sheer 309-m (1,014-ft) high cliffs form a dramatic landmark.

Trondheim is one of the larger ports of call.

0 kilometres 200
0 miles 100

The voyage in summer, while basking on deck, can be like a Mediterranean cruise. It may be rougher in winter, but the view is often even more beautiful and captivating. Whatever the weather, it is always comfortable on board.

The busy port of Narvik close to the border with Sweden

❻ Narvik

County of Nordland. 🗺 18,600. ✈
🚉 🚌 *i* Stasjonsveien 1, 76 96 56
00. 🎿 Winter Festival (2nd week Mar),
Black Bear Rally (4th week Jun).
🌐 destinationnarvik.com

Narvik developed as a shipping
port for iron ore from Kiruna in
Sweden. The Ofotbanen train line
to Kiruna was completed in 1902,
after which Narvik was given
town status. Heavy bombard-
ment by the Germans in 1940
destroyed most of the town.

After World War II, Narvik rose
again to become Norway's
second largest shipping town.
Activities connected with iron
ore are still form its economic base.
The Ofotbanen passes below
the mountains high above
Rombaksfjorden, offering
stunning views.

From Oscarsborg a cable
car, **Fjellheisen**, climbs up to
700 m (2,296 ft). In summer it
operates until 2 am (midnight
sun: 31 May–14 Jul).

Krigsminnesmuseet (the
War Memorial Museum), near
the main square, focuses on
the military campaigns fought
here in 1940. Allied as well as
German soldiers are buried
near Fredskapellet (the Peace
Chapel) in the cemetery.

From Narvik, the E6 runs
southward, crossing a number of
fjords either by ferry or bridges,
including the impressive 525-m
(1,722-ft) long bridge spanning
the beautiful Skjomenfjorden.
On Hamarøy, around 100 km
(60 miles) south of Narvik, is
the strangely shaped mountain
of Hamarøyskaftet and the
childhood home of Nobel

Prize-winning novelist Knut
Hamsun (1859–1952).

Environs
The scenic E10 road,
Bjørnfjellveien, starts at
Rombaksfjorden and ascends
to 520 m (1,706 ft) through
the wild mountains of Ofoten
to the Swedish border.

🏛 **Krigsminnemuseet**
Torvhallen. **Tel** 76 94 44 26.
Open daily. **Closed** public hols.
🎦 📷 by arrangement.

❼ Senja

County of Troms. 🗺 9,000. ✈ 🚌
i Ringveien 2, Finnsnes, 77 85 07 30.
🎿 Finnsnes Festival (4th week Jul),
Ocean Fishing Festival (late Jun),
Tranøy Festival (2nd week Aug),
Husøy Festival (2nd week Aug).

Norway's second largest
island, Senja, can be reached
by road (E6) from Bardufoss,
across the bridge at Finnsnes.
The landscape is green and
welcoming on the mainland
side, becoming harsher toward
the sea coast. **Ånderdalen**

Family of swans in Ånderdalen Nasjonalpark
on Senja island

Nasjonalpark has an unspoilt
landscape inhabited by elk
and eagles.

Back on the mainland, in the
south of Troms county large
areas of wilderness, including
Øvre Dividal national park,
are home to bears.

From Skibotn, about 100 km
(60 miles) east of Senja, the E8
passes near the point where
Finland, Sweden and Norway
meet, the Treriksrøysa.

🏞 **Ånderdalen Nasjonalpark**
35 km (22 miles) S of Finnsnes.
i Sør-Senja Museum, 77 85 46 77.

❽ Tromsø

See pp220–21.

Detail of rock engraving from Hjemmeluft,
near Alta

❾ Alta

County of Finnmark. 🗺 18,000. ✈
🚌 *i* Bekkefaret 3, 99 10 00 22.
🎿 Borealis Winter Festival (Mar),
Finnmark Race (Mar).

The original village of Alta, at
the mouth of the Alta river, has
grown and merged with its
neighbours to form the most
populated urban area in
Finnmark. It includes Bossekop, a
commercial market place rich in
tradition where Sami and Kvæn
people (immigrants of Finnish
origin) and Norwegians traded
goods. Apart from the church
in Bossekop, the entire area was
razed to the ground during the
German retreat in 1944.

Today, Alta is a growing
industrial and educational
centre, and an important
transport junction on the E6
with its own airport.

The lower part of the Alta
Valley is covered in spruce forests
and fertile agricultural land. The
Gulf Stream and sunny summer
nights provide fertile conditions,

Pikefossen, a waterfall on the Kautkeinoelva river in Finnmark

⑪ Karasjok

County of Finnmark. 🏔 3,000. ✈ 🚌
ℹ Leavnnjageaidnu 1, 78 46 88 00.
🎪 Easter Festival (Easter).

The Sami capital is Karasjok (Karásjohka in Sami). It is the seat of the Sami Parliament, **Sametinget**, opened in 1989. Its new building was inaugurated by King Harald in 2000. The architects, Christian Sundby and Stein Halvorsen, used elements from reindeer husbandry as a base for their design. A long hallway, Vandrehallen, reminiscent of the dividing fences used for the reindeer, winds through the building. The plenary hall is like a *lavvo* (pointed Sami summer tent) and decorated with a magnificent artwork in blue and gold by Hilde Skancke Pedersen.

Around 80 per cent of the population of Karasjok is of Sami origin. Their culture is the subject of **De Samiske Samlinger**, a museum featuring Sami handicrafts and way of life, clothing and building traditions.

The climate in these parts can be extreme. The record low temperature is –51.4° C (–60.5° F), and the highest temperature 32.4° C (90° F).

🚌 **Sametinget**
Kautokeinoveien 50. **Tel** 78 47 40 00. **Open** Mon–Fri. 🎫 🅰

🏛 **De Samiske Samlinger**
Museumsgate 17. **Tel** 78 46 99 50.
Open daily. **Closed** public hols. 🎪 🎫 🅰 🏠

even at 70°N. Altaelvar is one of the world's most attractive salmon rivers for fly-fishing. Every year salmon weighing more than 20 kg (44 lb) are caught.

In 1973, rock engravings between 2,000 and 6,000 years old were found near the village of Hjemmeluft. The engravings, now a UNESCO World Heritage Site, show wildlife and hunting scenes.

Alta Museum is also located at Hjemmeluft. It features ex-hibits relating to the Alta River from the Stone Age Komsa culture (7000 BC–2000 BC) through to the latest hydro-electric project. Close to the museum is the largest of the five open-air rock art sites.

🏛 **Alta Museum**
Altaveien 19, Hjemmeluft. **Tel** 78 45 63 30. **Open** daily. **Closed** some public hols. 🎪 🎫 🅰 🖥 🏠

⑩ Kautokeino

County of Finnmark. 🏔 3,000. 🚌
ℹ Siva Bygget, 78 48 65 00. 🎪 Easter Festival (Easter), Autumn Festival (Sep).

The name "Kautokeino" is a Norwegianized form of the Sami word, *Guovdageaidnu*. Kautokeino is a mountain town surrounded by barren plateaus where reindeer husbandry is the most important economic activity.

The town has a large Sami community and has become a centre for education with a Sami High School. Reindeer

husbandry is one of the courses on the curriculum.

Kulturhuset (the Culture House), opened in 1980, houses the Sámi Instituhtta, a co-ordinating organization for Sami politics and culture. It has a theatre and a library and also mounts exhibitions.

Easter is a time of transition for the Sami, just before they set off with their reindeer for summer pastures on the coast. It is marked by colourful celebrations, with weddings, a *joik* (Sami chanting song) festival and reindeer racing, all attracting large numbers of visitors.

🚌 **Kulturhuset**
1 km (half a mile) N of town centre. **Tel** 78 48 72 16. **Open** Mon–Fri: daily (library) and for cinema or theatre performances. **Closed** some public hols.

The striking Sami Parliament building in Karasjok

❽ Tromsø

Known as the "Paris of the North", Tromsø is the largest town in the polar region of Scandinavia. It is located 300 km (186 miles) inside the Arctic Circle, on the same latitude as northern Alaska. Central Tromsø covers an island in the busy Tromsøy-sund. There was a farming estate here in early Viking times, and the first church was built around 1250. During the Hanseatic period, trade and commerce boomed; Tromsø officially became a market town in 1794. From the 1820s it developed as a thriving port for sea traffic in the Arctic Ocean. Nansen and Amundsen started their polar expeditions from here. The world's northernmost university opened in Tromsø in 1972.

Tromsøy-sund with Ishavskatedralen and the peak of Tromsdalstind

🏛 Polaria

Hjalmar Johansens Gate 12. **Tel** 77 75 01 00. **Open** daily. **Closed** some public hols. 🐾 ♿ 🖥 📷

Polaria is a national centre for research and information relating to the polar regions, particularly the Arctic. It is also a great place to experience the Arctic landscape. In a fascinating panoramic film from Svalbard (*see pp224–5*), the viewer becomes a wanderer in a polar landscape beneath the Northern Lights, sensing what it feels like to be in the Arctic wilderness.

An aquarium features Arctic species of fish. Other creatures include the red king crab, *paralithodes camtschaticus*, which can weigh up to 10 kg (22 lb). This Arctic species has migrated from Russia and is spreading steadily southward along the Norwegian coast. Another attraction is the glass-bottomed pool for seals, which can be viewed from below.

🏛 Tromsø Kunstforening

Muségata 2. **Tel** 77 65 58 27. **Open** noon–5pm Wed–Sun. **Closed** some public hols. 🐾 📷 🖥 📷

Established in 1877, Tromsø Kunstforening is the oldest art society in Northern Norway. It exhibits Norwegian and international contemporary art, and arranges around 20 exhibitions every year. The society is based in a 19th-century building, which once housed Tromsø Museum.

Façade of Tromsø Kunstforening, built in 1894

🏛 Nordnorsk Kunstmuseum

Sjøgata 1. **Tel** 77 64 70 20. **Open** daily. **Closed** some public hols. 🐾 ♿ 🖥 📷

The regional art museum for Northern Norway, Nordnorsk Kunstmuseum, was established in 1985 primarily to show painting and handicrafts from the northern regions, including sculpture and textile art. The museum also arranges temporary exhibitions of work both past and present.

🏛 Polarmuseet

Søndre Tollbugata 11. **Tel** 77 60 66 30. **Open** daily. 🐾 📷 🖥 📷

Polar hunting and research expeditions are the focal points of Polarmuseet. Displays feature Fridtjof Nansen's journey to the North Pole in his ship *Fram*, the life of Antarctic explorer Roald Amundsen and Salomon Andrée's attempted balloon flight to the North Pole (1897).

There are exhibitions devoted to the first hunters on Svalbard, the trappers of polar bears, polar foxes and seals, who wintered in the icy wasteland. Everyday articles, utensils and a wealth of other material left by hunters, whalers and sealers around Northern Norway form part of the collection.

The museum is located in the harbour area of old Tromsø, surrounded by sturdy warehouses, fishermen's bunkhouses and wooden buildings from the 1830s.

⛪ Ishavskatedralen

2 km (1 mile) E of town centre. **Tel** 47 68 06 68. **Open** daily. 🐾 ♿

Consecrated in 1965, Ishavskatedralen (the Arctic Ocean Cathedral, also known as Tromsdalen Church) was designed by Jan Inge Hovig. It is built of concrete. The shape of its roof symbolizes the way in which the Northern Lights brighten up Tromsø's dark winter months.

A massive 23-m (75-ft) high, triangular stained-glass window by Victor Sparre (1972) fills the east wall. It comprises 86 panels of jewel-like glass pieces on the theme of the Second Coming of Christ.

The striking east wall of Ishavskatedralen, composed entirely of stained glass

⬚ Nordlysplanetariet

3 km (2 miles) N of town centre.
Tel 77 61 00 00 (Tourist Information).
Open 11am–4pm daily.

Situated on the university campus in Breivika, near Tromsø Botaniske Hage (Botanical Gardens), is Nordlysplanetariet (the Northern Lights Planetarium). It is known for screening the film *Arctic Light*, which provides a realistic experience both of the strange, blue aurora borealis (known as the Northern Lights) – often visible in the Arctic sky

during the dark winter months – and of the incredible midnight sun, responsible for the light nights of summer.

The renovated planetarium is part of the Northern Norway Science Centre complex. It should not be confused with the Nordlysobservatoriet (Northern Lights Observatory), a research centre in Skibotn in Lyngen.

⬚ Tromsø Museum, Universitetsmuseet

Lars Thøringsvei 10.
Tel 77 64 50 00. **Open** daily.
🎨 ♿ 🖥 🏠

Now part of the University Museum, Tromsø Museum is the regional museum for Northern Norway. Established in 1872, it holds considerable collections from the Stone Age, Viking era and early Middle Ages, including a reconstructed

Viking longhouse. Of particular interest are the late medieval church carvings from the Hanseatic period and those in Baroque style.

From its early days the museum specialized in Arctic landscape and culture. Sami history has a prominent place and there are comprehensive displays devoted to aspects of Sami life.

The museum also has a lot to offer younger visitors with regular film shows and a life-size replica of a dinosaur.

VISITORS' CHECKLIST

Practical Information
County of Troms. 🅜 63,600.
ℹ️ Kirkegata 2, 77 61 00 00.
🎦 Tromsø International Film Festival (2nd week Jan), Northern Lights Festival (3rd week Jan), Midnight Sun Marathon (mid-Jun), Beer Festival (3rd week Aug).
🆆 destinasjontromso.no

Transport
✈️ 🚌 Prostneset. 🚢 Prostneset.

Tromsø Town Centre

① Polaria
② Tromsø Kunst forening
③ Nordnorsk Kunst museum
④ Polarmuseet
⑤ Ishavskatedralen

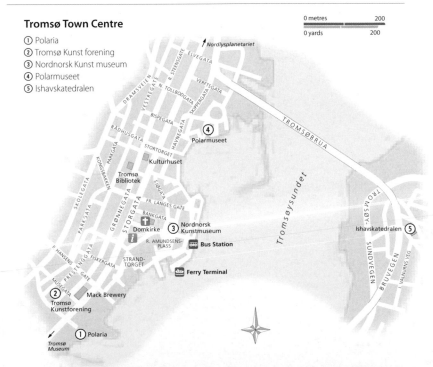

0 metres 200
0 yards 200

For keys to symbols *see back flap*

Verdens Barn (the Children of the World) sculptures at Nordkapp

⑫ Hammerfest

County of Finnmark. 🏔 9,200. ✈
🚌 ⓘ Hamnegata 3, 78 41 31 00.
📅 Hammerfest Days (3rd week Jul),
Polar Nights Festival (3rd week Nov).
Ⓦ **hammerfest-turist.no**

The polar bear on this town's
coat of arms recalls the days
when Hammerfest was a
hunting and trapping centre.
A settlement by the 9th
century, Hammerfest was
given town status in 1789.

It is the world's most
northerly town at
70° 39' 48"N, as recorded
on Meridianstøtten
(the Meridian Pillar),
which marks the
first international
measurement of the Earth
in the 19th century.

The town has endured
many catastrophes, inclu-
ding being destroyed
by a hurricane in 1856 and
being razed to the
ground in World War II.
Each time it has been
rebuilt in true pioneer
spirit. In 1890 it was
one of the first towns
in Europe to install electric
street lighting.

Hammerfest church is unusual
in that it has no altar. Instead, the
back wall is a monumental abstract painting in glowing colours.
The Polar Bear Club, **Isbjørnklubben**, has a museum illustrating the town's Arctic traditions.

🏛 **Isbjørnklubben**
Rådhusplassen 1. **Tel** 78 41 31 00.
Open daily. 🅿 ✅ ♿ 📷

The Meridian Pillar at
Hammerfest

⑬ Nordkapp

County of Finnmark. 🚌 summer.
ⓘ Northcape Tourist Information,
Honningsvåg, 78 47 70 30.
Ⓦ **northcape.no**

It was the English sailor, Richard
Chancellor, who named
Nordkapp (the North Cape) in
1533, during his attempt to find
the Northeast Passage to China.
Various important people
travelled to view the North
Cape, including the French king,
Louis Philippe of Orleans, in
1795, and Oscar II in 1873.
The latter was responsible
for encouraging tourist
ships to include the
North Cape on their
itineraries and tourism
grew rapidly. An impressive
road – part of it below the
sound of Magerøy – links
the cape to the mainland.

Every year, more
than 200,000 people
come to the cliff top.
Nordkapphallen (the
North Cape Hall),
inside the mountain,
offers a panoramic
view of the coast. A
videograph showing Finnmark's
changing seasons plays on a
225°-wide screen. Visitors also
have the chance to become
a member of the Royal North
Cape Club.

From the top of the North
Cape there is a signposted
path to the promontory of
Knivskjellodden, which is
Europe's most northerly point,
at 71°11'08"N. **Honningsvåg**,
35 km (22 miles) southeast of

the cape, is where Hurtigruten
(see p215) calls. It also has a
Nordkapp museum.

🏛 **Nordkapphallen**
35 km (22 miles) N of Honningsvåg.
Tel 78 47 68 60. **Open** daily. 🅿 ♿
📷 🖥 📷

⑭ Vardø

County of Finnmark. 🏔 2,400. ✈
🚌 ⛴ ⓘ Kaigata 12, 78 98 69 67.
📅 Winter Festival (Apr), Winter Blues
(Nov), Pomor Festival (4th week Jul).
Ⓦ **varanger.com**

Two events at the beginning
of the 14th century were to
enforce Vardø's position as a
bastion against incursions from
the east: Håkon V built a fortress
and Archbishop Jørund
consecrated the first church.
The fortress, **Vardøhus
Festning**, was rebuilt in the
18th century as a star-shaped
fortification with parapets of
earth and peat, eight cannons
and a mortar. There are tours
of the commanding officer's
residence, the old depots and
the barracks. Four kings have
written their names on a beam
from the original fortress.

Vardø is connected to the
mainland by a tunnel below
the sound of Bussesundet,
constructed in 1982. Fishing
and fish processing are the
basis of the local economy.

The fishing village of **Kiberg**,
to the south, was known as "Little
Moscow" because of partisan
activity during World War II. To
the north, the deserted hamlet
of **Hamningberg** lies in a moon-
like landscape made up of
strange rock formations.

🏛 **Vardøhus Festning**
Festningsgata. **Tel** 78 98 85 02. **Open**
daily. 🅿 📷 by arrangement. ♿

A sun salute, fired from Vardøhus Festning
on the sun's reappearance

Vadsø, on the Barents Sea, owing its development to Finnish immigration

⑮ Vadsø

County of Finnmark. 🏔 6,200. ✈
🚌 🚢 ℹ Kirkegata 15, 78 94 04 44.
🎪 Varanger Music Festival (mid-Aug)

Originally situated on the island of Vadsøya, the town of Vadsø was moved to the mainland around 1600. Remains of its 15th and 16th-century buildings still exist on the island. Also there is an airship mooring mast on Vadsøya, which was used by Amundsen's expedition to the North Pole in the airship *Norge* in 1926, and to launch Umberto Nobile's airship *Italia* in 1928.

Over the centuries many Finns have settled in Vadsø and the buildings bear the hallmark of Finnish workmanship. **Ruija Kvenmuseum** devotes considerable space to the Kvænene (as the Finnish were known). It is located in a Finnish-style farmhouse, Tuomainengården.

Invandrermonumentet (the Immigrant Monument), by the Finnish sculptor Ensio Seppänen, was unveiled in 1977 by King Olav in the presence of the Swedish king and Finnish president.

The so-called Pomor trade with the Russians, by which fish was exchanged for timber, also contributed considerably to the town's development in the 19th and 20th centuries.

🏛 Ruija Kvenmuseum
Hvistendahlsgate 31. **Tel** 78 94 28 90.
Open 20 Jun–20 Aug: daily; other times: Mon–Fri. **Closed** public holidays. 🈴 🎦 ⬛ summer only. 📷

⑯ Kirkenes

County of Finnmark. 🏔 3,500.
✈ 🚌 🚢 ℹ Parkveien 3, 78 99 80 11. 🎪 Barents Ski Race (Mar), Salmon Fishing Festival (1st week Jul). 🗓 4th Thu of the month.
🌐 **nordnorge.com**

At the head of Bøkfjorden is Kirkenes, the biggest urban centre in eastern Finnmark and the last port of call for Hurtigruten. Iron ore was once the cornerstone of the community and when the town was destroyed by the retreating German army in 1944, its 2,000 inhabitants fled to nearby mineshafts.

The mines closed in 1996, but their legacy lives on. Opencast pits at **Bjørnevatn**, south of the town, have created a vast artificial valley with a floor 70 m (230 ft) below sea level.

Kirkenes' proximity to the border with Russia draws tourists to the area. A popular excursion is via Storskog (the official crossing point) to the Grense Jacobselv river on the border, through forests of crooked birch trees overlooking the Barents Sea.

At the mouth of the river there is a chapel built in 1869 as a spiritual watchtower toward the East. It was named after Oscar II who visited the region in 1873. A road leads from Elvenes to Skafferhullet and the Greco-Russian chapel on the Russian side.

The pine forests and moorland of **Øvre Pasvik Nasjonalpark** (National Park), on the Pasvikelva river, extend to the Treriksrøysa monument, where Finland, Russia and Norway meet.

The river has been heavily developed for hydroelectricity.

The Midnight Sun

The expression "The Land of the Midnight Sun" is often used to describe Norway and northern Scandinavia. The concept of the "midnight sun" means that the uppermost arc of the sun stays above the horizon for 24 hours. This occurs north of latitude 66.5°N during a few summer months. Correspondingly, there is a period of darkness during the winter, when the sun never rises above the horizon during the day. As if to compensate for this, the Northern Lights may sometimes blaze across the sky. The midnight sun and dark days of winter are caused by the tilt of the earth's axis, and the earth's rotation around the sun. To see the midnight sun in these parts can be a magical experience.

Midnight sun shining over the North Cape

⑰ Svalbard

Known as the "Land of the Cold Coasts", Svalbard consists
of the Arctic Ocean islands of Spitsbergen (the largest),
Nordaustlandet, Edgeøya, Barentsøya, Prins Karls Forland and
several smaller ones. The archipelago lies 640 km (400 miles)
north of the mainland, about one hour by plane from Tromsø.
It was first mentioned in an Icelandic document in 1194.
A Dutch explorer, Willem Barents, arrived in 1596. He found
a magnificent landscape peppered with ragged peaks, and
named it Spitsbergen. To the east the mountains are plateau-
like. Glaciers calve noisily into the sea from their huge walls
of ice. Svalbard was placed under Norwegian sovereignty
in 1925, and in 1935 the Soviet Union became a party to
the treaty to share in the local coal mining rights.

Walrus
Since the 1950s the walrus has
been a protected species and
stocks have increased. It is
particularly prevalent on the
island of Moffen.

Magdalenefjorden
The scenery around the little fjord of
Magdalene on the northwestern coast of
Vest-Spitsbergen is awesome. About 60 per
cent of Svalbard is covered by glaciers.

KEY

① **Newtontoppen**, and the peak of
Perriertoppen are the highest
mountains at 1,717 m (5,633 ft).

② **The campsite of the fatal
Andrée expedition**, was found in
1930 on Kvitøya, 33 years after
Salomon Andrée lifted off the island
of Danskeøya in an air balloon in an
attempt to fly to the North Pole.

Ny Friesland

Haakon vii
Land

Andree
Land

Wildefj

SPITSBERGEN

Ny-Ålesund

Dickson
Land

Ola
La

Oscar ii
Land

Bünso
Land
Sab
La

Prins
Karls Forland

Isfjorden

Longyearbyen

Barentsburg

Nordenskiöld Land

Nathorst
Land

He
Lar

Wedel
Jarlsberg
Land

Torell
Land

Sørkapp
Land

Sør-Kapp

Longyearbyen
The capital of Svalbard
is named after the
American, J M Longyear,
who opened the first
mine on Svalbard in
1906. It has a
population of 2,000.

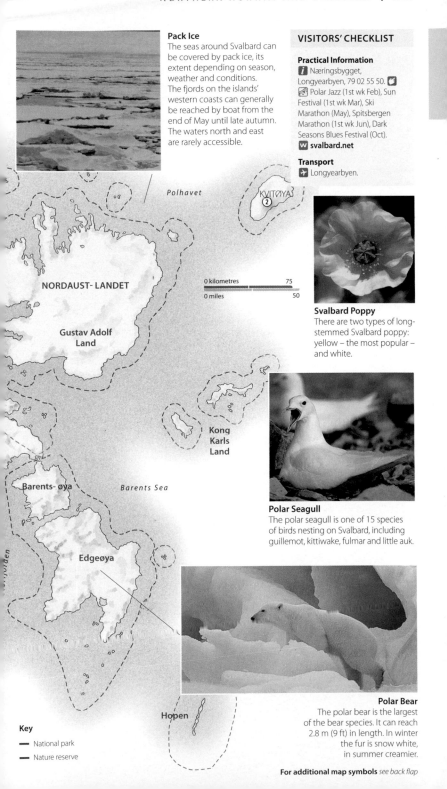

Pack Ice
The seas around Svalbard can be covered by pack ice, its extent depending on season, weather and conditions. The fjords on the islands' western coasts can generally be reached by boat from the end of May until late autumn. The waters north and east are rarely accessible.

Polhavet

KVITØYA ②

NORDAUST- LANDET

Gustav Adolf Land

0 kilometres 75
0 miles 50

Svalbard Poppy
There are two types of long-stemmed Svalbard poppy: yellow – the most popular – and white.

Kong Karls Land

Barents- øya

Barents Sea

Polar Seagull
The polar seagull is one of 15 species of birds nesting on Svalbard, including guillemot, kittiwake, fulmar and little auk.

Edgeøya

Hopen

Polar Bear
The polar bear is the largest of the bear species. It can reach 2.8 m (9 ft) in length. In winter the fur is snow white, in summer creamier.

Key
— National park
— Nature reserve

For additional map symbols *see back flap*

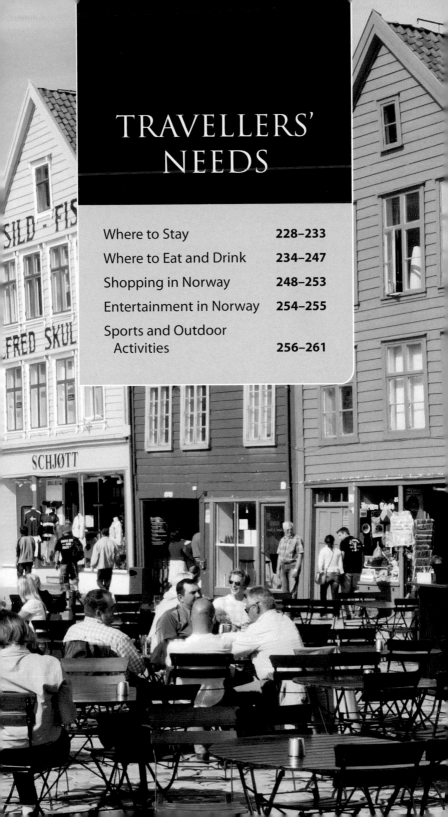

TRAVELLERS' NEEDS

WHERE TO STAY

Norway has a good selection of hotels covering all corners of the country, with a wide choice in terms of price and quality. Nevertheless, staying in a hotel is not always the best way of getting the most out of your holiday. In Northern Norway, for instance, it has become popular to stay in a *rorbu*, a small cabin once used by fishermen. Mountain huts, youth hostels, campsites, guest farms and mountain lodges are among the other types of accommodation on offer. Private homes along the highways often provide overnight accommodation. Many of these establishments offer bed and breakfast (B&B), and the price is usually displayed on a sign outside. If you are following a pre-planned route, it is advisable to book your accommodation in advance.

The distinctive Radisson Blu Plaza Hotel, Oslo *(see p231)*

Choosing a Hotel

The choice of accommodation options in Norway is as diverse as the country's scenery. There are large, fashionable hotels and chain hotels in the major towns and cities, modest lodges high in the mountains and B&Bs along the main roads. The best pick in terms of price is youth hostels.

In the outlying districts there are many comfortable *turisthoteller* (tourist hotels) and mountain hotels. The majority of these are situated in spectacular surroundings and are a good starting point for sporting activities. In Vestlandet, especially, many of the tourist hotels have been run by the same family for generations, and they maintain a tradition of good service.

The standard of cleanliness is very high in all Norwegian hotels while the size of rooms, facilities and service might vary depending on the price level of the hotel.

Booking a Hotel

It is easy to make reservations online. All of the hotels featured in this book have their own websites. Another option is the **Visit Norway** website, which lists all kinds of accommodation and also provides an online booking service. Most travel websites will offer deals when you book your hotel and flight together.

In towns and larger villages, the local tourist office can provide visitors with help when it comes to booking their accommodation even if it is outside the district.

Rooms can also be booked over the telephone enabling you to enquire about special rates or even negotiate a price reduction.

Hotel Groups

There are a number of hotel chains represented in Norway. These are located mainly in the towns and cities and tend to focus on the business market. However, in summer these hotel chains often offer advantageous rates for tourists.

The exterior of the elegant Hotel Bristol, Oslo *(see p230)*

All establishments offer central booking facilities, either by phone or online.

Best Western is a chain of more than 28 collaborating private hotels in the mid-price bracket. The hotels are small or medium-sized in both town and country locations.

The Scandinavian group **Choice Hotels** operates 85 hotels in Norway under four different brands: Comfort hotels, catering to business people and providing bed and breakfast; Quality hotels, for tourists and conferences; Clarion, high-end hotels; and the Clarion Collection, top-end luxury.

The **First Hotels** group is a chain with an environment-friendly ethos. It has business hotels in the upper price range located in towns and cities.

Radisson Blu has 20 hotels in Norway including the Radisson Blu Plaza in Oslo which, with its 37 floors and 676 rooms, is northern Europe's largest hotel. The group also has a hotel in Svalbard. Radisson Blu typically focuses on the business sector, and it also manages several tourist hotels.

Rica Hotels is a Norwegian-Swedish hotel chain with over 60 hotels in Norway, ranging from the Rica Dyreparken family hotel in Kristiansand to the Grand Hotel in Oslo. Rica operates a summer holiday pass as well, which gives discounts on rooms and attractions.

Thon Hotels is a Norwegian chain comprising 63 hotels catering to all price ranges, and offering excellent value, while **Scandic Hotels** is the leading hotel group in the Nordic region and has 22 hotels in Norway.

Junior suite, with a separate living area, at the Holmenkollen Park Hotel near Oslo *(see p231)*

Prices and Payment

Hotels in Norway vary greatly in price. Those in the cities and towns are generally more costly.

The majority of hotels offer special rates in summer and on weekends. Many operate discount schemes and hotel passes. A two-night stay is usually all it takes to justify the cost of a hotel pass.

All the major credit cards are accepted. Larger hotels will also change foreign currency, though it is easier and cheaper to do this at a bank *(see p268)*.

Youth and Family Hostels

There are more than 80 youth and family hostels in Norway. These are a part of **Norske Vandrerhjem** (the Norwegian Hostelling Association).

Hostels are designed to accommodate individuals as well as families. Most hostels are of a good standard with favourable prices, and many are situated in attractive areas. Pillows and duvets will usually be provided, and linen can be rented.

The association does not have a central booking office, but guests can visit its website to make a reservation.

DNT Huts

Den Norske Turistforening (DNT), the Norwegian Mountain Touring Association, operates a network of *hytte* or mountain huts in beautiful hiking areas *(see p256)*.

Many huts are staffed, provide meals and are reasonably comfortable with shower and toilet facilities. DNT also has self-service huts with necessities such as sheet sleeping bags and food supplies. Payment is based on the honour principle – you leave your money in the box provided. There are also some unstaffed huts which do not offer any provisions.

Reservations can only be made for the staffed huts, and for a minimum of three nights. Bookings can be made by telephoning the lodge. However, guests are usually given a place to sleep if they just turn up.

Camping

Norway's right-of-access regulation allows the freedom to camp almost anywhere in the countryside. Staying at a camp-site will, however, ensure a more comfortable stay, with better facilities. Visit the **NAF Camping** website for details. Campsites are graded on a scale of one to five stars. If you plan to camp in the summer it is advisable to book well in advance.

Recommended Hotels

The many different hotels in this book have been carefully selected for their excellent facilities, good location and value. A wide variety of accommodation is covered, from historic buildings in remote locations, to stylishly modern boutique hotels in Norway's towns and cities.

Entries labelled as DK Choice highlight establishments that are exceptional in some way.

They may be set in stunning surroundings, offer excellent service, have beautiful interiors and rooms, an inviting atmosphere or a superb on-site restaurant. Whatever the reason you will have a memorable stay. The majority of these hotels are very popular, so be sure to reserve well ahead.

DIRECTORY

Booking a Hotel

Visit Norway
W visitnorway.com

Hotel Groups

Best Western
Tel 80 01 16 24.
W bestwestern.no

Choice Hotels
Tel 22 33 42 00.
W choicehotels.no

First Hotels
Tel 80 01 04 10.
W firsthotels.com

Radisson Blu
Tel 80 01 60 91.
W radissonblu.com

Rica Hotels
Tel 66 85 45 60.
W rica.no

Scandic Hotels
Tel (+46) 8 517 517 20.
W scandic-hotels.com

Thon Hotels
Tel 81 55 24 40.
W thonhotels.no

Youth and Family Hostels

Norske Vandrerhjem
Tel 23 12 45 10.
W hihostel.no

DNT Huts

Den Norske Turistforening (DNT)
Youngstorget 1, 0181, Oslo.
Map 3 E3.
Tel 40 00 18 68.
W turistforeningen.no

Camping

NAF Camping
W scandic-hotels.com

Where to Stay

Oslo

Central Oslo West

Thon Hotel Munch Ⓚ
Modern   **Map** 3 D2
Munchs Gate 5, 0165
Tel *23 21 96 00*
🆆 thonhotels.com
Brightly decorated contemporary
hotel. Family rooms have bunk
beds for children.

Carlton Hotel Guldsmeden ⓀⓀ
Design   **Map** 2 B3
Parkveien 78, 0254
Tel *23 27 40 00*
🆆 hotelguldsmeden.dk
Close to the Royal Palace. Rooms
have unique and traditional
furnishings; some have four-
poster beds.

**Clarion Collection Hotel
Savoy** ⓀⓀ
Historical   **Map** 3 D3
Universitetsgata 11, 0164
Tel *23 35 42 00*
🆆 clarionhotel.com
Located in Oslo's theatre district.
All rooms are furnished in
Scandinavian style. Serves a
sensational buffet breakfast.

**Frogner House
Apartments** ⓀⓀ
Design   **Map** 2 B2
Skovveien 8, 0257
Tel *93 01 00 09*
🆆 frognerhouseapartment.no
Elegant, airy apartments with the
option of self-catering. Long- and
short-term rentals available.

Hotel Bristol ⓀⓀ
Luxury   **Map** 3 D3
Kristian IV's Gate 7, 0164
Tel *22 82 60 00*
🆆 thonhotels.com
Among Oslo's top hotels since the
1920s. Facilities include a spa and
fitness room. Offers one of the
best buffet breakfasts in town.

Radisson Blu Scandinavia ⓀⓀ
Luxury   **Map** 3 D2
Holbergs Gate 30, 0166
Tel *23 29 30 00*
🆆 radissonblu.com
Offers magnificent views of the
Oslofjord. Spa, pool and a play
room for kids.

Thon Hotel Cecil ⓀⓀ
Modern   **Map** 3 D3
Stortingsgata 8, 0161
Tel *23 31 48 00*
🆆 thonhotels.com
Modestly sized yet comfortable
rooms. Buffet breakfast and a
light evening meal served daily.

Hotel Continental ⓀⓀⓀ
Luxury   **Map** 3 D3
Stortingsgata 24–26, 0117
Tel *22 82 40 00*
🆆 hotelcontinental.no
World renowned deluxe hotel set
in a grand 19th-century building.

DK Choice

The Thief ⓀⓀⓀ
Design   **Map** 2 B4
Landgangen 1, 0252
Tel *24 00 40 00*
🆆 thethief.com
This amazing hotel located next
to the Astrup Fearnly Museet is
packed with pieces of art
curated by a former director of
the museum. The hotel's linen
also carries a top designer's
name. Magnificent views of the
Oslofjord on all sides.

Central Oslo East

First Hotel Millennium Ⓚ
Modern   **Map** 3 E4
Tollbugata 25, 0157
Tel *21 02 28 00*
🆆 firsthotels.com
Spacious rooms with separate
living areas. Private terrace for
top floor rooms.

Price Guide
Prices are based on one night's stay in
high season for a standard double room,
inclusive of service charges and taxes.

Ⓚ	under 1,000 NKr
ⓀⓀ	1,000 to 2,000 NKr
ⓀⓀⓀ	over 2,000 NKr

Rica G20 Ⓚ
Modern   **Map** 3 E3
Grensen 20, 0159
Tel *22 01 64 00*
🆆 rica.no
Close to the main shopping
street. Floor-to-ceiling windows.

**Best Western
Hotel Bondeheimen** ⓀⓀ
Historical   **Map** 3 D3
Rosenkrantz' Gate 8, 0159
Tel *23 21 41 00*
🆆 bondeheimen.com
A hotel that dates back to 1913
with modern interiors.

**Clarion Collection
Hotel Bastion** ⓀⓀ
Design   **Map** 3 E4
Skippergata 7, 0152
Tel *22 47 77 00*
🆆 nordicchoicehotels.no
Trendy boutique hotel with
a sauna and fitness centre. All
rooms are individually decorated.

**Clarion Collection
Hotel Folketeateret** ⓀⓀ
Design   **Map** 3 E3
Storgata 21–23, 0184
Tel *22 00 57 00*
🆆 clarionhotel.com
Bright rooms, a fitness centre and
a lounge. Complimentary dinner.

**Clarion Hotel
Royal Christiania** ⓀⓀ
Historical   **Map** 3 E3
Biskop Gunnerus' Gate 3, 0155
Tel *23 10 80 00*
🆆 nordicchoicehotels.no
Built for the 1952 Winter Olympics.
Impressive rooms with spacious
bathrooms. Great breakfast.

**Comfort Hotel Grand
Central** ⓀⓀ
Historical   **Map** 3 E3
Jernbanetorget 1, 0154
Tel *22 98 28 00*
🆆 nordicchoicehotels.no
Individually designed rooms in
an original train station building.

Grand Hotel ⓀⓀ
Luxury   **Map** 3 D3
Karl Johans Gate 31, 0159
Tel *23 21 20 00*
🆆 grand.no
Deluxe hotel that dates back to
1874. Gorgeous spa and pool.

Stylish suite at the Rica Victoria

Park Inn by Radisson Oslo ⓀⓀ
Modern   Map 3 D3
Øvre Slottsgate 2C, 0157
Tel *22 40 01 00*
Ⓦ parkinn.com
Centrally located. Most rooms
have balconies with good views.

**Radisson Blu
Plaza Hotel Oslo** ⓀⓀ
Luxury   Map 3 F3
Sonja Henies Plass 3, 0185
Tel *22 05 80 00*
Ⓦ radissonblu.com
Norway's tallest hotel set in a
glass skyscraper. Free Wi-Fi and
an indoor pool.

Rica Victoria ⓀⓀ
Modern   Map 3 D3
Rosenkrantz' Gate 13, 0121
Tel *24 14 70 00*
Ⓦ rica.no
Chic hotel with a glass atrium.
Well-sized rooms featuring wood-
en floors and huge bathrooms.

Thon Hotel Opera ⓀⓀ
Design   Map 3 F4
Dronning Eufemias Gate 4, 0191
Tel *24 10 30 00*
Ⓦ thonhotels.com
Overlooks the opera. Rooms offer
fjord or city views. Fitness centre.

Thon Hotel Oslo Panorama ⓀⓀ
Modern   Map 3 D4
Rådhusgaten 7B, 0151
Tel *23 31 08 00*
Ⓦ thonhotels.com
Good location. Most rooms on
the upper floors have balconies
with fjord views.

Further Afield

Comfort Hotel Express Ⓚ
Modern   Map 3 E2
Møllergata 26, 0179
Tel *22 03 11 00*
Ⓦ nordicchoicehotels.no
Stylish hotel with simple rooms
and a terrace bar. Good value.

**Clarion Collection
Gabelshus** ⓀⓀ
Design   Map 2 A3
Gabelsgate 16, 0272
Tel *23 27 65 00*
Ⓦ clarionhotel.com
A stylish boutique hotel close to
the Nasjonalgalleriet.

**Holmenkollen Park
Hotel Rica** ⓀⓀ
Luxury
Kongeveien 26, 0787
Tel *22 92 20 00*
Ⓦ holmenkollenparkhotel.no
An eye-catching hotel built in
the Norwegian 'dragon-style'.
Situated high above the city,
many rooms have great views.

'Dragon-style' architecture of Holmenkollen
Park Hotel

Rica Hotel Bygdoy Alle ⓀⓀ
Historical   Map 1 B1
Bygdøy Allé 53, 0265
Tel *23 08 58 00*
Ⓦ rica.no
Extraordinary hotel with turrets
and spires. Has large rooms and
an excellent location.

Saga ⓀⓀ
Design   Map 2 B1
Eilert Sundts Gate 39, 0259
Tel *22 55 44 90*
Ⓦ sagahoteloslo.no
Built in the 1890s and renovated
by a top design team. Great value
rooms and superb breakfast.

Lysebu ⓀⓀⓀ
Luxury
Lysebuveien 12, 0790
Tel *21 51 10 00*
Ⓦ lysebu.com
A fairytale-like hotel located on
Holmenkollen. Legendary
restaurant and wine cellar. Range
of room/meal/spa packages.

Around Oslofjorden

**FREDRIKSTAD: Quality
Hotel Fredrikstad** ⓀⓀ
Modern
Nygata 2–6, 1607
Tel *69 39 30 00*
Ⓦ nordicchoicehotels.no
Comfortable hotel in the heart of
the city. Bright, pleasant rooms.

**LARVIK: Quality Hotel
Grand Farris** ⓀⓀ
Modern
Storgata 38, 3251
Tel *33 18 78 00*
Ⓦ nordicchoicehotels.com
Centrally located. Some rooms
have balconies with sea views.

MOSS: Hotel Refsnes Gods ⓀⓀ
Historical
Godset 5, 1518
Tel *69 27 83 00*
Ⓦ refsnesgods.no
Set on the scenic Jeløy island.
Superb views and luxurious rooms.

**TØNSBERG: Quality Hotel
Klubben** ⓀⓀⓀ
Modern
Nedre Langgate 49, 126
Tel *33 35 97 00*
Ⓦ hotelklubben.no
Well-sized rooms and an on-site
café and restaurant. Bike hire
available from reception.

Eastern Norway

**DRAMMEN: Clarion Collection
Hotel Tollboden** ⓀⓀ
Design
Tollbugata 43, 3044
Tel *32 80 51 00*
Ⓦ nordicchoicehotels.no
Family-friendly hotel offering
decent rooms. Helpful staff.

**DRAMMEN: First Hotel
Ambassadeur** ⓀⓀ
Historical
Strømsø Torg 7, 3044
Tel *31 01 21 00*
Ⓦ firsthotels.com
Individually styled rooms with
some dating back to the 1870s.

HAMAR: First Hotel Victoria ⓀⓀ
Historical
Strandgata 21, 2317
Tel *62 02 55 00*
Ⓦ firsthotels.no
Hamar's oldest hotel with
modern rooms and free Wi-Fi.

HEMSEDAL: Harahorn ⓀⓀⓀ
Design
Hemsedal, 3650
Tel *32 05 51 10*
Ⓦ dvgl.no
Set at an altitude of 1,100 metres
(3,700 ft) with hotel comforts and
a mountain cabin atmosphere.

Traditionally styled restaurant at Uppigrad Natadal, Seljord

LILLEHAMMER: Clarion Collection Hotel Hammer Ⓚ Ⓚ
Luxury
Storgata 108B, 2615
Tel *61 26 73 73*
Ⓦ nordicchoicehotels.no
High-class hotel with large rooms. There is a sauna and solarium on site.

LILLEHAMMER: Mølla Hotell Ⓚ Ⓚ
Modern
Elvegata 12, 2609
Tel *61 05 70 80*
Ⓦ mollahotell.no
Simple yet comfortable rooms in a former mill. Bar with great views.

Sørlandet and Telemark

ARENDAL: Clarion Hotel Tyholmen Ⓚ Ⓚ
Modern
Teaterplassen 2, 4801
Tel *37 07 68 00*
Ⓦ clarionhotel.com
Situated in an idyllic building on the wharf. Rooms with views.

BØ: Lifjellstua Ⓚ Ⓚ
Design
Lifjellvegen 934, 3800
Tel *35 95 33 80*
Ⓦ lifjellstua.no
Inviting mountain lodge with delightfully furnished rooms.

DALEN: Dalen Hotel Ⓚ Ⓚ Ⓚ
Historical
N-3886, Dalen in Telemark
Tel *35 07 90 00*
Ⓦ dalenhotel.no
National romantic-style hotel from 1896, surrounded by forests.

KRISTIANSAND: Radisson Blu Caledonien Ⓚ Ⓚ
Modern
Vestre Strandgate 7, 4610
Tel *38 11 21 00*
Ⓦ radissonblu.com
Close to the sea. Large rooms and great on-site pub and restaurants.

LANGESUND: Quality Hotel & Resort Skjærgården Ⓚ Ⓚ
Luxury
Stathelleveien 35, 3970
Tel *35 97 81 00*
Ⓦ nordicchoicehotels.no
Beach hotel with well-equipped rooms and a massive water park.

DK Choice

SELJORD: Uppigrad Natadal Ⓚ Ⓚ
Historical
Natadal, 3841 Flatdal
Tel *35 07 34 25*
Ⓦ natadal.no
This collection of five traditional log farm buildings with grass roofs make for an unusual but memorable stay. The hotel's restaurant is one of Norway's best local produce eateries, specializing in game.

VRÅDAL: Vrådal Hotel og Hyttepark Ⓚ Ⓚ
Rural retreat
Tiurvegen 5, 3853
Tel *35 06 93 00*
Ⓦ straand.no
Quiet, family-run place with apartments and cabins. Indoor pool.

Vestlandet

BALESTRAND: Kviknes Hotel Ⓚ Ⓚ Ⓚ
Historical
Kviknevegen 8, 6898
Tel *57 69 42 00*
Ⓦ kviknes.no
Palatial 18th-century hotel with modern and luxurious rooms.

BERGEN: Clarion Hotel Admiral Ⓚ Ⓚ
Design
C. Sundtsgate 9, 5004
Tel *55 23 64 00*
Ⓦ clarionadmiral.com
Big and comfortable rooms. Surrounded by sea on three sides.

BERGEN: Radisson Blu Hotel Norge Ⓚ Ⓚ Ⓚ
Luxury
Nedre Ole Bulls Plass 4, 5807
Tel *55 57 30 00*
Ⓦ radissonblu.com
One of Bergen's most prestigious hotels. Health club and an indoor pool for guests.

HAUGESUND: Rica Maratim Ⓚ Ⓚ
Modern
Åsbygata 3, 5528
Tel *52 86 30 00*
Ⓦ rica.no
Family-friendly hotel. Ask for a room with a terrace that overlooks the harbour.

KRISTIANSUND: Comfort Hotel Fosna Ⓚ Ⓚ
Modern
Hauggata 16, 6500
Tel *71 57 11 00*
Ⓦ nordicchoicehotels.com
Waterfront location. Trendy rooms and a good restaurant.

DK Choice

MOLDE: Fjordstuer Ⓚ Ⓚ
Modern
Julsundvegen 6, 6412
Tel *71 20 10 60*
Ⓦ classicnorway.no
This hotel sits close to the ferry terminal on the shore of the Moldefjorden. The rooms are tastefully furnished with big windows and stunning views. The hotel's seafood restaurant is one of the best in the region.

SKODJE: Storfjord Hotel Ⓚ Ⓚ
Luxury
Øvre Glomset, 6260
Tel *70 27 49 22*
Ⓦ storfjordhotel.com
Set in private grounds in a forest. Huge rooms, most with four-poster beds. Excellent restaurant.

STAVANGER: Thon Hotel Maritim Ⓚ
Modern
Kongsgata 32, 4005
Tel *51 85 05 00*
Ⓦ thonhotels.com
A reasonably priced hotel with contemporary design. Spacious rooms and free Wi-Fi.

STAVANGER: Rica Park Stavanger Ⓚ Ⓚ
Luxury
Prestegårdsbakken 1, 4005
Tel *51 50 05 00*
Ⓦ rica.no
Large, well-equiped rooms. Offers a sauna, gym and scrumptious breakfast.

STAVANGER: Victoria Ⓚ Ⓚ
Historical
Skansegata 1, 4006
Tel *51 86 70 00*
🌐 victoria-hotel.no
Elegant hotel with traditional hospitality and tasteful rooms.

ÅLESUND: Radisson Blu Ålesund Ⓚ Ⓚ
Modern
Sorenskriver Bullsgate 7, 6002
Tel *70 16 00 00*
🌐 radissonblu.com
Art-Nouveau hotel on the water-front, with a Norwegian restaurant.

Trøndelag

HITRA: Dolmsundet Ⓚ Ⓚ
Design
Dolmsundet, 7250 Melandsjø
Tel *72 44 04 40*
🌐 dolmsundet.no
Located on an island, with stylish rooms and a great restaurant.

OPPDAL: Quality Hotel Oppdal Ⓚ
Modern
Olaf Skasliensvei 8, 7340
Tel *72 40 07 00*
🌐 nordicchoicehotels.no
Set in the Dovrefjell National Park. Good base for adventurers.

DK Choice

OPPDAL: Kongsvold Fjeldstue Ⓚ Ⓚ
Historical
Dovrefjell, 7340
Tel *72 40 43 40*
🌐 kongsvold.no
One of Norway's most prestigious hotels – the Queen of Denmark has her own room here. All rooms are exquisitely furnished and the on-site restaurant serves excellent local cuisine. The hotel also arranges wildlife-watching trips.

SELBU: Selbusjøen Hotel & Gjestegård Ⓚ Ⓚ
Design
Haverneset 15, 7580
Tel *73 81 11 00*
🌐 selbusjoenhotell.no
Situated on a peninsula with classically furnished rooms.

STEINKJER: Best Western Tingvold Park Hotel Ⓚ
Historical
Gamle Kongeveg 47, 7725
Tel *74 14 11 00*
🌐 book.bestwestern.com
Set in scenic grounds with stone formations from Viking times.

TRONDHEIM: Britannia Hotel Ⓚ Ⓚ
Historical
Dronningens Gate 5, 7011
Tel *73 80 08 00*
🌐 britannia.no
Luxury hotel dating back to 1897. Offers all the latest gadgets and facilities. Amazing spa.

DK Choice

TRONDHEIM: City Living Schøller Hotel Ⓚ Ⓚ
Modern
Dronningens Gate 26, 7011
Tel *73 87 08 00*
🌐 cityliving.no
Simple yet elegant rooms and self-catering apartments in a hotel right across from the Stiftsgården royal residence. The location is second to none. Perfect for longer stays, especially for families.

TRONDHEIM: P Hotels Trondheim Ⓚ
Modern
Nordregate 24, 7010
Tel *73 80 23 50*
🌐 p-hotels.no
A chic, comfortable hotel with family rooms. Breakfast is delivered to your room. Located close to the station.

Northern Norway and Svalbard

BODØ: Radisson Blu Hotel Bodø Ⓚ Ⓚ
Modern
Storgata 2, 8001
Tel *75 51 90 00*
🌐 radissonblu.com
Brightly furnished and well-sized rooms. Bowling alley, sauna and solarium on site. Rooftop bar with views of the Lofoten Islands.

HAMMERFEST: Hotell Skytterhuset Ⓚ
Modern
Skytterveien 24, 9600
Tel *78 42 20 10*
🌐 4service.no
Peaceful location amid a large garden in central Hammerfest. Basic, clean rooms.

LAKSELV: Lakselv Hotel Ⓚ Ⓚ
Modern
Karasjokveien, 9700
Tel *78 46 54 00*
🌐 lakselvhotell.no
Set above Porsangerfjord with countryside views. Simple, tasteful rooms. Facilities include a hot tub and sauna.

LONGYEARBYEN: Radisson Blu Polar Hotel Spitsbergen Ⓚ Ⓚ
Luxury
Rd 500, 9171
Tel 79 02 34 50
🌐 radissonblu.com
Deluxe accommodation located in the Arctic wilderness with superb dining options.

NARVIK: Breidablikk Guesthouse Ⓚ Ⓚ
Modern
Tore Hundsgt 41, 8514
Tel *76 94 14 18*
🌐 breidablikk.no
Narvik's top bed-and-breakfast since 1950. Contemporary and supremely comfortable rooms. Excellent food.

TROMSØ: Sydspissen Hotel Ⓚ
Design
Strandvegen 166, 9006
Tel *77 66 14 10*
🌐 sydspissenhotell.no
Good-value hotel overlooking a beach. Offers well-furnished rooms and serves an excellent breakfast.

DK Choice

TROMSØ: Rica Isavs Hotel Ⓚ Ⓚ
Design
Fredrik Langesgate 2, 9008
Tel *77 66 64 00*
🌐 rica.no
The metallic, space-age exterior of this hotel makes it the most remarkable in the whole of Tromsø. It is perfectly located on the harbour with well-appointed rooms. The Skipsbroenbar, on the top floor, is a must-visit even for those not staying in the hotel.

Façade of the luxurious Britannia Hotel, Trondheim

For more information on types of hotels *see page 229*

WHERE TO EAT AND DRINK

Norway's restaurant scene is incredibly diverse, with something on offer for even the most discerning of palates including exotic international cuisines. Norwegian specialities such as lamb and cabbage stew, *gravlaks* (marinated salmon), *kumle* (dumplings) and reindeer medallions are not to be missed. The best selection can be found in the towns. Look out for seafood dishes; there are daily deliveries of fresh fish from both the Barents Sea and the North Sea. From February to April, spawning cod from the Lofoten Islands, *lofotskrei*, is highly recommended. Before Christmas, *lutefisk*, cod marinated in a lye solution, is a speciality. Ethnic cafés and restaurants offer dishes from around the world and the food in less pretentious places is often good. The price of alcohol, however, is high.

Eating Out

Norway's cities offer the greatest choice of places to eat. In Oslo in particular, an entire spectrum of food is on offer – from truly Norwegian to the exotic – with a variation in standards and prices.

Most towns have a selection of ethnic restaurants and the quality of the fare is generally consistently good. In many of the towns and built-up areas, you will also find traditional pubs and bars serving mainly beverages.

In the internationally renowned restaurants presided over by Michelin-starred chefs, the menus normally feature international cuisine alongside Norwegian specialities that are focused on seafood. The best restaurants also have a good selection of game dishes that include reindeer, elk and wild fowl from the Norwegian forests and mountains.

It is standard practice to have dinner in the restaurants of the mountain and tourist hotels, as these are often the only places to eat in the vicinity. The food in both types of establishments is normally of a high standard.

A Great Buffet Lunch

The Norwegian buffet lunch is a substantial meal and consists of a variety of hot and cold food. The idea is to help yourself from a buffet table groaning with meat and fish dishes.

Norway is the world's largest producer of salmon, so salmon dishes are often well represented. In mountain hotels and tourist lodges the lunch table is one of the highlights of a stay, offering an extravagant choice of delicacies. Traditionally the buffet is approached in a certain order: start with eating fish and salads, go on to meat and hot dishes and finish your meal with cheese and/or dessert. Feel free to ask the waiters for advice.

Local Eating Habits

Norwegian eating habits are somewhat different from those on the continent, particularly with regard to meals such as lunch and dinner.

Lunch is normally served between 11am and 2pm, while dinner is usually eaten around 5pm in the home. When eating out, dinner is usually delayed until 7–8pm. In the evening restaurants open around 5–6pm. It is rarely necessary to reserve a table for lunch, but a reservation is recommended for dinner, particularly on Wednesday, Friday and Saturday in popular places. Most restaurants are usually close around 10pm or shortly afterwards.

Fast Food

The most common fast food is a *pølse* (hot dog) with a roll or a *lompe* (potato pancake). This traditional dish is topped with raw onion and various dressings and is often served from kiosks and food wagons. Some of the markets, such as the one in Bergen, have stalls that sell ready-to-eat delicacies. Most urban areas have a selection of hamburger chains and kebab cafés.

Paying and Tipping

Many eating places offer lunch at reasonable set prices. In the towns it is possible for guests to have a good meal for around 60–70 NKr. Drinks add considerably to the price and even mineral water can cost as much as 20–30 NKr. In a good restaurant, a three-course dinner with wine could

Alfresco dining at Glipp restaurant, Kristiansand *(see p243)*

Cosy bar area at Havfruen Fiskerestaurant, Trondheim *(see p246)*

cost 600–700 NKr per person.
A number of restaurants also
offer special deals, even for
dinner, which are usually
advertised on boards or posters
outside. In such cases, a good
main course can be had for less
than 150 NKr. Most restaurants
have menus displayed outside,
but this is not mandatory.

Service charge is always
included in the bill, but tipping
the waiter – approximately
5 to 10 per cent is still the norm,
especially if the service at the
restaurant has been good.
It is acceptable to complain
if the food does not live up
to your expectations; the
restaurateurs themselves
encourage guests to do so.

Children

Children are welcome in all
cafés and restaurants, however
parents are advised to take
noisy children outside to calm
them down. Most places offer
separate children's menus and
special chairs. If there is no
specific menu, one can usually
be arranged by talking to the
waiter. Children's menus will
often consist of meatballs,
sausages and chips or spaghetti.

What to Wear

There is no need to bring smart
clothes to wear when eating
out in Norway. Norwegians
have a highly informal dress
code, and only a few of the very
best restaurants will expect you
to make an effort to dress up:
even then, it is highly unlikely

that you will ever be turned
away from a restaurant for not
being correctly dressed.

Alcohol

Norway has a restrictive policy
on alcohol and the duty levied
is among the highest in Europe.

The minimum age for being
served wine and beer is 18,
and 21 for spirits. Restaurants
need a licence to serve alcohol,
and some establishments often
have a licence for beer and wine
but not for spirits. Most big
restaurants have full licences,
and many of them offer a good
selection of wine at all price
ranges. In bars, people usually
pay for their own drinks; buying
a round is not.

All wines and spirits are sold
in special state monopoly
outlets known as *Vinmonopolet*.
These are often closed on
Sundays, and on and around
public holidays. The state
monopoly shops are only
found in the larger towns and
urban areas.

Smoking

Norway has very strict smoking
laws, similar to its neighbouring
European Union countries. It is
illegal to smoke in any restaurant, pub or café, unless there is
a separate, screened-off section
for smokers.

Recommended Restaurants

The restaurants featured on
the following pages have been
carefully selected to give a
cross-section of options in every
region: you will find everything
from Michelin-starred fine
dining and traditional restaurants
to contemporary Norwegian,
international cusine and bistro
fare. The entires are divided
into seven geographical areas
corresponding to the chapters
in this guide, the entries are
then organized by town.

The fine-dining options
include some of the best
restaurants in Norway, often
in atmospheric and scenic
locations. Scandinavian cuisine
relies on fresh ingredients with
an emphasis on fish, seafood and
game. The international options
serve mostly global favourites,
while bistros generally offer
a range of cuisine alongside
Norwegian fare.

The DK Choice entries
highlight exceptional establishments that offer more than
just excellent food. The majority
of these are popular with
local residents and visitors,
so be sure to inquire regarding
reservations well in advance,
or you may face a lengthy
wait for a table.

Contemporary interior at Emma's Drommerkjokkem, Tromsø *(see p247)*

The Flavours of Norway

Dominated by mountains, wilderness and the open sea, Norway has a vibrant cuisine rich in fresh seafood and wild game, offering scrumptuous plates of smoked, pickled or fried fish, along with reindeer, elk, seal and whale meat. You'll also find many dishes based on potatoes – baked, boiled or mashed – while popular vegetables include cabbage, carrots, swede (*rutabaga*) and broccoli. For dessert, try the fruits and berries from the Hardanger region, most notably *tyttebær* (lingonberry, which accompanies roast meats), *blåbær* (blueberries or blackberries), gooseberries, red- and blackcurrants.

Geitost and Jarlsberg cheeses

Fish drying in the pure air of the Lofoten Islands

Smørbrød

Once served as an appetizer, the classic Scandinavian open sandwich (*smørbrød*) is now a meal in itself, often served buffet-style. Prepared fish, meats and vegetables are neatly arranged on slices of freshly-baked grainy bread or flatbread and elegantly garnished. The most common ingredient, herring, comes in several dozen varieties, such as pickled, curried, fried and prepared in a spicy mustard or horseradish sauce. Salmon also features prominently – smoked, roasted, poached or cured in a salt, sugar and dill mixture. Accompanying the *smørbrød* may be salads, eggs, breads, terrines, marinated mushrooms, spare ribs and even oddities such as jellied eel and delicacies including smoked reindeer and caviar.

Fish & Seafood

With 24,000km (15,000 miles) of coastline, 150,000 lakes and 50,000 islands, it is no surprise that fish and seafood predominate in Norwegian kitchens. Most popular are herring and salmon, both of which come grilled, cured or smoked (*røkelaks*), while herring, once a peasant staple but now quite pricey, is usually served pickled

Ham, onion and tomato

Smoked herring with raw egg yolk

Prawns, caviar and lemon

Plaice with asparagus and caviar

Rare roast beef with onion and horseradish

Cured herring

Aquavit

Selection of typical Norwegian *smørbrød*

Norwegian Dishes and Specialities

Norway's culinary traditions developed as a result of the country's isolated rural economy and its climate. Its people had to develop methods by which they could preserve the harvest through the long winter months. One result was a vast and inventive range of dried, smoked, salted and pickled meats (*spekemat*) and fish. Some of the country's seminal dishes are based on this produce, including *fenalår* (cured leg of mutton) and *pinnekjøtt* (steamed salted lamb ribs served with either mashed swede or turnip). Other traditional favourites include *morr*, a smoked and cured sausage, and the delicate *smalahove*, smoked lamb's head, which is a Vestlandet speciality. Game dishes include breast of pheasant served with mushroom sauce, and marinade of rabbit.

Dill fronds

Gravlax, salmon preserved in a dill, sugar and salt mix, is served with a piquant dill and mustard sauce.

Fishing boats moored in snowy Svolvaer

Cheeses

Norway's most famous cheese export is Jarlsberg, a mild white cheese produced in rural dairies. However, many Norwegians prefer *geitost* (goat cheese), which is technically not cheese but caramelized goat's and cow's lactose. The most popular type is the sweet, brown *gudbrandsdalsost*. A more acquired taste is *gammelost* ("old cheese"), an over matured, highly pungent brown cheese – mere mention of it will make some Nordmen wince. Norwegian cheese is best served on Ryvita crispbread, another Scandinavian staple you'll find everywhere.

with mustard or onions. *Lutefisk* is a chewy fish marinated in lye. Other catch includes shrimp, haddock, mackerel, Arctic char and cod, which is often split and dried *(klippfisk)*. Fish soup is a very popular appetizer.

Norway is one of only two countries with a commercial whaling industry, resumed after decades of moratorium and boycott. With a small annual quota, whale *(hval)* meat is seen as a delicacy here and you'll hear little controversy over the ethics of eating it. Seal is also eaten, but normally only in Tromsø.

Game

Elk, reindeer and woodland fowl have been staples of the Norwegian diet for centuries. Reindeer, still herded by Sámi semi-pastoralists, is often served thinly sliced in a thick cream sauce, although fillet of reindeer with lingonberries is also very popular. Game is often accompanied by chunky root vegetables and wild mushrooms, making hearty dishes fit for a cold climate.

Punnets of Norwegian gooseberries and redcurrants

What to Drink

Norway's most famous drink is Linie Akevitt (Aquavit), a potent brew of caraway and potatoes spiced with anise, fennel and coriander. Along with pilsner or red beer, Aquavit is the traditional accompaniment to many Norwegian dishes including mutton, cabbage, *smørbrød* and *lutefisk*. The Linie brand is aged in large oak sherry barrels, then shipped off in the hull of a Norwegian tanker on a round-the-world voyage to traverse the equator (the "linie"); the rocking effect produced by the waves is said to give it a finer taste. At Christmas, Norwegians enjoy *gløgg*, warmed red wine flavoured with cinnamon, raisins, ginger and cloves.

Lapskaus is a traditional stew of various meats and vegetables, flavoured with bay and nutmeg.

Reindyrstek, roast reindeer fillet, is served with boiled potatoes, rich gravy and a lingonberry sauce.

Tilslørte Bondepike ("veiled farm girl") is layers of apple purée with sweet cinnamon crumbs and whipped cream.

Where to Eat and Drink

Oslo

Central Oslo West

Egon Karl Johan Ⓚ
International **Map** 3 D3
Karl Johans Gate 37, 0162
Tel *22 41 77 90*
Located in the Paléet shopping complex, Egon is part of a family-friendly chain. Serves salads, Tex-Mex, fish and pizzas. Good children's menu.

Olivia Aker Brygge Ⓚ
Italian **Map** 2 C4
Bryggegangen 4, 0252
Tel *23 11 54 70*
Authentic pizzas, pasta and *antipasti* feature on the menu here. This is the best located of Olivia's three branches in Oslo.

Brasserie 45 ⓀⓀ
Norwegian **Map** 3 D3
Stortingsgata 20, 0161
Tel *22 41 34 00*
One of Oslo's most competitively priced restaurants, Brasserie 45 offers delicious, high-quality fare. The restaurant menu is a mix of seafood and meat.

Coco Vika ⓀⓀ
Asian **Map** 2 C3
Dronning Mauds Gate 1, 0250
Tel *22 83 18 18*
Reasonably priced restaurant, popular with locals who come here for lunch or after work for sushi and tapas. Good wine list.

Hard Rock Café Oslo ⓀⓀ
American **Map** 3 D3
Karl Johans Gate 45, 0162
Tel *40 00 62 60*
Well-located branch of the popular chain offering everything from superb burgers and Tex-Mex food to great cocktails and regular live music.

Alex Sushi ⓀⓀⓀ
Japanese **Map** 2 C3
Cort Adelers Gate 2, 0254
Tel *22 43 99 99*
Considered by many food critics to be the best sushi restaurant outside of Japan, Alex Sushi is a must for all sushi fans. Booking ahead is essential.

D/S Louise ⓀⓀⓀ
Scandinavian **Map** 2 C4
Stranden 3, 0250
Tel *22 83 00 60*
Located over a number of floors, this place has great views of the harbour. Serves terrific food; the fish soup is an Oslo legend.

Fru K ⓀⓀⓀ
Scandinavian **Map** 2 B4
Landgangen 1, 0252
Tel *24 00 40 40*
An exciting upscale restaurant with a Michelin-starred chef and a waterfront location. The seven-course menu is a tempting offer.

Lorry Restaurant ⓀⓀⓀ
Bistro **Map** 2 B3
Parkveien 12, 0350
Tel *22 69 69 04*
Serves simple and well-priced Norwegian food. The reindeer burger is the house dish and a favourite with almost everyone.

Oro ⓀⓀⓀ
Norwegian **Map** 3 D3
Tordenskiolds Gate 6, 0160
Tel *23 01 02 40*
Michelin-starred eatery that uses locally sourced Norwegian ingredients to create an exciting culinary experience. Great set menus and excellent wine list.

Theatercaféen ⓀⓀⓀ
Norwegian **Map** 3 D3
Stortingsgata 24, 0117
Tel *22 82 40 50*
Opulent Viennese-style eatery. Serves good food, coffee and excellent wine. Seasonal menu. Very popular, so book ahead.

Tjuvholmen Sjømagasin ⓀⓀⓀ
Seafood **Map** 2 B4
Tjuvholmen Allé 14, 0252
Tel *23 89 77 77*
Simple yet elegant fish restaurant perched on the edge of hip Tjuvholmen. Serves Norwegian seafood delicacies, enhanced by creative side dishes.

Price Guide
Prices are based on a three-course meal for one, with half a bottle of house wine inclusive of tax and service charges.

Ⓚ	under 300 NKr
ⓀⓀ	300 to 600 NKr
ⓀⓀⓀ	over 600 NKr

Ylajali ⓀⓀⓀ
Scandinavian **Map** 3 D2
St Olavs Plass 2, 0165
Tel *22 20 64 86* **Closed** *Sun*
Enjoy sensational food in a grand 19th-century building with a great ambience. Some of the tasting menus appear to be endless.

Central Oslo East

Vega Fair Food Ⓚ
Vegetarian **Map** 3 D4
Akersgata 74, 0180
Tel *47 92 12 14*
One of the very few vegetarian eateries in Oslo, Vega has a good hot and cold buffet with plenty of variety. Close to the city's main train station.

Café Christiania ⓀⓀ
French **Map** 3 D3
Nedre Vollgate 19, 0158
Tel *22 01 05 10* **Closed** *Sun*
Simple yet elegant bistro located in the freemasons' building opposite the Stortinget. Set menu for lunch and dinner, plus afternoon tea.

Dattera til Hagen ⓀⓀ
International **Map** 3 F3
Grønland 10, 0188
Tel *22 17 18 61*
The fare here includes burgers with creative toppings, warm and cold tapas and vegetarian options.

Modern dining room at Ylajai, a Scandinavian restaurant

Grilleriet ⓀⓀ
Norwegian **Map** 3 E3
Størgata 21–23, 0184
Tel *22 83 56 00*
Watch the chefs prepare your grilled main, from spare ribs to halibut, in the open kitchen. Seasonal ingredients are the focus here, but the chefs also experiment to create exciting dishes.

Håndverkerstuene ⓀⓀ
Bistro **Map** 3 D3
Rosenkrantz' Gate 7, 0159
Tel *22 42 07 50*
Rustic charm, modern design and a Belgian-influenced menu that offers comfort food such as hearty sausages and fish soup.

Kaffistova ⓀⓀ
Scandinavian **Map** 3 D3
Rosenkrantz' Gate 8, 0159
Tel *23 21 42 10*
One of Oslo's top lunch spots. Bright and open, it serves big portions of classics such as meatballs and reindeer burgers.

Olympen ⓀⓀ
Norwegian
Grønlandsleiret 15, 0190
Tel *24 10 19 99*
This pub and bistro offers an amazing selection of beer and food that is a cut above ordinary pub grub.

Ricebowl ⓀⓀ
Asian **Map** 3 E3
Youngs Gate 4, 0181
Tel *22 41 20 06*
A good choice for lunch or dinner. Plenty of dishes to choose from, all served quickly.

Brasserie France ⓀⓀⓀ
French **Map** 3 D3
Øvre Slottsgate 16, 0157
Tel *23 10 01 65* **Closed** *Sun*
Fine selection of classic French cuisine prepared by a team of top chefs. Unpretentious and charming spot. Book ahead.

Det Gamle Raadhus ⓀⓀⓀ
Seafood **Map** 3 E3
Nedre Slottsgate 1, 0157
Tel *22 42 01 07*
An Oslo legend open since 1641 in what was once Oslo City Hall. Known today for its fish and game dishes. Try the cheek of monkfish.

Engebret Café ⓀⓀⓀ
Seafood **Map** 3 D4
Bankplassen 1, 0151
Tel *22 82 25 25*
This café has played host to some of Norway's famous writers. Seafood and game dominate the menu. There is a great mid-morning buffet too.

Det Gamle Raadhus in the former City Hall

Fiskeriet ⓀⓀⓀ
Seafood **Map** 3 E3
Youngstorget 2, 0181
Tel *22 42 45 40* **Closed** *Sun*
Fiskeriet is a must for all seafood fans. Delicious food includes a Norwegian take on fish 'n' chips, fish soup and a seafood stew. Guests are served at the bar.

Grand Café ⓀⓀⓀ
Seafood **Map** 3 D3
Karl Johans Gate 31, 0159
Tel *23 21 20 00*
This famous café is where Henrik Ibsen dined each day. Located at the Grand Hotel, the bar-lounge is perfect for pre-theatre drinks. Great outdoor seating area in summer.

DK Choice

Maaemo ⓀⓀⓀ
Fine dining **Map** 3 F3
Schweigaards Gate 15, 0191
Tel *91 99 48 05*
Michelin-starred Maaemo is perhaps Norway's best restaurant. Spend an entire evening enjoying their landmark 25-course seasonal menu which comes accompanied by fine wines. The dishes are all beautifully presented and take diners on an adventure through the flavours of Scandinavia with twists from around the world. The food is worth every penny.

Palmen ⓀⓀⓀ
Norwegian/International **Map** 3 D3
Karl Johans Gate 31, 0159
Tel *23 21 20 00* **Closed** *Sun*
An architectural gem, complete with a glass roof and antique furniture. The food here is a mix of light lunches, evening meals and a superb selection of cakes. Good coffee, too.

Solsilden ⓀⓀⓀ
Seafood **Map** 3 D4
Akershusstranda 34, 0150
Tel *22 33 36 30*
A relaxed and friendly place right on the waterfront. Forgo the menu and ask the chef what is good that day.

Stortorvets Gjæstgiveri ⓀⓀⓀ
Norwegian **Map** 3 E3
Grensen 1, 0159
Tel *23 35 63 60* **Closed** *Sun*
The exterior of this 18th-century building has remained almost unchanged. The restaurant, offering traditional Norwegian food such as roasted reindeer, retains a historic feel as well.

Further Afield

Mathallen ⓀⓀ
Norwegian **Map** 3 F2
Maridalsveien 17, 0175
Tel *40 00 12 09*
A popular food destination between central Olso and trendy Grunnerlokka. Over 30 eateries and boutiques grace this food court, which is a great spot to dine on Norwegian cuisine.

Contemporary Michelin-starred restaurant Maaemo

For more information on types of restaurants *see page 235*

Tables set up ready for diners at Bølgen & Moi, Høvikodden

Bagatelle (Kr)(Kr)(Kr)
Fine Dining **Map** 1 B1
Bygdøy Allé 3, 0257
Tel *22 44 40 40* **Closed** *Sun*
Michelin-starred restaurant with a luxurious menu and a formidable wine list. French fare dominates but the ingredients are locally sourced.

Ekeberg Restaurant (Kr)(Kr)(Kr)
Scandinavian
Kongsveien 15, 0193
Tel *23 24 23 00*
Oslo residents flock to this classy eatery for seasonal cuisine with a contemporary edge. Chanterelle salad with duck egg and deer sirloin stand out.

Feinschmecker (Kr)(Kr)(Kr)
French
Balchens Gate 5, 0265
Tel *22 12 93 80* **Closed** *Sun*
One of Oslo's top restaurants. The cuisine is fantastic. There is also a set vegetarian tasting menu, which is superb. Make sure you leave room for dessert.

Frognerseteren (Kr)(Kr)(Kr)
Scandinavian
Holmenkollveien 200, 0791
Tel *22 92 40 40*
This eatery offers lovely, sweeping views of the city and the Oslo-fjord. The kitchen serves up seasonal food.

Holmenkollen Restaurant (Kr)(Kr)(Kr)
Norwegian/International
Holmenkollveien 119, 0787
Tel *22 13 92 00*
Built with logs and stone, this place is perched near the summit of a hill close to the ski jump, so the views are stunning. Don't miss the apple pie.

Restaurant Sawan (Kr)(Kr)(Kr)
Thai **Map** 2 B2
President Harbitz' Gate 4, 0259
Tel *40 00 90 60*
An upscale Thai experience with inventive dishes made from quality ingredients. A glass of wine from the award-winning list cools the after-effects of the fiery curries.

Smalhans (Kr)(Kr)(Kr)
Scandinavian
Waldemar Thranes Gate 10, entr.
Ullevåsvein 41, 0171
Tel *22 69 60 00*
Traditional cuisine is the draw at Norwegian celebrity chef Tom Victor Gausdal's eatery. Open sandwiches and stews shine, and there are local craft beers on tap.

Around Oslofjorden

ENGALSVIK: Engelsviken Brygge Fiskerestaurant (Kr)(Kr)(Kr)
Seafood
Engelsvikenveien 6, 1628
Tel *69 35 18 40* **Closed** *Mon & Tue*
Great views and superb seafood make this a real favourite. Book ahead on weekends.

FREDRIKSTAD: Shiki Sushi Bar (Kr)(Kr)
Seafood
Storgata 10, 1607
Tel *69 33 88 28*
Highly regarded sushi restaurant. The range is extensive and there are set menus. Takeaway available.

FREDRIKSTAD: Major Stuen (Kr)(Kr)(Kr)
International
Voldportgaten 73, 1632 Gamle
Tel *69 32 15 55*
Folksy eatery with a wide range of light lunches and substantial dishes. Good-value set lunch.

Banquette seating at stylish Thai Restaurant Sawan

FREDRIKSTAD: Tobias Steakhouse (Kr)(Kr)(Kr)
International
Nygaardsgata 44, 1607
Tel *69 38 57 84*
Although expensive, the meat here is of the highest quality. There are plenty of other options, such as pizza and seafood. Play area for children as well.

HALDEN:
Café Spisekroken (Kr)(Kr)
Italian
Svenskegata 2, 1776
Tel *69 18 02 02*
Family-owned Italian café that uses fresh ingredients. Serves great pizza and has a nice terrace. Opens early for breakfast. Good value for money.

HØVIKODDEN:
Bølgen & Moi (Kr)(Kr)
International
Henie-Onstad Art Centre, Sonja Henies vei, 1311
Tel *67 52 10 20*
Nationwide chain that offers tasty food in a quirky setting. This branch is housed in an arts centre and hosts changing exhibitions. Try the delicious five-course meal.

LARVIK: Farris Bad Restaurant (Kr)(Kr)
Norwegian/French
Fritzøe Brygge 2, 3264
Tel *815 58 700*
This eco-friendly restaurant with stunning sea views serves locally sourced, delicate, raw dishes in an elegant atmosphere.

LARVIK:
Becks Brasserie & Bar (Kr)(Kr)(Kr)
Bistro
Fritzøe Brygge 1, 3264
Tel *480 51 111*
Trendy restaurant with one of the region's better wine selections. Serves mainly meat and fish dishes with a Scandinavian twist.

Skutebrygga restaurant on Dramme's waterfront

LARVIK:
Trudvang Gjestedaard Ⓚ Ⓚ Ⓚ
Norwegian
Gårdsbakken 43, 3256
Tel *33 16 52 70*
Elegant restaurant in a grand
building dating back to 1881.
Serves traditional food.

SANDEFJORD: Brygge 11 Ⓚ Ⓚ Ⓚ
Seafood
Brygga 11, 3222
Tel *95 55 91 91*   **Closed** *winter*
Contemporary Scandanavian
restaurant on the harbour front.
The highlights on the menu are
the delicious salmon dishes.

SANDEFJORD: SMAK Ⓚ Ⓚ Ⓚ
Scandinavian
Thor Dahls Gate 9, 3210
Tel *33 46 27 41*   **Closed** *Mon & Sun*
Widely viewed as Sandefjord's
finest eatery. Outstanding seafood
and meat often prepared with
real invention.

SARPSBORG:
Festiviteten Ⓚ Ⓚ Ⓚ
Fine Dining
Sandesundsveien 2, 1724
Tel *69 13 30 00*   **Closed** *Sun*
Stylish dining in a grand building.
The food is beautifully presented
and served with real pomp.

STAVERN: Skipperstua Ⓚ
Seafood
Skippergata 8, 3290
Tel *33 19 92 15*
Bargain deli serving a wide range
of dishes. Terrific value and
massively popular. Takeaway too.

TØNSBERG: Conradis Bar
& Restaurant Ⓚ Ⓚ Ⓚ
Seafood
Nedre Langgate 18, 3126
Tel *33 37 09 00*
Mainly serves seafood in a
contemporary setting, but there
is also some game on the
extensive menu. Good wine list.

TØNSBERG: Esmerelda Ⓚ Ⓚ Ⓚ
International
Nedre Langgate 26C, 3126
Tel *33 31 91 91*
Restaurant, pub, piano bar and
pizzeria rolled into one on the
harbour jetty. Portions are
generous and there's a good
choice of vegetarian dishes
available. Family-friendly.

Eastern Norway

DK Choice

BÆRUMS VERK: Værtshuset
Bærums Verk Ⓚ Ⓚ Ⓚ
Norwegian
Vertshusveien 10, 1353
Tel *67 80 02 00*
Norway's oldest restaurant, built
in the mid-17th century, is
located in romantic surrounds at
the entrance to the Lommedalen
valley. The restaurant serves
locally sourced and traditional
Norwegian dishes, featuring
seafood and game. Try the elk
carpaccio or fillet of reindeer. A
truly memorable experience.

DRAMMEN: Pigen Ⓚ
Bistro
Bragernes Torg 9, 3017
Tel *32 83 45 50*
Pigen is a centrally located,
unconventional bistro in a
historic building. It offers a varied
and changing range of fare,
including an excellent children's
menu. Good coffee, too.

DRAMMEN: Aroma India Ⓚ Ⓚ
Indian
Torggate 4, 3017
Tel *32 83 82 50*
A good-value restaurant where
the chef will happily spice things
up for diners who like their curries
hot. Top-notch onion bhajis.

DRAMMEN: Elvebredden Bar
& Restaurant Ⓚ Ⓚ Ⓚ
Italian
Grønland 54, 3045
Tel *32 82 74 00*
Bright, spacious bar and grill with
a more formal section upstairs for
special occassions. Food is served
with a local twist.

DRAMMEN: Glass Grill
& Bar Ⓚ Ⓚ Ⓚ
International
Nedre Strandgate 4, 3015
Tel *32 82 00 70*
Waterfront restaurant with huge
windows that offer great harbour
views. Food is modern with the
emphasis on steaks and burgers.

DRAMMEN:
Skutebrygga Ⓚ Ⓚ Ⓚ
Seafood
Nedre Strandgate 2, 3015
Tel *32 26 88 01*
Trendy place packed with
pictures from Drammen's past.
Separate lunch and dinner
menus are mainly centred on
seafood and grilled meats.

GEILO: Capri Ⓚ
Italian
Vesleslåttvegen 19, 3580
Tel *32 09 09 03*
One of the very few places in
Geilo serving pizza and pasta at
reasonable prices. Great service.
Particularly popular during the
skiing season.

GJOVIK: Skibladner Ⓚ Ⓚ Ⓚ
Norwegian
Jernbanegate 2, 2802
Tel *61 14 40 80*
Restaurant on board a restored
paddle-steamer that continues
to run a service across Lake Mjøsa
during the summer. Traditional
Norwegian fare.

Inviting festive entrance to Værtshuset
Bærums Verk

Stunning mountain views at the Skarsnuten Hotel's restaurant, Hemsedal

HAMAR: Hamarstua Spiseri ⓀⓀ
Bistro
Strandvegen 100, 2315
Tel *62 52 34 62*
Historic location at Domkirke-odden. Traditional Norwegian fare is made with local produce.

HAMAR: Irishman ⓀⓀ
Pub
Strandgata 31, 2317
Tel *62 52 33 92*
Serves vast portions of pub grub including steaks, eggs and bacon, as well as sandwiches. Best draft beers in town.

HAMAR: Nagomi ⓀⓀⓀ
Japanese
Strandgata 21, 2317
Tel *62 52 11 02*
This excellent restaurant offers a full range of sushi. Other dishes include miso soup. Great cocktails.

HEMSEDAL: Skarsnuten ⓀⓀⓀ
European
Skarsnuten Hotel, 3560
Tel *32 06 17 00*
The hotel's futuristic dining room at a height of 1,000 m (3,280 ft) offers great views. The food is delicious, especially the soups.

HEMSEDAL: Skogstad Hotell ⓀⓀⓀ
Norwegian
Skogstad Hotell, 3561
Tel *32 05 50 00*
Visit this à la carte restuarant for amazing food. There is a bar and an inexpensive buffet eatery too.

LILLEHAMMER: Blåmann Restaurant & Bar ⓀⓀ
Norwegian/Mexican
Lilletorget 1, 2615
Tel *61 26 22 03*
The food is a bizarre but good mix of Norwegian and Mexican, such as beef and reindeer quesadillas. Everything is cooked to order in a large open kitchen.

LILLEHAMMER: Café Stift ⓀⓀ
Café
Kirkegata 41, 2609
Tel *61 27 00 40* **Closed** *Sun*
One of Lillehammer's best-value eateries serving burgers, sandwiches and salads. Doubles as a trendy bar/club on Fridays and Saturdays.

LILLEHAMMER: Egon Restaurant ⓀⓀⓀ
International
Elvegata 12, 2609
Tel *61 25 23 40*
Restaurant in a milling house that dates from 1863. Food is simple but tasty: sausages, burgers, salads and pizzas.

LILLEHAMMER: Nikkers ⓀⓀⓀ
Bistro
Elvegata 18, 2609
Tel *61 24 74 30*
Superb bistro serving Italian fare and a range of local game and seafood. Look out for the daily specials, served until they run out. Vegetarian options and a children's menu available too.

LILLEHAMMER: Telemarkstunet ⓀⓀⓀ
Scandinavian
Kantveien 135, 2618
Tel *90 64 13 67*
Inside this traditional homestead guests are served outstanding food, as well as a selection of fine wines from around the world. Good set lunch menus.

LILLEHAMMER: Victoriastuen ⓀⓀⓀ
Scandinavian
Storgata 84B, 2609
Tel *61 25 00 49* **Closed** *Sun*
Located at the Rica Victoria hotel, this restaurant offers fine food. Specialities include mountain trout and *kjøttboller* (meatballs). Great people-watching spot.

TRYSIL: Laaven ⓀⓀ
Bistro
Trysilfjell Turistsenter, 2420
Tel *62 45 26 00*
Boasts a large open fire and rustic decor. The menu is varied and there is an all-you-can-eat buffet lunch. Crowded on weekends.

TRYSIL: Big Horn Steakhouse ⓀⓀⓀ
Steakhouse
Trysilfjell Apartment Hotel, 2420
Tel *62 45 23 55*
Seriously good steaks that can be ordered in a variety of sizes, up to a whopping 400 g (0.8 lb). Try the house speciality – Mexican pepper steak.

Sørlandet and Telemark

ARENDAL: Madam Reiersen ⓀⓀ
Bistro
Nedre Tyholmsvei 3, 4836
Tel *37 02 19 00*
Friendly restaurant on the quayside with an adjoining bar. Offers an international menu and has live music some evenings.

ARENDAL: Nidelv Brygge ⓀⓀ
Seafood
Vesterveien 250, 4817
Tel *37 01 14 24*
Superb little restaurant located at a campsite south of Arendal. Serves simple yet delicious seafood. Perfect summer setting to enjoy a meal.

ARENDAL: Solsiden Brasserie ⓀⓀ
Tapas
Langbryggen 7, 4841
Tel *40 00 07 03*
There is something for everyone at this great tapas bar that also offers pizza, pasta, salads and burgers. Suitable for big groups.

ARENDAL: Mør
Steakhouse (Kr)(Kr)(Kr)
Nedre Tyholmsvei 2, 4836
Tel *37 02 02 02*
Good steakhouse serving a
wide range of top beef including
the sensational 800 g (2 lb)
Porterhouse. Fish dishes and
salads as well. There is another
branch in Grimstad.

GRIMSTAD: Apotekegarden
Restaurant & Bar (Kr)(Kr)(Kr)
Scandinavian
Skolegaten 3, 4876
Tel *37 04 50 25*
A stylish eatery famous for its
seven-course gourmet menu
that takes diners on a delicious
culinary journey of Scandinavia.
Beautiful setting.

HAMRESANDEN:
Lanternen Restaurant (Kr)
Scandinavian
Hamresandveien 3, 4876
Tel *38 14 42 80*
A charming spot serving
breakfast, simple lunch dishes
and more sophisticated à la
carte dinners.

HOVDEN: Eminent Hovdestoylen
Hotel (Kr)(Kr)
Scandinavian
Hovdestoylen Hotel, 4756
Tel *37 93 88 00*
This restaurant, set in the rustic
Hovdestoylen Hotel, serves
delicious food from a lava stone
grill. Good-value set menus.

KRISTIANSAND:
Café Dronningen (Kr)(Kr)
Norwegian
Dronningens Gate 5, 4610
Tel *38 17 40 00*
This popular eatery, at the Hotel
Norge, is located in the heart of
town. Come here for breakfast,
lunch or dinner. The homemade
bread is excellent.

KRISTIANSAND:
Brasserie C (Kr)(Kr)(Kr)
Norwegian
Vestre Strandgatan 7, 4610
Tel *38 11 21 00*
Located in Radisson Blu, this
restaurant offers a great buffet
breakfast and an à la carte dinner.
The hotel also has a lively pub,
the Telford.

KRISTIANSAND: Glipp (Kr)(Kr)(Kr)
International
Rådhusgata 11, 4611
Tel *38 02 96 20*
Small and pleasant restaurant
specializing in dishes such as
tapas, bagels, pasta, pizza, wok
dishes and great soups. There is
something for everyone.

KRISTIANSAND:
Sjøhuset (Kr)(Kr)(Kr)
Seafood
Østre Strandgate 12 A, 4610
Tel *38 02 62 60*
This waterfront eatery is located
in a former salt warehouse that
dates back to 1892. The emphasis
here is on fish and shellfish
dishes, paired with a terrific
selection of wines. Guests relish
the delicious fare in a surprisingly
casual atmosphere. The huge
terrace is a great place for
relaxing, summer meals.

LANGESUND: Wrightegaarden
i Langesund (Kr)(Kr)
Norwegian
Tordenskjolds Gate 2, 3970
Tel *40 24 63 30*
Artists such as Bob Dylan have
graced the stage at this venue that
also has outdoor performances
on most weekends during the
summer. The on-site restaurant is
perfect to grab some food before
the show.

PORSGRUNN: Becks Brasserie
& Bar Osebro Porsgrunn (Kr)(Kr)(Kr)
International
Storgata 16, 3915
Tel *48 05 11 11*
Set in an 18th-century manor
house located by the river. The
menu is based on fish and steaks.
Ideal setting for alfresco dining
in the summer.

RISOR: Kast Loss (Kr)(Kr)(Kr)
Seafood
Strandgata 23, 4950
Tel *37 15 07 77*
Balanced on the edge of a jetty,
Kast Loss is one of the most
fashionable seafood restaurants
in town. Pizzas and steaks are
also featured on the menu.
Terrific views.

Informal interior at Glipp restaurant,
Kristiansand

SKIEN: Becks Brasserie (Kr)(Kr)
Bistro
Langbryggene 6, 3724
Tel *48 05 11 11*
Good food at a decent price
from one of Norway's smaller
restaurant chains. The braised
lamb with parsley, bacon and
cognac gravy is excellent.

SKIEN: Jacob & Gabriel (Kr)(Kr)(Kr)
Scandinavian
Langbrygga 5A, 3724
Tel *35 70 72 91*
The region's best restaurant
serves fine and flavourful food in
a quirky and charming setting.
Good set menus with a choice
of four, five or six courses meals,
as well as à la carte dining.

VRÅDAL:
Straand Sommerland (Kr)(Kr)
Scandinavian
Quality Straand Hotel & Resort, 3853
Tel *35 06 90 00*
Sit out on the terrace surrounded
by forests and mountains and soak
up the endless views of the lake as
you feast on a vareity of tasty
dishes. There is a pub – allegedly
Norway's smallest – here as well.

Sjøhuset waterside restaurant, Kristiansand

For more information on types of restaurants *see page 235*

Spectacular views at Cornelius restaurant in the Byfjorden

Vestlandet

BERGEN: Bryggeloftet & Stuene Restaurant ⓚ ⓚ
Scandinavian
Bryggen 11, 5003
Tel *55 30 20 70*
Enjoy a meal in the fascinating atmosphere of the old wharf. Food is mainly fish and game. On Thursdays *Saltjøtt* and *Ruspeballer* (salt meat and potato dumplings) is the house specialty.

BERGEN: Dickens ⓚ ⓚ
Bistro
Kong Olav Vs plass 4, 5014
Tel *55 36 31 30*
Close to the Festplassen, this eatery is one of Bergen's dining landmarks. Good value food. Try the trademark Dicken's Burger.

BERGEN: Big Horn Steakhouse ⓚ ⓚ ⓚ
Steakhouse
Lodin Lepps Gate 2B, 5003
Tel *55 36 60 60*
Reliable chain of steakhouses. Try the ribeye bone served with béarnaise sauce or the immense New York striploin.

BERGEN: Bryggen Tracteursted ⓚ ⓚ ⓚ
Scandinavian
Bryggestredet 2, 5003
Tel *55 33 69 99*
This has been an eating place since 1701. It feels like a Hansa merchant's house, with the staff dressed up in period costumes. Serves exquisite food.

BERGEN: Cornelius ⓚ ⓚ ⓚ
Seafood
Cornelius AS, 5174 Mathopen
Tel *56 33 48 80*
Glorious restaurant on an island in the Byfjorden that can only be reached by boat, but it is worth the effort. It is essential to book in advance.

BERGEN: Holbergstuen ⓚ ⓚ ⓚ
Norwegian
Torgallmenningen 6, 5014
Tel *55 55 20 55*
Traditional restaurant in central Bergen. Quotes from the Bergen poet Holberg embellish the interiors. The delicious menu mainly features fish dishes. Try the grilled scampi and scallops.

BERGEN: Potetkjeleren ⓚ ⓚ ⓚ
Bistro
Kong Oscars Gate 1A, 5017
Tel *55 32 00 70*
A tiny place with a pretty courtyard and cellar located close to the fish market. The set menus with wine are great value for money.

BERGEN: To Kokker ⓚ ⓚ ⓚ
Scandinavian
Enhjørningsgården 29, 5003
Tel *55 30 69 55*
The best place in town for steaming pots of mussels and much more. A pub and restaurant rolled into one.

BERGEN: Wesselstuen ⓚ ⓚ ⓚ
Fine Dining
Øvre Ole Bulls Plass 6, 5012
Tel *55 55 49 49*
One of Bergen's legendary dining rooms, catering to the rich and famous since 1957. The menu is a delight – unpretentious Norwegian food including treats such as fillet of reindeer served with pickled red onion and creamy Bergen-style fish soup.

HAUGESUND: Bestastua Mat Prat & Vinhus ⓚ ⓚ ⓚ
Bistro
Strandgata 132, 5527
Tel *52 86 55 88*
This large restaurant situated in an old building is both an eatery and a piano bar. Diners can expect traditional Norwegian fare and a good range of cognacs in the bar.

KRISTIANSUND: Onkel & Vennene Hans ⓚ
Café
Kaibakken 1, 6509
Tel *71 67 58 10*
Chilled out place with a trendy crowd sipping on cocktails, coffee and cognac. Offers wraps, bagels and salads.

KRISTIANSUND: Smia Fiskerestaurant ⓚ ⓚ ⓚ
Seafood
Fosnagata 30B, 6509
Tel *71 67 11 70*
A wonderful little restaurant with charm, a varied menu, and an open fire in winter. The building dates back to 1787.

MOLDE: Molde Fjordstuer ⓚ ⓚ
Seafood
Julsundvegen 6, 6412
Tel *71 20 10 60*
Traditional and popular seafood restaurant. Try the creamy fish soup. The menu also features meat dishes. Book ahead in summer.

STAVANGER: Café Sting ⓚ
Bistro
Valbergjet 3, 4006
Tel *51 89 38 78*
Coffee, cakes and light meals in a simple yet pleasant café that has become a Stavanger legend. Good choice for a cheap lunch.

STAVANGER: Sjokoladepiken ⓚ
Café
Øvre Holmegate 27, 4006
Tel *47 20 19 83*
A bright pink house with a little chocolate factory. Coffee, bakery snacks and sandwiches on offer.

STAVANGER: Ostehuset ⓚ ⓚ
International
Hospitalgata 6, 4006
Tel *51 86 40 10*
A popular deli and bakery that serves a variety of sandwiches, salads and soups alongside good fruit juice and great coffee.

STAVANGER:
Bevaremegvel ⓚⓚⓚ
Fine Dining
Skagen 12, 4006
Tel *51 84 38 60*
The Bevaremegvel offers exquisite food and drinks with great views of the city. There is a choice of a varied à la carte menu, as well as more simple meals.

STAVANGER:
Harry Pepper ⓚⓚⓚ
Mexican
Øvre Holmegate 15, 4006
Tel *51 89 39 59*
Norway's first and best Mexican restaurant. Hot and spicy food is a real treat in a city not famed for non-traditional food.

STAVANGER: Sjohuset
Skagen ⓚⓚⓚ
Scandinavian
Skagenkaien 16, 4006
Tel *51 89 51 80*
This old restored bunkhouse on the wharf, next to the harbour, incorporates a range of inviting rooms over eight different floors. Come here to feast on good-value local food.

DK Choice

STAVANGER: Straen
Fiskerestaurant ⓚⓚⓚ
Seafood
Nedre Strandgate 15, 4005
Tel *51 84 37 00* **Closed** *Sun*
Amusingly touted as being "world famous throughout Norway", this is indeed one of the best seafood restaurants in the land. The old-fashioned interior is straight out of the 1950s and the windows open out to give fantastic harbour views. In addition there is a hip nightclub upstairs and the restaurant downstairs offers more of a bistro-type menu.

Café Lyspunktet bistro in Ålesund

VOSS: Elysée ⓚⓚⓚ
Bistro
Uttrågatta 1-3, 5700
Tel *56 51 13 22*
The on-site restaurant of the Hotel Park offers an inventive selection of food, including French and Norwegian dishes. It also boasts one of Europe's best-stocked wine cellars.

VOSS: Magdalene ⓚⓚⓚ
Fine Dining
Evangervegen 13, 5700
Tel *56 52 05 00*
The best restaurant in Voss is at the fairytale-like Fleischers Hotel. Choose from the set or à la carte monthly menus. Has a truly spectacular terrace.

ÅLESUND:
Café Lyspunktet ⓚⓚ
Bistro
Kipervikgata 1A, 6003
Tel *70 12 53 00* **Closed** *Mon*
Simple yet tasty food and great coffee. Reasonable prices, lovely atmosphere and a great staff. No alcohol is served.

ÅLESUND: Orient ⓚⓚ
Asian
Kongens Gate 30, 6002
Tel *70 10 71 71*
Tasty Japanese and Chinese food in a bright setting where the service is prompt and food appears in minutes. Best bet for a bargain lunch or dinner in town.

ÅLESUND: Taj Mahal ⓚⓚ
Indian
Kongens Gate 18, 6002
Tel *70 12 03 00*
Taj Mahal is in a modern building with a street terrace for summer. The menu is unfussy with a decent choice of dishes including many favourites, such as chicken tikka masala. The prices are good for this part of the world.

Sjohuset Skagen overlooking the harbour at Stavanger

ÅLESUND:
Hummer & Kanari ⓚⓚⓚ
European
Kongens Gate 19, 6002
Tel *70 12 80 08*
A cosmopolitan spot with high ceilings and magnificent views over the harbour. Serves Italian-based modern European food made with local produce. Pasta, fish, burgers and salads all feature and are well cooked.

ÅLESUND:
Sjobua Fiskerestaurant ⓚⓚⓚ
Seafood
Brunholmgate 1, 6004
Tel *70 12 71 00*
Outstanding fish restaurant situated in a renovated warehouse by the Brosundet Canal. The menu changes daily, but there is always a delicious assortment of dishes for diners to choose from.

ÅLESUND: XL Diner ⓚⓚⓚ
Bistro
Skaregata 1, 6002
Tel *70 12 42 53*
This place not only boasts the best views in town but also serves what it modestly calls "the best fish soup in town". Diners will be inclined to agree. Fish is also the main course.

Trøndelag

LEVANGER:
Backlund Brasserie ⓚⓚⓚ
Norwegian
Kirkegata 41, 7600
Tel *74 08 15 55*
Gorgeous brasserie serving classy food. The seasonal menu makes use of available local ingredients. Waterside location.

For more information on types of restaurants *see page 235*

DK CHOICE : Havfruen Fiskerestaurant

OPPDAL: Café Ludvik   Ⓚ
Café
Inge Krokannsvei 21, 7340
Tel *72 42 01 40*
One of Oppdal's most price-friendly eateries. Serves breakfast, lunch and light meals.

ORKANGER:
Bårdshaug Herregård ⓀⓀⓀ
Fine Dining
Orkedalsveien 102, 7300
Tel *72 47 99 00*
Dating back to the 19th century, this elegant place has hosted kings and queens. Today, it serves great dishes from a weekly menu.

RØROS:
Vertshuset Røros   ⓀⓀⓀ
Mediterranean
Kjerkgata 34, 7374
Tel *72 41 93 50*
The chefs here take inspiration from the Mediterranean but use mainly local ingredients, often from the nearby mountains.

STEINKJER: Brod & Cirkus ⓀⓀ
Bistro
Sannangata 8, 7713
Tel *74 16 21 00*
This bakery and confectioners offers simple but tasty lunch dishes and a wider range of meals during the evening.

TRONDHEIM:
Bakgarden Bar & Spiseri ⓀⓀ
Tapas
Kjøpmannsgata 40, 7011
Tel *45 22 24 88*
Terrific location for tapas and light meals, and one of the best-value places in town.

TRONDHEIM: Credo   ⓀⓀⓀ
Seafood
Ørjaveita 4, 7010
Tel *73 53 03 88*
Gourmet restaurant with a changing menu. The five-course dinner is a must. There is a bistro upstairs.

DK Choice

TRONDHEIM: Havfruen
Fiskerestaurant ⓀⓀⓀ
Seafood
Kjøpmannsgata 7, 7013
Tel *73 87 40 70*
The best fish restaurant in Trondheim, nestled in an old warehouse on the waterfront. Any type of fish that swims in Norway's waters can be found here. The top chef also whips up excellent meat dishes. Go for the superb multi-course gourmet set menus which allow diners to try a variety of flavours. There is a terrace for summer dining.

TRONDHEIM: Palmehaven ⓀⓀ
Norwegian
Dronningens Gate 5, 7011
Tel *73 80 08 00*   **Closed** *Sun lunch*
Large dining room at the Britannia Hotel, serving a fantastic all-you-can-eat buffet for breakfast and lunch. The buffet always features a wide range of of fish and meat dishes.

TRONDHEIM:
Emilies et Spisested ⓀⓀⓀ
Fine Dining
Erling Skakkes Gate 45, 7012
Tel *73 92 96 41*
This small eatery close to the central square offers a fixed five-course menu with individual options. Cuisine is Italian and French, and the food comes exquisitely presented.

TRONDHEIM: Fem Bord ⓀⓀⓀ
Norwegian
Dronningens Gate 37, 7012
Tel *454 88 889*   **Closed** *Sun & Mon*
A quiet little restaurant serving amazing food. Choose from a five- or eight-course set menu and prepare yourself for some outstandingly original cuisine.

TRONDHEIM: Vertshuset
Grenaderen   ⓀⓀⓀ
Norwegian
Kongsgårdsgata 1, 7013
Tel *73 51 66 80*   **Closed** *Mon*
The menu at this restaurant in a former forge highlights traditional Norwegian food. There is a folklore floorshow some evenings. In the summer, sit outside on the terrace.

Northern Norway and Svalbard

BODØ: Kafe Kafka   ⓀⓀ
Café
Sandgata 5B, 8006
Tel *75 52 35 20*   **Closed** *Sun*
Popular, elegant eatery that serves light meals such as upmarket sandwiches with fries and wine.

BODØ: Bryggerikaia   ⓀⓀⓀ
Bistro
Sjøgaten 1, 8006
Tel *75 52 58 08*
Look out for the specials at this great bistro, with a friendly atmosphere. Lovely location by the waterfront. Superb staff.

BODØ: Restaurant Smak ⓀⓀⓀ
Scandinavian
Dronningens Gate 26, 8006
Tel *45 23 11 00*   **Closed** *Sun*
Smak means taste and there is plenty of flavour on the menu here, which mainly consists of seafood. Wines complement each dish. Reservations are essential.

HAMMERFEST: Peppes Pizza Ⓚ
Italian
Sjøgata 6, 9600
Tel *22 22 55 55*
Part of a Norway-wide chain offering a good meal. Choose from pizza, pasta or salads. Eat in, take away, or ask for home delivery.

A flaming torch welcomes diners to Bryggerikaia, Bodø

HAMMERFEST:
Redrum Café ⓀⓀ
Café
Storgata 23, 9600
Tel *78 41 00 49*
Contemporary place serving a
good range of snacks and light
meals at reasonable prices. It also
doubles up as a live music club
on weekends.

HARSTAD: Hoelstuen ⓀⓀ
Norwegian
Rikard Kaarbøs Plass 4, 9405
Tel *77 06 55 00*
Superb little restaurant which
packs a serious punch, both in
terms of style and the high
quality food. A real gem.

HARSTAD:
Restaurant de 4 Roser ⓀⓀⓀ
Fine Dining
Torvet 7, 9405
Tel *77 01 27 50*
French-Italian food cooked in an
open kitchen at a chic restaurant.
Also operates a café for lighter
and less expensive meals.

KARASJOK: Storgammen ⓀⓀ
Scandinavian
Leavnnjageaidnu 3 9730
Tel *78 46 88 60*
For a unique experience try this
place serving centuries-old Lapp
recipes. The building itself is
made of wooden logs with a turf
roof. Book in advance.

DK Choice

LONGYEARBYEN: Huset ⓀⓀ
Scandinavian
Longyearbyen 9171, Svalbard
Tel *79 02 25 00*
It is worth splurging at this
restaurant, one of the most
amazing in the whole of Norway.
Many of the country's top chefs
have worked here since it
opened in 1977. The polar bear
on the wall was shot in 1982
and eaten at the restaurant. The
seasonal menus are dedicated
to the flavours of the north, and
the extensive wine list is
sensational. Huset also has a
café dating back to 1951 that
serves bistro-style dishes.

MO I RANA:
Meyergården Hotel ⓀⓀⓀ
Scandinavian
Fridtjof Nansens Gate 28, 8622
Tel *75 13 40 00*
The kitchen here focuses on the
use of local ingredients and
produce. Look out for reindeer and
the superb cheeses supplied by
a nearby farm. The varied menu
ranges from snacks to à la carte.

Colourful façade of Emma's
Drommerkjokken, Tromsø

NARVIK: Linken
Restaurant og Bar ⓀⓀⓀ
Norwegian
Kongensgate 64, 8500
Tel *76 97 70 00*
Feast on lots of interesting small
dishes made with local produce.
Choose either the 9- or 14-course
meal. Fantastic view over Narvik.

SVOLVÆR:
Du Verden Restaurant ⓀⓀⓀ
Seafood
Torget 15, 8300
Tel *76 07 09 75*   **Closed** *Sun*
A contemporary yet casual
restaurant in an amazing loft
where tradition meets style. There
are set menus every Thursday and
Friday, based on the fresh local
ingredients that are available.

TROMSØ: Blå Rock Café ⓀⓀ
Pub
Strandgata 14, 9008
Tel *77 61 00 20*
Friendly staff and locals make all
the guests feel like regulars at this
pub. The food consists mainly of
tasty burgers and fries. Guests can
pick from a top range of beers.

TROMSØ: Skarven Kro Ⓚ
Bistro
Strandtorget 1, 9008
Tel *77 60 07 20*
A highly popular pub serving
daily specials such as fish stew
alongside various local dishes.
Halibut and reindeer are
popular with locals at lunchtime.

TROMSØ:
Fiskekompaniet ⓀⓀⓀ
Seafood
Killengrensgate, 9007
Tel *77 68 76 00*
Elegant and stylish restaurant
located on the quayside. Serves
traditional cuisine based on dried
and salted fish.

TROMSØ:
Aunegården ⓀⓀⓀ
Norwegian
Sjøgata 29, 9008
Tel *77 65 12 34*
Made up of a number of different
rooms, all with a different feel
and history. Serves a full range
of dishes from snacks and light
meals to gourmet cusine. Good
wine selection, too.

TROMSØ: Emma's
Drommerkjokken ⓀⓀⓀ
Norwegian
Kirkegata 8, 9008
Tel *77 63 77 30*   **Closed** *Sun*
Anne Brit, known as "Emma",
operates this dream kitchen
and is the best-known chef in
northern Norway. Dishes are
made using local ingredients
infused with exotic flavours.

TROMSØ: Steakers ⓀⓀⓀ
Steakhouse
Fredrik Langes Gate 13, 9008
Tel *77 61 33 30*
Inspired by 1930s Chicago, this
is the best place in town for
steaks, which come in a range
of sizes. Informal but trendy, it
is situated at the quayside.

Huset, one of Norway's top restaurants

For more information on types of restaurants *see page 235*

SHOPPING IN NORWAY

Norway's larger towns have a wide selection of shopping centres and department stores. Generally, prices are high, but there are often good buys to be had when it comes to gold and silver items, watches, glass and leather articles. VAT on sales is particularly steep in Norway, but foreign visitors can reclaim a percentage of the total amount that they spend by taking advantage of the tax-free facility. Among the best buys are hand-knitted sweaters and cardigans in traditional patterns, known as *lusekofte*. Specialist craft shops in all the towns offer a good selection of beautiful hand-crafted articles made of wood, pewter, silver and linen. Sámi crafts and jewellery make exquisite gifts, while Norwegian food specialities and the famous aquavit always makes a good gift. Shopping in Oslo is covered on pp102–103.

Opening Hours

Opening hours vary, but most shops are open between 9am and 5pm on weekdays. Shopping centres and department stores open at 9–10am and close between 6–9pm. In many towns it is becoming standard practice to stay open until 2–3pm on Saturday, while shopping centres and department stores open at 9am and close around 6pm. There are often late openings on Thursday until 6 or 7pm, as well as the first Saturday of each month, known as *Super Lørdag* ("Super Saturday"). Shops are closed on Sunday, except in the run-up to Christmas when shopping centres and department stores open for business. Food stores generally remain open from 9am–10pm during the week and 9–6pm on Saturdays. Newsstands often stay open until 9 or 10pm.

Many towns have a local petrol station that remains open until midnight, or even around the clock, which can be useful as most have small supermarkets selling everything from food, gifts, flowers and music to coffee, sweets and hot dogs.

How to Pay

As a rule, department stores and shopping centres accept all internationally recognized credit cards, such as VISA, MasterCard, Diners, Eurocard and American Express. Travellers' cheques are on the decline as a form of payment and not all shops will accept them. If you are using travellers' cheques you must also have identification, such as a passport or driving licence. All shopping centres have cash machines (ATMs). Some Norwegian shopping centres may accept the euro on purchases.

Hand-crafted goods on sale in a Norwegian market

Sales Tax and Tax-free Shopping

Sales tax (*moms*) levied on goods currently can be up to 25 per cent of the purchase price. Since Norway is not a member of the European Union, residents of EU and non-EU states, with the exception of visitors from Sweden, Denmark and Finland, can reclaim the sales tax paid on goods over a specified amount.

More than 3,000 shops in Norway offer tax-free shopping, allowing you to reclaim some of the total price, depending on the type of item purchased. Most tourist-oriented shops in the country fall under the tax-free umbrella, but there are no tax-free concessions in restaurants or for car hire.

For information on how to reclaim tax, pick up the brochure "How to Shop Tax Free in Norway", available at many shops or look online at www.visitnorway.com.

Colourful shop-fronts in bustling Bergen

Stall-holders offering a selection of traditional Sami crafts

Shipping Items Home

If you find you need to ship purchased items back home, visit a local post office. The *Verdenspakke* rates are generally quite good and offer efficient delivery, usually in under two weeks to anywhere in the world.

Return Policy

Most shops offer an excellent exchange of goods service. If there is anything wrong with the item you have bought you have the right to have it replaced or the money refunded. If you want to return something just because you regret having bought it, most retailers will take it back – even if they are not obliged to do so by law. The article must not have been used, and should preferably be in its original packaging. Most shops ask to see the receipt and will give you a full refund, though some may insist that you buy something else in the shop instead.

Department Stores and Shopping Centres

Norwegians love shopping. On Saturday, in particular, you could be forgiven for thinking that the country's entire population is on a nationwide shopping spree. Streets, department stores and shopping centres all bustle with shoppers. Large shopping complexes, built in the 1990s on the periphery of towns,

experienced such a rapid growth that local politicians sounded a warning as smaller retailers in town centres began to suffer economically. Nowadays the development of shopping centres is regulated by local authorities in an attempt to achieve an acceptable balance between small shops and larger malls.

Most such centres hold several dozen restaurants and shops which comprise exclusive designer shops as well as cheaper chain stores. Norway's bigger centres include **Kløverhuset** in Bergen, and **Trondheim Torg** and **Nerstranda Senter**, both located in Tromsø.

Note that the sale of all wine and spirits in Norway takes place in specially designated state monopoly shops called Vinmonopolet.

Markets

April and May is a popular time for flea markets in Norway when jumble sales are held in practically every sports hall and school playground. They are organized to raise money for sports clubs and school brass bands, and are always advertised in the local paper. These get-togethers can be a very Norwegian experience, providing you

with an opportunity to meet the locals in a positive and entertaining way (as well as providing great tasting snacks such as homemade waffles and coffee). Often jumble sales will have a separate second-hand and antiques section where it is possible to find a bargain, though the most valuable antiques are usually auctioned.

Various market days are also arranged throughout Norway. One of the best-known is the market in Røros, held towards the end of February. This is a delightful experience, with everything from clothes to crafts and food on sale, but dress warmly as temperatures can fall to −20° C (−4° F).

Fresh fruit and vegetables on sale at a market in Bergen

What to Buy in Norway

If you are planning to take home a memento it is worth looking for something authentically Norwegian. The most popular souvenir is the traditional knitted cardigan, *lusekofte*. There is a wide selection of handcrafted articles such as pewter and glassware to choose from, and if you have a lot of room in your suitcase you could take home a reindeer hide. Sailing and outdoors enthusiasts will find high-quality sports clothes and equipment. Popular gifts for small children include Norwegian trolls, or cuddly toys such as snow-white polar bears and little furry seals.

Polar Bear
A soft little bear from the north is a lovely memento. You can also buy cuddly brown elk toys.

Slippers
Nothing beats felt slippers made from the matted wool of Norwegian sheep for warmth. The soles are leather. Such slippers are available in many mountain huts.

Knitwear
Knitting has a long tradition in Norway. All children, both boys and girls, learn to knit at school, though few acquire the skills required to knit a lusekofte. Good buys include hats, gloves and cardigans in traditional and modern designs, as well as ear warmers, mittens and scarves.

Silver and Pewter
Norway has many outstanding goldsmiths and silversmiths whose products can be found in shops such as Husfliden and Heimen in Oslo. Pewter products are particularly popular, especially authentic copies of old beer mugs, dishes and bowls. Queen Sonja sometimes chooses these to present to foreign dignitaries. Some shops offer an exciting range of modern jewellery.

Cheese Slicer
Invented in Norway, the practical cheese slicer comes in many shapes and forms, ranging from traditional to modern. The handle can be made of wood, metal or even reindeer horn.

Linen
Linen tablecloths, napkins and towels, often in traditional patterns, exude quality. Flax cultivation is on the increase in Norway.

Hand-Painted Wood and Porcelain
The painting of floral motifs on all kinds of objects from small boxes to large cupboards is known as "rosemaling" and follows a centuries- old tradition. Porcelain is available from glassware shops, which also stock tableware and ornaments.

Hand-decorated bowl

Porsgrunn porcelain

Glass Christmas Figures
Gnomes to decorate the Christmas table are available with either red or blue hats.

Sami Crafts

There are shops all over Norway selling excellent Sami products, but the best buys are probably to be had in Finnmark. Sami shoes (skaller) have a characteristic curled tip because they were worn for skiing. The Sami would slip the tip under a strap which was fastened to the skis. To keep moisture out of the shoes they packed them with dried grass.

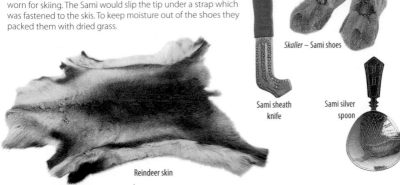

Skaller – Sami shoes

Sami sheath knife

Sami silver spoon

Reindeer skin

Pewter thread bracelet

Silver brooch

Traditional brooch

Sami Jewellery

Beautifully crafted and of excellent quality, traditional bracelets are made of thin pewter thread, plaited in different patterns on a base of soft reindeer skin. Brooches come in ancient and contemporary designs.

Norwegian Specialities

Norwegians cut geitost, their brown goats' cheese, into thin slices with a cheese slicer and use it as a sandwich topping. Norwegian smoked salmon is highly regarded by gourmets all over the world, and Norwegian milk chocolate is a perennial favourite.

Geitost cheese

Milk chocolate

Smoked salmon

Sailing Jacket

Helly Hansen is synonymous with quality, whether you want a thick winter fleece, a thin summer jacket or the proper gear for yachting. There is also a large selection of waterproof trousers for sport and leisure.

Aquavit in Miniature Bottles

Aquavit *(see p237)* can be bought as a set of miniatures, including the richly spiced oak flavoured Gammel, the strong Taffel (for heavier meals) and the moderately spiced Linie Aquavit.

Life Jacket

In Norway the law requires everyone on board a boat to wear a life jacket. These light life jackets are soft and comfortable to wear and are popular among sailors.

Oppland Aquavit

Gammel Aquavit

Taffel Aquavit

Oslo Aquavit

Linie Aquavit

Where to Shop in Norway

Bergen, Trondheim, Kristiansand, Tromsø, Stavanger, Ålesund and all the larger towns in Norway have department stores, shopping centres and markets. Even in Hammerfest, in the far north, there are numerous shops. Every self-respecting village or town has a local arts and crafts shop and there are souvenir shops in all the tourist centres. In summer you can visit bustling open-air markets where there are plenty of local items on sale.

Souvenirs

Norwegian souvenirs can be divided into two distinct categories: cheap, mass-produced items and hand-made high-quality articles. The mass-produced souvenirs include mugs, brooches, sew-on badges, fridge magnets, key rings, ashtrays and T-shirts, similar to those found all the world. Popular themes for gift items include the Norwegian flag, rotund trolls, Viking ships and helmets, and typical northern animals such as elk, reindeer, polar bear and seal.

Forest and mountain trolls are available in a multitude of different forms. The cheapest versions are made of rubber, the most expensive are hand-carved from local wood.

Hand-crafted items can be found in all the larger souvenir shops. Popular purchases include the troll figurines in wood, bowls decorated with hand-carved or hand-painted floral motifs in traditional designs, cheese slicers made from various materials, knitted hats, gloves and scarves, porcelain, linen tableware and small silver and pewter objects.

Arts and Crafts

Across rural Norway there are craftsmen and women carving in wood, doing joinery, embroidery, sewing, weaving and painting. The area around the historical Bryggen district in Bergen has at least a dozen arts and crafts shops, such as **Audhild Viken** and **The Viking Shop**. **Husfliden**, with more than 100 shops in Norway, also sells high-quality handi-crafts. Wooden articles decorated with hand-painted or carved floral motifs, known

as *rosemaling*, are popular gifts. The smallest items, such as napkin rings and little bowls and cups, are not expensive. *Rosemaling* is an age-old tradition. In the 17th and 18th centuries painters would travel around to the large farms in Norway offering to decorate cupboards, doors and ceilings. The patterns and colours of this craft have remained the same for hundreds of years.

Antiques

Should you be tempted to invest in an antique hand-decorated beer jug or wooden box you must be prepared to spend a lot of money. Visit **Kaare Berntsen AS** in Oslo or make enquiries about local antique shops.

In summer, shops often display their wares outside. Every year Hammerfest *(see p222)* holds a Sommertorg, a day-long open-air market at which souvenirs can be bought, including traditional knitted sweaters, Sami handicrafts, arts and crafts, reindeer hides, and fresh produce such as sausages and salmon. There are lots of good buys during Hammer-festdagene (the Hammerfest Festival) in July.

Glassware

One of Norway's most popular tourist attractions is **Hadeland Glassverk**, a 70-km (43-mile) drive northeast from Oslo. Here children are allowed to blow their own glass under expert supervision. Hadeland Glassverk is a lovely place to spend the day. The glassworks are set in a rural oasis, with a bakery and a café.

The selection of glass for sale is enormous and there are many splendid artifacts to admire.

Another glassworks that is worth visiting is **Magnor Glassverk**, where you can also observe how glass is produced. It is situated a couple of hours' drive east from Oslo, very close to the Swedish border.

Gold and Silver

Gold and silver items are good buys. Norway has many talented goldsmiths who produce jewellery in an assortment of classic and modern designs.

All the larger towns have a number of gold and silversmith shops to choose from. In Oslo, **Thune** and **David-Andersen** in Egertorget have the biggest selection. In Bergen there is **Bryggen Gull og Sølv** in Bryggen; in Trondheim, **Møllers Gullsmedforretning** is the recommended place to visit.

Watches and Clocks

According to the statistics from Global Refund Tax-Free Shopping, wristwatches and clocks are the fourth most popular items purchased by tourists. With a refund for the visitor of up to 18.5 per cent of the purchase price, it can pay to buy watches in Norway, including some of the exclusive Swiss makes.

Urmaker Bjerke has a number of shops in Oslo and Bergen.

Sami Design, Arts and Crafts

The best buys of Sami handicrafts can often be found by the roadside in the Finnmark region, where items are sold from private houses, tents or small outlets.

Popular souvenirs include traditional Sami shoes, jewellery and knives, as well as products made of reindeer hide and horn.

In Kautokeino *(see p219)* it is worth visiting Regine Juhl's **Juhls Silver Gallery**, a large jewellery and design workshop which is open to the public. There are outlets in Oslo and Bergen, too.

Clothing and Fashion

Every town teems with clothes and shoe shops. The widest selection will be found in shopping centres and department stores *(see p249)*, but if you explore the back streets you will find everything from designer boutiques to well-stocked fashion houses.

As Norway is a country with six months of winter, there is an emphasis on functionality and warmth. If you are looking for an overcoat there is an enormous choice. The same applies to outdoor shoes, which are stylish and water resistant.

Good and reasonably-priced ladies' clothing is widely available, for example at the **Lindex** stores. If you are planning to buy a sensibly-priced suit or blazer, go to one of the **Dressmann** shops. Childrens' clothing is sold in all the shopping centres – look for **Cubus** or **Hennes & Mauritz**.

A shop in Trondheim which is popular for its bohemian, eccentric clothing is **Namasté**.

Sports Equipment

There are no bad sports shops in Norway. The chain stores all stock similar products. There are frequent offers on sports equipment. Ask if any of the local sports shops are having a sale.

Gresvig and Intersport are the largest sports stores. Equipment for specialist activities can be found in **Skandinavisk Høyfjellsutstyr**, which has branches in Lillehammer and elsewhere, and a low price shop in Oslo is **XXL Sport og Villmark**. One of the best sporting shops in Bergen is the **G-Sport**.

Good Norwegian brands include Helly Hansen, Norrøna, Hjelle and sportswear collections from the Olympic cross-country skiing champions, Vegard Ulvang and Bjørn Dæhlies.

Fish and Shellfish

The best-known fish market is Bryggen in Bergen, which is renowned for its selection of cod, flounder, catfish, salmon and trout. Lobster is at its best in the winter months. Norwegians eat it with white bread and mayonnaise. Crab is highly recommended. A typical Norwegian activity is to sit on the wharfside eating fresh prawns. All these delicacies are expensive – but it is worth treating yourself and sampling them during your stay.

Fresh fish and shellfish are normally on sale in most coastal towns. If there isn't a market or shops at the harbourside, look for a local fishing boat.

It you are staying in Oslo, it is well worth taking a trip to **Vulcanfisk** in Mathallen Food Hall, where you can buy quality products from small-scale producers. The many options available here include fresh, seasonal seafood and prepared seafood for sale, as well as a seafood tasting bar.

DIRECTORY

Arts and Crafts

Audhild Viken
Holmedalsgården 1,
Bryggen, Bergen.
Tel 55 21 51 00.

Husfliden
Storgata 47–48,
Lillehammer.
Tel 61 26 70 70.

The Viking Shop
Bryggen, Bergen.
Tel 55 21 51 00.

Antiques

Kaare Berntsen AS
Universitetsgaten 12, Oslo.
Map 3 D2. **Tel** 22 99 10 10.

Glassware

Hadeland Glassverk
Jevnaker, County of
Oppland.
Tel 61 31 64 00.

Magnor Glassverk
Magnor, County of
Hedmark.
Tel 62 83 35 00.

Gold and Silver

Bryggen Gull og Sølv
Bryggen, Bergen.
Tel 55 93 13 69.

David-Andersen
Egertorget, Oslo.
Map 3 B3.
Tel 24 14 88 00.

**Møllers Gullsmed-
forretning**
Munkegatan 3,
Trondheim.
Tel 73 52 04 39.

Thune
Egertorget, Oslo.
Map 3 B3.
Tel 23 31 01 00.

Watches and Clocks

Urmaker Bjerke Karl Johans
Gate 31, Oslo. **Map** 3 D3.
Tel 23 01 02 10.

Urmaker Bjerke
Torgallmenningen 13,
Bergen.
Tel 55 23 03 60.

Sami Design, Arts and Crafts

Juhls Silver Gallery
Roald Amundsens Gate 6,
Oslo. **Map** 3 D3.
Tel 22 42 77 99.
Bryggen 39, Bergen.
Tel 55 32 47 40.
Kautokeino.
Tel 78 48 43 30.

Clothing and Fashion

Cubus
Stenersgata 1, Oslo City.
Map 3 E2. **Tel** 22 36 76 60.
Tel 66 77 32 00.

Dressmann
Stortorvet 3, Oslo.
Map 3 E3. **Tel** 22 33 71 73.

Hennes & Mauritz
Nedre Slottsgate 10 B,
Oslo. **Map** 3 E3.
Tel 22 47 30 70.

Lindex
Karl Johans Gate 27, Oslo.
Map 3 D3.
Tel 22 33 22 00.

Namasté

Beddingen 10,
Trondheim.
Tel 73 52 50 40.

Sports Equipment

**Skandinavisk
Høyfjellsutstyr**
Bogstadveien 1, Oslo.
Tel 23 33 43 80.

G-Sport
Stromgarten, Bergen
Storsenter, Bergen.
Tel 55 30 12 00.

**XXL Sport og
Villmark**
Storgaten 2–6, Oslo.
Map 3 E3.
Tel 24 08 40 25.

Fish, Shellfish

Vulkanfisk
Maridalsveien 17 A,
Mathallen, Oslo.
Map 3 F2.
Tel 21 39 69 58.

ENTERTAINMENT IN NORWAY

Norwegian cultural life is characterized by an excellent range of dramatic, musical, dance and artistic events, as well as a large number of festivals held throughout the year that feature performances by professional artists of national and international renown. While the larger theatres in the towns close during the summer (the new season begins towards the end of August), summer revues and historical plays, both indoor and outdoor, are staged throughout the country. A vibrant urban nightlife of bars and clubs is livened up by club musicians and stand-up comedians, and regional parks also offer a variety of popular, family-friendly attractions. Festivals are an important part of the nation's cultural life, ranging from rock, jazz and church music to food, theatre, folklore and film. Entertainment in Oslo is covered on pp104–105.

Information and Tickets

The **Visit Norway** website is a useful portal for tourist information in English.and offers details on many cultural programmes, activities and festivals. There are also 260 authorized tourist information offices in Norway, many of which have websites. Hotels and travel agents can also be of help, though if you intend to go to a festival, theatre or concert, visit the venue's website, as most prepare their programme (and sell tickets) in advance. Most towns have their own newspaper with up-to-date listings.

    Billettservice sells tickets (with added commission) to most large concert and per-forming arts events, though for some sold-out venues, it may be possible to buy unclaimed tickets on the evening of the performance at the box office.

Large Theatres and Cultural Centres

In addition to the permanent and mostly traditional theatres, many of the larger towns and cities in Norway outside of Oslo have multicultural performing arts centres offering a broad spectrum of events. Bergen's **Grieghallen**, Trondheim's **Olavshallen** and Stavanger's **Konserthus** are permanent homes for local symphony orchestras and varied programmes of classical music.

    The larger cultural arts centres host numerous music performances by international stars, while other venues may feature smaller dance events, classical music recitals, musicals and rock concerts, as well as family entertainment.

Traditional Theatre

Henrik Ibsen's plays are the most frequently performed works in the world after those

A play at Bergen's Den Nationale Scene

by William Shakespeare, making Ibsen the leading ambassador for Norwegian theatre. The country's best theatrical venues include Bergen's **Den Nationale Scene** and **Rogaland Teater** in Stavanger, both of which offer classic works, as well as more contemporary musicals, comedy and drama.

    There are also many outdoor summer theatre performances such as at the **Porsgrunn Internasjonale Teaterfestival**, which has a large street theatre element, and **Figurteater Festivalen i Kristiansand**, a puppet festival that is a great place to take the kids.

    Several towns have their own intimate comedy theatres, where the audience gets a chance to meet Norway's best entertainers.

Classical Music, Ballet, Dance and Opera

In Bergen, the **Musikkselskabet Harmonien** symphony orchestra puts on regular

The cast of a production at Trondheim's Trøndelag Teater

Members of the Carte Blanche company at Studio Bergen

concerts in the Grieghallen. Additionally, Trondheim, Tromsø, Stavanger and Kristiansand also have permanent orchestras and concert halls, providing year-round programmes of music.

Contemporary dance has a permanent home in Bergen at **Studio Bergen**, where the company, Carte Blanche, performs interesting new works by both Norwegian and foreign choreographers. First-rate international dance, opera and classical music concerts are on offer every year in late May and early June during Bergen's quality international festival, **Festspillene**.

Jazz, Rock and Country Music

Jazz enthusiasts have plenty of festivals to look forward to in Norway. In May and June, towns in the west of the country stage numerous jazz events, while the international jazz festivals, **Sildajazz** in Haugesund and **Molde International Jazz Festival**, are world-renowned.

For rock fans, **Odderøya Live** in Kristiansand is a must, with indoor and outdoor concerts all day and night. **Vestfold Festspillene** is a performing arts festival with around 50 performances of flamenco, blues and other music styles. Country music lovers should take a trip through the beautiful landscape of Telemark to **Seljord** in summer and the biggest country music festival in the Nordic region.

Folk Music and Dancing

Telemark is known for keeping alive traditions in Norwegian folk dancing and music, and July's **Telemark Festival** in Bø is the best event in the country to come and enjoy it. Other popular venues for seeing – and participating in – music and dancing are Ålesund's **Folkedansveka** in August and the **Førde International Folk Music Festival** in July, the latter of which also features interesting groups from Asia, India, South America. Another popular event is the **Jørn Hilme Festival**, held in late July in Fagernes, three hours north of Oslo.

Norway's two national orchestras are based in Bergen and Oslo

DIRECTORY

Information and Tickets

Billettservice AS
W billettservice.no

Visit Norway
W visitnorway.com

Theatre

Den Nationale Scene
Engen 1, Bergen.
Tel 55 54 97 00.

Figurteater Festivalen
Kongens Gate 2A,
Kristiansand.
Tel 38 07 70 50.

Grieghallen
Edvard Griegs Plass 1,
Bergen. **Tel** 55 21 61 00.

Konserthus
Bjergsted, Stavanger.
Tel 51 53 70 00.

Olavshallen
Kjøpmannsgata 44,
Trondheim.
Tel 73 99 40 00.

Porsgrunn Teaterfestival
Huken 3D, Porsgrunn.
Tel 35 93 21 00.

Rogaland Teater
Teaterveien 1, Stavanger.
Tel 51 91 90 00.

Classical, Ballet, Dance and Opera

Festspillene
Vågsallmenningen 1,
Bergen. **Tel** 55 21 06 30.

Musikkselskabet Harmonien
Grieghallen, Bergen.
Tel 55 21 61 00.

Studio Bergen
Nøstegaten 119, Bergen.
Tel 55 30 86 80.

Jazz, Rock and Country Music

Molde International Jazz Festival
Molde, Møre and Romsdal.
Tel 71 20 31 50.

Odderøya Live
Bygg 29, Odderøya,
Kristiansand.
W odderoyalive.no

Seljord Country Music Festival
Seljord, Telemark.
Tel 35 05 51 64.

Sildajazz
Knut Knutsens Gate 4,
Haugesund.
Tel 52 74 33 70.

Vestfold
Stoltenbergsgata 38,
Tønsberg.
Tel 33 30 88 50.

Folk Music and Dancing

Folkedansveka
S Bulls Gate 4,
Ålesund.
Tel 70 10 06 50.

Førde International Folk Music Festival
Angedalsvegen 5,
Førde.
Tel 57 72 19 40.

Jørn Hilme Festival
Fagernes.
Tel 61 36 46 71.

Telemark Festival
Gullbringveien 34, Bø.
Tel 35 95 19 19.

SPORTS AND OUTDOOR ACTIVITIES

It is said that Norwegians are born with skis on their feet and rucksacks on their backs. They love the fresh air and engage in outdoor activities all year round, probably more so than any other European nation. But then conditions in every region are ideal for participating in the great outdoors, whether on foot or by boat. There are superb national parks and large tracts of untouched terrain. In many places, including the wild high fells,

hiking trails and ski tracks are marked out. In the south of Norway, boating enthusiasts will find numerous visitor harbours providing all the necessary amenities. Norway is also well geared for more demanding pursuits such as hang-gliding and white-water canoeing. Although it is a very long country, there is never far to go to the nearest hiking area or boating haven. Even in the largest towns, the outdoor life is always close at hand.

Hiking

Norway is a paradise for those who love to experience nature on foot, in summer and in winter. The expression, *søndagstur* (Sunday walk), prompts Norwegians to fasten their rucksacks and go out into the woods and fields. Usually they will make their way along narrow forest paths and signposted hiking trails. Many also spend their holidays walking from hut to hut at any time of year.

In the most popular high fell areas you never have far to go between the huts, which provide overnight accommodation *(see p229)*. They are linked by a network of marked trails (and in winter, ski tracks). Most of these tourist huts and cabins are owned by **Den Norske Turistforening** (DNT; the Norwegian Mountain Touring Club) and the 50 or so local branches of DNT

situated around the country. There are some 400 huts and cabins in total. The huts vary in terms of standard and service, from the best-equipped, which are similar to a hotel, to the more spartan offering only basic facilities.

If you plan to hike from hut to hut it can pay to take out membership of DNT (445 Nkr in the Oslo area). An overnight stay in a one-to-three-bed hut costs 190 Nkr for members (95 Nkr for children) and 245 Nkr for non-members (125 Nkr for children). Breakfast costs 80 Nkr and supper 185 Nkr for members (prices apply to the Oslo area only). Lunch is normally a packed lunch and a drink from a Thermos provided by the hut.

The marked trails and ski tracks in the high mountains are generally positioned where the view is the most spectacular yet where the terrain is not overly challenging. Always enquire at

Trout fishing in Sysendal in Hardangervidda National Park

the hut you are leaving about the distance to the next hut and how demanding the walk is likely to be.

The snow lasts for a long time on the high mountain plateaus, and the best time to hike is from May to October. In August and September the mountains are bathed in a pageant of colour.

If you are hiking in the fells at other times of year, always obtain up-to-date information on the snow conditions. In the most popular areas, ski tracks are dug as soon as the first snows fall. They are usually accessible for people of average skiing ability.

DNT and most of the large bookshops stock a good selection of maps. Free maps are also available for planning routes and distances.

Safety

Nature can be beautiful and benign, but it can be challenging and dangerous

Accommodation at Rondvassbu Lodge, Rondane National Park

Mountain hikers on Besseggen in Jotunheimen National Park

if you overlook simple ground rules. It is important to read and follow the mountain guidelines known as *fjellvettsreglene*, which are a good reminder of how to act in variable conditions in the mountains, particularly during the winter months. The weather can change rapidly from sunshine to storms. The latest weather report is usually posted on the information board in hotels and huts.

Take clothes that will be suitable should the weather change for the worse *(see p267)*. Good maps are essential and remember to take a compass with you as well. Never go alone unless you are an experienced hiker.

Equipment

When out walking, it is important to have good equipment and an ample supply of food and drinks. At the same time, try to cut down on weight by selecting what is most appropriate, but take account of likely changes in weather conditions. Sturdy shoes, preferably robust boots, are a necessity. Include a change of clothing, ideally woollen, as well as garments that will insulate you against wind and rain. Pack your gear in a plastic bag before placing it in your rucksack so that it will remain dry.

You should take a standard first-aid kit containing such items as plasters and cream for treating blisters and cuts, as well as mosquito repellent. Sunglasses and sun cream will be needed in the fells in summer as well as winter.

Carrying sufficient energy-rich food and, in particular, adequate fluids is important for day trips. Very often you will come across streams along the way where you can refill your bottles. You can supplement your provisions at the tourist huts.

If you are camping, most of the gear, such as tent, cooking utensils and sleeping bag, needs to be purchased as there are no specialist rental companies for camping equipment in Norway.

Touring the National Parks

Norway has 32 national parks on the mainland; 85 per cent of which are mountains, and a further seven on Svalbard. The national parks have been designated as such because they contain unspoilt, unique or especially beautiful scenery, as well as being the natural habitat of flora and fauna. All activities liable to have an effect on the environment are banned. Information can be obtained from DNT branches, tourist information centres and visitor centres in the parks.

Hardangervidda is the largest national park, covering an area of 3,422 sq km (1,320 sq miles) *(see pp162–3)*. A large part of the park consists of a high mountain plateau. It is easily accessible from Eastern Norway as well as from Vestlandet by car, or by bus or train from Oslo or Bergen. The road and train connections between west and east access starting points for hikes of a moderate degree of difficulty.

A more demanding and spectacular national park is the mountain massive of Jotunheimen in central southern Norway *(see pp144–5)*. Jotunheimen has five peaks exceeding 2,300 m (7,546 ft), and has been an attractive tourist destination since the latter half of the 19th century. It is wild and majestic, with glaciers, lakes and valleys, and can be explored using its well-developed network of hiking trails and ski tracks.

Rowing on one of the many lakes in Hardangervidda National Park

Skiers in Rondane National Park, Eastern Norway

Skiing

There are good reasons why Norwegian skiers have won more gold medals in the Winter Olympics and World Championships than anyone else. In many parts of the country conditions are ideal for both cross-country and downhill (Alpine) skiing. Distances between ski tows and lifts are never far. Even Oslo is only a short distance away from the ski runs.

The main centres for winter sports are in Eastern Norway. The resorts of Beitostølen, Oppdal, Geilo, Hemsedal, Lillehammer and Trysil are hives of activity all winter.

Cross-country skiing, known as *langren*, is Norway's national sport. The mountains here are less craggy than in Central Europe and are most suited to this form of skiing. The prepared ski tracks comprise two lanes. Always remember to keep to the right to avoid on-coming skiers. The tracks are well marked and circumvent steep hills.

Many places also have illuminated trails for night-time skiing. These are normally 4–5 km (2–3 miles) long and circular. An evening run on a floodlit track is particularly atmospheric. Some skiers use headlamps to ski on unlit tracks.

There are facilities for downhill skiing all over Norway and the runs are graded in terms of difficulty. You can also try to master the Telemark technique – downhill skiing on cross-country skis. The larger ski centres have cross-country, downhill, Telemark and snowboarding equipment for hire. Do not be tempted to ski off-piste in unprepared areas, especially in unfamiliar terrain. It is possible to trigger an avalanche by off-piste skiing.

DNT provides information on cross-country conditions. **Skiforeningen** (Norwegian Ski Association) maintains the 2,600-km (1,616-miles) long network of ski-tracks in Oslo and its environs and provides updates on trail conditions on its website.

Mountaineering

With its mountainous terrain, Norway offers climbing for every ability from the less experienced to the serious mountaineer. Although the mountains are not as high as the Alps, they can be equally dramatic. The sharp peaks of Jotunheimen in the south of Norway are particularly appealing to climbers. Further north, popular climbing areas include Lofoten (see p214) and Lyngsalpene (Lyngen Alps) in Troms. Romsdalen's precipitous rock faces, which include Trollveggen (the Troll Wall), are among the most challenging.

The season for summer climbing is relatively short. Be prepared for harsh conditions, including snow and wind, at any time in the most exposed areas. Larger towns have training areas for climbers, such as at Kolsås, 15 km (9 miles) west of Oslo.

A number of books are available describing Norway's peaks and climbing routes. **Norges Klatreforbund** (the Norwegian Climbing Federation) has an informative website with details of mountaineering opportunities throughout the country.

A challenging climb high above a shimmering fjord

Boating, Rafting and White-water Canoeing

Norway has an enormously long coastline interspersed with fjords and islands, making it a boating paradise. Marinas hire out boats, including canoes, kayaks, yachts and motor boats. There are no special requirements to operate smaller craft, although you have to have basic seafaring skills.

The national centre for river sports is located in Heidal in Gudbrandsdalen. For people without their own

Summer snowboarding and skiing at Stryn Summer Ski-Centre

vessel (kayak or raft), guided tours can be arranged.

A number of rivers throughout Norway are great for white-water canoeing. **Norges Padleforbund** (the Norwegian Canoe Association) provides information on the best places to go.

Fishing

More than 50 per cent of Norwegians go fishing one or more times a year, a larger proportion than in any other country. But then the country has rich opportunities for both sea and freshwater fishing. The most common types of fish for sports anglers are cod and trout. There are 230 other salt-water species and 40 freshwater species.

Sports fishing is practised with a rod, hand reel and a single line with a hook. Along the coast, good catches can be made by fishing from the shore. If you have access to a boat it is possible to make excellent catches of cod, coley and mackerel. Norway also has a number of outstanding salmon rivers.

Be careful to observe the fishing regulations. Sea angling is free for recreational fishermen. Freshwater fishing is regulated; here, either state or private property rights need to be observed. Always check whether fishing is permitted in a particular watercourse. Rules and regulations vary from place to place. All anglers over 16 years must buy a fishing card, sold in shops, hotels, tourist offices and post offices. The cards are valid for specific areas by the day or for longer periods. Fishing with live bait is forbidden.

Information is available from **Norges Jeger-og Fiskerforbund** (Norwegian Hunting and Fishing Association) or Fylkesmannens Miljøvernavdeling (County Environmental Departments).

Whale Safaris

Every summer male sperm whales leave their families in the southern latitudes and migrate north to the coastal areas off Northern Norway. They visit the coast off the islands of Vesterålen to feed on fish and squid.

Whale-watching cruises operate from Andenes and Tysfjord, weather permitting. A whale safari usually lasts for six to eight hours.

The tours will almost certainly bring you close to these giants, which can measure up to 20 m (66 ft) long. Sometimes they will lounge on the surface of the water close to the boat while they take in air before descending to the depths of the ocean (see p211). You may be lucky and also spot humpback, minke, fin and killer whales in addition to dolphins.

Seal and seabird safaris are also available.

Hunting

Game hunting takes place all over Norway. It is regarded as having great utilitarian value and hunters value the experience of being with nature. Animals hunted include elk, roe-deer, stags, small game,

(see p211)

DIRECTORY

Useful Organizations

Den Norske Turistforening DNT
Youngstorget 1, Oslo.
Map 3 E3.
Tel 40 00 18 68.
W turistforeningen.no

Norges Jeger-og Fiskerforbund
Tel 66 79 22 00.
W njff.no

Norges Klatreforbund
Tel 21 02 98 30.
W klatring.no

Norges Padleforbund
Tel 21 02 98 35.
W padling.no

Skiforeningen
Tel 22 92 32 00.
W skiforeningen.no

Whale Safaris

Hvalsafari
Fyrvika, Andenes.
Tel 76 11 56 00.
W whalesafari.no

Tysfjord Turistsenter AS
Storfjord, Tysfjord.
Tel 75 77 53 70.
W tysfjord-turistsenter.no

forest birds and grouse. Regardless of whether you hunt on private land or common land, you will need to pay for the right to hunt.

The hunting season is strictly regulated. Generally it runs from August to December, but local regulations may permit the hunting of some species until May. Note that a number of species are protected throughout the year.

Enthusiastic tourists on a whale safari in Tysfjorden, Nordland, spotting a killer whale

Specialist Holidays and Tours

Nestled into the Scandinavian peninsula with a 24,140 km- (15,000 mile-) long coastline and some of the most pristine landscape in the world, Norway is a fantastic country for taking advantage of the great outdoors. Its alpine mountains, lengthy fjords, harbour-side towns and sprawling plains and steppes are havens for exploring flora and wildlife among some of the most untouched, remote parts of Europe. There are numerous well-organized excursions available for every type of interest, and this will enable you to immerse yourself in Norway's stunning landscapes.

The Northern Lights, clearly visible in the Arctic Circle

Coastal Steamer Fjord Tours

The **Hurtigruten** is a famous coastal steamer ship that offers one of the most popular activities for visitors to Norway, as it is an excellent way to see parts of the country that are virtually inaccessible on foot or skis. The "classic journey" departs from Bergen and follows the coastline all the way up to Kirkenes along the country's picturesque fjords, stopping at dozens of ports to pick up and let off passengers.

The ship offers a variety of accommodation options, ranging from inexpensive seats to more luxurious suites and cabins, as well as amenities such as restaurants, bars and movie theatres. Other outfits, such as **Fjord Tours** and **Fjell & Fjord**, offer a variety of trips around the fjords of the southwest, including the famous Norway in a Nutshell tour, while groups such as **Tide Sjø** offer more specialized fjord excursions with both day excursions and longer trips.

Reindeer Tours

Because reindeers are the stuff of childhood stories, it often comes as a surprise to realize that they actually exist in real life, herded year-round high up in the Arctic region. **Turgleder** runs an April tour that begins inland, in the heart of Arctic nomadic territory, and travels across windswept plateaus towards the coast, where reindeers graze and calve during summer. Participants take part in daily duties, eating, sleeping and travelling like local herdsmen, who share their vast knowledge of nature and outdoor life. In the evenings, the team decamps to an open fire in a Lávvu, a traditional Sámi tent.

Hurtigruten operates an excursion in February that combines a tour along the Norwegian coastline, with a visit to the annual reindeer racing championships in Tromsø and the Sámi National Day festivities in Lapland. It is an excellent means of learning about traditional Sami culture. The Sami Easter Festival, in April, offers another opportunity to observe reindeer racing.

Northern Lights Tours

The Northern Lights, or Aurora Borealis, is a defining attribute of the Arctic firmament. Throughout the winter months, the night sky is regularly lit up by bright, streaming tapestries of green, blue and red that flicker across the heavens. Created by the collision of solar particle emissions with the earth's atmosphere, the strips of light may shine on for hours or last no more than a few seconds – what sort of experience you have is entirely up to the heavens to decide. Aurora are at their most spectacular on clear evenings in early autumn and late winter, when the sky is at its darkest, and your best bet for observing them is in the rural countryside, far away from cities, since urban flicker reduces the effect. For a variety of tours, contact **Natur i Nord** or **Fjord Travel**. The latter's fantastic Northern Lights Cruise Trip consists of a scenic train ride, four nights' cruise across the Arctic circle, the Northern Lights (depending on the weather) and dog sledding excursions.

Reindeer racing at the Sami Easter celebrations in Lapland

Packs of dogs pulling sleds in the Norwegian countryside

Fjord, Mountain and Glacier Hikes

One of the best ways to experience Norway is to hike along a fjord up into mountain ranges and national parks. Along the way, you can stop off at *hytter* (cabins) that vary from large, staffed lodges to small, basic wooden huts. The hiking season is from early July to late September, and the best areas are the Rondane, Jotunheimen, Dovrefjell and Hardangervidda national parks. **Jostedalen Breførarlag** operates hikes on the nearby Jostedalsbreen glacier, while **Ice Troll** combines these hikes with glacier kayaking.

Dog-sledding

A unique way to experience the Norwegian countryside is by driving a pack of sled dogs across several hundred kilometres of otherwise unforgiving steppe and mountain plateau. The best outfit for tours on solo or tandem, guide-assisted sleds is Norway's most renowned husky farm, **Engholm Husky**, located in the heart of Lapland. Novices are catered for.

Arctic Adventure Tours and **Tromsø Villmarks-senter** offer similar tours that finish with a gourmet Arctic meal of reindeer stew served up in a Sámi tent.

Arctic Safaris

It is an unforgettable experience to ski across Norway's most remote Arctic regions, and **Polar Charter** runs an exciting "skiing by boat" adventure. Participants travel to the far north by yacht and dock each day at various island and fjord-side ports, then head out to ski on the fresh, alpine mountain terrain.

The Dive Center operates sea rafting and diving trips along the Arctic coastline. Another invigorating trip is a winter snowmobile safari that traverses the Arctic island of Spitsbergen. These are organized by **Barents Safari** and **Svalbard Wildlife Service**.

Walkers hiking on one of Norway's many glaciers

DIRECTORY

Coastal Steamer Fjord Tours

Fjell & Fjord
Gamlevegen 6, Gol.
Tel 32 02 99 26.
W fjellandfjord.com

Fjord Tours
Strømgate 4,
Bergen.
Tel 81 56 82 22.
W fjordtours.com

Hurtigruten
Kirkegt 1, Box 6144,
Tromsø.
Tel 81 00 30 30.
W hurtigruten.no

Tide Sjø
Møllendalsveien 1A,
Bergen.
Tel 55 23 87 00.
W tide.no

Reindeer Tours

Turgleder
Box 71, Rena.
Tel 91 16 73 03.
W turgleder.com

Northern Lights

Fjord Travel
Østre Nesttunvei 4–6,
Bergen.
Tel 55 13 13 10.
W fjordtravel.no

Natur I Nord
Nansenveien 34, Tromsø.
Tel 981 44 96 57.
W naturinord.no

Fjord, Mountain & Glacier Hikes

Ice Troll
Breheimsenteret,
Jostedal. Tel 97 01 43 70.
W icetroll.com

Jostedalen Breførarlag
Krundalen, Jostedal.
Tel 57 68 31 11.
W bfl.no

Dog-sledding

Arctic Adventure Tours
Kvaløysletta, Tromsø.
Tel 77 66 66 75.
W arcticadventuretours.no

Engholm Husky
Karasjok.
Tel 78 46 71 66.
W engholm.no

Tromsø Villmarkssenter
9100 Kvaløysletta.
Tel 77 69 60 02.
W villmarkssenter.no

Arctic Safaris

Barents Safari
Fjellveien 28,
Kirkenes.
Tel 90 19 05 94.
W barentssafari.no

The Dive Center
Stakkevollveien 72,
Tromsø.
Tel 77 69 66 00.
W dykkersentret.no

Polar Charter
Tromsø.
Tel 97 52 32 50.
W polarcharter.no

Svalbard Wildlife Service
Næringsbygget Pb 164,
Longyearbyen.
Tel 79 02 22 22.
W wildlife.no

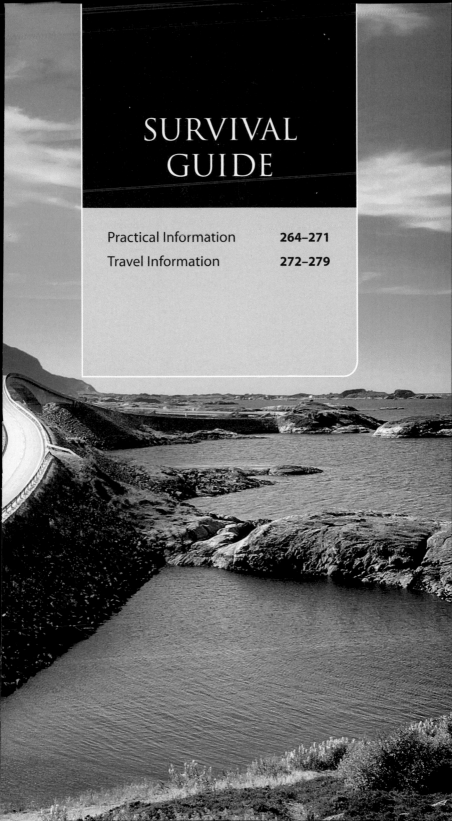

SURVIVAL
GUIDE

PRACTICAL INFORMATION

Norway is a vast country. The distance from Oslo to the North Cape is the same as from Oslo to Rome. It is therefore advisable to spend a little time planning your trip.

Most reasonably-sized towns in Norway have a tourist information centre. The country can be explored by car, plane, ferry and train. The road system is well developed and train connections extend as far as Bodø, north of the Arctic Circle. The coastline is indented with fjords, but a comprehensive ferry and tunnel network makes it easy to reach the islands and cross the fjords. The towns all have modern facilities for the traveller.

Many of the natural attractions such as national parks, skiing, hiking, fishing and mountaineering areas are situated off the beaten track, so good maps are a necessity.

Tourist information office in Bergen

Tourist Information

Norway has a number of tourist information offices abroad. **Visit Norway** provides practical information on the range of holidays available in the country on its website. It also lists the addresses and telephone numbers of the many local tourist offices throughout Norway.

Oslo has two main information centres – **Turistinformasjonen** near the Rådhus and Turistinformasjonen at Oslo Central Station. These offices have a joint website and you can obtain answers here to specific queries by e-mail. Brochures and travel tips may also be requested via e-mail or can be picked up from the tourist offices abroad or from local tourist offices in Norway. Every town has its own tourist office providing information on where to stay, where to eat and sightseeing options in the area.

When to Visit

The best time to visit Norway is in the summer between the months of May and September. Eastern Norway along with the Oslo area has the most stable weather. Nevertheless, it is advisable to pack some lightweight waterproofs.

If you plan to experience the midnight sun, you will need to travel north of the Arctic Circle. At Bodø the sun is visible at midnight from 20 May–20 July, in Tromsø from 16 May–27 July, at the North Cape from 13 May–29 July. In the rest of the country at this time the nights are very short and light.

Besides having good summers, Norway is a winter wonderland with lots of opportunities for sport and outdoor pursuits. The severity of the winter between November and April varies from region to region. Cold and snow prevail for long periods in the north of the country, in the mountains and in the inland parts of southern Norway. The climate is often milder along the coast.

Norway has the most snow in January and February. This is a popular time to visit the hotels and tourist huts in the mountains, especially when combined with a skiing holiday.

Passports and Customs Regulations

All visitors, with the exception of those from the Nordic countries, require a valid passport. Citizens of some countries also require a visa. Contact the Norwegian Embassy or consulate in your home country for the latest entry requirements.

Norway is one of the few European countries which is free of rabies, and every precaution is taken to maintain this status. You are advised against bringing a pet with you. If you do, it will have to be kept in quarantine for four months before being admitted.

Duty-free allowances on entering the country are 2 litres of beer, 1 litre of spirits, 1 litre wine and 200 cigarettes. The minimum age for bringing spirits into the country is 20; for wine and tobacco the age is 18. You are only permitted to bring medicines for personal use and you should have a letter from your doctor certifying your need for them.

Opening Hours and Admission Fees

In Norway you will need to pay an admission fee to visit most museums and art galleries. There is usually a discount for families, students, adolescents, pensioners and groups. Children are often admitted free of charge. In Oslo admission is free to the Nasjonalgalleriet (see pp56–7) and to Frognerparken with Gustav Vigeland's sculpture garden (see pp94–5). The opening hours of museums vary; they usually open sometime between 9 and 11am and

◀ A section of the Atlanterhavsveien (Atlantic Road) winding its way through spectacular scenery

close between 4 and 7pm. From September to May the opening hours can be shorter. Most attractions open daily; some close on Monday.

Norway's protestant churches are normally closed outside services. Churches of special importance, such as cathedrals and stave churches, have longer hours to accommodate visitors, especially during the summer months.

If you are planning to visit a number of sights in the capital, it is worth buying an *Oslo Kortet* (Oslo Pass) which, for a fixed price, gives admission to most museums and galleries and unlimited travel on public transport (except night buses and trams). Pass-holders are also entitled to discounts on other attractions. Available at tourist offices, most hotels, and Narvesen newsagents *(see p271)*, the pass can be bought as a single or family pass, for one or more days. A variation on the Oslo Pass is the Oslo Package, which also includes hotels. Towns such as Bergen and Trondheim have similar arrangements.

The Bergen Card

Disabled Travellers

It has become increasingly common for hotels to cater to the needs of disabled guests with improved access and specially adapted rooms.

NSB, the Norwegian State Railways, has special carriages to meet the needs of those with impaired mobility. The Coastal Express ships are equipped to accommodate disabled passengers. **Norges Handikapforbund** (the Norwegian Association for the Disabled) can supply details.

Etiquette

Norwegians are easy-going and informal. Following an initial introduction, people are generally on first-name terms, and this applies to men and women. When meeting someone for the first time it is customary to shake hands.

However, there are two special rules of etiquette. After a meal it is the practice to thank the host/hostess by saying *"takk"*.

In a slightly more formal context, at the beginning of the meal the host will propose a toast, *"skål"*. It is polite not to touch your drink before this toast is made.

After having spent a pleasant day or evening together with good friends, it is customary to ring the hosts a day or two later to thank them *("takk for sist")*.

Driving, Alcohol and Tobacco

In Norway it is illegal to drive a car if your blood alcohol level is more than 0.2 per mil. For most people this is equivalent to less than a glass of wine. This rule virtually equates to a complete ban on drinking and driving.

Norway also has relatively strict laws regarding the use of tobacco in communal rooms. In restaurants and bars smokers are directed to separate screened-off areas. Smoking is prohibited in all public buildings.

The sale of all alcoholic drinks is subject to special restrictions. Beer with an alcoholic content on a par with pilsner (lager) can be purchased in grocery shops and supermarkets. Wines and spirits, however, are only sold in the specially designated, state-owned Vinmonopolet outlets *(see p235)*.

The state-owned Vinmonopolet selling wines and spirits

DIRECTORY

Tourist Information in Norway

Bergen Turistinformasjon
Slottsgaten 3,
5003 Bergen.
Tel 55 55 20 00.
W visitbergen.com

Kristiansand Turistinformasjon
Rådhusgata 6,
4611 Kristiansand.
Tel 38 12 13 14.
W visitkrs.no

Lillehammer Turistinformasjon
Jernbantorget 2, 2609 Lillehammer.
Tel 61 28 98 00.
W lillehammerturist.no

Oslo Turistinformasjon Rådhuset
Fridtjofnansens Plass 5,
0160 Oslo.
Map 3 D3.
Tel 81 53 05 55.
W visitoslo.com

Tromsø Turistinformasjon
Kirkegata 2, 9253 Tromsø.
Tel 77 61 00 00.
W destinasjontromso.no

Trondheim Turistinformasjon
Munkegata 19,
7411 Trondheim.
Tel 73 80 76 60.
W visit-trondheim.com

Visit Norway
Akersgate 13, 0158 Oslo.
Postboks 448, Sentrum,
0104 Oslo.
Map 3 F3.
Tel 22 00 25 00.
W visitnorway.com

Disabled Travellers

Norges Handikapforbund
(information for disabled people)
Schweigaards Gate 12,
0185 Oslo.
Map 3 F3.
Tel 24 10 24 00.
W nhf.no

Personal Security and Health

Norway is a safe tourist destination, even in the cities and towns, with one of the lowest crime rates in Europe. But just as anywhere else, it is always sensible to take basic safety precautions. In all built-up areas there are places which are more exposed to crime than others and Oslo is no exception. According to statistics, however, the few violent episodes that do occur usually involve the criminal fraternity and rarely affect tourists. Nevertheless, it is always advisable to lock your car and avoid leaving valuables visible to passers-by, regardless of where you are in the country.

Policeman　　Policewoman

Fire engine

Personal Security

Pickpocketing can be a problem in Oslo. The capital is visited periodically by well-organized international gangs. They operate in crowded places, particularly in busy shops and airport terminals. Do not carry your wallet in your back pocket. Valuables should be kept close to your body so they are difficult to steal. In restaurants and cafés be careful not to hang your handbag over the back of a chair. Put it on the floor beside your chair and place a foot on the strap; alternatively, keep it on your lap.

Always keep your passport and tickets separate from your wallet, and keep your credit card and PIN number separate from each other.

Most hotels have safes that you can use to avoid carrying large amounts of money around. Even though theft from hotel rooms is unusual, avoid placing valuables where they are visible.

In Norway it is common practice to withdraw money from cashpoint machines (ATMs). Should you encounter technical problems when making a withdrawal, be on your guard for anyone standing behind you in the queue offering to "help" you. You should politely decline and look for another cashpoint or go into a bank.

Police and Sheriffs

Norway is divided into 27 police districts each with its own police chief *(politimester)*. Some police districts have a number of smaller sheriff offices *(lensmannskontorer)*, which also have police jurisdiction. The Directorate of Police is the body responsible for police administration.

Standard sign displayed outside Norwegian police stations

Norwegian police are generally unarmed. They are helpful and polite. Feel free to ask police officers on patrol for directions or advice. Remember that it is strictly against the law to drive when you have been drinking. Even a relatively moderate amount of alcohol in the blood can result in an unconditional prison sentence and a hefty fine. It can be expensive to infringe traffic regulations, especially speed limits.

Lost Property

Inform the police immediately if anything of value is lost or stolen. In order to make a claim with your insurance company you will need a document from the police to confirm that the item has been stolen.

It is possible that missing items will be found and handed in at a public lost property office. Bus stations, airport terminals and train stations usually have their own lost property offices.

If you lose your passport you are advised to contact your nearest embassy or consulate immediately.

Medical Treatment

The Norwegian health service is well developed across the whole spectrum, from private doctors to large public hospitals. In towns there are both public and private out-of-hours clinics for emergencies known as *legevakt*. Waiting times for private rather than public medical treatment are generally shorter, but private is more expensive. Emergency medical treatment is free in Norway for EU and EEA citizens. Treatment only covers urgent help, with the exception of renal dialysis and refilling visitors' own oxygen cylinders.

You are strongly advised to obtain a European Health Insurance (EHIC) card before you travel, as treatment of citizens from EU and EEA countries is conditional on you being able to produce this, along with a valid passport or other form of identification. Citizens of non-EU and non-EEA countries must meet the cost of medical treatment themselves if they do not have travel insurance.

Pharmacies

In Norway only pharmacies are permitted to sell medicines. Some remedies can be bought without a prescription, but most require a doctor's written instruction. If you are dependent on a prescription-only drug it is advisable to bring enough supplies to cover your entire stay. However, visitors are entitled to attend a doctor's surgery and request any medicines if necessary.

Pharmacies have similar opening hours to other shops.

Mountain rescue patrol equipped with stretchers and sleighs

·APOTEK·
Pharmacy sign

Larger cities have a 24-hour opening rota system – all pharmacies display a list.

Forces of Nature

Norway is a vast country with wide variations in its geographical and climatic conditions. Both at sea and in the mountains the wind and weather can change rapidly, and there is good reason to respect the forces of nature.

Unfortunately drowning accidents claim many lives. Those affected include tourists who have ventured out to sea in unseaworthy vessels or in bad weather. It is advisable to consult local people with a knowledge of the area and conditions before setting forth into unknown waters.

The mountains are renowned for sudden bad turns in the weather. Sunny, still conditions can change in just a few hours to heavy mist, snow or howling wind. Again, follow the ground rules and take advice from people familiar with the terrain and weather before setting off.

Staff at your accommodation will be able to recommend signposted paths and advise on how long it should take from one point to the next.

In summer mosquitoes are a problem in some areas and you will need to cover up. Mosquito sticks and sprays are widely available from pharmacies and grocery stores.

Although bears and wolves roam freely in certain areas, there is no need to be alarmed. They are timid and avoid contact with people. There have been no serious confrontations between humans and these animals in recent times.

Ambulance

Banking and Local Currency

Travellers to Norway may bring in and take out any amount of cash. However, you must notify officials at the red zone of the airport if you have amounts exceeding 25,000 Nkr. The use of credit cards is widespread. It is easy to use your credit card to obtain local currency, although traveller's cheques are a safer option. There are exchange bureaux at all the international airports. Many hotels will also change money, but for the best exchange rates and lowest commission charges go to a bank. Note that Norway is not a member of the EU.

Foreign exchange bureau at Oslo Central Station

One of the commercial banks' automated teller machines

Banks and Foreign Exchange Bureaux

The majority of banks have foreign exchange bureaux and there is little variation in the exchange rates they offer. Most banks also have ATMs, known as Minibanks, which accept major bank and credit cards, such as MasterCard, Bank Accept and Visa, to withdraw Norwegian currency. These cash machines usually have multilingual instructions. The amount of commission charged for withdrawals depends on the type of card you have. Normally, you can withdraw up to 9,900 Nkr over four days with a maximum of seven withdrawals. Alternatively, you can withdraw

cash at the counter using Visa. These withdrawals can take time because the bank must first obtain authorisation.

There are exchange bureaux on arrival at most airports, at the busiest border crossings and at the *flytog* terminal (for the express train between Oslo's Gardermoen airport and the city centre).

Banking Hours

Banks in Norway stay open from 9am to 3:30pm, although in summer they close a little earlier, at 3pm.

All banks are closed on Saturday and Sunday, but some have extended opening hours on Thursday, usually to around 5 or 6pm.

On days before a public holiday, such as New Year's Day, most banks close earlier than the usual time of 3:30pm.

Credit Cards

The use of credit cards is widespread in Norway. They are accepted in hotels,

restaurants, service stations and most shops. MasterCard and Visa are the most widely used cards. Some places do not accept American Express because of the high transaction fees that are charged to retailers.

DIRECTORY

Banks

DnB NOR
Stranden 21, 0250 Oslo.
Map 2 C4.
Tel 04 800.

Nordea
Akersgate 55, 0180 Oslo.
Map 3 E3.
Tel 06 001.

Postbanken
Post offices in most urban areas.

Foreign Exchange Bureaux

DnB NOR Oslo Lufthavn
Gardermoen Flyplass.
Tel 07 700.

Nordea Flytogterminalen
Sentralbanestasjonen, Oslo.
Tel 23 15 99 20.

American Express Card Services Unit
DnB NOR Bank ASA, 0021 Oslo.
Tel 66 98 43 71.

Lost Credit Cards

American Express
Tel 80 06 81 00.

Diners Club
Tel 21 01 50 00.

MasterCard/ Eurocard
Tel 21 01 52 22.

Visa
Tel 80 01 20 52.

The head office of DnB NOR at Aker Brygge in Oslo

It is possible to withdraw cash on a credit card in most banks. It is also possible to get cash back when making purchases in most shops.

Traveller's Cheques

Traveller's cheques can be purchased from your local bank at home. They are accepted almost everywhere in Norway. Remember to sign your traveller's cheques. If you do not they can be misused if they are lost or stolen, and you will be liable for the loss.

Traveller's cheques are steadily losing ground to credit cards. In terms of security, however, traveller's cheques are generally more secure than cards.

Telegraphic Transfers

Norwegian banks are helpful when it comes to receiving money transferred telegraphically from abroad. But this type of transaction can be slow and costly. The sender's bank abroad forwards money to its banking partner in Norway, which transfers it to a bank for the receiver to collect. Quicker transfers can be made via MoneyGram to American Express in Oslo

Currency

Norway's currency is the Norwegian *krone* (kr, Nkr or NOK). One *krone* equals 100 *øre*. The smallest coin is 1 *kroner*, the largest

is 20 *kroner*. Notes are issued in denominations from 50 Nkr to 1,000 Nkr.

Using the 1,000 Nkr note should not be a problem, but it is most practical to carry notes no larger than 500 Nkr.

In view of the fact that Norway is not a member of the European Monetary Union, the Euro is not legal tender, except in certain places such as at airports and tax-free shops. However, it is up to individual retailers how they stand with regard to the Euro. Time will tell if it becomes accepted in an increasing number of outlets.

50 Nkr

Bank Notes

Norwegian notes are issued in five denominations – 1,000, 500, 200, 100 and 50 kroner. They each carry a portrait of a well-known cultural figure.

100 Nkr

500 Nkr

200 Nkr

1000 Nkr

Coins

Norwegian coins are issued in denominations of 20, 10, 5 and 1 kroner. On the front is a traditional Norwegian design. The 1 Nkr and 5 Nkr coins have a hole in the centre.

1 Nkr

5 Nkr

10 Nkr

20 Nkr

Communications and Media

Telephone services in Norway are generally of a high standard. Norwegians are among the world's largest users of mobile phones; from a population of 4.8 million, there are around 5 million mobile phone subscriptions. The leading telecommunications company is the former state-owned enterprise, Telenor. It offers a wide range of specialist services. Payphones accept cash, Norwegian phone cards and most credit cards. Internet access can be found in most hotels throughout Norway, as well as in Internet cafés commonly available in all main towns and cities.

Public Telephones

The availability of public telephones in Norway has decreased considerably in the wake of the mobile phone. There are two types of payphones, both operated by Telenor. The red telephone boxes found in most large towns accept phone cards (*telekort*), a range of credit cards and Norwegian coins. Phone cards can be purchased in the Narvesen kiosks located throughout the country. The green telephone kiosks only accept phone cards and credit cards, not cash.

It is possible to be called back by the person you are talking to. Ask the person to ring the number given in the telephone box.

Telephone kiosk that accepts phone cards, credit cards and coins

Mobile Phones

Before you leave on your trip, it is wise to contact your mobile phone provider to ensure that international roaming is activated on your handset and to check how much it with cost to use your phone abroad. These charges can be expensive and so buying a pre-paid SIM card is one way to reduce costs. In order to do this you may need to ask your provider to unlock your phone.

It is easy to find cheap mobile packages and special call rates in Norway. The main mobile phone providers are Telenor, Netcom and Network Norway. Telenor run the **Telekiosken** shops that sell pre-paid SIM cards, handsets and other accessories. Alternatively, if you would rather purchase a mobile phone before your arrival **Telestial** sell international SIM cards and handsets online. The SIM cards come with pre-paid credit, a US and global UK telephone number and international roaming coverage in 270 countries. Rates for international calls start at just US$0.49 per minute, and it is free to receive calls in more than 70 countries on the UK Global number.

Mobile phones in Norway operate mainly on a GSM network, which covers 97 per cent of the population and 70 per cent of the country. NMT, also known as "the wilderness network" (*villmarkstelefonen*), has wider coverage than that of GSM and is used across Norway, Sweden and Finland. However it is advisable not to rely on GSM and NMT to provide a comprehensive nationwide service.

Mobile telephones are useful to have when travelling in wilderness areas, but remember that the coverage is not total, and you should not rely on a mobile phone as a guarantee that you will always be able to call for help.

Internet Access

Most hotels in Norway provide Internet access, and many offer rooms with wireless Internet. Charges do vary, so ask how much it will cost when checking into your room. If you are travelling without your own computer and need to access the Internet, there should be a terminal available for guests to use.

Public libraries commonly have free wireless Internet and computers available for use, although you may need to book a slot in advance in order to access the computers. The **Oslo Public Library** has a number of branches in the city that have Internet facilities. Many tourist offices throughout the country also have Internet access terminals. Internet cafés can be found in the main towns and cities,

Making a Telephone Call

- Norwegian telephone numbers have 8 digits; there are no area codes.
- To phone abroad from Norway dial 00, then the country code, area code (minus the initial 0), then the number.
- The country code for Norway is 47.
- Domestic directory enquiries: 1881; international directory enquiries: 1882.
- Telenor customer services: 05000.
- Telenor mobile phone customer services: 09000.
- Netcom mobile phone customer services: 05050.

such as **Accezzo Internetcafé** in Bergen and **Arctic Internet Café** in Oslo. They are typically open all day and charge between 50 and 80 Nkr an hour. Some cafés, for example **United Bakeries** in Oslo, provide free wireless Internet access to customers.

Red boxes for national and international post, yellow for local mail

Sending Letters

There are post offices in all towns and nearly all villages. In addition, some shops have postal services.

Post offices are usually open from 9am–5pm on weekdays and 10am–3pm on Saturday. Opening hours for postal services in shops are the same as the retailers' opening hours and vary from shop to shop.

You can buy stamps at post offices, in shops, kiosks and bookstores. The cost to send a normal letter or postcard weighing less than 20 g to a European country is 12 Nkr. Heavier letters, up to 50 g, cost 16 Nkr. Postage to the rest of the world is 14 Nkr for letters weighing less than 20 g and 27 Nkr up to 50 g. To send a letter within Norway costs 9 Nkr and 14 Nkr respectively.

There are postboxes everywhere. They are red and occasionally yellow. When a red postbox is on its own, letters to all addresses can be posted in it. When a red and yellow postbox stand next to each other, the red box is for national and international letters; the yellow box is for local mail and you need to check that the postal code on your letter corresponds to that on the box. Collection times are given on the postboxes.

Norwegian postal codes have four digits and the code precedes the place name. In addresses, the street number comes after the street name.

It is possible to receive mail via Poste Restante. Addresses should contain the name of the addressee, and the name and postal code of the post office where the letter will be collected. Courier services are provided by a number of international companies.

TV and Radio

Almost all hotel rooms in Norway are equipped with colour TV, and can receive both Norwegian and international programmes. The Norwegian channels are NRK1, which is state owned and non-commercial, and NRK2, an auxiliary channel. TV2 is Norway's leading commercial television channel. TV2 transmits weather forecasts periodically in the morning. The other Norwegian commercial channels are TV3 and TV Norge. All channels show foreign films and series in their original language (mostly English).

Hotels often have international channels such as Eurosport, MTV and CNN. The larger hotels also offer pay-TV with a choice of films.

The most popular radio stations are P1 and P2, which broadcast news and weather on the hour. There are a number of other Norwegian stations which broadcast music 24-hours a day.

Newspapers

Norway has an impressive number of newspapers. Most towns have one or more local or regional newspapers while the three national ones are *Aftenposten*, *Verdens Gang* and *Dagbladet*. VG is a daily tabloid newspaper with a large circulation. *DN-Dagens Næringsliv* is a daily business newspaper. One newspaper has an English version on the Internet, with up-to-date news and sports, business and feature stories, including upcoming festivals and concerts: www. norwaypost.no. International newspapers are available from **Narvesen** kiosks in larger towns.

DIRECTORY

Mobile Phones

Telekiosken
Stenersgaten 1, 0050 Oslo.
Map 3 E3. **Tel** 22 05 04 00.
One of several locations.

Telestial
Tel 1800 707 0031 (US).
Tel 0800 376 2370 (UK).
Tel 1800 795 252 (Aus).
w telestial.com

Internet Access

Accezzo Internettcafé
Galleriet, Torgallmenningen 8, Bergen. **Tel** 55 31 11 60.

Arctic Internet Café
Jernbanetorget 1, Oslo.
Map 3 E3. **Tel** 22 17 19 40.

Oslo Public Library
Harald Hårfagresgt 2, Majorstuen.
Tel 23 36 59 50.
Schous plass 10, Grünerløkka.
Map 3 F2. **Tel** 22 35 65 83.
w deichman.no

United Bakeries
by Vigelandsparken 58, Oslo.
Map 2 A1. **Tel** 22 17 19 40.
Karl Johan's Gate 39, Oslo.
Map 3 D3. **Tel** 22 41 27 53.

Main Post Offices

Bergen Postkontor
Småstrandgaten 3, Bergen.
Tel 81 00 07 10.

Posten Norge BA
Biskop Gunnerus' Gate 14, Oslo.
Map 3 E3. **Tel** 04 004.

Courier Companies

DHL Express
Tel 81 00 13 45.

FedEx
Tel 63 94 03 00.

TNT
Tel 81 00 08 10.

Foreign Newspapers

Narvesen
Stortingsgata 24–26, 0161 Oslo.
Map 3 D3. **Tel** 2 42 95 64.
Bystasjonen (bus station),
5015 Bergen.
Tel 55 32 59 06; route info: 177.
Trondheim Central Station,
7491 Trondheim.
Tel 73 88 39 20.

TRAVEL INFORMATION

The majority of visitors coming to Norway by plane arrive at Oslo's Gardermoen airport. Torp in Vestfold and some of the larger towns and cities in western Norway, such as Bergen, Stavanger and Trondheim, also have international airports. There are good car ferry connections to southern Norway and Bergen from Great Britain, Denmark, Sweden and northern Germany. Many visitors also travel to Norway by bus, car, train and cruise ship. Note that you are entitled to shop duty-free when travelling to and from Norway because it is not a member of the European Union (see p248). Despite the many natural obstacles such as fjords and mountain chains, travelling around Norway is easy thanks to the many car ferries, tunnels and bridges, and a good road network. Train and bus links are also well developed.

Interior of the terminal building at Oslo's Gardermoen airport

Arriving by Air

Many European cities and some in the USA have flight connections to Norway. Gardermoen, the country's main international airport, has excellent road and train connections into Oslo. The journey by bus takes 35 to 40 minutes. Flytoget, the express shuttle train to the city centre, departs every 10 minutes, and takes about 20 minutes. Taxis are expensive and take longer than Flytoget.

SAS (Scandinavian Airlines) is the leading airline in the region, with flights to and from Great Britain and other European countries. The services are either direct or routed via Copenhagen. SAS also has daily flights from the USA and the Far East. **SAS Norge** is a subsidiary of SAS,

with flights from London Gatwick, Manchester, Newcastle and Aberdeen to Oslo, Bergen, Stavanger and Trondheim. **Widerøe**, with its Dash 8 planes, operates from Aberdeen and Newcastle to Stavanger and from Manchester to Bergen with connections to a large number of smaller destinations throughout Norway.

International airlines with flights to Oslo include **British Airways**, Lufthansa, Finnair and Icelandair. The low-cost airline **Ryanair** operates from London Stansted to Moss Lufthavn Rygge, about 65 km (40 miles) south of Oslo, Haugesund and Torp near Sandefjord, about 130 km (81 miles) south of Oslo. Ryanair

SAS logo

offers discounted tickets for the two-hour bus journey to Oslo. **Norwegian Air Shuttle ASA**, know as **Norwegian**, is a low-cost airline operating domestic and international flights across Scandinavia and Europe.

Flight Prices

Ticket prices to and from Norway vary greatly. In addition to the cut-price deals offered by most airlines, there are large price variations for children, students, families and for booking well in advance.

A rule of thumb is that the nearer the date of departure a booking is made the more difficult it becomes to obtain a discount. Booking just prior to departure often means that only full-price tickets are available.

APEX tickets, which need to be booked well in advance, are reasonably priced, but be aware that they cannot be changed or refunded.

There is stiff competition between the airlines and it can often pay to look into what offers are available; check airline websites for special deals. Charter flights can sometimes be more favourable than individual flights.

Ask your local travel agent about the various package deals to Norway.

Arriving by Ferry

Norway's coastline is the longest in Europe and ferries have long been an important means of travel to and around Norway.

Flytoget, the fastest connection between Oslo and Gardermoen airport

Car ferry docking in Kristiansand harbour in southern Norway

DFDS Seaways operates between Oslo and Copenhagen, as well as to Gothenburg (Sweden), and from Harwich to Esbjerg (Denmark). **Fjord Line** operates between Newcastle and Stavanger, Haugesund and Bergen.

From Denmark, **Stena Line** sails between Frederikshavn and Oslo; **Color Line** runs services between Hirtshals and Oslo, Hirtshals and Kristiansand, Frederikshavn and Larvik and Kiel (Germany) and Oslo. There are crossings from Hanstsholm to Bergen, and Strømstad to Sandefjord.

All crossings are by means of large and comfortable car ferries with various categories of cabins. They usually have a good selection of restaurants and tax-free shops to make the crossing as pleasant and relaxed as possible.

Arriving by Train and Coach

Oslo is served by good daily train connections from Copenhagen and Stockholm. Trains from Copenhagen follow the route along Sweden's west coast.

From London, **Eurolines** operates a coach service to Copenhagen from where **NOR-Way Bussekspress** runs to Oslo. Nor-Way Bus Express also operates from Gothenburg and Stockholm to Oslo. In Northern Norway there are bus connections between Skellefteå in Sweden and Bodø, and Umeå in Sweden and Mo I Rana; and

from Rovaniemi in Finland to Tromsø, Tana Bru, Lakselv, Karasjok and Kautokeino.

Arriving by Car

Norway borders three countries and has a large number of border crossings from Svinesund in the south to Grense Jakobselv on the border with Russia in the far north.

All crossings are open to private vehicles. Most travellers by car enter from Sweden via the busiest border crossing at Svinesund.

It is not advisable to drive into Norway from Sweden on a Saturday or Sunday afternoon when traffic is often at its busiest with long queues on both sides of the border crossing. This is because Norwegians regularly travel to Sweden to shop, as the price of many items is lower across the border.

There are customs posts at the border, but if you have nothing to declare you can simply drive through. There are occasions when you may be waved over for a customs check. You should note that this can also happen a considerable distance from the border crossing.

Main entrance, Oslo Central Station

DIRECTORY

Airlines

British Airways
Tel 0844 493 0787 (UK).
W britishairways.com

Norwegian
Tel 0047 21 49 00 15 (Nor).
W norwegian.com

Ryanair
Tel 0871 246 0000 (UK).
Tel 0818 303030 (Eire).
W ryanair.com

SAS Norge
Tel 0047 91 50 54 00.
W sas.no

Widerøe
Tel 0047 75 80 35 68 (Nor).
Tel 0870 6072 7727 (UK).
W wideroe.no

Ferry Companies

Color Line
Tel 0047 81 00 08 11 (Nor).
W colorline.no

DFDS Seaways
Tel 0047 21 62 13 40 (Nor).
Tel 0870 533 3111 (UK).
W dfds.no

Fjord Line
Tel 0047 51 46 40 99 (Nor).
Tel 0191 296 1313 (UK).
W fjordline.co.uk

Stena Line
Tel 02 010.
W stenaline.no

Train and Coach Companies

Eurolines
Tel 0871 781 8178 (UK).
W eurolines.co.uk

NOR-Way Bussekspress
Tel 0047 815 44 444 (Nor).
W nor-way.no

Rail Europe
Tel 0844 848 4078 (UK).
W raileurope.co.uk

Travelling by Air, Train, Bus and Boat

Distances are so great in Norway that nearly all travel between the north and south of the country takes place by plane. There are comprehensive air services between the major towns with connections to outlying districts. To get the most out of your visit to Norway, it is often a good idea to combine flying with the train and ferry. In Northern Norway in particular, combining air travel with the Hurtigruten ferries *(see p215)* offers the chance to visit the more remote communities that lie outside the airline network. Bus travel is another option.

Widerøe flight calling at Svolvær in the Lofoten Islands

Domestic Flights

Nearly all the provincial towns in Norway have airports with daily domestic flight connections. There is also a good network of smaller airports so you are rarely far from an air strip. Travelling times are relatively short unless you are flying between the north and the south. The flights from Oslo to Bergen, Oslo to Stavanger and Oslo to Trondheim take 50 to 60 minutes. The Oslo-Tromsø route takes about one and a half hours. The longest flight is from Oslo to Kirkenes in the far north, a journey that takes just over 2 hours.

SAS is the leading airline and has taken over Braathens (now **SAS Norge**) and **Widerøe**. However, Widerøe still operates as an independent company. Also there are several small companies with limited scheduled flights.

SAS Norge serves 15 domestic airports. Widerøe runs flights to 35 mostly smaller destinations. Between them, the two airlines maintain a comprehensive network of flights. Airline tickets can be purchased at travel agents or directly from the airlines. Domestic travel in Norway is not cheap, but if you are flexible with respect to flight times, it is possible to get good discounts. Widerøe's Explore Norway Ticket offers unlimited air travel for 14 days.

Up-to-date flight times and information about delays are continually posted on page 320 of NRK1's *tekst-TV*. SAS also offers a text messaging service for checking arrival and departure times. Be aware that the timetables vary between summer and winter.

Travelling by Train

From Halden in the south to Bodø in the north there is an excellent train network. Services to the west of the country, such as to Stavanger and Bergen, are also good.

The trains in Norway are operated by Norwegian State Railways, **NSB** (Norges Statsbaner). Both the trains and the railway stations are of a generally high standard. Compartments are always clean and comfortable. There are special facilities for disabled travellers. Skis and bicycles can be carried as luggage, but on long-distance trains you need to make a reservation for your bike as well as for yourself. Luggage can also be sent in advance. The NSB website has detailed information.

Norwegian trains are divided into three categories. Local trains in the Oslo area, Bergen, Stavanger, Bødo and Trondheim serve the immediate vicinity. InterCity trains operate on medium distance routes between towns in Eastern Norway. Long-distance trains include Ekspress (express train) and Nattog (night train). For long-distance trains it is necessary to book tickets in advance, with a seat reservation. On regional trains, no seat reservation is required, and unless you wish to book in advance, you can buy your ticket at the station or on board the train (many smaller stations are unmanned).

Flåmsbanen, one of Norway's most dramatic stretches of railway line

M/S *Telemarken* at Akkerhaugen wharf on the Telemark Canal

The most spectacular train journey is that on the steeply winding Flåmsbanen *(see p186)*. This can be taken as part of the "Norway in a Nutshell" tour, a round trip from Bergen via train and bus, which also includes a fjord cruise. To book, contact Fjord Tours (Tel: 81 56 82 22, www.fjordtours.no).

Travelling by Bus

Most towns and regions have their own local bus companies, with frequent services in urban areas and less frequent services in rural districts. Oslo airport is served by *flybusser* (airport shuttles) from the towns around the capital.

NOR-Way Bussekspress operates the largest network of buses in the country with domestic and international routes. The company offers a seat guarantee scheme. This makes it unnecessary to reserve tickets in advance. If the bus is full, another bus will be put into service.

Buses offer a range of discounts, such as for children and pensioners, and for return journeys. There are frequent departures; between Oslo and Bergen there are three buses per day in each direction. Coffee and tea are served on board. On night buses the seats can be reclined. Blankets and pillows are available on some services.

Many of the bus companies arrange round trips in Norway and abroad. Ask your travel agent for information.

Travelling by Ferry

Car ferries and express boats link the islands and fjords along Norway's coast. Not only do they provide a vital means of communication for these areas, but they are also a splendid way of seeing the country.

The famous coastal express, **Hurtigruten**, offers daily cruises between Bergen and Kirkenes in both a northerly and southerly direction *(see p215)*. The boats make 34 stops along the way. The return journey takes 11 days and the route is planned so that the stretches which are covered during the day in one direction are passed at night on the return trip. The ships vary in terms of age and size, but all are of a high standard.

Some of the counties along the coast have their own ferry companies with car ferries *(see p277)* and express boats, providing the opportunity to experience the spectacular scenery of the fjords. On the majority of these, you pay once you are aboard the ferry. It is often possible to take a day trip, for instance on Sognefjorden, from Bergen

Boarding a fleet of sightseeing buses in Eidfjord

to Flåm, or between Svolvær in the Lofoten Islands and Narvik. Tickets for the Telemark Canal, from Skien to Dalen and Akkerhaugen *(see p152)*, can be purchased through **Telemarkreiser**.

DIRECTORY

Domestic Airline Reservations

SAS Norge
Tel 05400.
W sas.no

Widerøe
Tel 0047 75 80 35 68.
W wideroe.no

Train Operators

Airport Express Train
Tel 815 00 777.
W flytoget.no

NSB
Tel 815 00 888.
W nsb.no

Ferry Travel

Hurtigruten (NNDS)
Tel 810 03 030 (Nor).
Tel 020 8846 2666 (UK).
W hurtigruten.com
W norwegian coastalvoyage. com

Telemarkreiser
Tel 35 90 00 20.
W visittelemark.no

Bus Travel

NOR-Way Bussekspress
Tel 815 44 444.
W nor-way.no/nbeweb

Travelling by Car

Norway has an extensive road network. Most of the roads are of a high standard. The majority are tarred, but gravel roads may be found in more remote areas. A large number of highways are toll roads. With some planning it is possible to avoid the tolls in most cases. The journey may take a little longer, but almost certainly there will be more to see along the way especially if there is a sign for "Turistveg", indicating a scenic route. Below are details on how to pay the motorway tolls and information regarding the rules and regulations for driving and parking, as well as how to cope with road conditions in winter.

Automatic toll road station with sign displaying fees

Traffic Regulations

Traffic is well-regulated, and Norwegian motorists are law-abiding, possibly because there are stiff fines for breaking the rules.

Be particularly aware of the speed limits. Driving 20 km/h (12 mph) over the speed limit may cost you around 3,000 Nkr. If you exceed the speed limit by more, you risk having your licence confiscated on the spot, in addition to a hefty fine. Most main roads have cameras to catch speeding motorists.

The speed limit on highways is normally 80 km/h (50 mph). On motorways it is between 80 and 90 km/h (50–56 mph) and on certain stretches 100 km/h (60 mph).

You should also be aware of the strict regulations for drink-driving. The maximum legal blood alcohol concentration is 0.2 per mil, which means that you virtually cannot drink any alcohol before driving. Concentrations of 0.2–0.5 per mil will result in a very large fine. Driving with a blood alcohol level in excess of 0.5 per

mil warrants an unconditional custodial sentence of a minimum of 21 days, confiscation of driving licence and a big fine.

The use of seatbelts is compulsory for all passengers. Young children are required to sit in special child seats.

Dipped headlights have to be used at all times.

It is advisable to ensure your car is in good order before arriving as there are spot checks, albeit infrequently.

Be aware of the many roundabouts. Drivers entering the junction must always give way.

Traffic lights must always be observed. Under no circumstances should you drive through a red light.

Road Tolls

Several of the larger conurbations are surrounded by toll stations and you are required to pay to enter the town. Make sure you have some Norwegian coins to hand.

Most toll stations are automatic and you simply throw the coins

into a special receptacle. There are manned booths, too, for which you also need Norwegian money. Tolls vary between 20 Nkr and 30 Nkr per entry.

Tolls are also payable on a number of main roads and at some tunnels and bridges. A toll is levied in both directions. Most toll stations have both manual and automatic collection.

Certain private roads also charge tolls, particularly over mountain passes or in areas with holiday cabins. This is, however, more the exception than the rule.

Private road tolls are paid by putting a coin in an envelope marked with the registration number of the car, then placing the envelope in a special box. Envelopes are available at the barrier. There are controls to check that the fee for passing the barrier has been paid. The cost of the toll varies from 10 Nkr to 150 Nkr.

Parking

In most towns and urban areas there are parking meters or multi-storey car parks. In Oslo, if you exceed the allocated time on your meter, you will be fined 500 Nkr – the parking wardens are known for their efficiency. In car parks you pay on departure, so there is no risk of exceeding the time limit. Parking charges vary considerably; in the capital parking can cost 20–30 Nkr per hour.

Road Standards

Norwegian roads are divided into so-called Europe roads *(europaveier)*, national roads *(riksveier)* and smaller roads. The standard of the *europaveier* is often very high, especially in

One of Norway's spectacular bridges connecting islands and skerries

southern Norway. The *riksveier* are also good. Smaller roads vary in quality. In western Norway there are numerous tight bends, so adjust your speed.

Hiring a Car

There are a number of local Norwegian car hire companies, as well as the international chains, **Avis**, **Budget** and **Hertz**. Car hire firms can be found at the main airports and in the towns. Bookings can be made either through the international network of the big companies, or directly.

The minimum age for hiring a car is 19 (Avis). For the hire of more exclusive cars and for paying by credit card the minimum age is 25. The hire conditions are more or less the same as in other countries.

Prices, however, may vary significantly compared to other countries. The cost of car hire will often be higher in Norway, but there are a variety of special offers which are worth enquiring about.

Car Ferries

The Norwegian coastline is broken up by numerous fjords penetrating deep inland. In places car ferries are an indispensable means of transport. There is an extensive network of ferries, with frequent sailing times.

Usually tickets are bought either just before boarding, or from a ticket collector on board. During the summer months, however, it is best to book in advance for larger ferries to popular destinations, such as Lofoten. Reservations can be made by calling the ferry company OVDS. The cost of ferry tickets is heavily subsidised, and therefore low. Most car ferries have cafeterias serving simple food.

Petrol Stations

As a rule, it is never far from one petrol station to another in Norway. Many towns have manned 24-hour petrol stations and most have automatic credit

card payment facilities. If you are driving at night, however, start out with at least half a tank of petrol.

Even though Norway is an oil producing nation, neither petrol nor diesel is cheap.

NAF (Norges Automobil-forbund), **Falken** and **Viking** are the main vehicle recovery organisations. Members of the AA and RAC are able to obtain help from NAF in case of a breakdown or accident.

Road Signs

International road signs prevail in Norway. There are a few exceptions: a white M on a blue background denotes a passing place.

Don't be tempted to take an elk warning sign home as a souvenir. Elks are common in Norway and the signs serve an important purpose, indicating the risk of an elk crossing the road just ahead of you. You should adjust your speed accordingly. Collisions between elks and cars can result in serious damage and have even been known to cause death.

Winter Driving and Safety

Driving conditions during the winter vary considerably from one part of the country to another. In Oslo and the coastal areas of eastern Norway and Vestlandet the roads are normally free of ice and snow all year round. However, they may be slippery, and special winter tyres or studded tyres are strongly recommended for use between November and April. In the mountains and in the north of the country there is a risk of snow and ice for five or six

months of the year. Appropriate tyres and sometimes a set of chains may be necessary.

The most exposed roads are fitted with barriers. In case of difficult or impossible driving conditions, these roads are closed. Some mountain passes are shut for most of the winter season. Road closures are usually signed up well ahead.

On those mountain passes which are normally kept open throughout the winter, snowfalls may make driving difficult. At such times, a snowplough will drive through at set intervals with cars following in convoy.

It is always advisable to check on conditions before setting out. Take warm clothes and extra food with you when driving in the mountains during the winter.

Petrol station run by Norway's state-owned oil company

Getting Around Oslo

It is easy being a tourist in Oslo. Most places of interest are centrally situated, and the various museums, attractions and restaurants are close at hand. The best way to experience Oslo is on foot or by bicycle. From the principal thoroughfare, Karl Johans Gate, it is only a few minutes' walk or cycle ride to the main sights. The capital also has an extensive public transport network that branches out from the city centre. Frequent services mean that even the outskirts of the city are easily accessible. It is advisable to avoid using private cars during the morning and afternoon rush-hour when the roads can become very congested.

Pedestrian crossing on Oslo's Karl Johans Gate

Walking in Oslo

There is no better way to enjoy Oslo than on foot. This way you can experience the city from close quarters. Traffic is not a hindrance to pedestrians and in the centre there are several pedestrianized streets.

Note that you are not allowed to cross the road if the light is red, even if there are no cars nearby. In some places you need to press a button to get a green light. When the "green man" appears, you can cross. When crossing at a pedestrian crossing without traffic lights, cars must give way to pedestrians, but do take care.

The streets in Oslo are generally well signposted, and with the Oslo Street Finder (see pp108–13) it is easy to find your way around.

Karl Johans Gate (see p54) is Norway's street for parades and an attraction in itself. It leads from the Central Station past the Parliament building and the National Theatre to the royal palace. The area around it is pedestrianized.

A 10-minute walk from here brings you to the harbour and the commercial centre of Aker Brygge. The harbour teems with

life, with small boats and ferries coming and going. The best view of Akershus Festning, the historic fortress facing Oslofjorden, is from the harbour. Walk up to Akershus for an even more splendid view of the fjord.

Driving in Oslo

If you are used to driving in cities then driving in Oslo should not pose a problem. The traffic density in the capital is no greater than any other city. As in many other urban areas, however, there is an extensive

Rush-hour traffic causing long queues on the approach into Oslo

one-way system in the centre, which might be difficult to negotiate unless you have a map on which it is marked.

As long as you avoid the rush hour (7am–10am and 3pm–6pm) getting around Oslo is straightforward. The speed limit in the centre varies between 30 and 50 km/h (18–31 mph). Near schools and on some residential roads the limit is 30 km/h (19 mph).

Be aware of speed bumps. On smaller roads they are very close together, and if taken at speed the shock can be fierce enough to damage the car.

Tunnels make it easy to drive through the city. The largest tunnels are Rådhustunnel (along the fjord under Rådhuset) and Vålereng-tunnelen (from the east going in a northerly direction).

Oslo has numerous large multi-storey car parks, including those at Østbanen, Grønland, Ibsen and Aker Brygge. If you park on a controlled parking bay in the city centre between 8am and 5pm you will need to obtain a ticket from a pay-and- display machine. At other times and on Sunday parking is free. Parking becomes increasingly expensive the nearer the city centre you are. Do not forget to pay during the specified parking times. The fine for failing to pay is high. Private parking places and multi-storey car parks charge at all times.

Always lock your car and keep valuables out of sight, preferably by locking them in the boot.

Taxi Services

Getting a taxi in Oslo is easy, except at the height of the rush hour. Taxis have a sign on the roof. When the light is on, the taxi is for hire.

Official taxis can be hailed on the street or at special taxi ranks. They can also be booked in advance, usually for a small additional charge, up to 20 minutes before the required time. Most taxis can take four passengers, but it is also possible to request a larger vehicle for more people. Oslo has a number of cab companies – **Oslo Taxi**,

NorgesTaxi and Taxi 2. It is advisable to use official taxis for travel to and from the airports, as most offer fixed prices.

A market has also grown for so-called pirate taxis in the city, where private people offer to drive for an agreed price. However, they are not to be recommended.

Blue taxi operated by NorgesTaxi

Public Transport

Oslo has an efficient public transport system with trams, buses, trains and the Tunnelbane (metro), also known as T-bane, with frequent services between the city centre and the outskirts. There are also routes connecting outlying areas without crossing the city centre. Tunnelbane lines radiate from the city centre (see map, inside back cover). Call **Ruter** for information on routes, timetables and connections.

Tickets can be purchased from machines and from staffed Tunnelbane stations, or on buses and trams. If there is no conductor then you must stamp your ticket in the automatic machine. Penalties are high for travelling without a valid ticket.

A single ticket is valid for an hour after it has been stamped, on all forms of public transport within the city. It also allows an unlimited number of changes during this time slot.

You can also buy a ticket that is valid for several trips, a 24-hour ticket, known as a dagskort, or a weekly card which gives you unlimited travel for seven days.

The Oslo Pass (see p265) entitles the holder to free public transport (except on night buses and trams).

Ferry Services

A boat service operated by **Nesoddbåtene** runs between Aker Brygge and the peninsula,

Ferry connecting Bygdøy with Oslo city centre

Nesoddtangen, on the east of Oslofjorden, every hour. In rush-hour the service is more frequent.

From the end of April to early October you can take the **Bygdøyfergene** (Bygdøy Ferry) for a scenic trip across the water to the museums on Bygdøynes (see pp82–3), or to Dronningen Pier for a walk to the outdoor museum, Norsk Folkemuseum.

Cycling

It is easy, enjoyable and practical to cycle around Oslo, especially if you choose routes that pass through parks and quiet streets. Bear in mind, however, that Norwegian drivers are not particularly well-disciplined with regard to cyclists, so you will need to be cautious and not assume that drivers will stop automatically for you.

Sign for a bicycle route

You may walk with your bike on the pavement and you may cycle on the pavement if conditions require and you are not causing a nuisance to pedestrians.

Bicycles can be rented at **Kikutstua** or **Oslo Bysykkel**.

Sightseeing Tours

An alternative to touring the city on your own is to take a guided tour. A typical itinerary for a three-hour guided tour by coach arranged by **Båtservice Sightseeing or HMK**, for example, would include the centre of Oslo, Vigelandparken, the Holmenkollen Ski Jump and Museum and the museums in Bygdøy. Tailor-made tours with a personal guide can be arranged by companies such

as **Oslo Guideservice** or **Oslo Guidebureau**. They offer traditional itineraries as well as walking, cycling and themed excursions.

There are also cruises on Oslofjorden between May and September. **Båtservice Sightseeing** operates a 50-minute mini-cruise of the harbour every hour, and a 2-hour sightseeing trip around inner Oslofjorden departing three or four times a day. The boats depart from Bryggen in front of Rådhuset (City Hall) (see pp60–61).

General Index

Acknowledgments

Streiffert Förlag would like to thank the following staff at Dorling Kindersley:

Senior Map Co-Ordinator Casper Morris.
Senior DTP Manager Jason Little.
Managing Art Editor Jane Ewart.
Publishing Manager Anna Streiffert
Publisher Douglas Amrine.

Dorling Kindersley would like to thank all those whose contributions and assistance have made the preparation of this book possible.

Main Contributor
Snorre Evensberget, former chief editor at Gyldendal Norsk Forlag and author of *Thor Heyerdahl, Oppdageren (Thor Heyerdahl: The Explorer),* Norwegian and English Editions 1994, the reference works *Bevingede Ord,* 1967, and *Litterært Leksikon,* 2000. Evensberget has also edited works on Norway, including *Bygd og By i Norge, 1–19, Norge, Vårt Land, 1–9,* and many books on Norwegian nature, hunting and fishing.

Fact Checker Sharon A. Bowker.

Editor, UK Edition Jane Hutchings.

Revisions Team
Umesh Aggarwal, Emma Anacootee, Catherine Atundi, Claire Baranowski, Kate Berens, Julie Bond, Surya Deogun, Emer FitzGerald, Anna Freiberger, Rhiannon Furbear, Camilla Gersh, Taraneh Ghajar Jerven, Phil Hunt, Shobhna Iyer, Laura Jones, Phil Lee, Toril Lund, Alison McGill, Claire Naylor, George Nimmo, Catherine Palmi, Helen Partington, Susie Peachey, Pete Quinlan, Pure Content, Ellen Root, Susana Smith, Roseen Teare, Craig Turp, Conrad Van Dyk, Alison Vågen.

Additional Picture Research Rachel Barber.

Proof Reader Stewart J Wild.

Indexer Hilary Bird

Additional Photography
Catherine Atundi, Tim Ridley, Ian O'Leary, Alison Vågen.

Photography Permissions
Dorling Kindersley would like to thank all the churches, museums, restaurants, hotels, shops, galleries and other sights too numerous to thank individually, for their permission to photograph their establishments.

Picture Credits
Key: a = above; b = below/bottom; c = centre; f = far; l = left; r = right; t = top.

Works of art have been reproduced with the permission of the following copyright holders:

Shaft (1988) Richard Serra ©ARS, NY and DACS, London 2011 74b; Bust of Einar Gerhardsen Nils Aas © DACS, London 2011 79cl; Inner Room (1990) Per Inge Bjørlo © DACS, London 2011 74cl; Winter Sun (1966) Gunnar S. Gundersen © DACS, London 2011 74tr; The Rubbish Man (1935–95) Ilya Kabakov © DACS, London 2011 75tl; Tilted Form No 3 (1987) Sol Le Witt © ARS, NY and DACS, London 2011 75cra; Without Title (1990) Per Maning © DACS, London 2011 75b; The Night Wanderer Edvard Munch © ADAGP, Paris and DACS, London 2011 97b; The Scream (1893) Edvard Munch © ADAGP, Paris and DACS, London 2011 56clb; Høstens Promenade Ludvig O. Ravensberg © DACS, London 2011 62br; Winter Night in the Mountains (1914) Harald Sohlberg © DACS, London 2011 57cr; Wheel of Life Gustav Vigeland © DACS, London 2011 94ca; The Monolith Gustav Vigeland © DACS, London 2011 94cl; Triangle Gustav Vigeland © DACS, London 2011 94b; Fountain Gustav Vigeland © DACS, London 2011 95cr; The Clan Gustav Vigeland © DACS, London 2011 95tl.

4Corners Images: SIME/ Da Ros Luca 102cla; SIME/ Mezzanotte Susy 260bl; SIME/ Susy Mezzanotte 102bc.

Alamy Images: blickwinkel/ Baesemann 260tr; Bryan and Cherry Alexander Photography 249tl; charistoone-travel 126–7; Danita Delimont 64–5; Danita Delimont/ Russell Young 237c; eye35 stock 10cla; FAN travelstock/ Bildarchiv Friedrichsmeier 106br; PE Forsberg 267bl; imagebroker 245tr; Art Kowalsky 103cr, 106tr; Elisa Locci 237tl; NordicImages 15bc; Radharc Images 266cla; Pep Roig 130; Mike Sivyer 226–7; Dave and Sigrun Tollerton 236cl. **All Over Press:** 44c, 45br, 160br. **Amarok AB:** Magnus Elander, 25bl, 224tr, 225tl 225cra, 225cr, 225br, 259b. **Tom Arnbom:** 211br. **Liv Arnessen:** 30bc.

Barnekunstmuseet: 99bc. **Bergen Kunstmuseum:** *Bergens Våg, 1834,* by J. C. Dahl 177br. **Bergen Museum: De Naturhistoriske Samlinger:** 179cl. **Bergen Tourist Board (Bergen Reiselivslag):** 265ca. **Studio Lasse Berre AS:** 5clb, 28cla, 28ca, 28cra, 28clb, 28cb, 28crb, 28bl, 28bc, 28br, 29tl, 29tc, 29tr, 29cla, 29ca, 29cr, 29cb, 29crb. **Bølgen & Moi:** 240tl. **Britannia Hotel, Trondheim:** 233br. **British Museum:** Peter Anderson 38br, 39cb. **Bryggerikaia:** 246br.

Carte Blanche: Erik Berg 255tl. **C. M. Dixon:** 38tr. **Corbis:** Richard Cummins 12br; Tom Hansen/Demotix/Demotix 32cla; Gavin Hellier/Robert Harding World Imagery 158–9; John Hicks 50tr, op2/Peter Kleumann 28–31u; John Hicks 104cra; Douglas Pearson 18 / JAI 80, 92, 164; Radius Images 216–7. **Cornelius Restaurant:** 244tc.

Den Nationale Scene A/S: Thor Brødreskift 254cr. **Det Gamle Raadhus:** 239tr. **Dreamstime.com:** Chaoss 46–7; Serban Enache 182–3; Ermolenko 2–3; Alessandro Flore 206; Bjørn Hovdal 13tc; Plotnikov 114–5, 262–3; Natalia Rumyantseva 12c; Scanrail 14br; Seraph1703; Magnus Skjølberg 198–9; Zhukoff 138–9.

Emma's Drømmekjøkken: 235br, 247tc.
English Heritage: 38cl.

Fotolia: Morten Almeland 270bl.

Gamle Raadhus Restaurant: 73clb. **Getty Images:** Bongarts/ Christof Koepsel 100br; Mark Hannaford 15tr; MJ Kim 105tl; Nordic Photos/ Anders Ekholm 261tl; Nordic Photos/ Jorgen Larsson 261cr. **Glipp Restaurant:** 234bl, 243tr.

Havfruen: 235tl, 246tl. **Jiri Havran:** 55b, 181tr. **Holmenkollen Park Hotel Rica:** 229tl, 231tc. **Huset:** 247br.

Taraneh Jerven: 256bl.

Det Kgl. Bibliotek, København: 40t. **Knudsens Fotosenter:** 19b, 20t, 20b, 21b 29bl, 33cl, 33b, 35tr, 35b, 77t, 121b, 145cra, 147cl, 176cla, 185bl, 189tl, 203cla, 203cra, 203bl, 209cr, 219tl, 222tl, 222c, 223t, 223br, 224bl, 258cr, 267tr, 274cla. **Kulturhistorisk Museum, Oslo:** 58br. **Kunstindustrimuseet i Oslo:** *Baldisholteppet* 63tl. **Kviknes Hotell:** 229t.

Håkon Li: 187cl, 187cr, 187bl, 187br. **Lunds Historiska Museum:** 29t. **Lyspunktet Cafe:** 245bl.

Maaemo: 239br. **Maihaugen Museum:** 140cla. **Munch-Museet:** *Nattvandreren,* Edvard Munch 97b. **Museet for Samtidskunst:** *Vintersol* by Gunnar S. Gundersen 74tr, *Indre Rom* by Per Inge Bjørlo 74cl, *Søppelmannen* by Ilja Kabakov 75tl, *Form No 3* by Sol Le Witt 75cra, *Uten titel* by Per Maning.

Nasjonalbiblioteket: 43br. **Nasjonalgalleriet:** *Brudeferd i Hardanger* by A. Tidemand & H. Gude 8–9, *Leiv Eirikson Oppdager Amerika* by Christian Krohg 38–9c, *Fra Hjula Veveri* by Wilhelm Peters 43cl, *Fra Stalheim* by J. C. Dahl 53cra, *Larvik by Moonlight* by J C Dahl 56br, *The Golden Age* by Lucas Cranach 56c, *Portrett av Mme Zborowska* by Amadeo Modigliani 57cc, *Den Angrende St Peter* by El Greco 57cra, *Vinternatt i Rondane* by Harald Sohlberg 57cr, *Stetind i Tåke* by Peder Balke 57b, *Skrik* by Edvard Munch 56clb,. **Nordlysfestivalen:** 255cr. **Norgestaxi Oslo AS:** 279cla. **Norsk Folkemuseum:** 3, Anne-Lise Reinsfelt 87bl. **Norsk Hjemmefront Museum:** 45clb, 72bl. **Norway Designs:** 103tl. **The Norwegian National Opera & Ballet:** 76bl.

Oslo Bymuseum: *Prøvetur på Eidsvollsbanen* 43tl. **Oslo International Church Music Festival:** 104bl. **Oslo Spektrum:** 79b.

Photolibrary: Photononstop/ Dominique Lerault 249br.

Rica Victoria Hotel, Oslo: 230bl. **Sametinget:** 219br. **Samfoto:** Kim Hart 30c. **Restaurant Sawan:** 240bc. **Scanpix:** 31cra, 31br. **Garve Scott-Lodge:** 45tr. **The Sense Cocktail Bar & Lounge:** 106clb. **Smuget:** 205cl. **Mick Sharp:** 39cr. **Skutebrygga:** 241tl. **Tiu Similä:** 25tr. **Sjohuset:** 243br. **Skimuseet:** 30tr, 30cl.**Skarsnuten Hotel:** 242tc. **Statens Historiska Museum, Stockholm:** Peter Anderson 39tl, 39crb. **Statens Vegvesen:** 23br. **Stenersenmuseet** *Høstens Promenade* by Ludvig O. Ravensberg 62br. **SuperStock:** Hemis.fr 192; Brian Lawrence 248bl; Camille Moirenc/Hemis.fr 116; National Geographic 11br; View Pictures Ltd 148.

Thon Hotels: 228bc; **Tofoto:** 215cla, 215cr, 215cl, 215br. **Trøndelag Teater:** 254bl.

Universitetets Kulturhistoriske Museer: Ove Holst 38br. **Universitetets Oldsakssamling:** 37b; Peter Anderson 4br, 38bl, 58clb, 88b, 89bl; Ann Christine Eek 58ca; 58tr, Ellen C. holte and Lill-Ann Chepstow-Lusty 59bl; Eirik Irgens Johnsen 53tl, 58b, 88cl, 89tl, 89tc. **Uppigard Natadal Hotel:** 232tl.

O. Væring: *Birkebeinerferden* by K. Bergslien 30clb, *Håkon Håkonsson Krones* by Gerhard Munthe 36, *Bærums Verk* by C. A. Lorentzen 40br, *Sjøhelten Peter Wessel Tordenskiold* by Balthasar Denners 41c, *En Aften i det Norske Selskap* by Eilif Petersen 41t, *Torvslaget i Christiiania 17.5 1829* by H. E. Reimers 42br, *Nasjonalforsamlingen på Eidsvoll 1814* by O. Wergeland 42tl, *Christian Michelsen og Kongefamilien 7/6 1905* by H. Ström 44tl, *Akershus Slott* by Jacob Croning 70br. **Værtshuset Bæreums Verk:** 241br.

Linda Whitwam: 207b, 220cl, 220bc. **Staffan Widstrand:** 25bcl, 25br, 224cl.

Restaurant Ylajali: 238br.

Front Endpapers – **Alamy Images:** Pep Roig Lclb. **Corbis:** Doug Pearson/JAI Lc. **Dreamstime.com:** Chaoss Lcl; Alessandro Flore Rcra. **Superstock:** Hemis.fr Rca; Camille Moirenc/Hemis.fr Rbr; View Pictures Ltd Lbl.

Jacket
Front and spine – **Photoshot:** Bard Loken..

All other images copyright © Dorling Kindersley. For further information: www.dkimages.com

Transport Map of Oslo

Oslo kollektivtrafikk / Public transport / *Nahverkehr*

T-bane
Metro
U-bahn

Trikk
Tram
Straßenbahn

Hovedbusslinjer
Main bus services
Hauptbuslinien

Båt
Boat
Boot

Overgangsmulighet
Interchange stop
Umsteigemöglichkeit

Stoppested i én retning
One direction stop
Eine Richtung Haltestelle

Jernbane
Railway line
Eisenbahn

Informasjon
Information
Information
© **177**
trafikanten.no

#